W9-CMB-936

A.S.A. MONOGRAPHS

General Editor: MICHAEL BANTON

8

Socialization:

The Approach from Social Anthropology

SOCIALIZATION

THE APPROACH FROM SOCIAL ANTHROPOLOGY

Edited by Philip Mayer

TAVISTOCK PUBLICATIONS

London · New York · Sydney · Toronto · Wellington

First published in 1970
by Tavistock Publications Limited
11 New Fetter Lane, London EC4
This book has been set in Modern Series 7
and was printed by Butler & Tanner Ltd,
Frome and London

SBN 422 73190 0

This volume derives mainly from material presented at a conference on socialization sponsored by the Association of Social Anthropologists of the Commonwealth and held at the University of Birmingham in April 1967.

Distributed in the U.S.A. by
Barnes & Noble, Inc.

Contents

Editor's Preface

Socialization seemed a rather daring choice for the theme of the 1967 conference of the Association of Social Anthropologists, considering how little the subject has figured in British social-anthropological discourse in the last twenty or thirty years. This volume consists of the papers presented at the conference, which was held at the University of Birmingham in April 1967. Owing to the exploratory nature of the occasion it is perhaps not as closely woven as some previous A.S.A. symposia, or as representative of a common standpoint, but we hope it justifies the experiment none the less.

As the convener responsible for planning the conference programme I was agreeably surprised to find contributions forthcoming in such respectable numbers. It was agreed that wherever possible the focus should be on the socialization of adolescents or youth, rather than on child-training. As will be seen, two of the contributors have dealt with basic questions of theory and method (Richards and Jahoda). Of the rest, four have focused primarily on youth (La Fontaine, the Mayers, Spencer, Wilder), three primarily on child-training (Goody, Lloyd, Ward), and two on other specific topics (Forge, Loudon). As to regional interest, there are five Africanist papers, two on Southeast Asia, and one each on Tristan da Cunha and New Guinea.

Besides A.S.A. members we were fortunate in having at the conference an educationist, Rosemary Firth, as a discussant, and also the two social psychologists, Gustav Jahoda and Barbara Lloyd, whose contributions appear here. (Jahoda's contribution began as a discussant's comment on Richards's paper and was expanded into its present form after the conference.) We deliberately invited contributions from psychologists (rather than sociologists, for instance, or culture-and-personality analysts) because it seems that the fear of 'getting stuck in psychology' has had a good deal to do with British anthropologists' one-time reluctance to confront the subject of socialization – to recognize it as a fit subject for analysis in the British anthropological tradition, or even as a major theme of human society at all.

Ethnocentric preoccupation with this local problem, of relating socialization studies to the British anthropological tradition, helps to explain why the conference did not refer more to the abundant American literature on socialization. Perhaps the volume will prepare the way for more future transatlantic dialogue.

I am grateful to Professor John Rex for reading the introduction in draft, and to my wife, Dr Iona Mayer, whose suggestions, as always, have made an essential contribution.

PHILIP MAYER

Durham
November 1968

Philip Mayer

Introduction

SOCIALIZATION AND THE SOCIAL ANTHROPOLOGIST

Socialization may be broadly defined as the inculcation of the skills and attitudes necessary for playing given social roles. In this light it has unquestionable theoretical relevance for social anthropology. Roles and role systems are central to the anthropological field of study however one chooses to approach it, and they can scarcely be conceived of as existing or functioning without some provision for socialization, thus defined.

Socialization is more than the training of children and the immature. Immaturity is in any case a relative term: as some of the contributions in this volume remind us, there are cultures where it is normal for a person to remain marginal to all the major social systems up to the age of thirty or forty. But even where that is not the case, certain roles are normally recruited from among people who are grown up already (senior kinship roles, for example, and many functionally specific roles in ritual, judicial, political, etc., systems). Further, social mobility and/or major social changes, such as ongoing urbanization or industrialization, involve the resocialization of people of all ages. By and large, then, it is rare for individuals not to have to confront actual or potential new roles in adult life, which would require from them the acquisition of new role-playing skills and attitudes.

Today, of course, many parts of the world are undergoing a socialization crisis, owing to the scope and momentum of social change. In developing countries more and more children go to school, in developed countries formal education takes longer and longer, but there is much painful uncertainty about the roles for which the young are being or ought to be prepared, and about how the task should be divided between family, school, and peer groups. Resocialization of adults appears equally problematic. In regard to the study of developing countries especially, socialization would seem as much a key theme today as political structure was in the past generation for the study of countries then under colonial rule.

Within the general field of socialization we may follow Durkheim (1956, p. 124) in distinguishing 'education' as the 'systematic socialization of the young generation by adults'. Durkheim himself was much concerned with the sociology of education in this sense. *Inter alia* he suggested that by comparing different societies 'one could establish types of education as one establishes types of family, state or religion' and 'seek out the conditions on which the characteristic traits of each of them depended' (1956, p. 97). Max Weber, the other founding ancestor of social anthropology, likewise suggested that a 'typology of pedagogical ends and means' would be found related to his own typology of forms of domination (1948, p. 426).

It cannot be said that British social anthropologists did much to follow this early lead. Sociologists have pursued the socialization theme from family to peer group to formal organization, and it nearly always figures prominently in textbooks of sociology. Meanwhile some American social anthropologists have sought regularities and theoretical insights along the Durkheim-Weber lines (e.g. Aberle, seeking to relate the severity of obedience training to levels of political organization: 1961, p. 386). But in this country anthropological interest in socialization appeared to wane after the period when Firth, Fortes, and Nadel made their major contributions to the subject, as also Raum and Read by their more specialized studies. Textbooks of anthropology are published here which give the subject minimal treatment or none at all (e.g. Beattie, 1964; Lienhardt, 1964; Mair, 1965).

Not only has there been a dearth of theoretically interesting work on socialization here since 1940, but ethnographic documentation has been rather neglected too, considering the prevailing British emphasis on thoroughgoing fieldwork. Rarely has material been collected with a systematic focus on socialization as such. So while British social anthropologists have done much valuable work on age-sets or age-grades as structural systems, and on initiation ceremonies as ritual complexes, there has been little attempt to place either the age-sets or the initiations within the frame of reference of the people's educational institutions as a whole. Similarly, observations on the training of children in specific kinship behaviour have tended to be focused on the given kinship system rather than the given educational system.

This point is vividly brought out in Richards's excellent analysis of British anthropological attitudes to socialization (pp. 1–32 below). She remarks *inter alia* that initiation rituals have too often been assumed to have normative functions when the assumption has not been tested empirically in the field. Van Gennep's hypotheses on the functions of initiations have been largely taken on trust, as have Durkheim's on the functions of religious rites, although 'it would not have been beyond the wit of the fieldworker to devise experiments to test some of them, if he had had the requisite time and patience'. She applies her stricture even to her own work, recalling that she failed to speak to the two Bemba girls whom she watched being initiated in a three-week-long ceremony, 'yet I blithely declared that the rites were used to inculcate the values of marriage and parenthood' (p. 12 below).

It can be added that British social anthropologists have likewise dealt extensively with social control and apparently not been much interested in its implications for socialization. Radcliffe-Brown's much-quoted 'diffuse sanctions' are in fact mechanisms of socialization as well as of social control. Socialization – one may say – diverts the individual in advance from actions inappropriate to his roles; social control inhibits such actions; both can be seen as techniques of conflict resolution, the one operating ideally by prescription and the other by proscription (Spiro, 1961, p. 479). There seems to be no hard and fast line between them, and no good reason why one but not the other should be regarded as deserving of attention. It will be noticed that Loudon describes in his paper on Tristan da Cunha a kind of teasing which can be seen as serving either socializing or controlling functions (below, pp. 329–330).

Thus we have the paradox that, just when British social anthropologists were most intent on defining their discipline as comparative sociology, they failed to share the sociologists' interest in socialization; and that their rationale for abandoning the subject was apparently a devotion to Durkheimian social fact (as opposed to psychological reductions), whereas socialization practices had been explicitly claimed by Durkheim himself as social facts *par excellence*. Did he not specially cite 'the way in which children are brought up' as a 'characteristic example' to illustrate the 'definition of the social fact' (1938, p. 5)?

To explain this paradox fully would doubtless require quite an essay in the sociology of knowledge. But it seems beyond doubt that one of the more important factors has been what Richards calls the 'British fear of psychology' (below, p. 7) She shows that psychology had been accepted here as quite respectable up to the 1930s, but in 1953 Firth could write of its having become 'rather a scare word for anthropologists in this country' (Firth, 1964, p. 48 f.) The idea that socialization is a specially 'psychological' kind of subject, and the idea that psychology is not for us, were doubtless both reinforced by the way socialization was handled in some early culture-and-personality studies.

This volume has been undertaken in a different spirit – in the view, first, that it is possible to study socialization by regular social-anthropological means, without special recourse to psychology; and, second, that it is also possible to draw in psychological concepts, where desired, without necessarily distorting anthropological explanation.

THE PLACE OF PSYCHOLOGICAL EXPLANATION: 'PRACTICES' AND 'PROCESSES'

In this connection I believe it is helpful to distinguish conceptually between two main targets of study in the field of socialization. One is largely oriented to vernacular models, the other largely to observer models. The latter – not the former – is likely to require some use of psychological concepts supplied by the observer, but to my mind that does not make it less legitimate anthropologically. We may distinguish the two as socializing 'practices' and 'processes' respectively.

By socializing *practices* I mean vernacular activities for which socialization (inculcation of role-playing skills or attitudes) is explicitly claimed by the actors as a deliberate aim. Along with the activities properly so called I would include the associated vernacular beliefs or theories. Thus socializing practices include initiation rituals and all explicitly initiatory institutions and practices; explicit vernacular theory and practice regarding the training of children and young people for adult roles; the same regarding the training of adult aspirants to given roles; informal but deliberate exercise of socializing pressures, as by the teasing, etc. of those who seem to discharge their roles ineptly; vernacular opinions – not necessarily endorsed by the observer – about the suitability and effectiveness of socializing techniques.

In a given culture the body of conscious, deliberate socializing practice and theory, as just defined, constitutes a vernacular 'system', and the anthropologist can hope to deal with it by the regular techniques of his discipline. (Compare Durkheim's phrase 'systematic socialization', quoted on p. xiv above.) Psychological science is not required for recording it ethnographically, or for attempting cross-cultural typologies in the way suggested by Durkheim and Weber, or for noting (in the more familiar British manner) functional relations between such a system and other systems in the same culture. Thus Spencer (pp. 129–130 below) notes a functional interrelation between the Samburu mode of training for warriorhood, which keeps young men in the bush for years on end, and the gerontocratic organization, whereby all political, domestic, and ritual power is successfully engrossed by older men. This is an anthropological not a psychological observation.

Perhaps socializing practices are more easily observed in the complex societies studied by sociologists than in the simpler ones which anthropologists have generally studied. The complex society is likely to be richer in systematic socializing practices – e.g. varieties of occupational training – for the very reason that it is richer in functionally specific roles. But no culture or society could conceivably endure without *some* institutionalized procedures for training in *some* roles; and even where those are relatively few, people will have conscious ideas about them, and about the subjects of education, preparation for adulthood, and socialization generally. In principle, such ideas should be no more difficult to record than world views, for example, or verbalized kinship sentiments. They certainly would not be less significant anthropologically.

As a matter of fact we do not even know how far simpler

societies have or lack specialized educational institutions. We know only that anthropologists have often not reported any from their fields: an omission which might often be explained by preoccupation with other sectors such as the political, judicial, ritual, etc. The Hehe 'boarding schools' which the Culwicks described (from a now rather old-fashioned ethnographic standpoint) come to mind as an example of the kind of thing that might have been observed more often, had later fieldworkers been similarly interested (Culwick & Culwick, 1935). In my own fieldwork, it was chance that first led me to notice the weekend meetings of Red Xhosa youth, which the people themselves liken to 'schools' (p. 162 below).

Turning from 'practices' to what I would call 'processes' of socialization brings us to different methodological problems. By the 'processes' I mean all those social experiences that, one supposes, 'actually' advance people in their role-playing skills or attitudes, and the mechanisms whereby these socializing effects are 'actually' brought about. This, then, is an observer's model of 'what actually happens' in regard to socialization in the given field. It may coincide to a greater or lesser extent with actors' models – that is with people's vernacular accounts of their own vernacular socializing practices – but it is not likely to coincide exactly. Some of the practices may seem to the observer to have no 'actual' effect, or to have effects different from those claimed. Further, and more significantly, he may believe he sees socialization going on where the actors do not, or not consciously. Socializing messages, one would think, are often conveyed non-deliberately as well as deliberately – conveyed by a variety of agents in a variety of contexts. *A priori*, this would seem particularly likely in the case of the diffuse roles typical of the simpler society.

How is an anthropological observer to establish that experience A 'really does' contribute this or that towards a given skill apparently required in role B? And how, without guidance from the actors, can he claim to identify agents and occasions of 'unconscious', non-deliberate, diffuse socialization? Sometimes alternative patterns of experience can be compared as between reasonably matching groups, and then it may be possible to construct a statistical basis for comparing isolated aspects of role performance accordingly. Goody does this when she compares certain indices of marital and career success for Gonja who respectively did and did not undergo fostering in childhood (below, pp. 65ff.). More often, however, I believe that the observer simply 'sees' connections which he cannot prove. Having noticed what seems clearly to be a common motif running through situation A and role B, he postulates that they are somehow connected aetiologically. The connection (logically speaking) must be through some factor or process which supposedly operates within the psyche of the actors. Internalization, or conditioning, or habit-forming, or fear of sanctions, or reinforcement or blockage of drives, or displacement, or some other psychic mechanism, may be postulated. But, whichever it is, it will be a concept chosen by the observer for the sake of his own model, rather than a fact capable of being documented by observation in the field.

It is not being claimed that the line between socializing practices and processes is hard and fast, even in theory and still less in field situations. Nevertheless, the distinction seems to deserve consideration from anthropologists who object on principle to using any concepts drawn from psychology, lest they throw out the Durkheimian baby of social fact along with the (for them) psychologically dirty bath water.

My own attitude, and I think that of the other contributors, is that the water need not be dirty anyway. The rightful place of psychology in anthropological explanation is a subject that Nadel has discussed with characteristic logical rigour and thoroughness (Nadel, 1951, especially Chs. IV, XI, and XII). As may be recalled, his masterly analysis defends *inter alia* the form of hypothesis in which (social) 'experience' is held to produce (psychological) 'motivation' for subsequent (social) 'behaviour', provided that the insights so gained could not have been obtained by purely social analysis. This argument is clearly applicable to the study of socialization processes.

Admittedly, Nadel counsels great care with regard to the 'conversion factor' – the factor which the anthropologist postulates as converting the previous social experience into the psychological motivation for subsequent behaviour. Unless it is obvious or self-evident (he suggests) it ought to be specified very clearly, and possible logical pitfalls ought to be remembered, e.g. the fact that an 'unconscious' psychological mechanism is simply not susceptible of demonstration. This caution, too, will apply in the study of socialization process. And it raises another problem – what kinds of psychological concept to employ, seeing that the discipline of psychology affords different and often incompatible kinds. Nadel himself noted that 'conversion factors' may be envisaged in Freudian terms, but need not be; he preferred Janet's 'laws'. To some people a Freudian explanation of an allegedly socializing process (or for that matter of anything else) will fall within the 'self-evident' bracket, but other people will see it in an opposite light. One recalls a question that Turner has voiced in another context: how can the 'hapless anthropologist' hope to judge between rival psychoanalytic interpretations when psychoanalysts disagree among themselves (Turner, 1964, p. 213)? It becomes still more pressing when put into wider terms – how to choose between psychoanalytic models or concepts on the one hand, and those of (say) stimulus-response learning theory on the other.

One prescription would be that anthropologists who propose to study socialization process should have at least some first-hand acquaintance with psychological science. In this volume both Richards and Jahoda advocate more cooperation between anthropology and psychology. So far, cooperation has been difficult to achieve in this country – unlike America – because the disciplines have separate traditions here. Jahoda points out that British psychologists with active experience in cross-cultural research can be counted on the fingers of one hand (below, p. 33). He and Richards agree that it will be impossible to do anything much until further teaching is available on this interdisciplinary frontier. The anthropologist has his own job to do (says Richards) but should surely know what the research techniques of the psychologist are, and he might well gain by contact with 'hypothesis-testers' (below, p. 25). Psychology students, adds Jahoda, ought to be similarly enlightened about anthropology, 'especially as they are almost certainly more ignorant about it than vice versa'. 'The ideal solution would be a joint degree' (such as has been established at Swansea and at Durham), 'with subsequent specialization' (below, p. 39). Richards and Jahoda agree, too, that 'one of the areas of co-operation that ought to be developed might relate to social change in general and educational change in particular, since in these spheres [illegible] could learn a great deal from each other' (below, p. 40).

Gluckman and Devons took a rather different view in their discussion of the anthropological approach to problems that fall within the territory of another discipline. To master the task of the 'other' social scientist (they argue) may mean neglecting one's own; on the other hand, if one approaches it without mastering it, the 'undisciplined trespass on fields one is not competent to traverse produces more obscurity than it does creative inspiration' (Gluckman, 1964, p. 161). They advocate abstemious policies: 'naivety' (willingness to disregard the other scientist's researches and conclusions as being irrelevant to one's own problems); and 'abridgement' (acceptance of the other's results and conclusions, where they seem appropriate, in shortened form and without too much inquiry as to how he reached them).

Incidentally, like British authors in general, Richards and Jahoda on the one hand, and Gluckman and Devons on the other, all imply a firm belief in the autonomy of social anthropology as a distinct discipline, as against the suggestion that has sometimes been raised that the behavioural sciences might profitably ignore conventional demarcations and work towards a general, inclusive 'science of behaviour'. In the same spirit, Nadel too observed that transition from one discipline to another is like 'stepping into another order of existence, governed by regularities peculiar to it' (Nadel, 1951, p. 212).

To sum up, then, authentically social-anthropological approaches to socialization would seem to include the following: (1) To record a vernacular system of conscious socializing practice, relating it to other systems within the society and/or comparing it cross-culturally. (2) To construct one's own model of 'actual' socializing processes, in a given field, being duly explicit about the kinds of psychological mechanism one postulates. (3) If psychological concepts have to be used, either (a) to inform one's choice by advanced interdisciplinary study, as suggested by Richards and Jahoda, or (b) to remain deliberately 'naïve' or practise 'abridgement', as recommended by Gluckman.

All these approaches are used in this volume. For instance

Wilder, the Mayers, Goody, and Loudon all rely wholly or mainly on the first. Wilder's account of Malay youth represents their inactivity in its social aspect. He has no need to resort to psychological categories. The Mayers' account of Red Xhosa peer groups notes the apparently low incidence of sexual and violent misbehaviour among participants (in comparison with that among non-Red Xhosa youth, who do not participate), and suggests some of the social mechanisms that may be involved. There is no need to introduce psychological dimensions such as internalization. Goody, too, can dispense with psychological concepts in reaching her conclusion that being fostered in Gonja is perfectly compatible with success in marriage and career. She has social facts and figures to demonstrate it. Again, Loudon (though himself trained in psychology) needs to make only minimal reference to the psychological processes his analysis implies. Tristan da Cunha children are strictly trained to avoid open display of aggressive feelings and are remarkable for their docility and quietness. Loudon suggests that the sometimes vicious teasing common among adults is an 'outlet for repressed hostility', but he does not attribute to this hypothesis any 'explanatory value of an aetiological kind' over and above the 'social' explanation deducible from the social facts – the kind of authority exercised in the domestic family, the emphasis on preserving at least an appearance of cheerful cooperation (p. 313 below).

Forge's presentation of Abelam material, on the other hand, rests on assumptions about psychological learning processes, though he chooses to remain 'naïve' about these too. He is concerned with learning to see, and with the transference of what is learnt to later and different situations. Painted objects are the foci of Abelam initiation ceremonies, and boys have to suffer painful experiences before being shown them. Forge argues that this produces a set of expectations about two-dimensional images and permanently prevents the Abelam from 'seeing' (i.e. making sense of) anything two-dimensional that is not part of the closed system of ritual connotations; he holds that the initiation system teaches the young man to see the art, not so that he may interpret it consciously, but so that he is affected by it directly (p. 290 below). In discussion, Leach compared the experience of attending school chapel:

> 'It is a peculiarity of Church of England services that although they use the ordinary words of the English language the sentences into which these words are composed are wholly unfamiliar to the small boy initiate . . . Listening to this curious form of gibberish day after day . . . although we may not recognize it at the time (does nevertheless) affect our adult use of language in secular life.'

Ward's paper on Kau Sai also exemplifies the deliberately naïve (in Gluckman's sense) use of psychological concepts in explaining socialization process. Her data were 'certainly not collected systematically with the object of testing the validity of hypotheses in social psychology' (p. 109 below), though she hopes that what she calls her 'speculations' may stimulate others to a more systematic study. She was struck by the occurrence of extended temper tantrums among boys aged five to ten. The children are left to scream themselves out – their rages bring them no reward. Ward relates this common childhood experience to the strict playing down of aggressiveness in Kau Sai, where people have to live in extremely crowded conditions and without benefit of strong-armed external social controls, so that much depends on 'the successful repression of aggressive impulses within each individual'. Ward is trying to link childhood experience (treatment of tantrums) not with adult personality characteristics, in the culture-and-personality tradition, but with specific phenomena of social organization.

Spencer draws on Sargant's *Battle for the Mind* for a particular behaviourist psychological theory, and applies this theory in detail to Samburu material, along with the concept of rituals of intensification, drawn from the behaviourist-oriented work of Chapple and Coon. Spencer is deliberately 'trespassing', or, in less loaded language, crossing the boundary; but this is done in pursuit of a 'social' not a 'psychological' or 'personality' question. The question is how the Samburu elders manage to keep the young men socially marginal, and in many senses deprived, yet accepting their lot well on into manhood. Spencer finds a key in the periodic inducement of stress and anxiety in the young men, in ceremonial situations, which on Sargant's model would be likely to produce a 'brainwashing' effect. He is not evaluating Sargant's theory as psychological theory, but is content to find a psychologist independently arguing along lines which seem to fit the Samburu situation so exactly (Gluckman's 'abridgement' procedure).

Lloyd's paper is the only one falling within the American tradition of psychological-anthropological child-rearing studies. She draws on previous work by Doob, the Whitings, R. LeVine, and others. She is investigating 'methods of socialization in a number of behaviour systems deemed important to the mature adult personality' (especially as regards aggression, achievement, obedience, responsibility, sexuality, and sociability). Her subjects were a sample of traditional Yoruba mothers and one of elite Yoruba mothers. Both were interviewed and their answers coded. Lloyd notes both the strengths and the weaknesses of this kind of method, e.g. in her remarks on the problems encountered in coding semi-structured open-ended interview material along psychological dimensions. Thus she accepts warmth (of parent–child relations) as a central concept in terms of her psychoanalytically oriented learning theory, but admits disarmingly that 'my own attempts to scale warmth were abortive'. She cautiously refrains from relating her child-rearing material to adult Yoruba personality as such. Her concern is rather with identifying particular qualities, such as those that make some adults more adaptable to change than others, and then seeking to understand the socialization process which produces the qualities: a procedure in line with the thinking of McLelland and Hagen, for example.

SOME ETHNOGRAPHIC THEMES

Taken all together, these papers seem to me to present a good deal of new and interesting material, and a number of ideas (e.g. Richards's scheme for the study of values) that deserve to be followed up at length. However, I shall confine myself to noting a few of the ethnographic themes which invite attention by the way in which they crop up from one paper to another.

Marginality of youth

The four papers that deal with adolescent socialization all show the young people as being socially marginal or experiencing rather marked deprivations.

Spencer's Samburu data and the Mayers' data on Red Xhosa are particularly similar in this respect. These are two African gerontocracies where the young men have traditionally been denied all power whether domestic, political, legal, ritual, or economic. The Samburu gerontocracy seems to have been the more extreme, and to have undergone less erosion. (As Gluckman noted in discussion, it is important for Xhosa youth that they are no longer in a closed system; unlike Samburu youth, they can and do leave home nowadays to earn money in town.) Spencer's paper shows Samburu moran being socialized for prolonged dependence and deference, while the Mayers' material shows Xhosa of about the same age allotted a 'play' sphere in which *inter alia* they practise a 'play' version of later gerontocratic roles. The Samburu young men, though not nowadays required to be warriors, still have to live out in the bush as previously, till the age of thirty or thirty-five; they still cannot marry; they still have to settle their internal disputes by fighting, without benefit of legal processes; they still receive ceremonial harangues from their elders. Xhosa young men, on the other hand, spend a few months in the bush nowadays (as part of initiation) at around eighteen to twenty-two years old, and are then able to return home, to marry, and to own property; once initiated they are to settle disputes in the 'manly' (judicial or legalistic) way and not by fighting; and they receive no more harangues after the one given at initiation; nevertheless they remain largely without the power of initiative in judicial and ritual contexts and in public affairs generally. The striking thing about the Samburu situation is that the elders manage to 'brainwash' active young men into accepting such prolonged deprivation and dependency; the striking thing about the Red Xhosa is that the youth, being allowed pleasurable substitute activities (which count as youthful play), use these voluntarily to re-enact the values and habits of their elders.

La Fontaine's paper on Kinshasa shows the moratorium between physical and social maturity in a different form. The colossal influx of population from the provinces since independence has produced tremendous unemployment. Poverty weakens the authority of the head of the household, and the reciprocal obligations of obedience and respect fall away. Only rich parents can wield the sanction of withholding pocket money or school fees. The young themselves are sharply divided into those who attend school (about 29 per cent) and those who do not, but both categories share some diacritical features of youth culture, which are signs of defying adult mores: a 'secret' language of teenage slang, an active sexual life and ideas of romantic love, as well as drug-taking. Although the schoolgoers' activities are generally 'respectable' (avoiding serious clashes with adult values), the unoccupied youth are seen as 'bandits'.

Among Wilder's rural Malay, again, youth are excluded from 'real' adult activities to a remarkable degree, especially from work and sex. The sexes are practically segregated (except close kin), whereas among the Xhosa and Samburu, as well as in Kinshasa, premarital sexuality is a major feature of the marginal period. Moreover, youths between circumcision (at about twelve) and marriage (in the twenties) are supposed to be maintained by their families, and are discouraged from working to earn an income, or even helping adults in their work; it is only the very poor who cannot afford to keep their sons idle and well dressed. Thus what is an age of liveliest peer-group activity among the Xhosa, or the people of Kinshasa, with vigorous playing, fighting, flirting, and roaming, is here a period of 'standing or sitting silently' (Wilder, p. 234 below), of 'playing a waiting game'. One is tempted to see playing, fighting, etc. as 'innate urges' of the young, and to suspect the Malay of having these 'socialized out' before puberty; but (after all) this may be an ethnocentric stereotype based on the fact that urban Western youth generally appear closer to the activist pattern.

In striking contrast there is little evidence of any truly 'marginal' youth period in Ward's Kau Sai fishing community. Although fathers continue to exercise authority even over their married sons (a recognized source of potential hostility – p. 119 below), the boys are active economically from an early age. Their marriages are arranged when they are about sixteen; the marriage ceremony confers adulthood 'publicly and without any doubt' (p. 115). There are 'no sharp discontinuities' for these boys at any stage. Ward notes that much remains to be learnt about adolescence and the assumption of adult roles in Chinese cultures.

Extra-domestic contexts of socialization

The papers by La Fontaine, Goody, Mayer, Spencer, and Forge are all concerned with socializing experiences undergone by children or young people outside the parental home.

In principle, one might distinguish three main ways of transferring socializing responsibilities outside the home. One is to place children or young people within another domestic family, not the parental one; a second is to assign them to special extra-domestic institutions, under adult leadership or supervision, e.g. schools or church youth groups; and a third is to encourage or allow them to form youth peer groups proper, free of adult control.

Goody's paper exemplifies the first way. Gonja children of about six to eight are claimed by foster parents, and stay with them until marriage about ten years later. Adult Gonja claim advantages for this system similar to those sometimes imputed to British boarding schools by their admirers. It involves the young with a wider circle than the parental family, and it ensures that 'the frustrations attendant on giving up the freedom of childhood are . . . experienced not with their own parents but with other kin on whom they are not so emotionally dependent' (p. 72 below). There is widespread evidence of similar arrangements from other societies (both simple and complex) though the implications have seldom been explored as closely as by Goody. For example, Red Xhosa favour 'kin-rearing' as against 'parent-rearing', and often prefer that children should live with grandparents even when this is not necessitated by labour migration (see I. Mayer in P. Mayer, 1961, Ch. 17).

Whereas the schools of Western cultures are *eo ipso* adult-led as well as extra-domestic, the extra-domestic initiation 'schools' of simpler societies may combine features of the adult-led group and the true peer group. Among both Samburu and Xhosa (for example) initiation procedure combines the experience of living among peers, right away from the adult world, with the experience of receiving ceremonial harangues from adults, forcibly stating adult values. If the peer-group aspects of the experience (one might say) are designed to encourage manly independence, the haranguing is designed to encourage conservatism and continued 'respect' for elders, and to socialize the young to play adult roles in broadly the same ways as their elders have done.

This question of functional relation to later adult roles becomes far more complex with peer-group activities in the narrower sense. Youth peer groups, it seems, can be either radical or conservative in tendency. One tends to expect the former in situations of rapid change, e.g. in the modern city: an example is the 'antisocial' youth peer groups of Kinshasa. The peer groups of rural Red Xhosa youth, on the other hand, both pre- and post-initiation, are eminently 'respectable'; but the equally rural and culturally closely related Pondo have 'anti-social' youth peer groups as well. (p. 186 below). In all these instances the youth groups are equally free from adult supervision or control, but some defy whereas others uphold conservative adult values, particularly in regard to sex and aggression.

However, as La Fontaine shows, even the apparently anti-adult Kinshasa youth groups offer some socialization towards later adult roles in so far as the behaviour being practised is competitive. Is this practice in competition perhaps a general characteristic of associations of marginal youth? One recalls *inter alia* Nadel's illustration of Nupe 'playing' at the kind of political dominance which only a few will achieve in the 'real' context; elsewhere, youth seem prone to compete in such fields as sexual success, physical prowess, and personal adornment. This is a speculation which might perhaps lend itself to cross-cultural checking.

Circumcision: levels of meaning

Circumcision as a socializing experience is referred to in the papers on the Malay, Xhosa, Samburu, and Abelam. At the most general level of interpretation one wants to consider the 'meaning' of genital mutilation and of sublimation of pain as a symbol of rising status. Here, as Leach suggested in discussion, we as social anthropologists may well feel 'out of our depth', though the puzzle 'continues to intrigue'. At a further level, however, we may note that whereas Samburu, Xhosa, and Malay circumcision is seen as separating the sexes (males are made more male, females more female), the Abelam rite is seen as merging them (men are circumcised to prove that they too can bleed like women). Here, Leach suggested, we would be 'involved in relational problems, and the social anthropologist is on territory where he has something useful to say'.

At a still further level, distinctions must be made between the three instances where circumcision is seen as adding to the maleness of males (Samburu, Xhosa, and Malay). What constitutes maleness in each case? Among the Samburu, initiation is an ordeal, a test of bravery; and flinching during the operation results in irretrievable loss of honour for the novice and his kin. For this initiation is oriented to the immediately ensuing life-stage as moran, wherein honour and bravery are key values. Among the Xhosa, on the other hand, circumcision is regarded as a hard but not frightening test, for it is seen nowadays primarily as making boys into men who can marry. An uncircumcised boy cannot marry, and is allowed only restricted sexual relations. Xhosa initiation is believed to transform the 'irresponsible' and 'uncontrolled' boy into a man with adult dignity and self-respect. The anticipatory aspect is much more marked among the Malay. The operation is performed on pre-adolescent boys. It is not an ordeal: the boys are not forbidden to cry, and many do. Fathers are at hand to comfort their sons. The anticipated virility which the operation is supposed to promote seems to be narrowly conceived as better performance in sexual intercourse, rather than as involving a maturing of the personality. But sexual activity remains forbidden till marriage, many years later. The rite marks the beginning of the 'marginal' period, but seems otherwise unrelated to it.

REFERENCES

ABERLE, D. F. 1961. Chapter 13 in F. L. K. Hsu (ed.), *Psychological Anthropology*. Homewood, Ill.: Dorsey.

BEATTIE, J. 1964. *Other Cultures*. London: Cohen & West; New York: The Free Press.

CULWICK, A. T. & CULWICK, G. M. 1935. *Ubena of the Rivers*. London: Allen & Unwin.

DURKHEIM, E. 1938. *The Rules of Sociological Method*. Eighth edition. Chicago: University of Chicago Press; Cambridge: Cambridge University Press.

—— 1956. *Education and Sociology*. Glencoe, Ill.: The Free Press.

FIRTH, R. 1936. *We, the Tikopia*. London: Allen & Unwin.

—— 1964. *Essays on Social Organization and Values*. London: Athlone Press (University of London).

FORTES, M. 1938. *Social and Psychological Aspects of Education in Taleland.* (Supplement to *Africa* **11** (4).) London: Oxford University Press.

GLUCKMAN, M. (ed.). 1964. *Closed Systems and Open Minds.* Edinburgh: Oliver & Boyd; Chicago: Aldine.

HSU, F. L. K. (ed.). 1961. *Psychological Anthropology.* Homewood, Ill.: Dorsey.

LIENHARDT, G. 1964. *Social Anthropology.* London: Oxford University Press.

MAIR, LUCY. 1965. *An Introduction to Social Anthropology.* Oxford: Clarendon Press.

MAYER, P. 1961. *Townsmen or Tribesmen.* Cape Town: Oxford University Press.

NADEL, S. F. 1942. *A Black Byzantium.* London: Oxford University Press.

— 1951. *The Foundations of Social Anthropology.* London: Cohen & West.

RAUM, O. F. 1940. *A Chaga Childhood.* London: Oxford University Press.

READ, M. 1959. *Children of their Fathers: Growing up among the Ngoni of Nyasaland.* London: Methuen; New Haven, Conn.: Yale University Press, 1960.

RICHARDS, A. I. 1956. *Chisungu: A Girls' Initiation Ceremony among the Bemba of Northern Rhodesia.* London: Faber & Faber.

SPIRO, M. E. 1961. Chapter 15 in F. L. K. Hsu (ed.), *Psychological Anthropology.* Homewood, Ill.: Dorsey.

TURNER, V. W. 1964. Chapter 2 in M. Gluckman (ed.), *Closed Systems and Open Minds.* Edinburgh: Oliver & Boyd; Chicago: Aldine.

WEBER, MAX. 1948. *From Max Weber: Essays in Sociology.* Translated, edited, and with an introduction by H. H. Gerth & C. Wright Mills. London: Routledge & Kegan Paul.

Audrey I. Richards

Socialization and Contemporary British Anthropology

RETROSPECT

Socialization in its broadest sense was once considered to be an integral part of the ethnographer's field of study. During the first part of this century tribal monographs commonly contained chapters entitled 'The life-cycle of the individual', 'From birth to puberty', or 'From marriage to death'. In societies in which there is little variety of occupation and life-experience, and in which the biological and social stages of the individual's life tend to be ritually marked, the birth – growth – puberty – marriage – death – cycle forms a useful method of presenting a large section of the ethnographer's field data. It was certainly a practise very uniformly followed, as anyone who runs his hand along his collection of classical anthropological monographs will agree. The life-cycles presented in this fashion gave only general descriptive material of course. I cannot call to mind any individual case histories illustrating growth and maturation in British field studies of the first quarter of the century; nor do I believe that any empirical studies of the process of socialization were carried out at this time. The birth to death method was merely a way of presenting data on ritual, and on what would now be called 'role assumption'.

The second quarter of the century saw the appearance of the books which resulted from those intensive studies of particular peoples that were considered characteristic of the British anthropology of the time. They were mainly the work of Malinowski and his pupils, and covered the period from 1922 to 1935. In these monographs, socialization was also considered part of the programme of study for the fieldworker. A genetic approach to kinship was a fundamental aspect of Malinowski's studies of the subject since he was concerned with the child's extension of the primary terms for Father, Mother, Brother,

Sister, Son, and Daughter to groups of relatives of the same generation, sex, and descent. For this reason his students were encouraged to collect data on the kinship attitudes thought proper in the communities studied and to watch carefully to see how far these were reflected in daily behaviour. Most of us thought this an essential type of work at the time. Firth's *We, the Tikopia* (1936) is still quoted by psychologists and educationists. Observations on child-rearing are prominent in the work of Fortes (1938, 1949), Powdermaker (1933), Read (1959),[1] and myself (1932, 1939). They feature in the work of two South African pupils of A. E. Hoernle, who also joined the London group, E. J. Krige (1943) and M. Wilson (1936), and in that of Kaberry (1939). Such observations of child behaviour are not now commonly included in British monographs.

Malinowski taught, too, the importance of the body of knowledge and belief essential to the success of each system of activities, and many of his pupils described the dogma or theory attached to each institution such as agriculture or family life. Some made observations of the process of handing on the necessary knowledge and technical skills. But it must be emphasized that none of the observations made by this group of British anthropologists were systematic or continuous or of a type that would satisfy a social psychologist testing a hypothesis. Malinowski never made experiments on a random sample of Trobriand children as to the degree to which they actually did extend their attitude towards their mother, to their mother's sisters, or to her brothers. We made statements about the educational functions of ritual but did not consider the possibility of testing them.

More extraordinary, however, was Malinowski's failure to draw up a scheme for the study of the educational institutions of the Trobriand islanders as he did for their economic, political, or religious institutions. The handing on of knowledge, technical skills, and traditions is a task fulfilled by a group, a family, clan elders, age-mates, village or territorial authorities, priests or magicians. Such groups are responsible for a body of knowledge, not committed to writing, which may be esoteric or alternatively open to all, and which may concern myths, history, magic formulae or prayers, patterns of organizing economic activities, or a knowledge of the environment. The responsible groups can often claim charters of ownership for the handing on of knowledge, and observe rules for the passing on of esoteric knowledge or for the sale of, say, magic formulae. They may use a specific language for instruction, and mnemonic devices, such as ritual actions and songs, or emblems or designs associated with traditions or knowledge. The sociology of education could have been handled fruitfully by Malinowski's concept of the institution, but he did not in fact do this himself. I suggest below that it is a type of work that could usefully be done. It is certainly one that has considerable practical importance at a time when the whole mechanism of education is changing in many developing countries as well as in our own.

I have said enough, I hope, to show that at one time anthropologists in this country considered the subject of socialization to be an important part of their ethnographic work, however imperfect and unsystematic their initial observations were. In the 'thirties, lectures on primitive education for university students and teachers in training were given by social anthropologists and not by educationists.

First presentations of the culture pattern concept, obviously closely related to studies of socialization, appeared in the works of Benedict (1934), Mead (1928, 1930, 1935), Bateson (1936), and Linton (1936). The theories now described under the heading of 'culture and personality', which are no longer seriously studied in this country, were a source of considerable stimulus in the early days, in spite of the critical and often jocular comments with which they were sometimes greeted. As early as 1936 the Royal Anthropological Institute held a full-scale symposium on the subject with the medical section of the British Psychological Society (*Man*, July 1936, 150–152). C. G. Seligman was in the chair and the psychoanalyst Flugel and myself represented our different disciplines. This was a much quicker British reaction to a new theoretical import-product than took place, for instance, in the case of Lévi-Strauss's work. The occasion shows, furthermore, that there was a closer relationship between psychologists and anthropologists in the 'thirties than can be said to exist in the 'sixties. The culture pattern idea was also quickly recognized as a good introduction for first-year students of anthropology, and Mead's *Coming of Age in Samoa* and *Growing up in New Guinea* were included in book lists for first-year students at British universities, together with Benedict's *Patterns of Culture*. Questions appeared in the examination papers of the University of London, and, I believe, of other universities. They perhaps fell under the category of those interrogatives that were listed in the old Latin grammars as 'questions expecting the answer "No" ', but they nevertheless appeared!

The concept of the basic or modal personality of the members of a culture came to England rather belatedly after the Second World War. Psychological theories were then in the ascendant in the study of culture in America. Behaviourist hypotheses formed the basis of this work, together with an enterprising application of psychoanalytical theories to anthropological data. The *Gestalt* concept was used as support for the existence of patterns of culture. Learning theories, particularly perhaps those developed by Dollard, Doob, Miller, Mowrer, and Sears (1939) and by Dollard and Miller (1950), were beginning to be applied in cross-cultural studies of socialization. This was the heyday of the use of projection tests in cross-cultural comparison – the day of the Rorschach, thematic apperception tests, Lowenfeld's mosaics, dolls' play, and the rest of the battery. From this side of the Atlantic there seemed to be a positive explosion of experimental energy among our American colleagues. By 1953 Jules and Spiro had listed twenty-four experiments in cross-cultural comparisons of personality, which had taken place in societies ranging from those of the North American Indians to those of China and Japan (Jules & Spiro in Kroeber, 1953). In those days even pre-doctoral students of anthropology who arrived in England from the United States were trained in the administration of Rorschach tests, to the amazement of their English counterparts.

British psychologists of the time seemed little interested in cross-cultural comparison. There were perhaps too few of them and they were too much in demand for projects in applied psychology, in education or in industry for instance. This may well account for the ignorance of the British anthropologists of those days with regard to the use of projective and other tests in cross-cultural studies.[2]

In America, meanwhile, anthropologists interested in psychological problems had abandoned their first crude formulations of the culture pattern theory. Some were cooperating with psychologists in describing the basic or modal personality of the majority of the members of a given culture. Linton, Cora DuBois, and West collaborated with Kardiner in this way, for instance (Kardiner, 1939, 1945). Margaret Mead and her war-time research colleagues were at work on a somewhat similar concept, that of 'national character', estimated by means of interviews carried out in New York with samples of individuals belonging to the nation studied, with the use of a life-history schedule drawn up for the purpose (Mead, 1951, 1953). Kluckhohn and a group of psychological and anthropological colleagues were working jointly on studies of the personality of the Navaho from 1936 to 1948. Later this work was extended in the form of a comparative study of five Mexican cultures, which became known as the Five Cultures Values project (Kluckhohn, 1951a).

All these projects, novel and interesting as they were, seemed to British anthropologists to rely too greatly on Freudian hypotheses in interpreting differences in personality, patterns of values, and preferences, the *ethos*, *eidos*, or whatever term was used. There seemed to them to be too much talk of weaning, swaddling, and bowel-training, and too little of economic activities, social structure, and social roles. The comment was probably unfair in that a number of the American anthropologists had referred to personality or values determinants other than these first infant experiences[3] and yet the Freudian-type hypotheses were certainly the dominant ones.

The work of Kardiner and DuBois seemed somewhat nearer to the British outlook since they stressed, in addition to the effects of infant training, the importance of economic activities, such as the food quest; of structural characteristics, such as primogeniture and the authority system; and of life-goals and ritual patterns, in determing the basic personality. It was for this reason that their work aroused considerable interest here in the late 'forties. It was discussed together with that of Kluckhohn and his Harvard colleagues at a series of lectures and at seminars which E. Shils and I held at the London School of Economics in 1948 and 1949. Looking again at the notes I prepared for these lectures, I suppose I must have been typical of the cautious British attitude then current in that I accepted the notion that there might be such a composite picture as a basic personality, but suggested that the hypothesis could be tested only on the basis of much more detailed and systematic studies of the major structural features of the societies concerned. I wanted an emphasis on family forms and authority patterns influencing the formation of personality, as well as on their major institutionalized activities, economic, military, or political, and their associated targets and preference scales. I accepted the notion that values often seemed to form a system but urged that social anthropologists should attack the problem of values by means of a much more systematic study of structure, activities, and beliefs as a complement, or an alternative, to the Freudian-based studies then current in personality and culture studies. I suggested in fact that we should base our deductions on the type of structural–functional study of single societies on which we were all engaged at the time. This would have led, I think, to a correlation of structure types and values types rather than to the construction of basic personalities for each culture.

In 1950, when I became Director of the East African Institute of Social Research at Makerere College, I hoped that I would be able to try some such experiment based on the structural differences between the major ethnic groups in East Africa. Here were monarchies, segmentary societies, and age-set peoples in close proximity in Uganda, Kenya, and the then Tanganyika. With what now seems to me to have been an almost insane optimism, or even naïveté, I believed that it would be possible for the anthropologists attached to the E.A.I.S.R. to do the pioneering work by providing an outline account of the social structure of each tribe and of its major activities and values. I hoped that psychologists would then follow and either test the pattern of values we had so constructed by means of their own attitude tests; or apply projective tests to see if samples of the community seemed to reveal a basic personality congruent with these values; or add empirical studies of child-rearing practices to the anthropologist's analysis of family types. I give later some account of our failure to achieve this form of interdisciplinary cooperation and of the reasons for it, since I believe this will prove instructive in relation to our conference subject.

CURRENT LACK OF INTEREST IN SOCIALIZATION

By the 'fifties and 'sixties 'culture and personality' had ceased to be considered a reputable subject of study by anthropologists in this country. Nor is there much attention given to child-rearing or to the whole subject which Hsu describes as *Psychological Anthropology* (1961). I do not know of any university department in Great Britain that now gives a course on culture and personality. Some recent textbooks on anthropology fail to mention this approach even under the heading of the history of the subject.[4] It is not that students have weighed the concept and found it wanting but that they do not know what there is to go on the scales. An analysis of the research interests of A.S.A. members (1961) shows that, out of 125 members, eight mentioned 'culture and personality', of whom five hold posts overseas: three specifically stated that they were interested in 'education'; and three in 'values studies'.

On socialization itself, present-day field monographs contain less information on child behaviour, on children's attitudes to pivotal relatives or their use of kinship terms, than do those of twenty years ago, although some current anthropological controversies raise such questions (Needham, 1962, p. 37).

The reasons for this retreat from the study of socialization and the formation of values are not far to seek. I think it could be said that the shock of the impressionism of the first crude statements on culture and personality made by some American authors was particularly great in the case of a national group of anthropologists which prided itself on unusually intensive field studies of small communities. Many British anthropologists expressed their scorn of this early work, but did not follow up the more rigorous methods in the study of culture patterns evolved by their American colleagues in subsequent years. It must be admitted, of course, that these rigorous methods consisted mainly in the adoption of psychological testing techniques as has been mentioned above, but there has also been considerable prejudice on the subject.

Perhaps the traditional British fear of psychology has been responsible. It is reflected in the staffing of our universities and in popular suspicion of all 'trick cyclists', 'head-shrinkers', or testers.[5] This fear may, or may not, underlie the specifically anti-psychological stance taken up by social anthropologists in this country in the last twenty years or so. It is easy to understand Durkheim's motives in trying to isolate a 'social fact' in its purity and it was a good thing for sociology that he did so. It is less easy to understand the almost defensive statements of some British anthropologists of recent years that they are *not* concerned with psychological explanations or concepts – often a difficult balancing act when structural–functionalists in this country have been so much concerned with group identification, group conflicts, tensions and aggressions, and have recently been so much occupied with descriptions of ritual and symbolism and the analysis of the functions of witchcraft and spirit possession.[6]

But the main reason why socialization has been relegated to the background in our studies is probably the simple fact that most British anthropologists have been concentrating their attention for thirty years or so on studies of social structure and the making of kinship and political typologies. Many have in fact claimed that social relations, social groups, and social roles form the sum total of social anthropology. Hence the practising of what Turner has called 'a self-denying ordinance' as regards a number of subjects formerly considered to fall into the anthropologist's court. He was writing about the study of cosmologies (Turner, 1965) but self-denial has been practised in many other fields, whether by conscious effort or under the influence of prevailing fashion. Child-rearing, children's attitudes to kinsmen, and educational processes in general have been among them. If our anthropologists had wanted help from the psychologists there would have been few people available to give it. But the fact is that very few of them asked for it!

REAPPRAISALS AND CLARIFICATION

I think it is time to consider again the related, but distinct, subjects known as socialization, culture patterns, values systems, and basic personalities. I urge this because I believe that social anthropologists have a distinct contribution to make to this type of study and one that is entirely congruent with the intensive structural–functional studies which have been traditional in this country.

One aspect of this contribution I have described as the institutional study of education (p. 3 above), that is to say, the sociology or structure of education and the mechanisms by which socialization is achieved. This means, in effect, the regular inclusion of socialization in schemes for general cultural or 'tribal' studies, or in those devoted to field studies of special aspects. An analysis of political structure, for instance, would require a special consideration of the question of education in political values and of the mechanisms for teaching administrative skills, decision-making, or the enforcement of a legal code. A study of economic structure, that is to say of the groups involved in organizing or carrying out economic activities, would similarly involve methodical observations on the transmission of economic values and the knowledge of economic practices. The structure of religious activities could, and I think should, be associated with a consideration of the mechanisms for handing on to the next generation the magico-religious beliefs, the associated ethical codes, and the meaning of symbols as described below. The use of sanctions, negative and positive, in socialization is also, of course, involved. An institutional study of socialization is a field of inquiries which I believe the social anthropologist is particularly fitted to carry out. Child-rearing practices properly belong to it, but lack of comparative knowledge of child growth and development would probably hamper the ordinary field ethnographer. He or she would require specialist training or alternatively the help of a child psychologist (see p. 19).

The second aspect of socialization which I believe is very much the anthropologist's concern is one that is of current interest. The rigidity of the kinship and political typologies which have absorbed the energies of so many members of this Association is now under fairly constant attack. British anthropologists seem to be branching out in new directions. One of these reflects a renewed interest in symbolism, in ritual, myth, and language; and another a marked concern with world views and cosmologies[7] and with systems of knowledge and taxonomies; in fact with the whole field which was described, at a recent conference organized by the American Social Science Research Council Committee on the Development of Intellectual Processes, as 'cognitive systems'.[8] Related, but of course of a different order of abstraction, are the studies of thought categories and universal thinking processes to which Lévi-Strauss beckons more and more of the younger social anthropologists in England and America as well as in France.

The third aspect of the field broadly described as culture and personality, for which I believe social anthropologists should be responsible, is the study of values systems, another essential part of the process of socialization. There is evidence that values too are becoming a current interest after a considerable period of neglect in this country. Firth has long been concerned with values considered as the basis of choices of groups and individuals (Firth, 1953). Barth's work leans in the same direction (Barth, 1966, p. 5). Recently, Peristiany and his colleagues (Peristiany (ed.), 1965) and Campbell (1964) have returned to the use of the dominant value concept – in this case 'honour' – as they have studied it in various Mediterranean communities, although they explain this moral preference in terms of institutional factors such as lineage structure, sibling relationships, and client-patron ties, and not as a function of child-rearing. Fürer-Haimendorf's recent work on South Asian societies is concerned with moral codes (Fürer-Haimendorf, 1967).

I propose to discuss two of these problems, first, that of symbolism and cognitive systems and, second, that of values, in terms of possible new developments. I shall in each case try to ask what is the social anthropologist's contribution to these studies and what is his overlap with that of the psychologist. This will lead the way to a discussion, in rather concrete terms, of the planning of schemes of joint research in the field by anthropologists and psychologists, which will be based on the East African experience I have already referred to.

Studies of symbolism and cognitive systems

Some of the recent studies of symbolism are limited to the symbolic systems of particular peoples or to special aspects of them (Douglas, 1957; Richards, 1956; Rigby, 1966; Turner, 1962, 1964; Wilson, 1957). They are mainly concerned with the symbolism of ritual, but they also deal with the myths of single cultures (e.g. Burridge, 1967). The ritual studies have been based on informants' statements of what the rite in general or particular parts of it 'mean', 'teach', or 'say'.[9] To these are added in some accounts the alternative explanations given by different members of the community (Richards, 1956, pp. 112–134). Also important in analysis have been the anthropologist's hypotheses as to some of the secondary and pragmatic values of the rites, and his deductions concerning the meaning of a symbol to a particular people from examination of this symbol as it is used in other rites of the same society, as Radcliffe-Brown did in his work on the Andaman Islands.

Such studies of ritual are entirely congruous with the traditional British structural–functional monographs since they assume a correlation between a society's symbol system and the background of its physical environment, activities, structure, and beliefs. They merely require a second-level concentration on symbolism based on this first-level outline study. It is, in fact, interesting that some of the younger members of the A.S.A., who took part in the 1964 conference on Lévi-Strauss, definitely expressed this traditional view on the subject. Douglas, for instance, advises us to proceed from 'the known culture to the interpretation of the obscure myth' (1967, p. 66). She argues (p. 68) that richly abundant mythical material should be analysed against a known background of equally rich ethnographic records, and suggests that it is necessary to understand sufficient about a culture to know what residues are left when the systematic behaviour has been isolated for structural analyis (ibid., p. 67) and also to enable us to understand how myths sound to different native listeners (p. 65). Burridge talks of symbolic systems 'in terms of interrelated clusters of ideas which are themselves quite clearly tied to, or more closely associated with, particular sets of activities' (1967, p. 109). Such comments seem to me to indicate that the writers still want to start by immersing themselves in a culture, but that they want a new concentration on symbolism and a new standard of fieldwork as to this aspect of life. Yalman, in fact, specifically mentions the need for 'new directions in fieldwork' and an analysis based 'not on general impressions and the opinions of the informants on various subjects haphazardly collected but on a systematic analysis of a body of very detailed material, such as a collection of myths or an entire series of rituals' (1967, p. 85).

The study of ritual and myth from the socialization point of view is another such new direction in fieldwork. A major concern should surely be the testing of the fundamental assumption by which so many anthropologists have interpreted the function of ritual, that is to say the assumption that ritual has normative value. How far does the child acquire his moral values through participation in religious rites and how far are these values kept alive in the community by this means? Durkheim's hypotheses as to the function of religious rites have never been subjected to empirical verification, though it would not have been beyond the wit of the fieldworker to devise experiments to test some of them, if he had had the requisite time and patience. Even Van Gennep's hypotheses as to the function of initiation ceremonies are largely taken on trust. I am most open to rebuke in this respect since I failed even to speak to the two Bemba girls I saw initiated in a three weeks' ceremony in 1934 which I described in great detail afterwards (Richards, 1956). Yet I blithely declared that the rites were used to inculcate the values of marriage and parenthood. British anthropologists are sufficiently empirical in their viewpoints to irritate Leach, but they are certainly not empirical enough in the eyes of a number of other social scientists.

I am thinking, of course, not of a giant series of attitude tests designed to give 'yes' or 'no' answers as to the rightness of Durkheimian views, but of a concentrated study on the possible normative effects of the performance of ritual in pre-literate societies, which have few other means of preserving rules, precepts, and views. There is African material on the normative importance of the constant repetition of rites which supports some of Forge's observations on New Guinea peoples (see his paper, pp. 269–291 below).[10] This is a suggestion that needs testing. What is the spread of knowledge of symbolic meanings through the community? At what stages of childhood and adolescence are the deeper levels of meaning associated with each symbol passed on? Who hears myths recited, when, and how often? When it comes to a detailed study of the spread of knowledge of this sort throughout the community, systematic planning is required and the use of many of the psychologist's techniques, if not his actual help. Such an experiment might form perhaps a third level of study, following a first-level primary outline, and a second-level concentration on symbols in myth or ritual. It would be a topical study since the normative functions of ritual are beginning to be called into question.

Cognitive systems may also be studied in single cultures. Such work has produced accounts of cosmologies, as well as the descriptions of taxonomies and systems of classification of objects in the physical environment, which a group of American anthropologists have subsumed under the term ethnoscience.[11] Such studies are naturally culture-bound and based on empirical data. They have not been prominent in British ethnography since the 'thirties when we referred somewhat vaguely to ethno-botany, ethno-zoology, or ethno-astronomy, following Malinowski's attempt to prove that savages were not as ignorant and superstitious as people currently made out. But these inquiries were never systematic as those of the American group bid fair to be. Leach has turned our attention to methods of measurement of length, breadth, weight, and capacity, and of course time (Leach, 1954), and there have been occasional discussions of differences between European and, say, African methods of estimating quantity (e.g. Wallman, 1965) or of differences in their scientific thinking, as in Musgrove's accounts of the teaching of science in African schools (Musgrove, 1952) and in Horton's recent articles (Horton, 1967). The whole question is obviously an important aspect of socialization and one that deserves more specialist study, especially in relation to the introduction of Western systems of science into the schools of people who have up to date been largely illiterate.

I have reserved till the end a mention of the studies of symbolism and cognitive systems, made by Lévi-Strauss, Leach, and others, because they are concerned not with the functioning of individual cultures but with the structure, in Lévi-Strauss's sense of the term, of human thought processes, as revealed by a particular type of cross-cultural study. Field studies will of course be, and are being, affected by the hypotheses Lévi-Strauss has enunciated. But the demand for the cooperation of psychologists seems to me to be particularly great in the case of this kind of work. Many of these new hypotheses are surely based ultimately on assumptions about human perception, categorization, associational processes, and methods of overcoming emotional distress caused by intellectual conflicts or contradictions by processes such as censoring or 'mediating devices'. All these characteristics of the human thought processes are subjects which traditionally fall to the psychologist. All are connected quite directly with socialization. Let me display immediately what Gluckman and his colleagues call my 'limits of naivety'. Binary opposition, thesis, antithesis, and synthesis are postulated. Are these universal cognitive processes at the conscious, subconscious, or unconscious level? How soon do children become conscious of these and other categories recognized by their societies? Are anomalies in a system of classification always distressing? Do children accept the myth content before being aware of the anomaly which it is supposed to resolve? What relation does Lévi-Strauss's 'unconscious' bear to that of the pyschologist with its infinite variety of censoring and, I suppose, mediating devices? What can the psychologist tell us of the relation between affective systems and cognitive systems, or even perception? Lévi-Strauss's human being is a thinking man and not a suffering, anxious, or jubilating one. Is there such a human being? What are the processes of multiple association underlying the use of symbols in human society? Do they make it possible to believe in the single, rigid, structural explanations of Lévi-Strauss? These are only a few of the questions to which I have a persistent hope that some of the psychologists' experiments in this country will give, if not answers, yet considerable stimulus.

Studies of values systems

Anthropologists commonly use the term 'values', but they do not often attempt to define it. Firth made comments to this effect as long ago as 1953, and the situation has not changed materially since that date (see Firth, 1964, pp. 178–224). In fact, of course, the term is exceedingly difficult to define with any clarity. Sentiments, ethical codes, preference scales, and activity targets are closely associated concepts. Such behaviour patterns as gait and stance, or the tempo of activities and personal relationships which Mead has used in cross-cultural comparisons, may well be related to the values system. They certainly strike the fieldworker forcibly. The basic personality of the inhabitants as revealed by psychological tests has been related to their values system and is often confused with it, though the data used to construct the basic or modal personality are of a quite different type. Even Albert, who brings the clarity of the philosopher to the problem, is obliged to describe 'value' as 'a general label for a heterogeneous class of normative factors and not a single conceptual unit' (Albert, 1956, p. 221), and, since normative factors and preferences are exerted in many fields of behaviour – political, economic, legal, religious, or aesthetic – the class is bound to be very heterogeneous indeed.

Most anthropologists deduce a people's values from their expressed views and overt behaviour and these data are inevitably of a mixed-bag type. Albert lists empirical evidence based on life-histories, statements of approval and disapproval of the behaviour of others, legal rules, myths, sentiments formulated in folk-tales, records of conflicts, and, finally, 'socialization and other instructional situations' (Albert, op. cit., p. 222). Most anthropologists would accept such a list and possibly add to it. They would also probably admit that they had worked perforce in a grab-all, hit-or-miss fashion when studying values in the course of everyday life in a village and had got their major clues in this way.

Because of these difficulties of definition and empirical observation it is not surprising that the field has been largely handed over to the psychologists or to the psychological anthropologists with their more clearly framed psychoanalytical and learning theory hypotheses; and that basic personality studies and cross-cultural investigations of child-rearing processes are more numerous than studies of values systems themselves. The ambitious Harvard Five Cultures Values project was directed by an interdisciplinary team, but seems to have been dominated by psychoanalytical thinking, and the same is true of Whiting's Six Cultures series of child-rearing studies (see Whiting, B. B., 1966), to which I return.

To me it seems, on the contrary, that the study of values systems is essentially a task for the anthropologist, and for the structural-functional anthropologist at that. I say this because I use 'values' to mean the principles or unconscious assumptions (Homans, 1950) which form the basis of the preference scales by which we rank individuals or categories of individuals according to their performance of social roles, their attributes, possessions, or ways of living; by which we rate those ways of living themselves; and which determine our willingness to expend effort in economic, ritual, or other activities. They are also the assumptions which lead us to value or despise intellectual processes, aesthetic enjoyments, or emotional and other psychological states. Since these preference scales are based on a whole complex of structural principles, role concepts, activities, and beliefs – in fact Albert's 'heterogeneous class of normative factors' – the anthropologist's holistic approach, with his customary use of the concept of systems to describe a people's structure, activities, symbols, and beliefs, seems to me to be the most fitted for the initial task. A man rates his fellows or chooses his leaders according to multiple factors – the individual's success as a father, neighbour, workmate, political agent, or chief. He selects his course of action by weighing up multiple factors in the same way, balancing the advantages of spending his time in hoeing additional land, doing tribute for a chief who might subsequently reward him, fishing, making bark-cloth, or performing ritual to a supernatural being who may also reward him, according to his beliefs. It is for this reason that it is so difficult in practice even to distinguish clearly between subsystems of values.

We are looking therefore for an operational method of describing a series of related values and for a method which will enable the field ethnographer to proceed in as orderly a fashion as the student of social structure has learnt to do. It may be that the society in question has some dominant interest, such as military victory, the amassing of cattle, or the meticulous performance of ritual – an 'orientation', as Linton called it. This is an anthropological bonus, so to speak. I do not despise the dominant value approach because it is as useful a starting hypothesis as any other, but it is not universally applicable because some societies do not seem to have a single orientation of interests of this kind. They are not Dionysiac or Apollonian. Their activities are not dominated by a desire to succeed in a potlatch or to excel in the possession of cattle. Yet we cannot assume that the men and women of such societies have no values at all because they have no single or striking one. The successful use of the dominant value idea depends also, to my mind, on a particular type of intuitive flash which, again, I do not despise, but it is my experience that some fieldworkers simply do not possess this quality.

We need, I think, an empirical scheme for the collection of systematic observations in the field. My own scheme is based on an acceptance of the fact that there are universal forms of social relationship, and universal types of activity and institution – the inevitable aspects of culture, the 'cultural imperatives' in fact – and that the basic values of a society must centre on these. I cannot describe the scheme in detail here. Briefly, it consists of an examination of the traditional emotional attitudes centred on such inevitable features of the culture as the following: (a) First there is the environment, and the securities and insecurities it occasions either by virtue of its natural features or by dint of the culturally determined rules that govern its use. Different types of land or water are rated according to preference scales, whether on economic, political, or ritual grounds, and the social status of individuals may depend on their possession or lack of land. (b) Biological processes such as sex, food, health, disease, and death are also inevitably the source of emotional experiences and invariably the subject of cultural rules and normative influences. Sex success and the accumulation of food may become targets of activity, or the cult of physical health, hardihood, or physical abstinence. Cleanliness or dirt may become a desideratum. (c) Structural values develop in the first instance from the relations of dependence, interdependence, and authority in the primary family and kinship groups and become extended within residential, descent, generation, or political groups and to postulated supernatural beings. Correct performance in the resultant social roles becomes the target of endeavours and the basis of a preference rating by the rest of the community. (d) Preferences and objectives are associated with the major institutional activities, economic, political, religious, military, or educational. Each society has consumption targets and 'standards of living'. (e) There seem to be aesthetic values in each community, standards of design, music, or oratory for instance, and a patterning of logical thinking and judgement which is approved by the community.

Such sub-systems of values can, and should, be examined

against the composite terms used for values as a whole. This can be done by arranging the material in various ways. (1) It can be ordered, say, under ideal types as recognized by the society. 'The good man' is a compound figure who is a good father, son, husband; a chaste man or a Don Juan; an ascetic or sensitive man, or alternatively a hearty or strong man. He may be a good mixer, a good worker, an organizer, or an accumulator of goods; a 'religious man', or a good citizen, judge, or orator. (2) The system of social ranking, and hence of social mobility in the society, can also be considered in terms of the values sub-systems described above. On what attributes are the classes in the society based? (3) Individual life-targets, conceived as the normal progress of a man from stage to stage, can be studied. The cycle of his objectives is another way of checking the material collected under the sub-system heads. (4) Group targets such as conquest or village expansion and the community's identification with past forms of the society, future forms desired, or special reference groups, possibly outside the community, are a further check.

These categories are not distinct. In fact the point of the method is to arrange the same material in a series of different and often overlapping schemes, which as easily show incongruities between two sub-systems of values as they do congruities. It is a slow, extractive process, a version of what Douglas called the lemon-squeezer technique, with acknowledgement to T. S. Eliot (Douglas, 1967, p. 62), but it might also, and perhaps more appropriately, be called a holerith technique by which different selections of punched cards can be lifted on a steel prong at will to illustrate different sets of values.

This is an operational field scheme for the collection of data rather than an analytical scheme such as those of Kluckhohn (1951a, 1951b) or Albert (1956), or Firth, who specified technological, economic, aesthetic, normative, and ritual values in his list (Firth, 1964, p. 221). It is only one of many such schemes that can be used to get systematic observations on a system of values. It is given here to show how clearly such work falls into the traditional sphere of the British social anthropologist and not within the, to him, unfamiliar world of suckling, swaddling, and bowel-training, or studies of basic personality. I think, for instance, that my rather superficial attempt to describe the political values of the Ganda (Richards, 1964, Ch. VII) shows that the characteristics attributed to this people by a series of travellers from 1862 onwards can be interpreted no doubt in terms of child-rearing processes, as I hope they will be, but that they can also be explained by means of an institutional analysis. A people described as neat, prudish, meticulous over appearances, secretive, distrustful, treacherous, touchy over status, aggressive, competitive, lively, adaptable, quick, polite, and far-seeing may fall into the anal-erotic or some other psychological type, but their behaviour can also be accounted for in terms of the jealousies due to the absence of primogeniture, the concentration of authority in the father's hands, the highly competitive nature of this society, and a particular system of clientship, chieftainship, and landownership. It is this type of analysis of values which I believe to be the anthropologist's contribution to the study.

Such a systematic study of values could probably be undertaken only by what I have called a second-level field study and it goes without saying that subsequent or separate psychological studies, say attitude or projection tests designed to check or interpret the anthropologist's findings, would be invaluable. I believe that such a detailed anthropological examination of values would lead to a breakdown into a series of correlations between different political or economic systems and their characteristic values. An example is the hypothesis that certain values are associated with client-patron institutions and this was prominent in our minds during the investigations which Fallers and I carried out among some of the Interlacustrine Bantu. Campbell is now engaged on a similar study in the case of Mediterranean peoples. We should, in other words, find ourselves trying to correlate the structure and institution type with the values type. This does not disturb me, since large-scale schemes for comparative work inevitably and often usefully break into smaller units of comparison in this way.[12]

EXPERIMENTS IN COOPERATION

It was a comparative study of values I had in mind when I planned the programme of the East African Institute of Social Research in 1950. I hoped to get outline studies of the structure and institutions of the major ethnic groups in an area not more than two days' drive from Kampala, the seat of Makerere University College, of which the E.A.I.S.R. was part. The peoples initially selected for this and other reasons were the Interlacustrine Bantu, the Ganda, Soga, Nyoro, Toro, and Ankole, as well as some other Bantu tribes in Uganda, the Bamba, Gisu, Kiga, and the Nilotic Alur. I hoped also to find psychologists who would be ready to study the child-rearing practices of these groups, to be tested against the values systems of the adult members of the same groups; or, alternatively, to find a psychologist willing to apply personality tests to adults, to be correlated with the results of the anthropologists' descriptive accounts of their values system.

But in practice it proved difficult to arrange for the anthropologists to spend sufficiently long in the field to complete a first-level outline study and a second-level values study of the type I have described earlier. In addition, we had a number of competing interests and a series of assignments in applied research to be carried out for the then Protectorate government of Uganda. In the end, the anthropologists concerned themselves mainly with studies of comparative political structure in the tribes listed above and were not able to concentrate specially on values. We found it difficult to recruit psychologists at the time, and never had more than one on our staff except for a brief period.

Furthermore, cooperative work proved difficult for anthropologists and psychologists trained in the current British fashion. Neither our first psychologist (1952–54) nor the second (1954–55) had had previous experience in cross-cultural studies, and neither had practice in field techniques of the type required. One possibility would have been to ask the psychologist to learn a vernacular language and to make himself familiar with anthropological techniques – to become, in other words, a psychologist of a special kind. This would have been difficult to do in the course of a two-year appointment. My conviction that psychologists need special training for this type of work is confirmed by the fact that, of Whiting's team of twelve fieldworkers employed on his Six Cultures study of socialization,[13] seven were anthropologists, three were trained in the Harvard Institute of Social Relations, and only two were psychologists. The second alternative, and the one that I favoured at the time, was for the psychologist to work in an ethnic group already studied by a social anthropologist or for the two to work in cooperation. My suggestion raised unanticipated difficulties. Two at least of our psychologists were unwilling to work in this way because they felt that the anthropologist's descriptive work was impressionistic. They wanted to write on their own clean slate.[14] In the end, fieldwork of the type I had in mind was abandoned.

One psychologist (A. Laird) did a study of self-perception among Makerere students belonging to the Ganda, Kikuyu, and Luo, and collected fifty sets of responses to a specially constructed thematic apperception test, forty sets of Rorschach responses, and thirty life-histories. The work was afterwards extended to the upper forms of Maseno Secondary School (unpublished). The second psychologist (L. H. Ainsworth) applied a variety of tests – such as the Rorschach, Rozensweig frustration, thematic apperception, sentence-completion, and water-jar tests – to a school and a non-school population in Buganda and the Nyanza Province of Kenya (Ainsworth, 1959). The third psychologist, M. Ainsworth, who worked for a shorter period with us, undertook a study of weaning and other infantile experiences in a sample of twenty-eight Ganda babies (Ainsworth, 1967). Professor L. W. Doob was a guest of the E.A.I.S.R. during 1954–55 and was invaluable to us as a critic and a stimulator, but his main work was concerned with establishing indices of 'civilization' and testing his hypotheses in this subject among a group of 139 Ganda and forty-seven Luo (Doob, 1960).

There were also, naturally, differences in theoretical approach. In order to devise tests suitable for cross-cultural comparisons the psychologist has to select a few variables for definition. Whiting and his colleagues have used a variety of these in their studies of aspects of socialization affecting personality. Their selected 'behaviour systems' were initially five in number – oral, anal, and sexual training, dependence (in the sense of parental reactions to demands for help), and aggression (in the sense again of parental reactions to aggression) (Whiting & Child, 1953, pp. 45 ff.). Belief systems and rituals were used in addition as dependent variables and carefully defined. The definitions made possible the coding of the material for seventy-five societies. In the later Six Cultures study, nine behaviour systems were used: the parents' attitudes to succourance, nurturance, self-reliance, achievement, responsibility, obedience, dominance, sociability, and aggression (Whiting, B.B., 1966, p. xxiii). Yet such selectivity inevitably involves the danger that the data will be misinterpreted when detached from the culture of which they form part – a danger to which the anthropologist is especially sensitive since he is working in terms of systems whether of structural relations, activities, or symbols. Each of Whiting's Six Cultures studies, it is true, is preceded by an account of the environment of the people concerned, and of their history, economic activities, and what are called 'the elementary variables of social structure', which are defined in two interesting charts showing household composition and the nature of groups larger than households 'sharing intimate space' (Whiting, B.B., 1966, p. xii). Religious beliefs, the cures of disease, recreations, and fantasies are also mentioned (op. cit., p. xiii), but it must be confessed that these data do not mesh in very closely with the rest and the psycho-anthropologist probably has not time or opportunity to study the culture itself in any depth[15] or to make the necessary correlations between one aspect and another.

Again, the psychologist has to define his selected traits very exactly for comparative purposes. When Whiting wanted to compare forms of weaning in the seventy-five studies selected from the cross-cultural survey conducted by the Institute of Human Relations at Yale University (1937, continuing), he had to rate severity of weaning on a 21-point scale to be able to score his results. The *Gestalt*, beloved of the anthropologist, of course disappears. Hence the eternal dialogue in which the psychologist says to the anthropologist, 'What *exactly* are you trying to find out?', and the anthropologist replies, 'I can't extract weaning from the whole institution of parenthood like that.' Even the improvement of empirical work on socialization by the introduction of specialists, say in child-rearing, thematic apperception tests, or psychoanalysis, raises many of the same difficulties. With the appearance of many specialists the *Gestalt* again splinters up. The report on Kluckhohn's Five Cultures Values project lists sixty-eight fieldworkers and twenty-four analysts as engaged intermittently during a period of six years on the work (Kluckhohn, 1951a). The British anthropologist is inclined to gasp with envy at such a lavish provision and then to recoil and ask himself whether we know as much about the society and values of the Navaho, or any other of the selected groups, as we think we do in the case of the products of an intensive study made by one worker – what Fortes has called the best form of interdisciplinary cooperation, that which takes place within an individual mind.

Lastly, of course, there is the salient difference between the psychologist who arrives in the field to test a hypothesis and the anthropologist who is initially, at any rate, trying to describe a system, whether of social relationships, activities, symbols, or world views. Mary Ainsworth was, for instance, interested in testing Bowlby's hypothesis as to the harmful effects of weaning and other forms of maternal deprivation on the human young, whereas the anthropologists in the area were interested in the whole institution of parenthood and the family, the people's theories of child-rearing and values, the structural relationship of the two generations, and the system of activities in which the young were to play their part, and all this within a single culture. Roger Brown makes quite clear the difference in approach between anthropologists and a number of other social scientists in a discussion of methods used in transcultural studies, which I unfortunately read after our conference and not before. After distinguishing between hypothetico-deductive and descriptive work he writes, 'Hypothesis-testers are not interested in total cultures or the total minds of respondents but only in those fragments that figure in a theory' (Brown, 1964, p. 246). In such a case the anthropologist is liable to become distressed again by the possibilities of misinterpretation resulting from the selected hypothesis.

We were in fact struggling in a field situation to deal with the age-old problem of the Whole and the Parts which troubles all scientists and many philosophers. A distinguished botanist has written of her own methodological problems:

> 'the botanical and the human concepts, which we have taken as examples, each had a conspicuous unity before we tried to dissect it analytically; . . . In analysing them out

of the primary concept, we have destroyed their relation and it was this relation which was the guarantee of the original unity. No one can doubt that analysis is an essential tool of biology, but it is also, alas, a lethal weapon' (Arber, 1954, pp. 95–96).

The parallels with the anthropological field are evident, and I think it worth noting that it was an eminent historian (W. K. Hancock), also interested in scientific method, who called Mrs Arber's work to my attention. The problem is one that will remain in perpetuity, both as an insoluble difficulty and as a stimulus for scholars of many disciplines.

CONCLUSIONS

I end this discursive and rather hortatory paper with some suggestions which I believe to be practical in the present state of anthropological and psychological research in England.

1. Elaborate schemes of cooperation between anthropologists and psychologists seem to me to be out of the question at the moment owing to the shortage of personnel and funds as well as to our lack of tradition in this kind of cooperation. To my mind, however, this is no reason for anthropologists to avoid the study of socialization, which used to be considered an integral part of their work some thirty or forty years ago. Indeed, I have submitted that such studies have a major contribution to make in the case of two problems of topical interest, that of symbolism and cognitive systems and that of values. On these subjects I have tried to indicate that the type of intensive structural–functional study which has been regarded as the distinctive contribution of British anthropologists would be the best basis for the work but that it should be given a new direction by students wanting to specialize in socialization.

I have suggested that one such new field of work is the study of the educational institutions, among mainly pre-literate peoples, and I have urged that the educational processes of a group should be studied as a whole, or that the socialization aspect of each institution normally investigated by anthropologists – such as kinship, politics, law, economics, or religion –

should be looked at from the educational point of view (see p. 9).

Lastly, I have tried to show that social anthropologists have a particular part to play in the systematic study of expressed values and that such systematic analyses of systems of values, though likely to help the psychologist and educationist, will probably lead to sociological generalizations and typologies rather than to personality studies.[16]

2. I have pointed out from time to time the value of the psychologist's help in the testing of some anthropological hypotheses, in the use of attitude surveys, and in the carrying out of special investigations concerning, for instance, child-rearing (p. 19) and perception and cognition (p. 14). Cooperation between these two disciplines is difficult in this country owing to their separate traditions, and in this the situation here is different from that in America. It will, however, be impossible to do anything at all unless further teaching on this interdisciplinary frontier is available. The anthropologist has his own job but should surely know what the research techniques of the psychologist are, and he might well gain, in my experience, by contact with 'hypothesis-testers' as well as with his colleague 'describers' and analysers. The social psychologist would also, I dare to prophesy, find his work enriched by cross-cultural studies; by a knowledge of the great variety of family, kinship, and political groups that exist, of the differences in authority patterns, the wide range of incentives to human activity, and the methods by which pre-literate peoples educate their young, symbolize their values, and deal with conflicts. He might also learn from an anthropological course what the anthropologist means by systematic description as distinct from impressionism and how he uses models for the analysis of social structure and thought categories. The provision of suitable teaching for psychological-anthropologists or anthropological-psychologists is a subject this Association might usefully discuss.

NOTES

1. Read's work was published in 1959 but on the basis of fieldwork done in 1935. Fortes's fieldwork was done in 1934.
2. Nadel made an experiment of the kind in the comparison of a group of

Yoruba and Ibo children in Nigeria, but he never continued this work (*British Journal of Sociology*, 1937, vol. 28, no. 2).

3. E.g. Mead (1937), Kardiner (1939, 1945), DuBois (1944), Benedict (1947), Gillen (1948), Landes (1937), and Linton (1936). Whiting's later studies of socialization include a number of cultural determinants of personality as distinct from infant experiences.

4. See Pocock (1961) and Mair (1965). Beattie (1964), however, mentions some of the literature.

5. Since writing this paper I have heard a BBC announcer describing a programme on methods of selection for British army officers. He said soothingly, and at once, that no psychologist would appear!

6. See LeVine's useful article on psychological anthropology as applied in the African field (R. A. LeVine, 1961).

7. E.g. Fortes & Dieterlen (eds.), 1965.

8. See Romney & Andrade (eds.), 1964.

9. What I have called the 'expressed purposes' of the rite (1956, p. 112) and Turner the 'exegetic' (1962, p. 130).

10. Baxter (1965, p. 70); E. J. Krige (1943, p. 128); Richards (1956, pp. 125–128).

11. Sturtevant, 'Studies in Ethnoscience', in Romney & Andrade (eds.), 1964.

12. Bateson's essay on the value system of a steady state is an experiment in this type of correlation.

13. Kenya (Gusii): R. A. and B. B. LeVine; India (Rajputs): L. Minturn and J. T. Hitchcock; Mexico (Mixtecans): K. and R. Romney; USA (Orchard Town): J. L. and A. Fischer; Philippines (Tarong): W. F. and C. Nydegger; Okinawa (Taira): T. W. and H. Maretzki.

14. The Whiting Six Cultures project evidently struck the same difficulty. B. B. Whiting explains that the fieldworkers were meant to choose known communities but she found that their 'temperaments and motivations' were such that 'they tended to choose groups who were relatively unknown' (see her Introduction to LeVine & LeVine, 1966, p. vii).

15. Three or four months are allowed in the field schedule for 'work with informants on cultural data' (Whiting, B. B., *et al.*, 1966, p. 5). Would the British pattern of two to three years of intensive field study have produced better results or not? We do not know.

16. Spiro, himself a specialist in culture and personality studies, evidently agrees, for he suggests in a recent 'overview' of psychological anthropology that the important task for anthropologists is 'the analysis of sociocultural systems rather than personality systems' (Spiro, M., in Hsu, 1961, p. 467).

REFERENCES

AINSWORTH, L. H. 1959. Rigidity, Stress and Acculturation. *Journal of Social Psychology* **49** (2): 131–136.

AINSWORTH, M. D. S. 1967. *Infancy in Uganda*. Baltimore, Md.: The Johns Hopkins Press.

ALBERT, E. 1956. The Classification of Values: A Method and Illustration. *American Anthropologist* **58**: 221–248.

ARBER, A. R. 1954. *The Mind and the Eye: A Study of the Biologist's Standpoint*. Cambridge: Cambridge University Press.

BARTH, F. 1966. *Models of Social Organization*. Royal Anthropological Institute Occasional Paper No. 23. London.

BATESON, G. 1936. *Naven*. Cambridge: Cambridge University Press.

—— 1949. Bali: The Value System of a Steady State. In M. Fortes (ed.), *Social Structure: Studies Presented to A. R. Radcliffe-Brown*. London: Oxford University Press.

BAXTER, P. T. W. 1965. Repetition in Certain Boran Ceremonies. In M. Fortes & G. Dieterlen (eds.), *African Systems of Thought*. London: Oxford University Press (for the International African Institute).

BEATTIE, J. 1964. *Other Cultures*. London: Cohen & West; New York: The Free Press.

BENEDICT, R. 1934. *Patterns of Culture*. Boston, Mass.: Houghton Mifflin; London: Routledge, 1935.

—— 1947. *The Chrysanthemum and the Sword*. Boston, Mass.: Houghton Mifflin; London: Secker & Warburg.

BIDNEY, D. 1953. The Concept of Value in Modern Anthropology. In A. L. Kroeber (ed.), *Anthropology Today*. Chicago: University of Chicago Press.

BROWN, R. 1964. Discussion of the Conference. In A. K. Romney & R. G. D. Andrade (eds.), Transcultural Studies in Cognition. *American Anthropologist* **66** (3, Part II): 1–253.

BURRIDGE, K. O. L. 1967. Lévi-Strauss and Myth. In E. R. Leach (ed.), *The Structural Study of Myth and Totemism*. A.S.A. Monographs 5. London: Tavistock Publications.

CAMPBELL, J. K. 1964. *Honour, Family and Patronage: A Study of Institutions and Moral Values in a Greek Mountain Community*. London: Oxford University Press.

DOLLARD, J. 1935. *Criteria for the Life History*. London: Oxford University Press.

——, DOOB, L. W., MILLER, N. E., MOWRER, O. H. & SEARS, R. R. 1939. *Frustration and Aggression*. New Haven, Conn.: Yale University Press; London: Oxford University Press.

—— & MILLER, N. E. 1950. *Personality and Psychotherapy*. New York: McGraw-Hill.

DOOB, L. W. 1960. *Becoming more Civilized: A Psychological Exploration*. New Haven, Conn.: Yale University Press.

—— 1964. Leaders, Followers and Attitudes towards Authority. In L. A. Fallers (ed.), *The King's Men; Leadership and Status in Buganda on the Eve of Independence*. London: Oxford University Press.

DOUGLAS, M. 1957. Animals in Lele Religious Symbolism. *Africa* **27**: 46–58.

—— 1966. *Purity and Danger*. London: Routledge & Kegan Paul; New York: Praeger.

—— 1967. The Meaning of Myth. In E. R. Leach (ed.), *The Structural Study of Myth and Totemism.* A.S.A. Monographs 5. London: Tavistock Publications.

DUBOIS, CORA. 1944. *The People of Alor: A Social Psychological Study of an East Indian Island.* Minneapolis: University of Minnesota Press.

FALLERS, L. A. (ed.). 1964. *The King's Men: Leadership and Status in Buganda on the Eve of Independence.* London: Oxford University Press.

FIRTH, R. 1936. *We, the Tikopia.* London: Allen & Unwin.

—— 1953. The Study of Values by Social Anthropologists (The Marett Lecture). *Man* **52.** Reprinted as Ch. VII in *Essays on Social Organization and Values.* London School of Economics Monographs on Social Anthropology 28. London: Athlone Press (University of London), 1964.

FORTES, M. 1938. Social and Psychological Aspects of Education in Taleland. (Supplement to *Africa* **11** (4).) London: Oxford University Press.

—— 1949. *The Web of Kinship among the Tallensi.* London: Oxford University Press (for the International African Institute).

—— & DIETERLEN, G. (eds.). 1965. *African Systems of Thought.* Studies presented and discussed at the 3rd International African Seminar held at Salisbury, Rhodesia, in 1960. London: Oxford University Press (for the International African Institute).

FREEDMAN, M. (ed.). 1967. *Social Organization: Essays Presented to Raymond Firth.* London: Cass.

FÜRER-HAIMENDORF, C. von. 1967. *Morals and Merit: A Study of Values and Social Controls in South Asian Societies.* Chicago: University of Chicago Press; London: Weidenfeld & Nicolson.

GILLEN, J. 1948. *The Ways of Men: An Introduction to Anthropology.* New York: Appleton-Century-Crofts.

HENRY, J. & SPIRO, M. 1953. Psychological Techniques: Projective Tests in Field Work. In A. L. Kroeber (ed.), *Anthropology Today.* Chicago: University of Chicago Press.

HOGBIN, H. I. 1939. *Experiments in Civilization.* London: Routledge & Kegan Paul.

—— 1963. *Kinship and Marriage in a New Guinea Village.* London: Athlone Press (University of London).

HOMANS, G. C. 1950. *The Human Group.* New York: Harcourt, Brace; London: Routledge & Kegan Paul, 1951.

HORTON, R. 1967. African Traditional Thought and Western Science. *Africa* **37** (1): 50–71; (2): 155–187.

HSU, F. L. K. (ed.). 1961. *Psychological Anthropology*. Homewood, Ill.: Dorsey.

JAHODA, G. 1961. *White Man: A Study of the Attitudes of Africans to Europeans in Ghana before Independence*. London: Oxford University Press.

KABERRY, P. M. 1939. *Aboriginal Woman*. Philadelphia, Pa.: Blakiston; London: Routledge & Kegan Paul.

—— 1967. The Plasticity of New Guinea Kinship. In M. Freedman (ed.), *Social Organization: Essays Presented to Raymond Firth*. London: Cass.

KARDINER, A. 1939. *The Individual and his Society*. New York: Columbia University Press; London: Oxford University Press.

—— 1945. *The Psychological Frontiers of Society* (in collaboration with R. Linton, C. DuBois & J. West). New York: Columbia University Press; London: Oxford University Press.

KLUCKHOHN, C. 1951a. A Comparative Study of Values of Five Cultures. In E. Z. Vogt (ed.), *Navaho Veterans: A Study of Changing Values*. Cambridge, Mass.: Peabody Museum of American Archeology & Ethnology, Harvard University.

—— 1951b. Values and Value-Orientation in the Theory of Action. In T. Parsons & E. A. Shils (eds.), *Toward a General Theory of Action*. Cambridge, Mass.: Harvard University Press; London: Oxford University Press, 1952.

—— & MURRAY, H. A. (eds.). 1948. *Personality in Nature, Society and Culture*. New York: Knopf.

KOFFKA, K. 1935. *Principles of Gestalt Psychology*. London: Kegan Paul.

KRIGE, J. D. & KRIGE, E. J. 1943. *The Realm of a Rain-Queen*. London: Oxford University Press.

KROEBER, A. L. (ed.). 1953. *Anthropology Today*. Chicago: University of Chicago Press.

LANDES, R. 1937. The Personality of the Ojibwa. *Character and Personality* **6**.

LEACH, E. R. 1954. Primitive Time Reckoning. In C. J. Singer *et al.* (eds.), *A History of Technology*, Vol. 1, pp. 110–127. London: Oxford University Press.

—— 1961a. *Rethinking Anthropology*. London School of Economics Monographs in Social Anthropology 22. London: Athlone Press (University of London).

—— 1961b. *Pul Eliya: A Village in Ceylon. A Study of Land Tenure and Kinship*. Cambridge: Cambridge University Press.

LEVINE, R. A. 1961. Africa. In F. L. K. Hsu (ed.), *Psychological Anthropology*. Homewood, Ill.: Dorsey.

— & LEVINE, B. B. 1966. *Nyansongo: A Gusii Community in Kenya*. Six Cultures Series 2. New York and London: Wiley.

LINTON, R. 1936. *The Study of Man*. New York: Appleton-Century.

MAIR, L. 1965. *An Introduction to Social Anthropology*. Oxford: Clarendon Press.

MALINOWSKI, B. K. 1929. Kinship. In *Encyclopaedia Britannica* (14th edition).

— 1930. Parenthood, the Basis of Social Structure. In V. F. Calverton & S. O. Schmalhausen (eds.), *The New Generation*. London: Allen & Unwin.

— 1931. Culture. In *Encyclopaedia of the Social Sciences*, Vol. IV. New York: Macmillan.

MEAD, M. 1928. *Coming of Age in Samoa*. New York: Morrow; London: Cape.

— 1930. *Growing up in New Guinea*. New York: Morrow; London: Routledge, 1931.

— 1935. *Sex and Temperament in Three Primitive Societies*. New York: Morrow; London: Routledge.

— 1937. *Co-operation and Competition among Primitive Peoples*. New York and London: McGraw-Hill.

— 1951. The Study of National Character. In D. Lerner & H. D. Lasswell (eds.), *The Policy Sciences*. Stanford, Calif.: Stanford University Press.

— 1953. National Character. In A. L. Kroeber (ed.), *Anthropology Today*. Chicago: University of Chicago Press.

— & GORER, G. Tentative Questionnaire for Handbook of Psychological Leads for Ethnological Workers' Life Cycle. (Mimeograph.)

MUSGROVE, F. 1952. A Uganda Secondary School as a Field of Cultural Change. *Africa* **22.**

— 1947. *The Nuba: An Anthropological Study of the Hill Tribes in Kordofan*. London: Oxford University Press.

NEEDHAM, R. 1962. *Structure and Sentiment*. Chicago: University of Chicago Press.

PARSONS, T. & SHILS, E. A. (eds.). 1951. *Toward a General Theory of Action*. Cambridge, Mass.: Harvard University Press; London: Oxford University Press, 1952.

PERISTIANY, J. (ed.). 1965. *Honour and Shame: The Values of Mediterranean Society*. London: Weidenfeld & Nicolson; Chicago: University of Chicago Press.

PITT-RIVERS, J. 1965. Honour and Status. In J. Peristiany (ed.), *Honour and Shame*. London: Weidenfeld & Nicolson; Chicago: University of Chicago Press.

POCOCK, D. F. 1961. *Social Anthropology.* London: Sheed.

POWDERMAKER, H. 1933. *Life in Lesu.* New York: Norton.

RAUM, O. F. 1940. *A Chaga Childhood.* London: Oxford University Press.

READ, M. 1959. *Children of their Fathers: Growing up among the Ngoni of Nyasaland.* London: Methuen; New Haven, Conn.: Yale University Press, 1960.

RICHARDS, A. I. 1932. *Hunger and Work in a Savage Tribe.* London: Routledge.

— 1939. *Land, Labour and Diet in Northern Rhodesia: An Economic Study of the Bemba Tribe.* London: Oxford University Press.

— 1956. *Chisungu: A Girls' Initiation Ceremony among the Bemba of Northern Rhodesia.* London: Faber & Faber.

— 1964. Authority Patterns in Traditional Buganda. In L. A. Fallers (ed.), *The King's Men.* London: Oxford University Press.

RIGBY, P. 1966. Dual Symbolic Classification among the Gogo of Central Tanzania. *Africa* **36** (1).

ROMNEY, A. K. & ANDRADE, R. G. D. (eds.). 1964. Transcultural Studies in Cognition. *American Anthropologist* **66** (3, Part II): 1–253.

STURTEVANT, W. C. 1964. Studies in Ethnoscience. In A. K. Romney & R. G. D. Andrade (eds.), Transcultural Studies in Cognition. *American Anthropologist* **66** (3, Part II): 99–132.

TURNER, V. W. 1962. Three Symbols of *Passage* in Ndembu Circumcision Rites. In M. Gluckman (ed.), *Essays on the Ritual of Social Relations.* Manchester: Manchester University Press.

— 1964. Symbols in Ndembu Ritual. In M. Gluckman (ed.), *Closed Systems and Open Minds.* Edinburgh: Oliver & Boyd; Chicago: Aldine.

— 1965. Ritual and Symbolism. In M. Fortes & G. Dieterlen (eds.), *African Systems of Thought.* London: Oxford University Press (for the International African Institute).

WALLMAN, S. 1965. The Communication of Measurement in Basutoland. *Human Organization* **24** (3).

WHITING, B. B. (ed.). 1963. *Six Cultures: Studies of Child Rearing.* New York and London: Wiley.

— 1966. Introduction to R. A. LeVine & B. B. LeVine, *Nyansongo: A Gusii Community in Kenya.* Six Cultures Series 2. New York and London: Wiley.

— *et al.* 1966. *Field Guide for a Study of Socialization.* Six Cultures Series. New York and London: Wiley.

WHITING, J. W. M. 1953. Field Manual for the Cross-cultural Study of Child Rearing. (Mimeo.)

WHITING, J. W. M. & CHILD, I. L. 1953. *Child Training and Personality: A Cross-cultural Study*. New Haven, Conn.: Yale University Press.

WILSON, M. HUNTER. 1936. *Reaction to Conquest*. London: Oxford University Press.

—— 1957. *Rituals of Kinship among the Nyakyusa*. London: Oxford University Press.

YALMAN, N. 1967. The Raw: the Cooked: Nature: Culture. In E. R. Leach (ed.), *The Structural Study of Myth and Totemism*. A.S.A. Monographs 5. London: Tavistock Publications.

Gustav Jahoda

A Psychologist's Perspective

The preceding paper by Dr Richards is very encouraging for those of us who wish for closer links between anthropology and psychology. There are of course great practical problems here, which are considered by Dr Richards, and in general I would agree with her diagnosis of the weaknesses on the psychological side. The number of social psychologists in Britain is very small, compared even with countries like Holland; among them, few are interested in cross-cultural research, and those with active experience of it can be counted on the fingers of one hand.

A majority of the psychology departments in this country have, until very recently, devoted little time and effort to the teaching of social psychology; hence it is not surprising that the exposure of psychology students to anthropological ideas is in practice negligible, usually confined to some casual and frequently ill-informed references in social psychology textbooks. Let me give an example from a current one (1967): there are a few sentences on the inevitable Kwakiutl, Zuni, Manus, and Trobrianders; the only recent work mentioned relates to the Tiz (*sic*); and the total adds up to some half-dozen pages out of more than 500; and yet this represents a relatively generous dose. It can hardly be expected, therefore, that psychology students shall have much inkling of the central issues with which anthropology is concerned.

The reason for the neglect of social psychology in general, and cross-cultural problems in particular, is not far to seek: psychology in this country has during the past two decades been striving for respectability and recognition as a science; and it was held, wrongly in my opinion, that such a goal could best be attained by concentrating on studies of man as a biological organism rather than as a social animal. This trend is now being altered, but the aftermath of two decades of neglect cannot be rapidly remedied. Owing to this situation, much of the research to which I shall subsequently allude has been carried out by American social psychologists.

Turning to anthropologists, I was surprised to learn of the interest shown by them in the culture-and-personality sphere during the 1930s and '40s. I am more familiar with the period of withdrawal described by Dr Richards, when any psychological approach seems to have been widely regarded as irrelevant. This still persists in some recent books, such as the one by Lucy Mair (1963) in which the potential usefulness of psychological explanations is dismissed in the following sentence: '. . . the training of infants in the first year of their life is not enough to account for all aspects of their behaviour as adults . . .' On the other hand, John Beattie (1964) in his recent textbook explicitly advocates cooperation. None the less, the long period of alienation has clearly left its mark. Psychologists are admittedly woefully ignorant about current anthropological thinking, and I am not claiming to be an exception. I do have a vague notion, however, that some sizable cracks have appeared in the once solid structure of kinship as a key concept; and I am wondering whether there might be some connection between this and the renewed interest in what psychologists might have to contribute. The question is whether, having been out of touch for a while (as indicated by the quotation), anthropologists are in a position to assess in what ways psychologists may be of assistance to them and vice versa, since there have been extensive changes.

The most important of these changes, in the present context, has been a movement away from Kardiner-type studies of culture and personality. The reason, briefly and too dogmatically, is that this approach starts by taking for granted (rather than demonstrating) the universal validity of the bulk of psychoanalytic theory. Field material is collected in accordance with the major variables postulated by the theory. The findings are then interpreted in terms of greatly oversimplified causal linkages, ending up invariably and not surprisingly with conclusions in harmony with the theory. This is because the theoretical framework has to be very loose, so as to accommodate highly complex data; at the same time, the looseness practically guarantees some kind of fit between theory and data, and one gets out what one has put in. All this is, of course, a caricature, though I believe it to be so in the sense of 'exaggeration of characteristic traits'.

RECENT PSYCHOLOGICAL WORK OF CROSS-CULTURAL INTEREST

The first line of retreat from Kardiner has been a partial rejection of the view that the functioning of a society depends on the sharing by its members of a substantial core of basic motives. It has always been difficult to reconcile this view with the striking diversity of individuals within the same culture, which even emerges from a careful reading of the case studies supplied by culture-personality theorists themselves. The middle-of-the-road opinion is that the need for common motives has been greatly overstressed. A far more radical departure is the thinking of an American anthropologist with a strong psychological and biological bias, Anthony Wallace (1961). He not only rejects common motives *in toto*, but goes so far as to claim that even cognitive structures need not be highly congruent. The minimum he postulates is what he calls 'partial equivalence structures', meaning the ability to predict a certain range of responses by other people to one's own actions in particular sets of situations. If true, this might have revolutionary implications for most of the social sciences; as far as I know, there has not as yet been any attempt to put this formulation to an empirical test.

The retreat from 'basic personality' does not mean any abandonment of interest in personality characteristics. What it has involved is a shift towards a study of more specific and restricted characteristics, their distribution within a population, and efforts to identify their child-rearing antecedents as well as other factors connected with them. An outstanding example would be McClelland's (1961) 'achievement motivation' (nAch), which denotes a latent disposition to strive towards a standard of excellence; it should not be confused with any broad notion of trying to better oneself and get on in life. Anthropologists could contribute greatly towards exploring this problem further, especially as regards the relationship between the outward manifestations of nAch and social structure; on the other hand, once it becomes further clarified and more widely reliable means of assessment have been devised, nAch might become a conceptual tool of some value for anthropologists (cf. LeVine, 1966).

Witkin's theory of field-dependence is less well known (Witkin *et al.*, 1962), though it has already gained some substantial empirical support in cross-cultural research. Field-dependence or -independence is not strictly a motive, but rather a general mode of orienting oneself towards the perceptual world, linked respectively with severity or permissiveness of child-rearing. Together with ecological features of the environment this seems to have a bearing on people's capacity for adaptation to technological change.

Perception as such is a field that has been lying fallow since the Torres Straits expedition, an early example of close co-operation between anthropologists and psychologists. Lately there has been a renewal of activity, and a large project on cultural differences in the perception of optical illusions has just been published (Segall, Campbell & Herskovits, 1966). It is perhaps worth recording that this started off with a controversy between an anthropologist (Herskovits), who predicted that people in different cultures would vary in their susceptibility to illusions, and a psychologist, who disagreed; the evidence supported the anthropologist. There is scope for work in less recondite areas than that of optical illusions, and studies like the fascinating one by Dr Forge in New Guinea (pp. 269–291 below) might well offer mutually rewarding possibilities of joint work.

The most rapid growth in cross-cultural research has been concerned with cognitive development, in the tradition of Piaget. Such studies of the stages through which children acquire concepts of space, number, and physical relationships, and generally come to categorize the world around them, would seem to be to some extent relevant to anthropologists concerned with what Dr Richards has called 'cognitive systems'.

All the lines of work mentioned so far have already been applied cross-culturally, including illiterate populations. There are a number of others where this has not yet been done, but which hold considerable promise. One is an extensive cross-national project dealing with patterns of socialization, in particular the relative influence at various ages of such agents of socialization as father, mother, teacher, and the informal peer group. These semi-experimental studies have already yielded interesting results: thus it was found that adolescents in the Soviet Union, in contrast to those in the United States or England, usually had an adult rather than a peer orientation in their values. If these methods could be adapted for use in pre-literate cultures, they might help to answer some important questions. Thus, in the case of the Samburu moran studied by Dr Spencer (see pp. 127–157 below), one might be able to discover whether the initiation rite does in fact result in a sudden dramatic shift towards an adult value orientation.

Lastly, there has been a great spurt in the experimental study of social behaviour in the laboratory, dealing with highly restricted segments of behaviour in a rigorous manner. Here are some examples of the problems tackled: the effectiveness of various kinds of social reinforcement (e.g. by adult of same or opposite sex, or by another child; using different kinds of verbal or non-verbal reinforcement) on the performance of various tasks; the effect on the subject of witnessing the behaviour of another person (the 'model'), and seeing this mode of behaviour rewarded or punished; the frequency and duration of 'eye-contact' as a function of sex and physical distance in a dyad. It will be evident, particularly from the last example, that such studies need to be replicated in different cultures in order to establish which aspects of the findings are generally applicable and which are culture-bound. At first sight all this might appear somewhat remote from the concerns of anthropologists, though some (e.g. Hall, 1959) have made substantial, even if impressionistic, contributions to the detailed study of small-scale person-to-person interaction. It seems to me that anthropologists could help us by describing the details of such interactions which are not found in our culture; moreover, by paying some attention to the results of such laboratory researches they might become sensitized to certain unobtrusive and yet potentially important aspects of behaviour (e.g. in the types of reinforcement employed in handling children) which could advance our understanding of the developmental process in different cultures.

I should like to emphasize that this unavoidably brief and superficial sketch can of course make no claim to comprehensiveness; there are many other fields, such as psycholinguistics or psychopharmacology, that may at one time or another serve the purpose of the anthropologist.

COOPERATION BETWEEN PSYCHOLOGISTS AND ANTHROPOLOGISTS: POSSIBILITIES AND LIMITATIONS

It is my firm belief that the disciplines of anthropology and psychology can be of mutual help to each other, but I suspect that many anthropologists are likely to experience some resistance (in the psychoanalytic sense), which requires analysis. It is rooted, I believe, in mistaken expectations as to what psychologists can do. Here is what commonly happens: the anthropologist collects his field material, and after his return goes to the psychologist with the question: can you help me to understand this? The psychologist either confesses his inability to illuminate the problem, or gives an interpretation which does not strike the anthropologist as either novel or helpful. Why?

In making his request, the anthropologist tacitly assumes that the psychologist has access to a store of universally valid generalizations relating to complex aspects of personality and behaviour which are not available to himself. Unfortunately this faith is unjustified. The only really all-embracing theory of this kind is psychoanalysis. Because this meets the need of anthropologists for what Kluckhohn called 'a theory of raw human nature', it has already been seized upon by them; in fact, a good deal of it has become so much part of their intellectual stock-in-trade that they are apt to forget its origins. Hence what is expected of the psychologist is really the same, but more of it; perhaps 'deeper', and conveyed with authority.

A somewhat similar misunderstanding exists regarding psychological tests, to which a certain mystique has come to be attached by outsiders which is not shared by psychologists. At the same time, outsiders delight in pricking the balloon they have themselves inflated. The inflation consists in the belief that tests can elicit information about people which would not be accessible in any other way. Now it must be admitted that this has been claimed for certain projective techniques like the Rorschach (by Kardiner among others), though it remains a moot question for psychologists. By and large, tests are essentially convenient time-saving tools, to be employed with a cautious awareness of their limitations, especially in cross-cultural situations. Given such care, they can be very useful. Thus when Dr Loudon thinks he is gently criticizing tests for not conveying a picture of the people of Tristan da Cunha substantially different from the one he has arrived at without the benefit of tests, he is unwittingly paying them a great compliment (see below, p. 313). If after a few hours of testing the psychologist arrives at conclusions which are congruent with those reached by the anthropologist after lengthy and intensive studies, he reckons himself most fortunate.

In general, my feeling is that anthropologists are apt to attribute to psychology a kind of omnipotence which, after the inevitable disappointment, turns into an accusation of impotence. As usual, the truth lies somewhere in between, and this brings us to the important question raised by Dr Richards as to how cooperation might best be achieved. (Perhaps I ought to stress at this point that my discussion of misunderstandings does not derive from the paper by Dr Richards, whose presentation is most sensible and balanced, but from some personal experiences.)

The first step is no doubt, as she suggests, the training of students. Budding anthropologists ought to be given at least a broad panorama of what is going on in modern psychology. My own personal view (not, I fear, shared by some of my colleagues) is that psychology students ought to be similarly enlightened about anthropology, especially as they are almost certainly more ignorant about it than vice versa. The ideal solution would be a joint degree, such as has been established at Swansea, with subsequent specialization.

The problem of field study raised by Dr Richards is a difficult one. I would certainly agree that psychologists ought to work in areas about which anthropologists know a great deal, and that it is highly desirable that they should learn the language. Both these conditions were fulfilled by Price-Williams (1962) in his study of concept development among the Tiv. As one who has failed to live up to this, it is worth mentioning that even the acquisition of a few common phrases helps enormously in achieving rapport. Although I may not be free from bias, I think there is a considerable difference here between the two disciplines. Anthropologists become intensely immersed in the life of a few communities, a concentration that persists throughout their career and indeed becomes the bedrock of their professional reputation. Psychologists, by contrast, are concerned with more limited aspects of behaviour which must generally be spread over a wider population. While it is of course desirable that they should learn the language, it can hardly be expected very often in practice. In the long run, one answer would be the training of indigenous psychologists.

Given these practical limitations, I have no magic formula to offer, but shall venture a suggestion so simple and obvious that I might hesitate to voice it, were it not for the fact that it seems rarely done: there ought to be more mutual consultation *before* setting out into the field. As regards any assistance that might be given by psychologists, the potentially most fruitful occasion would be prior to an anthropologist's second visit to his community, when he is in a position to give a detailed picture of the situation.

In conclusion, I should merely like to record my support for Dr Richards's view that one of the areas of cooperation that ought to be developed might relate to social change in general and educational change in particular, since in these spheres we could learn a great deal from each other.

PSYCHOLOGICAL PERSPECTIVES AND LÉVI-STRAUSSIAN POSTULATES

The full text of Dr Richards's paper did not reach me until after the writing of the preceding observations, which goes some way towards explaining their inadequacy. Unable to make another start that might do more justice to the broad sweep of her discussion, I decided to venture additional comments on a single theme, namely the questions she raises about Lévi-Strauss. When I read *La Pensée sauvage* (1962b), my reaction was a mixed one of fascination and irritation, admiration and puzzlement. Although the work is densely packed with ideas, it represents apparently no more than a milestone on the way to a massive treatise in which Lévi-Strauss is concerned to show their practical relevance. Since I have not read the two volumes which have so far appeared, my basis for arriving at a judgement is a slender one. With this reservation I shall attempt some reflections on the challenge Dr Richards has addressed to psychologists.

The burden of her argument seems to be that the theories of Lévi-Strauss deal with cognitive systems, making certain assumptions about human thinking, perception, and categorization. Now psychologists are the specialists whose business it is to study these problems. Hence they ought to engage in research designed to throw light on the validity of the hypotheses formulated or implied, However, the issue is probably a good deal less straightforward than this line of argument tends to suggest.

A preliminary question that must be raised is whether Lévi-Strauss is really concerned with subject-matter within the province of the psychologist. While the title of the work primarily considered here is primitive *thought*, he does not seem to be preoccupied so much with the process of thinking as with certain structural aspects. In particular, he claims to discern underneath the rich and seemingly chaotic patchwork of myths a common logical substratum. Armed with this knowledge one can break the code, so that the myths of any people, irrespective of their linguistic form, can be made to yield a coherent meaning. This claim is one for anthropologists to evaluate. However, if there is such a universal logic, common to humans irrespective of time and space, this is bound to have implications about corresponding psychological characteristics. In fact Lévi-Strauss, who is hard to pin down, freely talks about both.

If one looks at his discussion, it is immediately evident that he is not concerned with thought processes in the strict sense. The raw data on which he operates consist of the products of cognitive processes, embodied in a particular linguistic form. Moreover, they are not the product of a single human, but presumably the outcome of a series of interactions among people over a lengthy period of time, with all this entails in terms of accretions, elaborations, and condensations. The object of examination is therefore a *pensée collective*, a precipitate from a multitude of minds within a given culture. It is possible that such a collective product (a term I prefer to 'thought' or 'mind' in this context) may have properties *sui generis* not necessarily identifiable in the thinking of particular individuals. Similarly, the 'unconscious' mentioned by Dr Richards is an *inconscient collectif* (Lévi-Strauss, 1962b, p. 88), and, apart from the element of absence of awareness, appears to have little in common with the way in which the term is used in psychology. It is likely that a majority of psychologists, with the exception of Jungians, would not regard themselves as suitably equipped to handle this kind of problem. In other words, what follows should not be regarded as more than one psychologist's speculative venture, seeking to relate current psychological trends to the formulations of Lévi-Strauss. This could be justified in the following way: even though a collective product must be clearly distinguished from individual cognitive processes, one would expect lawful relationships to link these two levels; and some aspects of the former might be capable of being detected in the mental processes of individuals. On the other hand, there can be no assurance of this, since the dispositions could conceivably be so weak as to manifest themselves only collectively over an extensive time-scale.

With these qualifications, I take up Dr Richards's question as to whether anomalies in a system of categorization are always distressing. I do not think that there can be any direct answer to the question in this form. Categorizing behaviour is certainly characteristic of all normal individuals tested in a variety of cultures. If people are presented with a heterogeneous set of objects and asked to place them into groups that are in some way alike, they can and do comply; moreover, if any of the objects fails to fit they give every evidence (frowning, scratching, or other displacement behaviour, trying it out here and there) of suffering some discomfort or at least tension which is not relieved until they have fitted in the recalcitrant object at least to their own satisfaction. It is hard to tell how much, if any, bearing this might have on Lévi-Strauss's theory, since at any rate the basic system of categorization is a given for an individual within a culture at a particular time. It is only when anthropologists like Leach (1964) bring the anomalies to people's attention that they first realize their existence. Let me therefore try another approach, based on the alleged function of myth in overcoming contradictions, though it will be necessary to extend this notion to include all forms of inconsistency. During the past decade there has been great psychological activity in a field labelled 'consistency motivation'. A family of theories have engendered research leading to evidence that people have a need for consistency among their ideas and beliefs. If conditions are manipulated in such a way that strong inconsistency is experienced, there is a tendency either to take action, or to change one's ideas and beliefs in such a way as to reduce inconsistency (for a summary of one of the liveliest discussions on this, see Feldman, 1966). In actual practice the effect is not easily obtained, partly because on ethical grounds situations for generating sharp inconsistency cannot be readily contrived, but also because the tendency appears to be rather weak relative to other determinants of behaviour.

At this point the well-known studies of Bartlett (1932) could be recalled: he showed that unintelligible parts of a story become gradually modified towards greater meaningfulness and coherence during a series of transmissions from person to person; a finding frequently replicated since. Putting this together with 'consistency motivation', one might glimpse a possible psychological mechanism of how things could have happened, though it is obviously little more than a 'just so' story. Imagine the original creator of a myth, perhaps a man like the one described by Worsley (1967, p. 149). Owing to the nature of the indigenous category system, his story contains one or more contradictions, which cause some slight tension or unease to some of the people hearing and retelling it. Those affected in this way give it a slight, perhaps imperceptible, twist, until after multiple transmissions over generations a change has been wrought in the structure and content such that the originally felt inconsistency is overcome, or at least concealed.

This scheme is admittedly full of holes. First of all, it does not explain the genesis of the myth, as Lévi-Strauss would have it, but merely its modification. Then it assumes that individuals must be aware of the inconsistencies, since it is only under these conditions that their motivating power has been demonstrated. Lastly, it relies on a motivational principle, which Lévi-Strauss would be unlikely to accept. As this is germane to Dr Richards's criticism of his conception of humans as merely thinking and not feeling, a brief digression is appropriate to cite a passage where he justifies the exclusive emphasis on intellect (Lévi-Strauss, 1962a, p. 103):

> 'En vérité, les pulsions et les émotions n'expliquent rien; elles *résultent* [italics in original] toujours: soit de la puissance du corps, soit de l'impuissance de l'esprit. Conséquences dans les deux cas, elles ne sont jamais des causes. Celles-ci ne peuvent être cherchées que dans l'organisme, comme seule la biologie sait le faire, ou dans l'intellect, ce qui est l'unique voie offerte à la psychologie comme à l'ethnologie.'

Thus in a few bald phrases he eliminates motivation as a causal variable, except in so far as it pertains to the sphere of the biologist; thereby he takes us back to Comte and Mill, dismissing everything that happened in between. Perhaps this is not altogether a digression, since his views on this lead Lévi-Strauss to treat categorization as a purely intellectual operation. Yet there is evidence from psychological studies (e.g. Bruner, 1957) that motivational factors do enter into the process. The symbolism of the right and left hands (an example *par excellence*, it must be granted, of binary opposition) is heavily laden with positive and negative values. Of course, Lévi-Strauss would not deny this, and could defend his intellectualist emphasis on several grounds. Thus he might argue that from his perspective the values common to all human societies outweigh the relatively minor variations with which psychologists are concerned; he could point out that psychologists cannot and probably could not show how motivation affects *la pensée collective*, or he might justify it merely as a convenient heuristic device.

Another question asked by Dr Richards is whether the categories postulated by Lévi-Strauss are in fact universal cognitive elements, and can be traced as such in the developing thought processes of children. This happens to be one of the most flourishing areas of psychological study, and a vast literature is available which has been recently reviewed by Wallace (1965). The development of class concepts has been a major focus of interest, but none of the empirical studies surveyed points directly to the principles of classification postulated by Lévi-Strauss. My first reaction was to leave it at that, but further reflection[1] led me to the realization that such principles could not readily emerge at that level of abstraction. I recalled the at one time famous and now largely forgotten 'noegenetic' principles put forward by Spearman (1923), which he regarded as fundamental laws of human thinking. One of them is the so-called 'education of correlates', which has been a model for a particular type of intelligence test item ever since; and in the present context it has a familiar form, as the example below shows:

WARMTH : STOVE : : SHARPNESS : fireplace ? tool ? heat ? cut ?

More recently, the grand old man of developmental psychology, Piaget (: Lévi-Strauss : : psychology : anthropology), tried to show that towards the age of about twelve 'forms of classification tend to approximate more and more closely to logico-mathematical structures' (Inhelder & Piaget, 1964, p. 282). It seems to me that it might be possible to regard Lévi-Straussian logic as a special case within Piaget's system. However, both Spearman and Piaget have been severely criticized for allegedly offering epistemology and logic in the guise of psychological generalizations; and so we are back at the same dilemma.

At a more empirical and descriptive level Piaget and numerous other workers in developmental psychology have established that there are considerable changes in children's modes of classification, complexity, and abstraction, increasing with age, as one might expect. Similarly, within any given culture the categorization of various facets of the physical and social environment does not appear uniform in terms of the level of abstraction or coherence of the underlying principles. The kind of grid used by Lévi-Strauss to extract the 'significant message' fails to make allowance for such variations. In an attempt to meet this difficulty Worsley (1967) proposed a substantially modified scheme for 'classifying classifications', inspired by the work of Vygotsky. This entails a division of classifications according to whether the thinking involved is in terms of congeries, complexes, or concepts. There are a number of reasons for being somewhat sceptical about this kind of scheme. Vygotsky's work dates back more than a generation, and he held the then still prevalent view that the mental processes of the child, the 'primitive', and the insane are all alike in important respects, of which 'complex thinking' was supposed to be one.[2] In his actual investigations children were given the task of grouping and naming a set of objects, the aim being to identify the stages leading to the acquisition of advanced scientific concepts. If a child in such a situation employs arbitrary groupings, or ones founded merely on concrete relations, it is justifiable to characterize the individual as being at the stage of congeries or complex thinking. It is quite another matter to apply such terms to relatively permanent modes of classification which have arisen in large part out of specific historical circumstances. For instance, our own classification of occupations is far from constituting a logical system; the divisions within it into unskilled, semi-skilled, and skilled often reflect historically determined trade union practices nearly as much as real differences between jobs. Would it make much sense to describe this classification as being the outcome of complex as opposed to conceptual thinking? And whose thinking, one might well ask?

Thus one returns again to the earlier problem of the relation between the thought processes of individuals and this enigmatic entity, *la pensée collective*, being thereby led to wonder whether there is any way of breaking out of the circle. One possibility would be a direct empirical study. Presumably fresh classifications are being generated under our very noses in different parts of the world, if we only knew what to look for and how to handle it. Alternatively, one might examine recent classificatory anomalies in our society and trace their origins and consequences; one could think of the corporation as a quasi-person, or the hovercraft. On mere impressionistic grounds, these instances seem to point to the operation of socio- rather than psycho-logic; but then of course things may be radically different in a non-technological culture without highly specialized institutions. All this is probably not very realistic, but I feel that some effort is needed to deal with the aspect of Lévi-Strauss's scheme that troubles me most, namely that it remains largely a closed system: there is an almost complete reliance on evidence of internal coherence, based on selected materials. It is not sufficient that anthropologists should apply the scheme to their own field data and arrive at good formulae, just as it is not sufficient that psychoanalysts should find in their own patients the classical Freudian patterns; in both instances there is ample scope for bias to creep in. A more satisfactory approach would be to supply a group of anthropologists with the same material from a culture unfamiliar to them and see how far they would, using the prescribed procedure, arrive independently at similar formulae.

The comparison just hinted at between Freud and Lévi-Strauss was not arbitrary, because it seems to me that their systems have certain common characteristics, though located at opposite poles of the affect-intellect continuum. Without wishing to develop this into a thesis, as someone is bound to do, I should just like to point out one aspect: both built their theories in consonance with some of the dominant scientific ideas of their time – Freud the theory of evolution, and Lévi-Strauss communication theory. Both have elaborated key concepts which, because of this affinity, appear seductive but have so far largely eluded efforts to provide them with a solid empirical anchorage (it is of course early days yet for Lévi-Strauss). However, even trenchant critics of Freudian theory have had to concede that 'the brilliance of his mind has opened doors which no one now would wish to close again' (Eysenck); and whether or not his universal logic will stand the test of time, the same may well apply to Lévi-Strauss.

I fear that I have strayed a long way from my original path, entered in response to Dr Richards's searching questions. But it seemed necessary to explore at some length the reasons why I feel rather doubtful whether psychologists could at present contribute much towards the elucidation of these issues. This is of course only a personal view, which may well be wrong. However, on a broader plane I am convinced that an extension of the dialogue between the two disciplines could be mutually beneficial, even if it would be going too far to say 'l'ethnologie est d'abord une psychologie'.

NOTES

1. Stimulated by critical comments kindly made by Dr Leach.

2. Vygotsky (1962) tried to use the notion of complex thought to explain, or rather explain away, Lévy-Bruhl's account of totemism in terms of participation, by arguing that vernacular words designate groups of objects rather than concepts: 'The word for parrot is the word for a complex that includes parrots

and themselves. It does not imply identity any more than a family name shared by two related individuals implies that they are one and the same person' (p. 72). Thus he felt that he had cut the Gordian knot of totemism.

REFERENCES

BARTLETT, F. C. 1932. *Remembering*. Cambridge: Cambridge University Press.

BEATTIE, J. 1964. *Other Cultures*. London: Cohen & West; New York: The Free Press.

BRUNER, J. S. 1957. On Perceptual Readiness. *Psychological Review* **64**: 223–252.

FELDMAN, S. 1966. *Cognitive Consistency*. New York: Academic Press.

HALL, E. T. 1959. *The Silent Language*. New York: Fawcett.

INHELDER, B. & PIAGET, J. 1964. *The Early Growth of Logic in the Child*. New York: Harper; London: Routledge & Kegan Paul.

LEACH, E. R. 1964. Anthropological Aspects of Language: Animal Categories and Verbal Abuse. In E. H. Lenneberg (ed.), *New Directions in the Study of Language*. Cambridge, Mass.: M.I.T. Press.

LÉVI-STRAUSS, C. 1962a. *Le Totémisme aujourd'hui*. Paris: Presses Universitaires de France.

—— 1962b. *La Pensée sauvage*. Paris: Plon.

LEVINE, R. A. 1966. *Dreams and Deeds*. Chicago: University of Chicago Press.

MAIR, LUCY. 1963. *New Nations*. London: Weidenfeld & Nicolson.

MCCLELLAND, D. C. 1961. *The Achieving Society*. Princeton, N.J.: Van Nostrand.

PRICE-WILLIAMS, D. R. 1962. Abstract and Concrete Modes of Classification in a Primitive Society. *British Journal of Educational Psychology* **32**: 50–61.

SEGALL, M. H., CAMPBELL, D. T. & HERSKOVITS, M. J. 1966. *The Influence of Culture on Visual Perception*. New York: Bobbs-Merrill.

SPEARMAN, C. 1923. *The Nature of 'Intelligence' and the Principles of Cognition*. London: Macmillan.

VYGOTSKY, L. S. 1962. *Thought and Language* (edited and translated by E. Hanfmann & G. Vankar). Cambridge, Mass.: M.I.T. Press.

WALLACE, A. F. C. 1961. *Culture and Personality*. New York: Random House.

WALLACE, J. G. 1965. *Concept Growth and the Education of the Child.* Slough: National Foundation for Educational Research.

WITKIN, H. A. *et al.* 1962. *Psychological Differentiation.* New York: Wiley.

WORSLEY, P. 1967. Groote Eylandt Totemism and *Le Totémisme aujourd'hui.* In E. R. Leach (ed.), *The Structural Study of Myth and Totemism.* A.S.A. Monographs 5. London: Tavistock Publications.

Esther Goody

Kinship Fostering in Gonja

Deprivation or Advantage?[1]

Discussions of socialization tend to centre on the years of infancy and early childhood, and to concern the character of early emotional and 'caretaking' relationships and the learning of impulse control. Not only are those areas of special interest to the psychologist, but clearly, with the learning of language and the basic cultural repertoire of custom, gesture, and idiom, this period is a vital one for the formation of adult character in a given society. If, however, we are concerned with the technical skills and role structure of this same society, we must give more emphasis to the context of learning in later childhood and adolescence. Moreover, it seems clear that the pattern of expectations governing interpersonal relationships is not established once and for all during early childhood. In later years relations between parents and children are no longer dominated by physical dependency; these and the relations with peers only then begin to take the form which they will retain in adulthood. And it is during adolescence, with emerging self-awareness, that the individual's position in the wider kin group and the community comes to take shape.[2]

If the importance of socialization during later childhood and adolescence is accepted, then we must also take seriously the institution of kinship fostering as it is found in a number of West African societies. This is the practice of sending children, both boys and girls, to stay with relatives for several years. It has been reported for the Ewe, Fanti, Bariba, Mossi, Dagomba, Hausa, and probably the Wolof.[3] My own material on the Gonja of Northern Ghana sheds light on how fostering works in practice in one society.[4] The first part of this paper is devoted to a description of kinship fostering in Gonja. In the later sections I shall turn to a consideration of some indices of the effects of fostering on adults' adjustment. In European society one is accustomed to think of the removal of a child from his parents to be brought up elsewhere as potentially damaging to the child. And given the circumstances which usually make this necessary – family crises of one kind or another – and the difficulty of finding suitable foster parents, this may very well be the case. But is it necessarily so? In Gonja fostering is positively valued for a number of reasons. It seems worth asking whether, in these favourable circumstances, there is any evidence to suggest that fostering has adverse effects on the adjustment of individuals to the society in which they live.[5] And in Gonja we have an 'experimental' situation, with some children raised by parents and others by non-parental kin.

THE INSTITUTION OF KINSHIP FOSTERING

The Gonja form a weakly centralized state to the north of the Ashanti. The ruling group claims descent from Mande conquerors who invaded the country from the south-west probably during the sixteenth century. With the Mande horsemen came a group of Muslims whose descendants still live in the divisional capitals as advisors and traders. The third element making up the Gonja polity consists of the various commoner groups, speaking a number of Gur and Kwa dialects. Rulers, Muslims, and commoners alike are farmers – the freeing of the slaves has removed the major source of economic differentiation between them, since commoners appear to have owned slaves less often than the other two groups. Estate membership is through paternal filiation, though some offices go to sisters' sons. Marriage between all three groups is constant and assumed as normal; this is perhaps encouraged by the absence of unilineal descent groups in all three estates.

The traditional marriage payment is twelve shillings and twelve kola nuts. This amount is distributed among the kin of the girl as a 'witness' (lit. the eyes) that the marriage has taken place. Nowadays, money gifts are sometimes made to the girl's parents but traditionally parents would refuse to accept substantial gifts from a daughter's lover or husband because they wanted their child to be a free woman in his house and not subject to abuse from co-wives. These marriage payments are in practice non-returnable.

Associated with this absence of transfer of wealth to the girl's family is the absence of transfer of rights in a woman's children to the husband. Paternity is reckoned strictly biologically, and adulterine children are not subject to the social paternity of their mother's husband. A man is the father of those children he begets whether with his wife or outside of marriage. That is, rights *in genetricem* are vested in the biological parents and their kin.

As rights *in genetricem* are not alienated by the girl's family at her marriage, they are in a sense retained, and her siblings and parents claim rights in her children. But the extension of rights over children is not limited to the mother's kin. The father also has rights in his children and these are shared with his siblings and his parents. This claiming of rights in children is expressed in the institution of kinship fostering which is prevalent throughout Gonja, taking somewhat different forms in different parts of the country. The institutionalized pattern is for a daughter of the marriage to go to a father's sister and a son to the mother's brother.

A man who wishes later to claim a particular boy as a foster child can insist on paying the barber who shaves off the 'ghost hair' on the seventh day when the baby is named. It is the mother's brothers who have the right to do this (if they do not, it is the father's father or elder brothers who automatically assume the responsibility). The boy remains with his parents until the age of six to eight, when his foster parent (*nyinipe*) comes to claim him. From then on he lives in his foster home except for visits until he is old enough to marry, when his foster parent should in theory offer him the choice of a horse, a wife, or a gun. After this he is free to return to his father's house. That men do return to their father's house is insisted upon in discussion. But in fact the regularity with which this occurs varies in different parts of Gonja together with other aspects of the social structure.

Although descriptions of male fostering usually refer to the foster parent as the mother's brother, in the ruling estate it is held to be a good thing for 'brothers' to bring up one another's sons, so that father's brothers are often found as foster parents.

The father's sister has certain duties towards her brother's wife, both in the sequence of rites which establish the marriage, and when children are born. Her right to claim a daughter as a foster child is seen as directly related to this involvement in the affairs of the couple. And as she is often the one to bathe the new-born infants in the medicine which ensures their health and sturdy growth, she is in an excellent position to ask this favour. Alternatively, if she is living at a distance, the father may send her a message telling her of the birth of a daughter and announcing that when partly grown the girl will come and serve her. Thereafter the future foster parent (*chepe*) should send the first string of waist beads which mark the transition of the naked infant to the status of little girl, and she will also bring small presents when she comes to visit.

There is another formal claim which is made in eastern Gonja by a woman on the third child of her married daughter. If a woman bears two children, then the husband is expected to agree to send the next girl as *kinyipo pibi* (child of the breast) to his wife's mother as a foster child. As she grows she will assume the domestic tasks in which the daughter used to help her mother, and she is expected to make a marriage in the same village where her foster mother lives, thus remaining nearby to look after her in her old age. Her husband will also have special responsibilities towards his wife's foster mother in supplying food and shelter; he will, according to the formal expectation, be a kinsman.

INCIDENCE OF FOSTERING

But formal norms are only a part of the picture. We need also to ask how often people actually send children to be fostered, and whether fostering takes the form it is said to.

Although it varies in form and incidence in different parts of the country, fostering in Gonja is common. If we take the percentage of children currently reared as foster children, the figure for central Gonja is 18 per cent, with an even balance between boys and girls; for eastern Gonja it is 26 per cent, with a preponderance of girls. It is useful to compare these figures with Fortes's findings for a Tallensi sample of 170 children: only 2 per cent were living with neither parent; all of these were orphans (Fortes, 1949, p. 136).

A figure that represents the proportion of all children currently fostered inevitably excludes children too young for fostering. If we take instead the percentage of adults who were fostered in childhood, this is considerably higher. In a sample of 72 adults from northern Gonja, 53 per cent of the men and 64 per cent of the women had been fostered as children. Of a western Gonja sample of 166 adults, 53 per cent of the men and 56 per cent of the women had been fostered in childhood. With the exception of eastern Gonja, where the incidence of male fostering is very much lower, all the adult samples in *Table 1* show over 50 per cent of both men and women as having been fostered for part of their childhood.

TABLE 1 *Rearing experience of six adult Gonja samples*[6]

	Rearing experience					
	Fostered		*Reared by parents*		*Total*	
	No.	*%*	*No.*	*%*	*No.*	*%*
NORTHERN GONJA						
Men	16	(53·3)	14	(46·7)	30	(100)
Women	27	(64·3)	15	(35·7)	42	(100)
WESTERN GONJA						
Men	41	(53·2)	36	(46·8)	77	(100)
Women	50	(56·2)	39	(43·8)	89	(100)
CENTRAL GONJA						
Men	15	(51·7)	14	(48·3)	29	(100)
EASTERN GONJA						
Men	6	(15·4)	33	(84·6)	39	(100)

NOTE: The absence of adult women's samples from central and eastern Gonja is unfortunate. However, female fostering is certainly no less prevalent than male fostering in either of these areas. My impression is that girls are fostered slightly more often than boys in Busunu (central Gonja). In eastern Gonja (Kpembe), girls are fostered very much more often than boys.

Another measure adopted for its usefulness in making comparisons between societies is based on the full sibling group. In the western Gonja sample, four sibling groups in five had at least one member fostered in childhood. I would suggest that the significance of fostering for socialization lies in part in the position of the socializing agents – parent figures and peers – in the social system. That is, if the adolescent gains his view of himself in relation to the society through his participation in primary groups, and his primary groups differ from those of his siblings, but of course overlap with theirs, then for both fostered and home-reared siblings experience is widened. The fostered child is at home in two domestic families, and his siblings become familiar through reciprocal visiting with members of the fostering family as well.

To put this in another way, the sibling group is, under these conditions, an open group. Where first and second cousins, indeed all kin of one's own generation, are called either 'older sibling' (*nda*) or 'younger sibling' (*nsupo*), it is a matter of some members of the full sibling group living with one set of brothers and sisters while another, perhaps more than one, lives with a different set. And in western Gonja four-fifths of the sibling groups are split up in this fashion.

Fostering always means a change of residence. The fostered child sleeps in the room of the foster parent (girls) or with the youths of the foster parent's household (boys). Meals are provided by the foster parent and eaten with other children of that compound. It is in the domestic economy of the foster home that the child participates increasingly as he matures. If he is still living in the same village as his own parents he will see them regularly and may spend some of his leisure with the play group of his early childhood. However, fostering frequently means moving to a new village as well as to a different household. In these cases the break with the natal family of orientation is more radical and the dispersal of the sibling group is emphasized by the intervening distance. The proportion of cases in which fostering involves a move to a different village varies from one part of the country to another. In central Gonja, where the population density is low and villages are scattered, residence in a different village from the parents is very common. In an eastern Gonja sample of 79 currently fostered children, 49 (62 per cent) were living in a different village from both parents.

But does fostering actually take the form it is said to? This is really two different questions. First, do foster children go to father's sisters, mother's brothers, and mother's mother, the traditional foster parents? Second, are they sent in the circumstances specified by the formal norm? The brief answer to the first question is that in fact foster children go to a wider range of kin than is formally specified. In the Buipe sample of currently fostered children (central Gonja), for girls, the father's sister and the mother's mother were the most common foster parents, in that order. But together they accounted for less than two-thirds of all cases. The single most common category of boys' foster parents was father's maternal siblings and matrilineal cousins, followed by mother's brother and mother's father. In all, 19 out of 34, or 56 per cent, went to a real or classificatory sibling of the parents, while the remainder went to a real or classificatory parent's parent. These same 34 foster children were almost exactly evenly divided between maternal and paternal kin (16, or 47 per cent, were with maternal kin, and 18, or 53 per cent, with paternal kin). This is confirmed on the (very small) figures for the second central Gonja sample. The

TABLE 2 *Distribution of foster children between maternal and paternal kin in seven Gonja samples*

	Foster children sent to:									
	Maternal kin		*Paternal kin*		*Others**		*Not known*		*Total*	
	No.	%	*No.*	%	*No.*	%	*No.*	%	*No.*	%
NORTHERN GONJA										
Boys	6	(37·5)	9	(56·2)	1	(6·2)			16	(99·9)
Girls	13	(48·1)	14	(51·9)					27	(100)
WESTERN GONJA										
Boys	18	(43·9)	9	(22·0)	8	(19·5)	6	(14·6)	41	(100)
Girls	28	(56·0)	19	(38·0)	3	(6·0)			50	(100)
CENTRAL GONJA										
Busunu boys	4	(25·0)	5	(31·2)	5	(31·2)	2	(12·5)	16	(99·9)
Buipe girls & boys	16	(47·1)	18	(52·9)					34	(100)
EASTERN GONJA										
Boys	none		5	(83·3)	1	(16·7)			6	(100)

* The 'others' category includes those reared by own full siblings, by parents' master or mistress (i.e. children of ex-slaves), by a chief, or by a Koranic teacher.

proportions for western Gonja show a bias in favour of maternal kin. Girls in the northern Gonja sample went about equally to maternal and paternal kin, but there is a bias in favour of paternal kin as foster parents for boys in this group. There were no cases of boys fostered by maternal kin in the eastern Gonja sample (*Table 2*). These variations are all consistent with differing emphases on maternal and paternal lines in each area, which it is not possible to examine here. However, overall it is clear that, with the exception of the fostering of boys in eastern Gonja, children of both sexes are sent to maternal and paternal kin. That is, successful claims are made by kin of both spouses on the children of a marriage. They are, however, made more often than the norm suggests by the grandparental generation.

VOLUNTARY AND CRISIS FOSTERING

The second question to be raised about the fit between the formal picture of fostering and actual practice concerns the circumstances in which children are sent to foster parents. According to the actors' model, foster parents ask for a particular child at birth and then, when he is old enough to 'have sense', come and collect him from the parents. However, if fostered children are compared with other children, a disproportionate number of them are found to be from homes where the parents' marriage has been broken by death or divorce. Again from the Buipe sample: 40 per cent of all children and adolescents are from broken homes, but, of the foster children, 74 per cent (25) are children of parents whose marriages are no longer intact. Here two modifying factors should be mentioned: in the first place, some of these children were sent to be fostered before their parents' marriage ended. I know this to be so for some, but lack information on others. Second, only in two of these 25 cases were both parents dead. In the remaining 23, the child could have lived with a surviving parent rather than a foster parent.

It seems that the institution of fostering provides a charter which can be employed in placing children on the dispersal of the original family of orientation. While each parent may keep one or two children on divorce, and some children may stay with the surviving parent following a death, the dissolution of the conjugal family tends to bring about the placing of some or even all of the children with foster parents. It should be emphasized that this is a culturally patterned alternative, not a necessity, except in those few instances where both parents are dead. Where fostering follows the dissolution of the conjugal family it is convenient to designate it as 'crisis' fostering to distinguish it from 'voluntary' fostering, which is initiated while the parents' marriage is intact. In the western Gonja

TABLE 3 *Crisis and voluntary fostering among men and women of northern and western Gonja*

	Form of fostering:							
	Crisis		*Voluntary*		*Not known*		*Total*	
	No.	%	*No.*	%	*No.*	%	*No.*	%
NORTHERN GONJA								
Men	12	(75·0)	4	(25·0)			16	(100)
Women	18	(66·7)	9	(33·3)			27	(100)
WESTERN GONJA								
Men*	16	(43·2)	21	(56·8)			37	(100)
Women	26	(52·0)	23	(46·0)	1	(2·0)	50	(100)

* These data are taken from a different sample from that used in *Tables 1* and *2* (in which there was insufficient information to distinguish between crisis and voluntary fostering).

sample reported in *Table 3*, 43 per cent of the cases of male fostering and 52 per cent of the cases of female fostering were associated with the disruption of the parents' marriage by either death or divorce. For the northern Gonja sample, even higher proportions – 75 per cent and 67 per cent, respectively – of the cases of male and female fostering were associated with the breakdown of the parents' marriage.

SPECIFIC FUNCTIONS OF FOSTERING

The care of children in crises is an example of a functionally specific use of fostering. There are a number of other specific functions of this institution as well as the more diffuse, but equally important, functions that concern the maintenance of links between kin. Specific functions can be discerned at several levels: with respect to the moral and technical education of the child concerned; with respect to the foster parents; and with respect to the parents themselves.

Although there is a certain amount of variation, it is generally held that children should not be sent for fostering until they 'have sense' – about the age of six or seven. The period of the next ten years or more during which they live with foster parents is one of training in the skills specific to each sex as adults – cooking and other domestic tasks for girls, and farming for boys. It is the foster parents' task to provide precept and model for these skills, and they are felt to be in a better position to do so than a child's own parents because they will not hesitate to use disciplinary measures when necessary, as would a parent. Conversely, it is held that the child fears and respects a foster parent where he might take advantage of the affection and lenience of his own parent. In other words, parents are not expected to be good teachers for their own children, and fostering is seen as one way of making sure that a child gets a good education. The foster parent is held responsible for the moral as well as the technical education of the child, and difficult and proud children may find themselves sent to foster parents who should be able to teach them respect (*jirma*) and perhaps strengthen a wayward character (*da*).

Functions of fostering for the foster parent are varied. There is no doubt of the value of a girl to the domestic economy from an early age: fetching water, washing dishes and clothes, minding children, sweeping the compound, running errands, selling bits of condiment and produce around the town, and eventually cooking and gathering firewood – all these women's tasks are readily shared and even taken over by the older girls. Boys are useful at a later age, although they can run errands and scare birds from ripening grain when still young. However, in discussing these 'economic' functions of fostering one needs to remember that the children would have been equally useful at home. There are cases in which only children are sent to a foster parent who has children of her own; and there are boys who do nothing whatever on the farm of the foster parent. This is not the place for a detailed analysis of the Gonja economy: it is a relatively simple one based on hoe agriculture, with ample land owing to a willingness to farm several miles from the permanent villages. There is no ownership of resources other than a few cattle. I can say only that there is no evidence that economic necessity is a decisive factor in the allocation of foster children. If the labour of youths *were* at a premium one would expect to see stepfathers making more effort to retain their wives' sons to farm with them. This is very rare.

Where old women are concerned, the companionship of a foster child is reckoned as particularly valuable, and this is also true for childless women. However, the sending of children to barren women is not stressed by the Gonja – it certainly happens, but for them its importance is overshadowed by the other features of the institution.

The specific functions of fostering so far as the true parents are concerned are most evident in crisis fostering. It is assumed that a co-wife will not take the trouble to look after another woman's child, and following the death of the mother or the parents' divorce the safest place for young children is with a kinswoman. A woman does not like to enter a new marriage with several children, although she may take a daughter and any infants with her. There is a special term, *angola*, for a boy living with his mother's husband and the relationship is compared to that between sexual rivals. They are enemies and each is expected to wish the other ill. So awkward is this situation that even young boys are said to run away to their father or a kinsman rather than live with a stepfather.

The advantages to the parents of voluntary fostering are less evident. Where there are many children it is one way of reducing the number of mouths to feed. In this situation, too, there is danger of jealousy leading to attempts to injure the children through witchcraft and it is thought safer to disperse them. One youth I knew who had done very well in school lived with his classificatory mother's brothers in order to be safe from the supposed hostility of his father's wives whose own sons were less successful. The management of difficult children is often handed over to foster parents much as an English child might be sent to boarding school.

In view of the Dagomba practice of sending the children of chiefs to court officials for training (Oppong, 1965) and of the

Buganda custom of sending boys to court to serve as messengers and pages in the hope of later political advantages (Richards, 1964), it should be noted that there does not seem to be any specifically political function to Gonja fostering. There is no system of clientship in Gonja, and succession to political office is within the dynastic segment of one's father, so preferment can be only of an informal and limited nature. There is no important sense in which the child's family stands to gain by an alliance based on fostering.

There were a few cases in which a boy had been sent to cement the friendship of two chiefs, in much the same way that one might give the other a wife. Here again, this is done, but is not made much of by the people themselves – it is one special application of a general practice. Another similar application is the sending of a boy to his Koranic teacher. It is perhaps surprising how seldom this occurs, given the charter of fostering, but it does sometimes happen.

Nor is access to special skills gained by an apprenticeship based on the fostering relationship. In Gonja there are few such skills: ironworking, divining, weaving, and drumming just about exhaust the list. Of these the blacksmiths form patronymic groups, but not endogamous ones. They do exchange children in fostering, and a sister's son may occasionally thus learn and practise the craft. But there is no systematic utilization of fostering for recruitment, and a man may train either his own sons, or his brother's or sister's. For the rest of the skills, they may be taken up by anyone who wishes, weaving and divining in adulthood.[7] Most boys fool around with drumming, and those who find they have a special aptitude will attach themselves to an accomplished drummer to learn the intricacies of the art.[8]

The purpose of detailing the specific functions of fostering to the main actors concerned has been to make clear what fostering does not do, as well as what it does. Those functions that are most evident, and most emphasized, in Gonja are such as must be involved wherever fostering occurs – training, service, and companionship. There does not appear to be any single institutional feature which is closely related to the sending of foster children: economic and political advantages are limited, and certainly not stressed. What does seem to be the most outstanding feature of kin fostering in Gonja is its pervasive, widespread character. Except in eastern Gonja, something like 50 per cent of all adults in each sample had been fostered in childhood, and household censuses show no disproportionate concentrations of foster children, apart from at the households of important chiefs, which have larger numbers of attached residents of all sorts.

One final descriptive point might be made. While fostering of classificatory siblings' children does occur and occasionally of classificatory grandchildren, what does not happen, or happens so rarely as to be inconsequential, is the sending of a child to an affine of a parent's sibling. The foster-parent/foster-child tie is a direct one, based on the reciprocal relationship of service and training with respect to tasks which are central to the adult sex-typed role in this society. Men take their kinsfolk's sons, women take their kinsfolk's daughters. The role model is provided (as are discipline and instruction) by the child's kinsman or kinswoman, not by an affine.

Given the pervasiveness of the institution, and the general nature of the training which is its main rationale, I would argue that its major function lies in the way in which it reinforces ties between kin. Where, as in Gonja, marriage between members of different estates and different ethnic groups is common, and where there are no strongly corporate unilineal descent groups to organize rights and duties and claims on property, there is a constant centrifugal tendency among kin. This is most extreme in central Gonja where villages are relatively far apart and marriages across considerable distances add an element of spatial dispersion to the social and ethnic complexity. Under these conditions, rights in children assume the character of a joint resource. Claims on this resource are one way of expressing kin ties, for the kindred is not only unbounded, but there are strong pressures to keep it 'open'.

CHILDREN'S RESPONSES TO FOSTERING

I now want to turn to the question of the effect of fostering on those most directly concerned: the children being fostered and the adults who were fostered in childhood.

When a group of fostered children were asked how they felt

about it, the range of responses was very wide. Some said that they preferred to be with foster parents because they got more attention, more food, and more goods to take with them on marriage, and because, if the foster parent did not treat them well, their parents could intervene, whereas 'your own mother can do as she likes and no one will say anything'. Others said that they would rather be with their own parent because there they would not be forced to work, would not be disciplined so severely, and would get more food and more attention. Asked what they intended to do with their own children, the reaction was again mixed, although the majority replied that they would have at least one child fostered. Some of those who had previously stated that they would rather be brought up by their own parents said that they would send their child to a parent or sibling to be fostered. This would seem to indicate a sense of obligation to keep the system going, even at the age of six to sixteen. Interestingly enough, only a few of the fostered children spoke of sending a child to the person currently acting as their foster parent. There does not seem to be a direct chain of obligation set up by this relationship. It might also be argued that, where so many are prepared to send a future child to a parent and not to their current foster parent, there is a stronger attachment to parents, and a stronger sense of obligation with respect to them, than is felt towards foster parents, despite the fostering relationship. This fits with the picture of the fostering relationship as an additive one, not replacing that between parents and children, but experienced as something different and additional to it.

The mixed feelings held by foster children themselves raise the question of the effect of fostering on a child. What kinds of adult do fostered children become? It seems to me worth taking this question seriously also because in thinking of fostering in our own society we assume that it is a makeshift arrangement made necessary by some crisis in the parental family. It is expected that it will be to the disadvantage of the child and it is thought likely that maladjustment in adulthood may follow a history of fostering in childhood. The implication is that only the parents can provide that mixture of affection and guidance which is necessary for healthy adjustment while growing up. We are not here concerned with the problem of removing a child from his parents during the first four or five years. As Bowlby (1960) has shown, this may have special hazards and raises problems connected with development in infancy and early childhood which are not directly relevant to the Gonja situation where fostering normally is initiated after the age of five.

Any answer to the question as to what kinds of adult are created by Gonja kinship fostering presupposes a *measure* of adjustment. I have two such indices to offer, neither free from difficulties, but taken together providing, I think, some corroboration for what must otherwise be a mere impression that the fostered are not at a disadvantage compared with the non-fostered in their adaptation to the society in which they live.

'SUCCESS' IN ADULTHOOD AS AN INDEX OF THE EFFECT OF FOSTERING

The first of these indices is based on the rearing histories of 'successful' men, and compares the incidence of fostering in this group with that among 'ordinary' men. The question here is whether successful men are more likely than those who have not distinguished themselves to have been fostered as children. If fostering is related to success, this might be either directly, through offering greater opportunity of appointment to and advancement in office, or through rendering such achievement more difficult; or indirectly, through developing personality characteristics which either help or hinder success.

For the purposes of this inquiry, successful men have been defined as those holding positions in one of the three status hierarchies which operate in the two divisional capitals where these data were collected.

The traditional system is based on a hierarchy of chiefships. In Kpembe (eastern Gonja) these are open to men whose fathers were members of the ruling estate by patrifiliation. The ruling estate is divided into three dynastic segments – non-exogamous with only truncated genealogies, and thus not lineages. Succession to a chiefship depends on the support of a man's own dynastic segment – that is of his paternal kin. In the second capital, Bole (western Gonja), succession may be either by patrifiliation to one of the chiefships of the first rank, or by matrifiliation to the ruling estate – to a second-rank chiefship. In both divisions there are a few commoner chiefships, succession to which is by paternal filiation.[9] Most of the successful men in the samples from Kpembe and Bole held chiefships in the traditional system.

A second group of successful men was drawn from the officials in local government. These are achieved statuses, dependent for the most part on at least a middle-school education. This also introduced a bias in favour of the ruling estate, particularly in Bole which has had its own middle school only a few years.

The third category of successful men was made up of those who were respected elders in their communities but held no office in either the traditional or the modern system.

In all, 29 'successful' men from Kpembe and 25 from Bole were interviewed about their rearing histories. On another occasion, random samples of men from these two communities were interviewed concerning marriage histories and included in the interviews was a question on rearing history. If we compare

TABLE 4a *Comparison of rearing experience of 'successful' men and 'ordinary' men from eastern Gonja*

Rearing experience	*Ordinary men*	*Successful men*
Fostered	6	10
Reared by parents	33	19
Tota	39	29

$\chi^2 = 3{\cdot}42$; $p = < {\cdot}10$

TABLE 4b *Comparison of rearing experience of 'successful' men and 'ordinary' men from western Gonja*

Rearing experience	*Ordinary men*	*Successful men*
Fostered	41	13
Reared by parents	36	12
Total	77	25

$\chi^2 = {\cdot}008$; not significant

the incidence of fostering in these 'ordinary' populations with that among the 'successful' men it is possible to see whether successful men are more or less likely than others to have been fostered in childhood.

This comparison is made in *Tables 4, 5,* and *6.* It is immediately clear from the figures presented that in neither the eastern nor the western Gonja sample is fostering negatively associated with success: successful men have been more often fostered as children than have those who hold no position. This difference is only pronounced for the eastern Gonja sample (*Table 4a*). Indeed, the straight comparison between ordinary and successful men for western Gonja (*Table 4b*) shows no difference. However, while eastern Gonja 'ordinary' men were preponderantly

TABLE 5 *Comparison of rearing experience of 'successful' men and 'ordinary' men of ruling estate: western Gonja*

Rearing experience	*Ordinary men of ruling estate*	*Successful men of ruling estate*
Fostered	10	13
Reared by parents	16	12
Total	26	25

$\chi^2 = \cdot 916$; not significant

of the ruling estate, this was not the case in western Gonja where approximately one-third came from each of the three estates. In the latter area male fostering is more widely practised by commoners than by the other two estates. Yet if 'ordinary' men of the ruling estate (those who have attained no position) are compared with 'successful' men of the ruling group (*Table 5*), we again find that the successful men are more likely to have been fostered, although the difference here is not so pronounced as that in the eastern Gonja sample. Thus it seems unlikely that the experience of being reared by foster parents systematically gives rise to men who are handicapped in comparison with their home-reared peers in the pursuit of adult careers.

This still leaves open the question of why fostering should be related to success. Is it through the conferring of direct advantage, or indirectly through the development of such characteristics as independence and achievement drive which are an advantage in the struggle for position? To this question my material offers some clues, if no conclusive answer.

Fostering by paternal kin may operate to strengthen later claims to office by establishing personal links with agnates other than one's own father. This is how the Gonja themselves see it, and several of the chiefs in the Bole sample grew up with father's brothers (real or classificatory) who were themselves chiefs and thus in a position to influence appointments to vacant skins. However, judging from those instances I know well, the foster parent himself is often not alive by the time a protegé seeks chiefship – at the earliest in his thirties. Nevertheless, if the foster parent himself is no longer able to be of help, his sons and younger brothers with whom the protegé grew to adulthood are then among the vocal members of the family council which determines who among the men of the segment shall be put forward for office. Thus it may well be that fostering by patrilineal kin serves to strengthen a man's position with the group of agnates whose support is necessary if he is to obtain a chiefship.

It is, of course, also possible that the experience of being fostered tends to develop characteristics which give a man positive advantage in forming his career. Consideration of cases of fostering of successful men by maternal kin is revealing here (*Table 6*). In the Bole sample there were six holders of sister's son chiefships, four of whom had been fostered. But only one of these four had been brought up by his maternal kin. That is, for the other three men, fostering could not have led directly to chiefship (success as measured here) because, while they were reared by paternal kin, their chiefships were obtained through maternal connections. In the Kpembe sample there were two cases of successful men fostered by mother's brothers. One of these had been manoeuvred into a chiefship by his mother's brother. The other had been placed in a privileged position where he had minor jobs with the Medical Field Unit which led to his picking up a fair command of English. Now, in a different town and subdivision from that in which he grew up, and long after his foster parent's death, his own initiative had

TABLE 6 *Rearing experience of Bole 'successful' men related to type of position held*

Position held	*Reared by:* *Parents*	*Paternal kin*	*Maternal kin*	*Total*
Chiefship of the first rank	6	4	0	10
Chiefship of the second rank	2	3	1	6
Achieved position	4	1	4	9
Total	12 (48%)	8 (32%)	5 (20%)	25 (100%)

brought him to hold the job of court interpreter, which placed him among the 'new elite'. Thus it appears that fostering by maternal kin does not necessarily lead directly to the holding of a sister's son chiefship, although in some cases this does occur. There are other factors at work, and at least some of the time they take the form of individual initiative. It is perhaps significant in this regard that in the Bole sample none of those fostered by maternal kin later succeeded to chiefships of the first rank (patrifilial chiefships) but four of the five did *achieve* positions of importance. In fact, of these four men, one was the member of parliament for the district and a government minister, and another the District Commissioner.

It is clear from these data that the factors involved in successful careers are complex and the role played by fostering is by no means plain. However, it does seem fair to say that fostering does not *hamper* achievement in either the traditional or the modern system.

MARITAL STABILITY AS AN INDEX OF THE EFFECT OF FOSTERING

The second index concerns the relative frequency of divorce for women who have been fostered and for those who have been brought up by their own parents. In our own society divorce is considered to be both an indication of individual inability to form stable emotional relationships, and a response to pressures which render the establishment of stable unions difficult.

I have argued elsewhere (E. Goody, 1962; J. & E. Goody, 1967) that marriage in Gonja is unstable owing to institutional features – the strength of the sibling bond, the status of a woman in her natal home, the absence of widow inheritance, and the ousting of widows, all tend to precipitate a return of older women to their kin in what I have called terminal separation. These same features undermine marriage during the years of active childbearing – the middle years of a woman's marital career. Yet in this period there are counter-pressures supporting the maintenance of a marriage: affection, desire for children, and joint concern with the rearing of children and the domestic enterprise result in some stable unions of many years' duration. In comparing the divorce ratios of fostered and home-reared women, we are asking whether there is anything about the experience of being fostered that makes a woman more susceptible to the disruptive pressures which are built into the system. For it might be that the experience of being brought up away from home emphasizes instrumental relationships at the expense of close emotional ties, thus making it more difficult to establish a satisfactory conjugal relationship in adulthood. As one man put it, 'All foster children become liars because they want to please their guardians and they fear their anger.' [10]

Even if the institutionalized pressures leading to terminal separation affect the two groups similarly, more stable marriages in the early and middle periods could lead to significant differences in their divorce ratios.

The material for comparison comes from Bole, in western Gonja, and from Daboya, in northern Gonja. In Bole, of a sample of 89 women, 44 per cent had been reared by parents and 56 per cent by foster parents. This is an area with a somewhat higher incidence of divorce than central or eastern Gonja. For the Bole sample as a whole, the proportion of all marriages that ended in divorce was 31·9 per cent. For all marriages except those ended by death, the proportion terminated by divorce, Barnes's ratio C (Barnes, 1949), was 39·3 per cent. If fostering does in fact work to make settled emotional relationships more difficult in adulthood we would expect to find that, within this situation of overall high divorce, fostered women would have proportionately more divorces, and home-reared women proportionately fewer. In fact the data show no significant difference between the divorce ratios of the two groups

TABLE 7 *Comparison of the divorce ratios of fostered and home-reared women of two Gonja samples*

	Number of persons	*Number of unions*	*Number of divorces*	*Divorce ratio C*
WESTERN GONJA				
Fostered	50	79	26	38·2
Reared by parents	39	65	20	40·0
NORTHERN GONJA				
Fostered	27	40	10	32·3
Reared by parents	15	19	5	38·4

Western Gonja: $\chi^2 = \cdot 034$; not significant
Northern Gonja: $\chi^2 = \cdot 176$; not significant

(*Table 7*). The 39 women brought up by their own parents had among them 20 divorces, giving a figure for ratio C of 40 per cent. For the 50 women who were fostered as children there were a total of 26 divorces, giving a ratio C of 38·2 per cent. A comparison of the divorce ratios for fostered and home-reared women of northern Gonja shows slightly more divorce among those reared at home (a ratio of 38·4 as compared with 32·3 for fostered women). However this difference is within the range of variation to be expected by chance; the χ^2 is not significant. There is thus no basis for accepting the hypothesis that fostered and home-reared women have significantly different divorce ratios. While it cannot be suggested that fostering leads to an especially stable emotional life, it cannot be said to make divorce in adulthood more probable.

CONCLUSIONS

These two indices, incidence of fostering among 'successful' men, and incidence of divorce among fostered and not-fostered women, taken together suggest that, in a society where fostering is positively valued by adults and viewed by fostered children with at least mixed feelings, it does not produce adults who are at a disadvantage with respect to success in either marriage or career. Various features of the institution have been suggested which might be related to this: primary among these is no doubt that foster parents are kin, and that ties with own parents are usually maintained throughout childhood and adolescence. Parents are seen as taking a continued interest in their children's welfare, and as ready and able to interfere should things not go well. Also of importance here, I believe, is the definition of fostering as a situation involving service to the foster parent and training of the child. This view is held by children as well as adults: foster parents are not expected to be indulgent, whereas parents are. Therefore, when increasing demands are inevitably made by the foster parent with the coming of later childhood and adolescence, these are regarded by all concerned as legitimate. In any case, the frustrations attendant on giving up the freedom of childhood are, for the fostered, experienced not with their own parents but with other kin on whom they are not so emotionally dependent. Except in eastern Gonja, something like half of all adults have spent their later childhood and adolescence living and working apart from their own parents. For them, this period of education and gradual entry into adult roles, although still mediated by kin, takes place outside the nuclear family. They are involved already with the wider world of kin and community.

NOTES

1. The first period of fieldwork in Gonja (1956–57) was sponsored by a Foreign Area Fellowship of the Ford Foundation. Later work specifically concerned with the study of kinship fostering was sponsored by the Wenner Gren Foundation of New York, and by the Child Development Research Unit of the University of Ghana, again from Ford Foundation funds.

Comments by participants in the Cambridge, Manchester, and Birmingham research seminars have been of great help in clarifying my ideas.

2. This point is made by Meyer Fortes in his Introduction to *The Developmental Cycle in Domestic Groups* (J. Goody (ed.), 1958, p. 9).

3. For the Ewe and the Fanti, see E. Goody, 1966; for the Dagomba, see Oppong, 1965; for the Mossi, see Skinner, 1960, 1961; for the Bariba, see Lombard, 1957; for the Hausa, see Smith, 1955. My information on the Wolof comes from an interview conducted in Cambridge with a Wolof student.

4. In a state with an area of some 15,000 square miles, encompassing groups of differing ethnic and linguistic affiliation, some variation in form and content

is to be expected. I have somewhat different, but overlapping, information from central, northern, eastern, and western Gonja, and where variations are significant this is noted in the text. This paper makes no attempt to discuss regional differences: it is very much in the nature of a preliminary overview. As the analysis of this material is still in progress, some calculations have been made for certain samples and not for others. Information is more complete for some samples than others. No negative results have been omitted.

5. From the material I have gathered, this different attitude seems to account in part for the very high rate of fostering among West African students in this country; they are more inclined to view the 'parental' role as transferable to others.

6. The data in this and the following tables are assembled from several sources. The western Gonja women's sample is based on a stratified random sample of all the compounds in the old town of Bole. All adult women in twenty-four compounds were interviewed. The western Gonja's men sample used in *Table 3* consists of all the full brothers of the women interviewed in the Bole sample. The northern Gonja women's sample consists of all the adult women in nine Daboya compounds non-randomly selected to represent Muslim and ruling estates. The northern Gonja men's sample is based on all the full brothers of the Daboya women interviewed. The western and central Gonja (Busunu) men's samples are based on all the men in randomly selected compounds stratified to represent Muslim, ruling, and commoner estates. The eastern Gonja sample includes all the men of the Muslim section of Kpembe, plus all the men in randomly selected compounds in one of the sections of Kpembe dominated by the members of the Singbung gate of the Kpembe ruling estate. There were no refusals, although some permanent residents were absent on extended visits. The central Gonja (Buipe) sample consists of all the fostered children living in the village at the time of our census. The 'successful' men in both eastern and western Gonja were all those in the three categories discussed who were present in the two towns at the time the interviewing was done.

7. Weaving in the northern Gonja town of Daboya may be a partial exception to the rule elsewhere that anyone can learn a craft who wishes to do so. There is a section of weavers and families which specialize in this occupation. Sons here do learn their father's craft, but a very brief stay did not reveal a systematic use of fostering to train additional recruits.

8. The Kontunkuri drummer of the paramount, at Damongo, and the Mbontokurbi drummers attached to Kawsawgu and Mpaha, play items of traditional history (albeit in a form few can understand). The need to preserve these may have given rise to mechanisms to ensure sufficient players in each generation. I neglected to inquire into this point. However, in discussing the present situation with regard to the Kontunkuri, I was told that the only youth learning now is a brother's son of the drummer. As his interest is only lukewarm there are fears for the continuity of the drum history. So far as the drums which are found in all the divisions are concerned, a similar need to preserve traditional forms obtains with respect to the Ntimpani drums (copied from Ashanti), which drum the titles and exploits of previous chiefs on Fridays and Mondays. Despite this, drummers insist that anyone who is so inclined may learn, and no special provision is made for continuity. There is some evidence that in the past Ntimpani drummers were slaves. Bintiri drummers who led in war might belong to either ruling or commoner estate, and are recruited on the basis of personal inclination.

9. See J. Goody, 1967, for a discussion of the Gonja political system.

10. It is perhaps equally plausible to argue that the fostering experience would serve to make a woman less dependent on close emotional ties and for this reason better able to tolerate the inevitable strains of married life. Although the trend of the northern Gonja divorce ratios is in the direction of more stable marriages for fostered women, there is, in the absence of any significant difference between the ratios for the fostered and non-fostered groups, no confirmation of such a hypothesis.

REFERENCES

BARNES, J. A. 1949. Measures of Divorce Frequency in Simple Societies. *Journal of the Royal Anthropological Institute* **74**.

BOWLBY, J. 1960. Separation Anxiety. *International Journal of Psycho-Analysis* **41**: 89–113.

FORTES, M. 1949. *The Web of Kinship among the Tallensi*. London: Oxford University Press (for International African Institute).

GOODY, E. N. 1962. Conjugal Separation and Divorce among the Gonja of Northern Ghana. In M. Fortes (ed.), *Marriage in Tribal Societies*. Cambridge: Cambridge University Press.

—— 1966. Fostering in Ghana: A Preliminary Survey. *Ghana Journal of Sociology* **2**.

GOODY, J. (ed.). 1958. *The Developmental Cycle in Domestic Groups*. Cambridge Papers in Social Anthropology 1. Cambridge: Cambridge University Press.

—— (ed.). 1966. *Succession to High Office*. Cambridge Papers in Social Anthropology 4. Cambridge: Cambridge University Press.

—— 1967. The Over-kingdom of Gonja. In D. Forde & P. Kaberry (eds.), *West African Kingdoms in the Nineteenth Century*. London: Oxford University Press.

—— & GOODY, E. N. 1967. The Circulation of Women and Children in Northern Ghana. *Man* (n.s.) **2** (2): 226–248.

LOMBARD, J. 1957. Un système politique traditionnel de type féodal: les Bariba du Nord-Dahomey. *Bulletin de l'Institut français d'Afrique noire* **19** (ser. B): 464–506.

OPPONG, C. 1965. Some Sociological Aspects of Education in Dagbon. M.A. thesis, Institute of African Studies, Legon, Ghana.

RICHARDS, A. I. 1964. Authority Patterns in Traditional Buganda. In L. A. Fallers (ed.), *The King's Men*. London: Oxford University Press.

SKINNER, E. P. 1960. The Mossi *Pogsioure*. *Man* **60**: 20–23.

—— 1961. Intergenerational Conflict among the Mossi: Father and Son. *Journal of Conflict Resolution* **5**: 55–60.

SMITH, M. G. 1955. *The Economy of Hausa Communities of Zaria*. Colonial Research Studies 16. London: HMSO.

Barbara B. Lloyd

Yoruba Mothers' Reports of Child-rearing

Some Theoretical and Methodological Considerations

Studies of child-rearing practices, guided to a greater or lesser degree by a concern with psychological theory, have a venerable history within anthropology. Through Sigmund Freud and Whiting and Child it may be possible to forge links between this study of the child-training procedures of Yoruba mothers and Malinowski's investigations of Trobriand Island families. Rather than struggle to establish genealogical legitimacy I shall restrict this discussion to a description of the basic design and data collection, and to a presentation and analysis of the material in terms of the theoretical variables according to which it was formulated; I shall then proceed to a consideration of some methodological problems and of certain other interpretations and hypotheses to which this study might lead.

RESEARCH DESIGN, SETTING, AND PROCEDURES

The research reported here was carried out within Ibadan and is mainly based upon standardized interviews. These interviews formed part of a larger study concerned with diverse aspects of socialization and personality development. The location of the research in the Institute of Education at the University of Ibadan was in part determined by the availability of research facilities but proved fortuitous in giving certain direction to the investigation.

In April 1962, the Institutes of Education and Child Health began a combined longitudinal cross-sectional study of child growth aimed at comparing traditionally reared and Western-reared children. We had by then established a research base within a traditional Ibadan community, a neighbourhood centring on Oje market. It remained only to find the Westernized sample, since sufficient children of the required ages – from birth to three and a half years – could be found within Oje (B. B. Lloyd, 1967).[1] Concern with possible genetic differences, as evidenced by reported tribal differences in height, led to the decision to restrict the study to intracultural samples, i.e. to children both of whose parents were Yoruba (Talbot & Mulhall, 1962).

Though it is usual to assign social-class ratings on the basis of husband's occupation and education, the decision was made to use mother's education as our criterion for membership in the Westernized or elite sample. The rationale for this decision was based upon observations that in rapidly changing African societies men of considerable education and occupational status often have semi-literate wives who rear their children according to traditional patterns. In practice, the decision to recruit in terms of the wife's education meant that most of the fathers in the elite sample had had a complete secondary education and often had obtained professional qualifications. The sample included high-ranking civil servants, university staff, professional men, and wealthy merchants. An extensive survey was thus undertaken through schools, staff lists, and personal contacts to find children from Yoruba families in which the mother had had the equivalent of four years of secondary school education.

Support for the validity of the sample selection procedure which was designed to produce differences between a traditional and a materially advantaged group can be seen in the preliminary findings of the growth study (Janes, 1967). Results based upon elite and Oje samples of 200 children each, maintained by replacement over the past four years, indicate marked differences between the groups. From three months until three years, height curves for the two samples steadily diverge though after three years they run parallel. While the average height of elite children compares favourably with that of a general London sample, the Oje curves begin to fall away at six months and the disparity grows steadily. For weight, too, there is a noticeable divergence, with Oje and elite samples parting again at three months and diverging dramatically until a year, after which they run parallel. There is an interesting sex difference: elite boys first surpass and then equal London weight norms while elite girls cross the London sample at six months and then run slightly below it. Janes attempts to relate these clearly demonstrable growth differences to socio-economic differences in nutrition rather than to ethnic or climatic factors.

The interview study also sought to capitalize on the marked intracultural sample differences but in terms of rearing practices. The Oje sample was taken as a measure of traditional Yoruba modes of child-training, and these were compared with Western-educated mothers' modes of rearing to give an estimate of change based upon a cross-sectional approach. Census data collected for use in establishing the growth samples were employed to locate mothers for the child-rearing study. The study concentrated upon parents' reports of their attitudes and methods. In each sample there were thirty mothers and ten fathers of children aged five to six.[2] The interviews focused attention on diverse socialization practices as they affected a particular child but no attempt was made to relate the reported practices to actual behaviour in the children.

In designing a questionnaire for parents one has countless possibilities unless guided by theory. In this instance direction was sought in the earlier work of Sears and colleagues who had studied the practices of American mothers (Sears, Maccoby & Levin, 1957) and in the related Six Cultures study of Whiting *et al.* (Whiting, 1963). In the study of personality development from a social learning viewpoint account is taken of methods of socialization in a number of behaviour systems deemed important to the mature adult personality. Thus the interview was constructed to yield information on differing Oje and elite methods of training aggression, achievement, obedience, responsibility, sexuality, and sociability. Previous research has indicated that the emotional relationship of dependence developed in early infancy and childhood and techniques of discipline are especially important in developing internalized standards of morality. Thus considerable attention was given to these dimensions also.

In addition, questions particularly useful as direct measures of change were included. Among these were items concerning adherence to a long list of traditional Yoruba customs such as circumcision, head-moulding, and lengthy breast-feeding, and questions concerning maternally perceived changes in the family and in child-training practices. Mothers were also asked the source of any advice they had sought in rearing their children. Results from a small part of the interview will be presented in this report to illustrate the theoretical and methodological points being considered.

The questionnaire was administered in English by myself and an American assistant, by appointment, in the homes of elite mothers. Payment was not offered or given to parents for their help. The taped interviews were transcribed verbatim. The Yoruba version used for the Oje sample was double translated by two Yoruba speakers and administered in my presence by a Yoruba assistant. Again, the interview was arranged at the mother's convenience by appointment, but, to avoid the distractions of compound life, it was held in the research office, a fairly ordinary building facing Oje market. The interviews were carried out entirely in Yoruba by an assistant who was familiar to the mothers, but they were transcribed from tape into English by the interviewer and another well-educated Yoruba woman.

Although all available measures were taken to ensure the comparability of the elite and Oje interviews, the responses of elite mothers are significantly longer than those of Oje. The statistical test (Student's *t*) significant at the ·001 level is hardly necessary. The difference between the Oje mean length of seventeen pages and the elite mean length of twenty-nine pages is marked. This difference did not appear to reflect any lack of rapport with Oje women. The interviewer was clearly of higher status in Yoruba society (some mothers curtseyed to her), yet the mothers seemed to joke with her and appeared at ease. The interviews were not shortened in translation, because the actual amount of tape required for the Oje interviews was considerably less than for the elite ones. Furthermore, the typescripts of the standard questionnaire, in English and Yoruba, are almost identical in length. Thus one is left wondering whether the difference in the length of the responses can be accounted for by anything other than differing styles or modes of verbal behaviour. Perhaps we have a process similar to class differences in speech patterns noted in Western societies (Bernstein, 1960).

Adherence to traditional practices among Oje and elite

As the design of this study assumes that Oje responses represent a measure of traditional modes of child-rearing, it is important to ask whether elite and Oje mothers differ in their reports of adherence to various traditional practices. According to the accounts of informants, there are a number of procedures relating to the treatment of children in early infancy which are relatively rare in Western child care but which are seen as essential to older, uneducated Yoruba women. These can be conveniently grouped into three categories: practices involving cutting the infant's body (*Tables 1a, 1b, 1c*), methods of manipulating the body (*Tables 2a, 2b, 2c*), and customs relating to infant-feeding (*Tables 3a, 3b*).

TABLE 1a

Face-marking, boys and girls

	Oje	*Elite*
No. practising	3	0
No. not practising	27	30

TABLE 1b

Ear-piercing, girls only

	Oje	*Elite*
No. practising	15	15
No. not practising	0	0

TABLE 1c *Circumcision*

	Boys		*Girls*	
	Oje	*Elite*	*Oje*	*Elite*
No. practising	15	15	10	1
No. not practising	0	0	5	14

$\chi^2 = 10{\cdot}3$; $p < {\cdot}01$

Findings in the first category are the most equivocal but are also interesting for further interpretations we might wish to make of the interview data. Only one statistically significant difference in the proportions of elite and Oje mothers who adhere to practices involving cutting the infant's body emerges from the χ^2 tests (*Table 1c*).[3] We may thus conclude that while it is traditional for female infants to be circumcised in Yoruba society there is a significant shift away from this practice among educated mothers. The question remaining is how do we interpret lack of difference? According to our model of change, Oje practice is taken as representing traditional methods: thus we ought to conclude that traditionally the Yoruba (a) did not usually mark infants' faces, (b) did pierce girls' ears, and (c) circumcised male infants. Should one then ascribe ideas of face-marking to the category of 'old wives' tales'? Fortunately, in this instance external evidence in the shape of thousands of Yoruba adults bearing face marks attests to the existence of the practice in the recent past. The equivalence of Oje and elite practice may pose more difficult questions when we seek validation for less readily observed variables.

Evidence within the remaining two categories is less equivocal. *Tables 2a, 2b,* and *2c* represent adherence to various

TABLE 2a

Head-moulding, boys and girls

	Oje	*Elite*
No. practising	20	3
No. not practising	10	27

$\chi^2 = 16{\cdot}4;\ p < {\cdot}001$

TABLE 2b

Hip-moulding, boys and girls

	Oje	*Elite*
No. practising	30	15
No. not practising	0	15

$\chi^2 = 16{\cdot}1;\ p < {\cdot}001$

TABLE 2c *Limb-stretching, boys and girls*

	Oje	*Elite*
No. practising	29	15
No. not practising	1	15

$\chi^2 = 13{\cdot}3;\ p < {\cdot}001$

practices of body-shaping. In all the comparisons concerning the manipulation of the infant's body the proportions for the two samples are significantly different statistically. Where there is some Oje movement away from the traditional Yoruba custom of shaping the infant's head to ensure that it will be round, the elite have almost completely abandoned the practice (*Table 2a*). *Tables 2b* and *2c* indicate that there is significant abandonment of hip-moulding and limb-stretching as part of routine baby care among the elite. It is interesting to note that those elite mothers who reported employing these practices often offered the explanation that a grandmother had come to help with the new baby and that it was she who carried out the manipulation.

The remaining comparisons concern procedures of feeding and weaning. Informants report that in the past infants were breast-fed for at least two years and that during this time, until the child was weaned, the parents refrained from sexual intercourse. Furthermore, when supplementary feeding such as a thin maize or millet gruel was introduced, it was common to force the child to eat by holding the nostrils. On all these practices a clear distinction between the two groups of mothers appears. First of all there is a significant difference (Student's t, $p < \cdot 001$) in the length of time mothers breast-feed: the Oje mean is 22·2 months whereas that for the elite is 7·4 months. *Table 3a*, which concerns the explicit statement of adherence to the post-partum taboo, indicates that along with a radical drop in length of breast-feeding has come a significant shift away from compliance with the taboo. Force-feeding is common in Oje and rare among the elite (*Table 3b*).

TABLE 3a *Post-partum taboo, boys and girls*

	Oje	*Elite*
No. practising	30	15
No. not practising	0	15

$\chi^2 = 16 \cdot 1;\ p < \cdot 001$

TABLE 3b *Force-feeding, boys and girls*

	Oje	*Elite*
No. practising	18	3
No. not practising	12	27

$\chi^2 = 16 \cdot 3;\ p < \cdot 001$

With the exception of face-marking, then, a significant proportion of Oje women still adhere to the list of practices concerning body-marking and manipulation, and infant-feeding and weaning, which we might describe as traditional. Again, the contrast between the groups in terms of these very specific practices is as marked as that found on dimensions of physical growth, and again supports the assumptions concerning extreme socio-economic and educational differences between the groups which were the guiding hypotheses in sample selection.

COMPARISONS OF CHILD-REARING

There remains the rather more elusive task of examining and interpreting differences among psychological variables. A strictly empirical approach might suggest seeking all Oje-elite differences on psychological dimensions and then constructing a model of traditional patterns of Yoruba socialization and personality development. Although this method has the appeal of making few *a priori* assumptions, it runs the risk mentioned whereby all differences found are ascribed to change among the elite, and all similarities to a lack of change in Oje child-care procedures.

Rather than hazard these assumptions regarding change, clues to the direction of differences will be sought in the findings of other researchers. First, studies reporting distinctly African emphases in socialization practice will be examined. From these reports predictions about the direction of change can be made. Any predicted differences that do appear can be viewed as the effects of Westernization in modifying elite practices. It is possible, of course, that, as the proponents of *négritude* suggest, it is just these dimensions that are most resistant to change. A second source of guidance is to be sought in studies of social change specifically relating to child-rearing practices. As the sources of change, industrialization and Western education, are similar in various parts of the world one can assume that reported changes in methods of child-rearing will be reflected in changes in a similar direction among the elite of Ibadan.

Comparisons with African societies

The first question raised, how African societies compare on a number of socialization practices with societies in other areas of the world, has been answered quantitatively by Doob (1965) and more intuitively by LeVine (1963). Doob employed a cross-cultural analysis of seven socialization practices in 110 societies, choosing these for completeness of information available rather than as a truly representative world sample. No statistically significant differences were found on five of the dimensions on which he compared African practices with those of Oceania, North America, and a residual category of societies. From this evidence Doob concluded that, because of considerable variability among African samples, their socialization practices do not appear extreme when compared with a world sample. The five non-significant dimensions included overall infant nurturance, anxiety about dependence in the transition from infancy to childhood, overall childhood indulgence, overall nurturance, and the learning of achievement.

Significant differences did, however, occur on the dimensions of learning obedience and learning responsible behaviour. Along both of these dimensions training in African societies was rated stronger than that in societies in Oceania and North America. For the residual group of societies the difference was significant only for learning obedience. Obedience learning is defined by Doob as 'learning to do as he [the child] is told by his parents'. 'Learning to perform the tasks, duties or routines which are demanded by the culture' (Doob, 1965, p. 99) is the definition of learning responsibility behaviour. Thus at the behavioural level it may be difficult to differentiate obedience and responsibility. However, we may predict that, although all parents expect their children to obey them generally speaking, Oje mothers will place greater emphasis on obedience than will elite mothers.

Question 25 in the interview (see Appendix, pp. 98–105 below, for questionnaire) furnishes one measure of maternal attitudes towards obedience: 'Some parents expect their children to obey immediately when they are told to do something – other parents leave it to the child to do things when he can. How do you feel about this?' *Table 4* presents frequencies for almost unequivocal

TABLE 4 *Expectations concerning obedience: boys and girls*

	Oje	*Elite*
Immediate obedience	27	15
Qualified obedience	3	15

$\chi^2 = 9{\cdot}6;\ p < {\cdot}01$

demands for immediate obedience and for qualified expectations of obedience. The proportions differ significantly in the predicted direction, i.e. more Oje mothers expect immediate obedience. Two of the three Oje mothers who qualified their responses stated that it takes time to develop obedience; thus presumably they would expect it in an older child. The remaining Oje mother pointed out that she does not flog her daughter the first time she fails to obey immediately but only on repeated failures. Elite qualifications concerning immediate obedience take account of the nature and urgency of the request and the belief that the child will know enough to do it when he can reasonably manage it. The responses to question 25 thus lend further support to Doob's finding that traditional African societies tend to exert greater than average pressure in the socialization of obedience.

To pursue this notion further and to consider the socialization of responsibility behaviour, question 15b was analysed. This analysis also indicates some of the difficulties encountered in the content analysis of interview material from distinctly different samples. Question 15b asks: 'What do you expect of a well-behaved child of [your son's or daughter's] age?' The question appeared at the end of a sequence concerning disciplinary techniques, which started with a discussion of naughty behaviour and its punishment and then progressed to pleasing aspects of the child's behaviour and corresponding rewards. Although question 15b was open-ended and posed special problems in scoring owing to marked differences in the length of replies, it is considered particularly useful to elicit areas of socialization which are of special concern to the mother. On the hypothesis that the first item of behaviour mentioned in reply to the question represented something particularly important to the mother, a ranked scoring system was devised. The first behavioural item mentioned by the mother was thus given a score of 1; the second, even though it might also be the last of two items, and the third were given a score of 2; and subsequent items were scored 3. Very few mothers produced more than three codable items.

As the question about the well-behaved child was answered in a fairly limited number of quite concrete ways, it was decided to reject a method that scored obedience only in terms of explicit statements, and responsibility in terms of any reference to tasks, duties, or routines, and to develop a system of categories which allowed greater specification of the responses. Explicit statements of maternal demands for obedience were coded as such, but the learning of tasks, duties, and routines demanded by the culture, i.e. responsibility training, was subdivided into categories for (a) errands, (b) household chores, (c) personal tasks for oneself, (d) intellectual tasks, and (e) tasks involving sociability. Although all of these categories might fall under the general rubric of responsibility it is worth noting special considerations. Evidence points to early emphasis on training for self-reliance – performing tasks such as washing oneself and dressing – as important in the socialization of high need achievement (Winterbottom, 1958). Stress on intellectual performance, i.e. asking intelligent questions or reading well, probably relates to achievement socialization too. Explicit mention of formal and informal saluting of elders can probably be classed as sociability learning as well as responsibility and/or obedience learning. Errands were coded separately because mothers mentioned them often without specific content and appeared to interpret their willing and prompt execution as evidence of obedience. Before pursuing the interpretation of demands for children to perform errands we ought to examine the results from the coding of question 15b (*Table 5*).

TABLE 5 *Expectations concerning the well-behaved child*

	Obedience	*Errands*	*Household chores*	*Self-reliance*	*Intellectual achievement*	*Sociability*	*Totals*
Total codable replies							
Oje	9	18	4	3	5	5	44
	20%	41%	9%	7%	11%	11%	
Elite	11	6	9	13	7	13	59
	18%	10%	15%	22%	11%	22%	
Category mentioned first							
Oje	5	15	1	1	2	4	28
	18%	55%	3%	3%	6%	15%	
Elite	6	1	2	7	4	9	29
	21%	3%	6%	24%	14%	31%	

Inspection of *Table 5* indicates that an analysis of replies to the question on the well-behaved child which examined only explicit statements about obedience and which regarded the remaining categories as aspects of responsibility learning would reveal no difference between Oje and elite mothers' attitudes on the training of these systems. Roughly 20 per cent of mothers in each group either mention obedience explicitly first or mention it somewhere in their replies. Thus nothing can be said about the direction of change and thus, too, nothing about traditional African emphases on responsibility and obedience learning.

However, an argument could be made for the validity of combining explicit obedience references and mentions of doing errands. A more interpretative reading of the interviews suggests that mothers' concern in the running of errands, usually simple tasks such as carrying a message or buying a pennyworth of salt, is with willingness and promptness, and that skill learning is not involved. The mother's attention appears to be focused on the child's doing what she has requested, which approaches our definition of obedience learning. When the explicit obedience and errands categories are combined, the previously established difference in obedience learning between Oje and elite mothers reappears. Furthermore, the remaining categories, which specify particular sorts of tasks or routines,

TABLE 6 *Obedience learning*

Explicit obedience & errands combined	*Oje*	*Elite*
No. mentioning first	20	7
No. not mentioning first	8	22

$\chi^2 = 12{\cdot}1;\ p < {\cdot}001$

may be combined to produce a measure of responsibility learning. *Table 6* is based upon mothers' first comments to the question on the well-behaved child and employs as a measure of obedience socialization the combined categories, explicit obedience and errands. A significant difference in the proportions of mothers emphasizing obedience appears as predicted, i.e. the more specifically African stress upon obedience learning is now not present in the elite sample.

Following on the analysis of obedience, the results of responsibility training are puzzling. The table for responsibility training based upon the remaining four categories is the mirror image of that for obedience. Thus the difference would again be significant but it would indicate that elite mothers place greater stress on responsibility training than do Oje mothers, and would fail to support the prediction that it is distinctly African practice to put stronger than average socialization pressure on responsibility learning. If Oje practice were still to be assumed to equate with traditional African methods, it would follow that elite socialization for responsibility must be extreme.

If attention is restricted to the socialization of achievement, i.e. to intellectual tasks and those involving self-reliance, we can refine our notions of responsibility learning and support a previously observed difference in Oje and elite socialization (B. B. Lloyd, 1966). The proportions of Oje and elite mothers who give first mention to tasks involving achievement socialization are significantly different (*Table 7*). However, an analysis

TABLE 7 *Achievement socialization*

Intellectual achievement & self-reliance combined	*Oje*	*Elite*
No. mentioning first	3	11
No. not mentioning first	25	18

$\chi^2 = 4{\cdot}32;\ p < {\cdot}05$

of total expectations is less conclusive. Among Oje mothers 8 out of 44 responses, and among elite mothers 20 out of 59 codable responses, mention achievement (*Table 5*), and thus lend support to the view that considerable achievement socialization occurs throughout Yoruba society.

The foregoing analysis is intended to indicate the very considerable problems encountered in coding semi-structured, open-ended interview material along psychological dimensions. A major problem is the behavioural definition of categories, but this may be solved more readily than difficulties imposed by the unequal length and content of replies, which seem to be part of the fundamental difference between the groups. These problems make it difficult to construct identical category systems (Frijda & Jahoda, 1966). A system whereby the entire question was repeatedly rated on a number of dimensions would perhaps have solved the immediate problem posed by exhaustive categories, but it would not have dealt with omissions, and would have raised further questions of reliability and interpretation. These points may appear trivial in comparison with the overall support the findings lend to the conclusions cited by Doob from a conference report on the basic psychological structures of African populations. He quotes the general conclusion that 'the common factor in the "Ideal Personality" sought in African society is "respect for elders and ancestors, and for accepted forms of behaviour" ' (Doob, 1965, p. 402). In another sense, however, this conclusion raises further questions concerning the functional equivalence of our categories. A possible interpretation is that, for the elite family, achievement may be considered the accepted form of behaviour and could be regarded as functionally equivalent to the running of errands.

Viewing socialization procedures from a sociological perspective, LeVine has considered features characteristic of African societies (LeVine, 1963). He derives these from social structural factors, i.e. the mother-child unit embedded in a markedly polygynous context wherein considerable importance attaches to women for subsistence agriculture. His three African dimensions are: casual infant nurturance, emphasis on obedience and responsibility, and the use of corporal punishment. Evidence in support of the second factor has been discussed but it is interesting, in view of the quotation just cited, to note that in the LeVine hypothesis its origins are sought in the age-status system of African societies, which favour elders and man and within which menial labour falls to the lowest in rank. There is considerable convergence of interpretations, for LeVine suggests that it is the importance of child labour that leads to stress upon obedience and responsibility. The availability of paid servants to perform menial tasks in the elite family supports the decreasing emphasis on obedience training *per se* (P. C. Lloyd, 1967).

Casual nurturance is a complex concept which is employed to correct the implicit assumption that African infant nurturance, because it includes breast-feeding on demand, mother-infant bed-sharing, and late weaning, must be indulgent. These practices are seen as congruent with the high value African societies place on fertility. Support for a lack of anxiety or emotional intensity in infant nurturance is drawn from mothers' willingness to leave infants with assorted caretakers, young and old, who employ force-feeding in the mothers' absence, from the lack of attention they give to infants while nursing, and from the abruptness of weaning. Economic necessity is seen to determine the traditional pattern.

The evidence already cited on age of weaning, force-feeding, and the observance of the post-partum taboo, indirectly focusing on infant-mother bed-sharing, presents a superficial picture of an elite shift away from traditional patterns. Functionally it could be argued that artificial feeding has replaced mothers' milk and the need to force-feed the elite child; the question remains whether it has changed the affective quality of the mother-child relationship. An interesting anomaly appears when evidence concerning maternal work patterns and caretakers in infancy is examined. Approximately two-thirds of each sample of mothers returned to work before their child was a year old: 19 elite women and 22 Oje mothers. A statistically significant difference is found in the age the children had attained when the 41 mothers resumed work, the elite children being on average 2·6 months old and the Oje children having a mean age of 5·6 months (Student's t, $p < \cdot 001$). It is perhaps worth noting that 4 of the 19 elite women weaned their infants at about eight weeks and then placed them with English foster mothers to enable themselves to complete training courses in Britain. This evidence is congruent with a hypothesis of low anxiety about infant nurturance and incidentally would seem to indicate considerable maternal achievement motivation among the elite.

A final item of evidence on patterns of infant nurturance is obtained from the question concerning primary caretakers in infancy. *Table 8* shows a significant difference in the proportions of Oje and elite mothers reporting that they were the infant's primary caretaker.

TABLE 8 *Primary caretakers in infancy*

	Oje	*Elite*
Mother	22	7
Other(s)	8	23

$\chi^2 = 13{\cdot}1$; $p < {\cdot}001$

The availability of modern feeding techniques has freed the elite mother from prolonged demand-feeding. Her education or pursuit of education gives work outside the home priority over infant care. However, this analysis does not mean to suggest that elite mothers have little emotional involvement in their children, but intends to support a notion of casual nurturance in African societies and to question beliefs about greater emotional warmth among elite mothers. It would seem that fertility, as LeVine suggests in an analysis of traditional societies, is still a prime concern to the elite, and thus educated young women in the early years of marriage produce children even when they will have to be cared for by foster mothers or semi-literate girls. Evidence to support this argument comes from responses to a question on birth control and family planning. Only four elite mothers, predominantly older women, were opposed to birth control, but even such knowledgeable young women as trained nurses only considered the matter seriously after they had had two or three children. Functionally the elite mother's attitudes towards her infant and towards her work appear little different from those of the Oje mother. The need for money to educate her own children or her siblings probably places considerable economic stress on the educated mother and may explain the large proportion of this group who return to work shortly after childbirth. From this cursory analysis it seems unlikely that the affective relationship has changed either.

Finally, we may ask whether corporal punishment is more widely used in traditional African than in other societies. My analysis is based upon responses to a series of questions dealing with naughty behaviour, punishment in general, and the mother's reactions when her child irritates her just a little, does something more serious, and finally does something really serious. LeVine suggests, though not completely to his own satisfaction, that extensive use of corporal punishment may be an outcome of casual nurturance. The lack of a close emotional bond between mother and child may in a situation demanding strict obedience result in the mother's inability to control behaviour without resorting to physical punishment. Among Oje and elite fathers, LeVine, Klein, and Fries (1967) report no difference in the use of physical discipline, scolding, and isolation. The maternal measures based upon differing degrees of transgression appear to be more sensitive. There is a significant difference in the proportions of Oje and elite mothers who use physical punishment for slight offences (*Table 9*).

TABLE 9 *Punishment for slight offences*

Type of punishment	*Oje*	*Elite*
Physical	12	1
Other	18	29

$\chi^2 = 9{\cdot}8;\ p < {\cdot}01$

Group differences are not significant for more extreme offences. Perhaps these differences represent the beginnings of a change in the use of physical punishment among all Yoruba mothers, with most elite and some Oje mothers abandoning its use for minor offences. Again, a situational caution seems relevant: in the privacy of the isolated, neolocal, nuclear family of the elite, minor naughtiness may be more easily tolerated and our psychological differences may be situationally determined.

Comparisons with other changing societies

A second method of interpreting differences between Oje and elite practices is through an analysis of studies of social change undertaken in other parts of the world. LeVine has recently employed this strategy in an analysis of the responses of Oje and elite fathers, linking psychological change closely to socio-economic variation (LeVine *et al.*, 1967). He uses, essentially, three models in building his own. These are a model of value change based upon Inkeles's studies of Tsarist and Soviet Russian personality and child-rearing (1963); another stemming from a modernization study in Lebanon carried out by Prothro (1961); and, finally, Bronfenbrenner's overview of change and social class in America (1966). The propositions that are deduced relate modern child-rearing values and practices to the style of life and circumstances of a professional and bureaucratic class. Highly mobile elite parents wishing to produce a few well-qualified children to replace them in the social system must, it is argued, rear children with considerable inner resources to enable them to complete the long years of schooling and to perform adequately in their occupation roles. They need to be more independent than their more traditional peers. A psychoanalytically oriented, social learning theory of personality development which explains elite learning in terms of a warm parent–child relationship, which places few restrictions upon the child and in which psychological techniques of discipline are employed, is utilized to predict differences in the practices of Oje and the professional and bureaucratic elite. Changes in the authority pattern of the family leading to a more egalitarian interaction in the elite home are also predicted.

Returning, then, to psychological dimensions of child-rearing, it is essential to the theory to be able to assess emotional warmth both in infancy, when the emotional bond between mother and child is established, and in childhood, when it is manipulated to shape the child's behaviour. It is necessary to assess disciplinary techniques, the amount of restriction placed upon the child, any freedom of expression he is allowed, and possibly socialization for self-reliance and achievement. Sociologically, one would wish to measure authority patterns within the family. In the responses of fathers, LeVine *et al.* (1967) find considerable support for their predictions. In comparison with Oje men, elite fathers appear to be warmer, less restrictive of their children's aggressive behaviour, less demanding of household tasks, more permissive in occupational choice, and more egalitarian in their relations with their wives. The lack of significant differences in choice of disciplinary techniques and in paternal authority failed to support predictions.

Analysis of the mother interviews is generally congruent with findings based upon the fathers' reports, but equivocal on a number of points. Although LeVine reported no differences in the proportions of children who greet their fathers in the traditional fashion, i.e. girls by kneeling and boys by prostrating, a significant difference does appear when mothers' reports

TABLE 10 *Daily greeting to father*

	Oje	*Elite*
No. greeting father daily	20	29
No. not greeting father daily	10	1

$\chi^2 = 7{\cdot}1$; $p < {\cdot}01$

of daily greeting are compared for the two groups. *Table 10* shows the numbers of mothers who report that their children always greet the father, albeit some elite children only come into the bedroom, stand up, and say good morning. The Oje failures represent children who are reported to greet their fathers when they remember or when he is available, children who are believed to be too young to observe the custom, and one child for whom the mother had no information because the child slept with the father. Despite the unexpectedly significant difference in the proportions based upon mothers' reports, it should probably not be concluded that elite children are more deferential towards authority. Although an elite mother explicitly stated that greeting 'is a way to show respect and regard; I still do it', the difference may represent a tendency of elite mothers to report what ought to be rather than actual behaviour. If a valid behavioural difference exists it may relate to the evidence of greater elite pressure in the socialization of sociability, presented in *Table 5*.

Results of the punishment analysis based upon the mother interviews indicate a slight shift in the use of physical punishment for minor offences among elite mothers. The difference between fathers' and mothers' reports is probably attributable to the refined design of the mother interview. It did not seem readily possible to assess scolding techniques to measure psychological or love-oriented punishment.

We can now examine mothers' evidence on those variables for which the father interviews provided positive results in LeVine's change model. Mothers' replies support the finding that elite fathers see their child's career choice as dependent upon the child's inclinations, whereas Oje fathers specify an occupation. LeVine's conclusion that this supports the view that elite fathers are more likely to see their children 'as sentient beings who will develop will and judgement on their own' (LeVine *et al.*, 1967) is, it could be argued, open to question. When response styles are considered, it seems likely that concreteness of reply may be part of the style of Oje parents just as reporting what one ought to do may be an aspect of elite style. It is also possible that the elite parents' own education may sensitize them to the difficulties of predicting meaningful occupational choices for the future. Without some test of external validity it is difficult to interpret these replies. One can only wonder whether the elite parents would sanction their sons' becoming farmers, carpenters, or drummers.

Additional evidence for greater permissiveness in the elite home concerns parental attitudes towards aggression. LeVine rated responses on a three-point scale as low, moderate, or high permissiveness, and found that elite fathers tended to be moderate whereas Oje fathers were all rated low in permissiveness. Here a different analysis is applied to questions dealing with aggression. The questions analysed concern the mother's reaction should she come upon her child teasing another child or fighting with another child (*Tables 11a* and *11b*), and her expectations concerning the reporting of fights (*Table 11c*). The coding for the first two items was designed to differentiate statements implying that the mother would always intervene from those in which intervention was in any way qualified. This mode of analysis was also applied to the mother's expectation about reports of fighting.

Although the only significant difference in maternal modes of

TABLE 11a *Mother's response to child's teasing of others*

Intervention	*Oje*	*Elite*
Always	30	21
Qualified	0	9

$\chi^2 = 8{\cdot}3$; $p < {\cdot}01$

TABLE 11b *Mother's response to child's fighting with others*

Intervention	*Oje*	*Elite*
Always	27	26
Qualified	3	4

TABLE 11c *Child's reporting of aggression*

	Oje	*Elite*
Usually reports	21	19
Sometimes reports	8	10

dealing with aggressive behaviour occurs in the response to teasing (*Table 11a*) this difference and trends in the predicted direction may be sufficient to support the analysis based upon father interviews. Of course, Oje fathers may be stricter than mothers. Again, the question of validity arises: does this difference in the handling of verbal aggression represent a freer attitude towards children's impulse expression or does it relate more directly to differing Oje and elite uses and attitudes towards language? Our evidence does not permit an answer, but it is interesting to note that 18 Oje mothers specifically mention teasing as leading to fighting, and that only half this number of elite mothers justify their intervention on these grounds.

Most mothers report that they would intervene in fighting and the majority in both groups state that they would do so to avoid physical harm. Eight Oje mothers stated explicitly that they would stop the fighting to prevent trouble with the other child's parents or dissension within the compound. This explanation is not found among elite mothers and it is a bit surprising, considering the situational demands for harmony that the Oje mothers' explanation implies, that there are not sharper differences in mothers' attitudes towards physical aggression.

Although a central concept theoretically, warmth has been left to the end of the discussion owing to difficulties encountered in trying to code it. LeVine had raters scale replies to six questions, including those on the well-behaved child, on pleasing aspects of the child's behaviour, and on the father's reception on returning home, on a three-point scale for emotional warmth. The six highly reliable ratings were then combined to produce a measure of warmth for each father. Group comparisons showed elite fathers to be significantly warmer, thus supporting other research on changes in socialization due to Westernization.

My own attempts to scale warmth were abortive. An experienced researcher among the Yoruba felt unable to assign ranks of 0, 1, or 2 degrees of warmth to unidentified replies to the question on the well-behaved child. He was able, however, to sort the statements into two categories, one of elite mothers' replies and the other of Oje responses. Twenty out of the thirty statements thus assigned were correct. These results raise various questions of blind sorting and coding.

All the replies are in the English of educated Yoruba women, either the elite mother, or the interviewer and translators in the case of Oje protocols. However, this does not rule out noticeable differences, as we have already seen. Elite interviews are significantly longer than those of Oje mothers. No systematic assessment has been made of linguistic style but there is qualitative evidence suggesting that Oje mothers tend to be more concrete in their replies and that elite women may tend to report what their children ought to do rather than what they do. Although these considerations of differing linguistic characteristics are not sufficient to rule out the possibility of different affective styles, they apply, of course, only to the mother interviews, and the information available on maternal behaviour during infancy would hardly support a hypothesis of differential emotional interaction in infancy. Evidence concerning warmth in childhood could not be produced though, of course, once the child uses language these very differences in style may well affect socialization processes.

SUMMARY AND SUGGESTIONS FOR FUTURE RESEARCH

This analysis of intracultural differences in Yoruba child-rearing patterns set out to illustrate some of the difficulties to be encountered in attempting comparisons of markedly different groups. In one sense the basic research strategy, the choice of groups of widely differing socio-economic levels, makes control on a very large number of variables impossible. Thus it might be tempting to follow the lead Leach furnishes in his attack on a recent attempt to define the units for cross-cultural comparisons and to abandon the undertaking. Leach states:

> 'I have previously argued that any system of cross-cultural comparisons which can be so used as to make "the Tikopia" and "the Chinese" units of comparable type is self-evidently

> absurd, and I do not see that the absurdity is reduced by calling the units "cultunits" instead of "tribes"' (1964, p. 299).

Rather than counsel the complete neglect of socialization in anthropological and social-psychological research, I shall attempt to suggest some possible avenues of further exploration in the cross-cultural study of child-rearing practices.

Perhaps the most important question to raise is how valid are mothers' reports of their own behaviour. This issue has received a good deal of attention recently within psychology and has prompted renewed interest both in experimental studies of processes such as identification and in more naturalistic observation. Certainly greater reliance ought to be placed on observation in the cross-cultural setting.

Of course observation needs to be directed. My own difficulties in grappling with the concept of warmth as a rating of affect to be made either from an assessment of an entire interview, as Minturn and Lambert (1964) did in their analysis of the Six Cultures study, or from specific replies to assorted informational questions, as described in the Oje-elite father study (LeVine *et al.*, 1967), has led me to seek observational evidence of differing maternal patterns of warmth. The work of Schaffer (1963) on early attachment behaviour should offer helpful guidelines. Jahoda (1967) also has recently suggested that the study of early infancy might prove productive in a cross-cultural setting. If Eleanor Maccoby's (1966) view that maternal warmth varies with different stages in the child's development is correct, it may well prove useful to extend the observational study of maternal affection beyond infancy, even though many new problems would be encountered once the child became linguistically proficient.

Certain formidable conceptual problems flow from the nature of the differences we seek to measure and to explain. In the analysis of mother interviews in the Six Cultures study only twenty-eight ratings are utilized (Minturn & Lambert, 1964). Many other variables on which there is little or no intracultural variability had to be discarded. Thus the problem of constructing a system of identical categories appears yet again. Perhaps problems of the measurement of individual variation are most properly those of the psychologist but it remains a hope that careful ethnographic observation can be employed to reveal differences which could be meaningfully measured, or at least to indicate behaviours of functional equivalence where categorical identity is impossible.

Throughout this discussion the question of perhaps greatest importance has been neglected. One is still left puzzling – what does it all add up to? It is usual in studies of this general design to claim that the child-rearing procedures have certain demonstrable effects on adult personality, national character, and the like. Certainly the claims of this study are considerably more circumspect; though I think it still pertinent to ask questions about ultimate effects. In answer to this very important question I should like to offer the very similar recent suggestions of Inkeles (1966) and Jahoda (1967). In a discussion of competence Inkeles suggests that experts in the study of socialization have for too long been primarily concerned with the process rather than with the end-product. He notes that in the current era of extremely rapid social change throughout the world it might be more productive to try to assess and understand those skills, aptitudes, traits, and cognitive processes which make some adults able to adapt to change, 'to move to new status and to elaborate new roles' (1966, p. 265). Our aim, he maintains, should be to seek first to identify these qualities and then to seek to understand the socialization processes which produce them. How valuable a contribution to problems of change could be made if social scientists had this information in hand.

Appendix

Mother Interview: English Version

We are interested in getting a general picture of how different Nigerians bring up their children, but we would like to place our main emphasis on children about the age at which they begin school. For certain questions we will ask you in particular to tell us about __________. (Space left for name of designated child, aged five to six years.)

To help us to understand the child-rearing practices you describe we would like to get some idea of the setting in which you bring up your children. The first group of questions will concern the physical and personal environment.

1. Would you describe your house – the various rooms – who uses each of them?
   1a. Are there any other adults living in the house? – approximate age, sex, and relationship to parents.
   1b. Are there any other children living in the house? – age, sex, and relationship to parents.
2. How many housegirls, boys, or babynurses live with your family or serve them? – approximate age, sex, and any relationship to family.
   2a. Where do they sleep?
   2b. Where do they cook?
   2c. Where do they eat?
3. (May be omitted if clear from Question 1)
   Where do the various members of the family sleep?
   3a. Do the mother and father each have a room or do they share a room?
   3b. Do any of the children sleep with the mother?
   3c. Which children sleep together?
4. We would like to get an idea of meal-times at your house.
   4a. At what time do you usually eat? – breakfast, lunch, dinner.
   4b. Do you eat any of these meals together? Where? When? Mother and father together? With the children?

CARETAKERS

In answering the next questions I want you to think mainly about __________. If you want to mention things about your other children *please* do after answering my question.

5. Since __________ was born have you been working at all? If *yes*:
   5a. How old was __________ when you began to work after his birth? Have you worked continuously?
   5b. What time would you usually go to work in the morning? Did you return for lunch? At what time would you come home for the day?
   5c. How far was your work from your home? How long did it take you to get there?
6. Who would usually look after __________ when you were not at home?
   6a. When he was a baby?

6b. Nowadays?
6c. How old would ________ have to be before you would leave him by himself, without a babynurse, for an evening?
6d. Is there any one else who looked after ________ occasionally?

7. Has ________ been with you all his life or have you been separated from him at any time? If *yes*: a, b, c. For all mothers: d, e.
7a. For how long? Why?
7b. How old was ________?
7c. With whom did he stay?
7d. Why do people believe in sending children away to live with other people?
7e. Do you feel that sending children to live with others is a good practice?

8. Has ________ been with his father all of his life or have they been separated. If *yes*: a, b.
8a. For how long? Why?
8b. How old was ________?
8c. Has the father ever been separated from the family?

9. When your husband is at home does he spend much time with ________?
9a. What sorts of things do they do together?
9b. Does ________ greet his father in the morning – the traditional greeting – prayers together?
9c. Does your husband try to correct ________'s behaviour? Discipline him?

10. When ________ was a baby who took care of him mostly?
10a. Where did ________ sleep? For how long?
10b. Were there any things your husband did to look after the baby?
10c. We know that some mothers pick up a baby as soon as it cries; others fear they may spoil it. What do you think about this? What did you do when ________ was a baby?

DISCIPLINE

We would like to know about some of the things that children of ________'s age do which you would consider naughty.

11. Can you think of anything ________ did yesterday which you felt was naughty?
11a. In general, what does ________ do which might lead you to discipline him?

11b. Does he ask too many questions sometimes? What do you do about it?

12. What sorts of discipline might you use when __________ is naughty?

12a. What do you do when he irritates you just a little?

12b. What do you do for something more severe?

12c. For something really serious?

13. Some people feel that fathers can give more serious discipline than mothers. What is your opinion?

13a. Would your husband usually discipline __________ for a very serious offence?

13b. What discipline might he use?

13c. Are there any other people who might discipline ______?

14. All children get on their parents' nerves sometime. Are there any things which __________ does that annoy you especially?

15. We have talked so much about things that might bother you, I was wondering, are there some things which __________ does that please you particularly?

15a. Do you reward him in any way?

15b. What do you expect of a well-behaved child of ______ 's age?

AGGRESSION

16. Does __________ play roughly – like wrestling with other children?

16a. Does __________ fight with other children?

16b. What do you do about it?

17. Does __________ play roughly with his brothers/sisters?

17a. Do they fight with each other?

17b. Do you do anything about this? What?

18. Does __________ come to tell you when someone has hit him?

18a. Do you encourage him to do this? How?

19. If you saw __________ teasing another child would you interfere? Why?

19a. If you saw __________ fighting with another child would you do anything? Why? What?

20. Do you mind __________'s answering back to you? To other adults?

20a. What do you do when __________ strikes at you? If *never*, what would you do?

TRADITIONAL PRACTICES

21. We are interested to know whether you have observed certain traditional practices in rearing (raising) __________.
    - 21a. Did you have his face marked or ears pierced? Why?
    - 21b. Did you shape __________'s head after birth? Why?
    - 21c. Was __________ circumcised? Why?
    - 21d. Did you stretch his arms and legs? Why?
    - 21e. Did you try to mould __________'s hips? Why?
    - 21f. Did you ever force-feed __________ as a baby? Why?
22. How old was __________ when you weaned him from the breast?
    - 22a. How long did it take you to wean him? From the bottle – how long?
23. We have learned that it is traditional for the husband not to have sexual relations with his wife during the period she is nursing a baby. Did you observe this practice when __________ was a baby?
    - 23a. For how long?
    - 23b. What do you think of this practice? (Any questions on birth control which might be fitted in.)

RESPONSIBILITY AND OBEDIENCE

24. What sorts of things does __________ do to help you? Tasks? For himself? For you?
    - 24a. How often does he do these things?
    - 24b. What do you do when he fails to do these things?
    - 24c. Are there others you might expect him to do when he gets older?
25. Some parents expect their children to obey immediately when they are told to do something – other parents leave it to the child to do things when he can. How do you feel about this?
    - 25a. How does your husband feel about immediate obedience?

ACHIEVEMENT

26. How old was __________ when he began to walk?
    - 26a. Had you done anything to encourage him?
27. How old was __________ when he began to say words? Sentences?
    - 27a. Had you done anything to help him to learn to talk?
28. Has __________ started school?
    - 28a. Have you done anything to prepare him for school?

29. When __________ starts school do you expect him to show you his weekly reports? If there are older children, ask: Do your older children?
    - 29a. What will you do if he has a good report? A bad one?
    - 29b. Will you/do you do anything to check on __________'s homework? The other children's? Does your husband check?
    - 29c. Do you expect __________ to be coached or to have private lessons outside his class work?
    - 29d. Are there any lessons outside of school work you would like __________ to have?
30. What would you like __________ to be when he grows up? What qualification would you like him to obtain?
    - 30a. What do you think you should do to see that he achieves this?

SOCIABILITY

31. Who does __________ usually play with? His brothers/sisters? Other relatives?
32. Are there any children you would discourage __________ from playing with?
    - 32a. Who are these children?
    - 32b. What do you find objectionable about them?
33. Does __________ ever prefer to play alone rather than with other children?
    - 33a. What do you think of this – should children be encouraged to play on their own?
34. Do you ever tell __________ not to play so much but to do other things? What sorts of things would you want him to do?
35. What kinds of games and things does __________ play?
36. Do you give __________ any particular training for how to act when visiting other people? What sorts?
    - 36a. Do you train him how to eat in other people's houses?

SOURCES OF INFLUENCE

37. In bringing up your children, what kinds of problems did you encounter that you felt you needed advice or help with?
    - 37a. Where did you get most of your advice on how to care for __________? Books, own mother, husband's mother, friends, older women?
    - 37b. Did you ever get advice from the hospital? What sort?

38. Have you ever had any disagreements with older women in the family about how to bring up ________? What were they about?
    38a. Eventually how were these disagreements settled?
39. Sometimes when faced with problems in bringing up children people look back to their own childhood and the methods of their parents. Have you ever done this? Why? About what sorts of things?
    39a. Are children brought up the same ways now as in your own childhood? What are some differences?

MARRIAGE AND FAMILY

40. How did you meet your husband? Did the families know each other before? Arrange the marriage? Approve of it once you decided? Disapprove and why?
41. Do you think it would be better if marriage became monogamous? For the wife? The children? The husband? Why? Was your father a polygamist?
    41a. Do you think educated women will agree to polygamy? Why?
42. What is the ideal family size? Same number of boys and girls? How many years between children? Do you believe in planning (deciding beforehand how many children and when) your family? Did you do this?
43. How do you feel about wives working when the children are babies? Later on?

SEX AND MODESTY

(Little introduction depending on rapport)

44. Do you see any differences in the ways boys and girls are brought up? What are they?
45. At what age do you think it is important for ________ to be clothed in the house? When he is outside?
    45a. What would you do if he went about without his clothes in the house? Outside?
46. At what age did ________ stop wetting his bed at night?
    46a. Have you had any difficulty about this? What did you do?
47. What do you do when ________ explores his own body (plays with his private parts)? Handles his sex organ?

47a. What do you do when ________ indulges in sex play with other children?

47b. What do you do when ________ uses obscene language?

48. Does ________ know how babies are made? If *yes*: How did he learn this?

48a. Do you feel it is your responsibility to teach him about sex? Your husband's? The school's? Leave it to chance?

48b. What do you do when ________ asks you questions about sex?

NOTES

1. I am indebted to the following for support and criticism. In Ibadan this research was financed by the National Institute of Mental Health, Grant M-4865 to Professor R. A. LeVine, and by Ford Foundation funds to the Universities of Ibadan and Chicago. Aid in the preparation of this paper was generously supplied by the Department of Psychology, the University of Birmingham, and valuable criticism was given by Drs P. Rosenblatt, P. C. Lloyd, and Alistair Chalmers.

2. The interviewing of fathers was supervised by Professor R. A. LeVine and that of mothers by Dr B. B. Lloyd. Mrs V. Demos and Mrs O. Akinkugbe assisted with the mother interviews, and Mrs E. Roberts aided in translation and transcribing. Mr D. O. Oyerinde helped in the father interviews.

3. All values of χ^2 are corrected for continuity.

REFERENCES

ATKINSON, J. W. (ed.). 1958. *Motives in Fantasy, Action and Society.* Princeton, N.J.: Van Nostrand.

BACKMAN, C. W. & SECORD, P. F. (eds.). 1966. *Problems in Social Psychology.* New York: McGraw-Hill.

BERNSTEIN, B. 1960. Language and Social Class. *British Journal of Sociology* **11**: 271–276.

BRONFENBRENNER, U. 1966. The Changing American Child – A Speculative Analysis. In C. W. Backman & P. F. Secord (eds.), *Problems in Social Psychology.* New York: McGraw-Hill.

DOOB, L. W. 1965. Psychology. In R. A. Lystad (ed.), *The African World: A Survey of Social Research.* New York: Praeger.

FOSS, B. M. (ed.). 1963. *Determinants of Infant Behaviour*, Vol. 2. London: Methuen.

FRIJDA, N. & JAHODA, G. 1966. On the Scope and Methods of Cross-cultural Research. *International Journal of Psychology* **1** (2): 109–127.

INKELES, A. 1963. Social Change and Social Character: The Role of Parental Mediation. In N. J. Smelser & W. J. Smelser (eds.), *Personality and Social Systems.* New York: Wiley.

INKELES, A. 1966. Social structure and the socialisation of competence. *Harvard Educational Review* **36** (3): 265–283.

JAHODA, G. 1967. Some Research Problems in African Education. Paper presented at a Conference on Social Psychology in Developing Countries, Ibadan, Nigeria.

JANES, M. D. 1967. Report on a Growth and Development Study on Yoruba Children in Ibadan, Western Nigeria. Prepared for a Conference on Rural Nutrition, Dakar, Senegal.

LEACH, E. 1964. Comments on Naroll's 'On Ethnic Unit Classification'. *Current Anthropology* **5** (4): 299.

LEVINE, R. A. 1963. Child Rearing in Sub-Saharan Africa: An Interim Report. *Bulletin of the Menninger Clinic* **27** (5): 245–256.

—, KLEIN, N. H. & FRIES, C. H. 1967. Father–Child Relationships and Changing Life Styles in Ibadan. In H. Miner (ed.), *The City in Modern Africa*. New York: Praeger.

LLOYD, B. B. 1966. Education and Family Life in the Development of Class Identification among the Yoruba. In P. C. Lloyd (ed.), *New Elites of Tropical Africa*. London: Oxford University Press (for the International African Institute).

— 1967. Indigenous Ibadan. In P. C. Lloyd, A. Mabogunje & B. Awe (eds.), *The City of Ibadan*. Cambridge: Cambridge University Press.

LLOYD, P. C. (ed.). 1966. *New Elites of Tropical Africa*. London: Oxford University Press (for the International African Institute).

— 1967. The Elite. In P. C. Lloyd, A. Mabogunje & B. Awe (eds.), *The City of Ibadan*. Cambridge: Cambridge University Press.

—, MABOGUNJE, A. & AWE, B. 1967. *The City of Ibadan*. Cambridge: Cambridge University Press.

LYSTAD, R. A. (ed.). 1965. *The African World: A Survey of Social Research*. New York: Praeger.

MACCOBY, E. E. 1966. The Choice of Variables in the Study of Socialization. In C. W. Backman & P. F. Secord (eds.), *Problems in Social Psychology*. New York: McGraw-Hill.

MINER, H. 1967. *The City in Modern Africa*. New York: Praeger.

MINTURN, L. & LAMBERT, W. W. 1964. *Mothers of Six Cultures: Antecedents of Child Rearing*. New York: Wiley.

PROTHRO, E. T. 1961. *Child Rearing in the Lebanon*. Cambridge, Mass.: Harvard University Press.

SCHAFFER, H. R. 1963. Some Issues for Research in the Study of Attachment Behaviour. In B. M. Foss (ed.), *Determinants of Infant Behaviour*, Vol. 2. London: Methuen.

SEARS, R. R., MACCOBY, E. E. & LEVIN, H. 1957. *Patterns of Child Rearing*. Evanston, Ill.: Row Peterson.

TALBOT, P. A. & MULHALL, P. 1962. *The Physical Anthropology of Southern Nigeria.* Cambridge: Occasional Publications of the Cambridge University Museum of Archaeology and Ethnology.

WHITING, B. B. (ed.). 1963. *Six Cultures: Studies of Child Rearing.* New York and London: Wiley.

WINTERBOTTOM, M. R. 1958. The Relation of Need Achievement to Learning Experiences in Independence and Mastery. In J. W. Atkinson (ed.), *Motives in Fantasy, Action and Society.* Princeton, N.J.: Van Nostrand.

Barbara E. Ward

Temper Tantrums in Kau Sai

Some Speculations upon their Effects

The following paragraphs are offered with considerable diffidence. The fieldwork upon which this paper is based was directed primarily towards the analysis of a socio-economic system as such.[1] As a result, the data on child development and adult attitudes which appear in my notebooks do so almost by accident. They were certainly not collected systematically with the object of testing the validity of hypotheses in social psychology. They did, however, appear to me to have some intrinsic interest at the time, and my thinking about some of the major puzzles in Chinese social patterns – in particular, the marvellous ability of Chinese to 'live in crowds and keep their virtue' – has been partly influenced by them. An unpublished version of this paper has already provoked some useful rethinking, and it is my hope that if a wider audience may be reached others may be moved to look further and more scientifically into these and similar matters. The ensuing observations are therefore offered simply as speculations for discussion. I should add that they apply strictly to one particular fishing village in the British crown colony of Hong Kong, but I believe that such truth as they may contain has a much wider validity for Chinese families in general.

The village, Kau Sai, is situated on an island in the eastern waters of the colony. This paper begins in the period 1952–53 when the population was about 450, nearly all of them living on small boats anchored just offshore. Ten years later there had been a number of changes, notably an increase of population to about 600, the beginning of a move to living ashore, the building of a fine new school (with three teachers and more than 100 pupils), and a generally marked rise in the standard of living. All these things were connected with the completion of the mechanization of all but one or two of the fishing boats, which had brought also much greater physical mobility, knowledge of the ways of the big city, and so on. I do not think there have been, or are likely soon to be, concomitant changes in the patterns of child behaviour described here.

THREE KINDS OF TANTRUM

Both in the village and in Hong Kong generally I noticed very early that it was quite a common thing to see children, especially small boys – between the ages of, say, five and ten – in a screaming rage: lying on the floor or the pavement (sidewalk), kicking and screaming, red in the face and making no end of noise – an obvious tantrum, and nobody taking any notice. Usually these tantrums just petered out into sobbing, and the child finally picked himself up and went away; sometimes an elder brother or someone else, usually but not always a parent or sibling, would come and pull the child up, scold him and tell him to stop. Now in England I think it is true to say that children's tantrums tend to occur at rather younger ages and that they are much more usually a matter of adult concern. Either by comforting or by scolding the mother will usually try to stop her child screaming, and also it would, I think, be unusual for any adult to notice a screaming child and do just nothing about it at all – and this whether the child was any relation of his or not – whereas here they were just left to scream themselves out.

Later, I made a tentative classification of tantrums observed in Kau Sai village, as follows:

1. There was the kind of tantrum that occurred when a child felt himself left behind or deserted by his parents or others. This was especially common among the boat children who sometimes found themselves left on the shore while others went out to the boats – they were scared of being abandoned and they yelled their feelings very loud in order to make their presence known. This kind of tantrum happened to both boys and girls, and at any age from about three to six, seven, or eight; that is, from the time they were able to wander about on their own, and so run the risk of getting left behind, to the time they were able to scull a boat for themselves and so need not fear being

left behind. This seems to me to be a very ordinary kind of rage: any small children fear being abandoned and react to situations in which they think this is likely to happen in much the same way – the only difference here was that the pattern of living on boats made this situation a little more common, perhaps, than it is in other kinds of community. I feel myself that this fact may have some effect on the personality development of the boat people as such, but that is not my present concern.

2. The second kind of tantrum consisted of the crying and stamping that a child might break into if he did not get what he was asking for immediately. For example, a small girl wanting ten cents to buy sweets might stamp and shout until her father gave it to her just to keep her quiet. This again is not at all an unusual thing in any family where the children have been indulged. It was not a common type of tantrum in Kau Sai and is probably commoner in all societies among richer families who often have more time and opportunity to 'spoil' their children than have poorer ones.

3. The third type of tantrum was the one that interested me most. It was likely to affect both boys and girls, but boys more often. Though closely connected with the second type, it was not exactly the same in origin. For example, a group of small children is playing ball, a bigger boy comes along and kicks the ball away from them. The owner of the ball, a little boy about six years old, rises and runs after this bigger boy but fails to catch him. Finally, the bigger boy lets him have the ball back. The small chap, Ah Kam, picks it up again and goes off with it, but before he has gone very far an adult comes along and knocks it out of his hands. This causes laughter among the onlookers, and Ah Kam laughs too as he goes to pick up his ball once more. Later in the same morning he is playing with other children who have a skipping rope. Ah Kam tries to help to turn the rope for others to skip, but he is called away by his mother who wants him to bring the baby to her. A bit later still he starts playing at 'cooking' – with scraps of straw for firewood and broken-up pots for rice and dishes – with another group of his age-mates. This game goes on quite successfully for about fifteen minutes until along comes another adult who, with a sweep of his hand, knocks the pretence rice and the

pretence pots and pans flying. The adult laughs and the children laugh too. By then it is nearly noon and Ah Kam is hungry, so he trots off to the shop to spend his ten cents on biscuits. After collecting them he runs out of the shop and collides with another child coming in. One of the biscuits falls on the ground and is smashed. Ah Kam also falls to the ground in an apparently uncontrollable rage. He yells for some time. Nobody takes any notice of him except perhaps to look in his direction once or twice. Gradually his sobs grow quieter until, after about ten minutes, he picks himself up, still clutching his biscuits, and wanders off sobbing to himself. His slightly older sister comes up to him and takes two of the biscuits away from him. He makes no protest. About twenty minutes later he is playing with the other children again – the tantrum apparently forgotten.

Now the points I want to notice here are three:

1. In the first place, this third kind of rage springs from an accumulation of frustrating situations. Ah Kam, aged six, has already learnt to put up with a great deal of outside interference – he laughs at the ball being knocked out of his hands, for example – but he cannot yet put up with too much. In the end he simply screams.

2. Second, these frustrations are some of them accidental (running into another child) and some of them apparently deliberately caused (knocking over the cooking game). This apparently deliberate interference in the children's affairs is not in any sense considered unkind or unusual in the village. The general adult attitude if expressed would be: these are only children and it doesn't matter.

(There is here, by the way, an interesting difference between English and Chinese views on children's sensitivity. When a child falls down or hurts himself in Kau Sai, nobody makes any fuss about him, though of course if there is serious injury there is considerable alarm and great care is taken. As a result, one may guess, of the lack of fuss, children who have tumbles and minor hurts seldom cry. They appear to know they will get no attention if they do. Western children tend to behave in just the opposite way, crying loudly and unnecessarily over the smallest injury because they usually get much attention from doing so. Western and Chinese adults' explanations of their differing behaviour in this matter are interesting. The Westerner says: because he is a child it is more difficult for him to bear pain, he has not yet learnt to control his reactions. The Chinese villagers I know say: because he is a child he does not *feel* pain as badly as an adult would, so there is no need to fuss. Once I asked a woman how she knew that children felt pain less than adults do. She said: 'But of course you don't feel pain so badly when you are a child; if you did you would remember, but look at this' – she showed me some deep scars on her chest – 'that happened when I was about two years old and it was very serious as you can see, but I can't remember anything about it at all. So it can't have hurt very much.')

But to go back to the adult's frustration of children: I repeat there is absolutely no intention of being unkind. Children's affairs are not considered important and the children themselves are naturally expected to share this view (to which there is only one exception: going to school is considered important). Nevertheless, everybody is interested in children, and everybody likes to watch them; they provide, indeed, a common form of entertainment and pleasure. The same is true of small babies, who are continually being played with and talked to. Many, if not most, fathers like to carry a small child around with them almost wherever they go – particularly, of course, a boy baby. Now this great interest in small children leads very often to a desire to provoke them to some reaction. In very much the same way as a small child himself when playing with a live animal will poke it with a stick just to see what happens, so adults who play with live children tend to like to poke them in the ribs just to get a reaction. It does not much matter what the reaction is: the baby may smile or he may cry, in either case he has *provided a reaction*, and the person who provoked him is satisfied. Thus very early indeed babies in the village are subjected to adult provocation of one kind or another.

This continues into childhood, but by that time there are two differences to be taken into consideration. First, the child is more likely to be aware of frustration than the baby, because the ways in which adults can provoke a reaction from him are different. For example, a baby may be asleep and an adult may wake him up. The baby has been provoked and he will cry but he will probably fairly soon go back to sleep. But a child may be concentrating intently and deliberately on some game which an adult destroys, and this is a much more consciously frustrating experience than simply being woken up out of sleep. Second, a baby suffers less than a child in this matter because a baby if crying will always be comforted, picked up, fondled, given the breast, and generally soothed down. The change to being left alone to cry oneself out comes at about two and a half years or so, and is probably closely connected with weaning and with the arrival of another child in the family – situations themselves likely to provoke distress in the displaced child, especially if he is a boy and has therefore been particularly well noticed before.

Thus the frustrations that appear to be deliberately brought to children of, say, three years old and upwards are not intended to be unkind; they are in some ways simply the ordinary expression of interest in children, but they are none the less often very painful in their effects.

3. The third point about these tantrums that I want to stress is that, as a general rule, the child is left to cry himself out. Normally no one goes to deal with him either by scolding or by comforting. It is my belief that one result of this is that the child fairly quickly learns that such rages bring no reward (just as crying after being physically hurt does not pay), and it is probable that at the same time he also learns that he can expect no sympathy from others in his private despairs. As a result the village children I know do seem to learn remarkably quickly to accept frustrations, and to be peculiarly self-composed and in emotional matters self-reliant.

Although I have said earlier that tantrums occur rather later than in my experience with English children, they do not continue past the age of nine or ten.

So far the data; now for the speculation. The following arguments are not of a kind that is fashionable at present among either social psychologists or social anthropologists. It does not follow that they are entirely without validity. At the very least, speculation upon them may provoke others to develop more adequate hypotheses. I therefore wish to examine here the possible connection between the observations just recorded and certain other observed features of village social life, namely: the relatively problem-free period of adolescence; the strict playing-down of aggression; and the ability to live in extremely crowded conditions.

ADOLESCENT ADJUSTMENTS FOR BOYS AND GIRLS

First, then, I should like to postulate that there may be some connection with later individual development. The village of Kau Sai contains a community in which problems of adolescent adjustment appear to be minimal, especially for boys. There were in 1950–53 a number of circumstances relevant to this: children grew up with a clear idea of exactly what their place in the socio-economic system was to be; they lived always in the very midst of the cottage-industry type of fishing business which occupied all their neighbours and in which they themselves took an active and useful part from a very early age; the necessary skills were acquired gradually and at home; marriages were arranged when the children were about sixteen years old. Thus there were virtually no alternatives offered to adolescents, no choices they could make, and for boys there were no sharp discontinuities at any stage. As far as skills were concerned there was a gradual assumption of adult roles with increasing maturity and physical strength, and none of the necessary skills was beyond the achievement of any ordinary individual; as far as status was concerned, the ceremony of marriage conferred adulthood publicly and without any doubt; and early marriage gave adolescent sexual activity both limitation and legitimation. These are all structural features that point to a relatively stress-free adolescence. The period of greatest emotional strain, for boys at least, appeared to be much earlier – in the tantrum years from about five to ten.

The pattern for girls was different, for the obvious reason that they experienced the complete, sometimes traumatic, discontinuity of leaving home at marriage. Because of this, they were usually given clearly to understand – from the time they could understand speech at all – that they were 'goods on which profit is lost', which gave them from the start a position very different from that of their brothers. Generally less indulged when very young, and earlier introduced to responsible domestic tasks, girls appeared in 1953 to accept their frustrations more readily than did boys. I certainly observed fewer tantrums in girls, and they seemed not to persist beyond the age of five and six. The major problem for girls at adolescence was, of course, adjustment to the new family after marriage. I have very few observations to offer on this, beyond the obvious point that there were considerable differences between, say, a marriage with the boy next door (this is a mixed surname village)[2] and a marriage into an unknown family living at a distance, and, of course, between different individual mothers-in-law. A few (very few) recently married girls did try to run away, but a young bride is very unlikely to have anywhere to run to, and most accepted their new situation with much the same apparent readiness as that with which they had accepted their earlier frustrations. Perhaps these latter served the useful purpose of providing habituation. At any rate there is no doubt in my mind, after many conversations, that village girls were entirely realistic in their attitude towards their own situation, accepted it as inevitable, did not (I am speaking of a time about ten years ago) question its essential rightness, but did know that with luck, the successful production of children,[3] and the passing of time they too might have a more prestigeful, somewhat more restful, and much gayer future to look forward to.

To a lay observer all this appears to be a reversal of the usual developmental sequence. Both sexes exhibit in adolescence a marked degree of emotional control, in other words a successful adjustment to their structural situation. Is it fanciful to regard this as, in part at least, an outcome of the earlier period of stress and frustration which both undergo though in rather different ways? My own inclination is to argue that there is a connection but that it is in no sense causative. The psychological stability of the adolescent period in Kau Sai is to be explained in the situational terms I have just listed, including, at the time of which I am so far writing, the lack of alternative choices and the relative prosperity of the fishing industry there (a youngster is assured of a reasonably good living if he stays at home). At the same time, the kinds of childhood experience that most adolescents have undergone have led them to suppress the outward manifestations of emotional frustration and not to expect any deep emotional sympathy from others. They have also, of course, been deliberately taught the rightness of familialism and of the whole going concern into which they have been born, and, once again, at this level too, no alternatives have been put before them. They are therefore psychologically fairly well adapted to accepting the actual situation when it develops. It must be remembered, too, that adolescence in Kau Sai brings very real satisfactions, for it is during the age-period fifteen to twenty that nearly all members of this community marry and begin their economically productive careers, thus entering into the two most highly valued of the universally available statuses in traditional Chinese villages.

In the summer of 1963 I went back to Kau Sai. I noticed no changes in the parental treatment of children. The same temper tantrums could be observed. Indeed, it was laughable to see the younger brothers of today's strapping young married adolescents repeating their elders' behaviour patterns in almost identical ways. But there had been some changes in adolescent behaviour, if not in general then for certain individuals. Four girls had married, rather later than would have been usual ten years ago, *landsmen* of their own choice; five boys had gone away to work for wages ashore. In other words, the possibility of choice had now appeared. With it also had come a new school and, for the first time, an education which made it possible for some of the new choices to be taken up. Nowadays young people do discuss the alternatives to accepting arranged marriages and staying at home to work in the family business. A girl who leaves the community still does so only on marriage, and gains much the same status as she did before – or, because she can now more easily marry 'up',[4] a better one. A boy who leaves is less likely to marry early. He gains independence, but may well lose economic advantage, at least for a time. He may, perhaps, return to the family fishing business later on and settle down, or he may not. In any case he faces a period of uncertainty which does not exist in the village. It seems to me that his childhood experiences fit him just as well for that.

If I have dwelt overlong upon adolescence this is simply because it is a subject not yet much discussed in the Chinese context. The other two topics I wish to draw attention to have been more frequently described.

THE AVOIDANCE OF VIOLENT BEHAVIOUR

As I have explained elsewhere (Ward, 1954, 1965, 1966), village organization in Kau Sai (which is a small community in which there have never been any 'gentry' and both the standards of living and the sources of livelihood are more or less identical for all members of the population) is markedly anarchic. Leadership roles are shunned rather than sought, and on the one annual occasion on which organized leadership is required (at the annual festival in the 2nd moon) leaders are always selected by lot at the village temple. To push oneself forward in an open effort to dominate others is considered wrong in much the same way that any openly aggressive behaviour, including verbally aggressive behaviour, is considered wrong. One of the actually most influential men in the village is one of the most retiring, and he owes his influence (the existence of which he denies) largely to this fact. He has never been known to quarrel with anyone, and has several times been held up to me as an example of good character because of this. His reputation was enhanced rather than the reverse during the period immediately preceding family partition,[5] when fairly frequent noisy arguments broke out between his brothers; whenever this happened he quietly, and in obvious distress, absented himself and went to bed.

But then the phrase 'I was so angry that I went home to sleep' is one that I have heard more than once, and from different people of both sexes. Withdrawal from a situation in which aggressive feelings are likely to break into open expression is highly approved behaviour, and a good temper and a controlled tongue are among the most valued personal qualities. A good deal of the local gossip centres upon these qualities and a young person who lacks them, or whose horoscope or other magical properties indicate their absence, is difficult to marry off.

All this is part of what appears to many Westerners to be an exaggerated fear of violence. Children are constantly told not to fight each other and are quickly restrained if they do. There is absolutely none of the 'hit him back next time' kind of advice, but rather a warning to keep out of the way or run a bit faster. Adults who show signs of coming to blows are separated at once and the theme of one of the most usual lines of criticism of foreigners is the appalling violence of their behaviour.

Actually, quarrels or any sort of open expression of aggression between Kau Sai villagers appear to be exceedingly rare. There is no local mechanism for dealing with them, and it is unthinkable that any Kau Sai person should take another (or indeed anybody) to court. Potential hostility is not usually allowed to develop into open aggression, and is constantly played down. Young men in their late twenties, or even thirties, whose fathers still exercise complete authority over them, may grumble to an anthropologist, but they are careful to see that no one else overhears them. Brothers whose joint property is still undivided may squabble in public, but usually only after drinking; and everyone hastens to point out that drunken words carry no real significance. Within the village these are the two sets of relationship most loaded with potential hostility.

Relationships with non-Kau Sai people tend to be thought of in terms of general potential hostility mitigated by special circumstances. For example, the villagers of X across the water are nearly always described as being bad people, quarrelsome and thieving, yet there has been continued intermarriage between the two settlements and probably every individual in Kau Sai has close and amicable ties of both kinship and friendship with some individual(s) from X. Similarly, the local Hakka-speaking Chinese in general[6] are said to be 'no good'; again, it is significant that this is elaborated in terms of their alleged quarrelsomeness and thrusting. Most of the landsmen (including fish dealers) with whom the Kau Sai fishermen come into contact locally are in fact Hakka, and all fishermen in Kau Sai do have particular Hakka friendships. This distrust of other people when seen generally as groups, along with a willingness to accept close ties with particular individuals from those groups, goes along with what I have described elsewhere (Ward, 1965) as the lack of intergroup relationships between communities as such and the development of a series of dyadic relationships between Kau Sai individuals and non-Kau Sai individuals.

One consequence of the lack of intergroup relationships as such at the village level is that there is no local mechanism for dealing with disputes if they do arise. From time to time thefts of nets are reported in Kau Sai; usually the villagers of X are blamed, but there is no machinery for dealing with the matter other than through formal complaints to the police and through the courts. It is needless to say that no one follows this course. But the lack of machinery for the local settlement of disputes, together with the believed-in inaccessibility of the courts, means (as Smith remarked in his study of Chinese villages years ago: Smith, 1890) that there is very wide scope for the local bullies. In fact, the Hong Kong Marine Police maintain a close patrol in local waters and frequently visit outlying villages, but even so nets can be stolen with impunity, temples are robbed from time to time, and memories of successful piracies are very much alive. Every fishing boat carries sticks of dynamite, and these are not always used only for the (illegal) stunning of fish. The fear of violence is by no means without foundation.

CONCLUSIONS

What has any of this to do with temper tantrums in childhood? I can give only a common-sense suggestion: we have here a structural situation which offers few effective sanctions against aggressive behaviour; the people appear to rely mainly upon the successful repression of aggressive impulses within each individual. This is secured during the period of socialization partly by direct verbal teaching, partly by physical restraint, and partly, though not I assume by conscious intent, through the kinds of childhood experience of frustration and the failure of aggressive behaviour to obtain its objectives that I have described above. There may well be other contributory factors.

But except for particularly meek individuals (like the admired man of influence previously mentioned, who in most English villages would probably be the object of amused derision) it is impossible to rely solely upon the internalization of the values of non-aggression. As a result, the maintenance of public order is likely to be rather a chancy business.

Self-control may break down for various reasons. Some of them are psychological. For example, individual consciousness may be, as it were, in abeyance – in drunkenness, for instance, or hysteria (including mob hysteria). It has, of course, often been remarked how relatively peaceable Chinese drunks are, which suggests that the control of aggressive behaviour is pretty deeply imbedded. Nevertheless, I have frequently observed that people in Kau Sai and elsewhere are afraid that a drunken man may turn nasty; a careful watch is usually kept on a man who is drinking, and drunken quarrels do sometimes occur – only to be hushed up and explained away as quickly as possible by everybody else. It may well be that the very fact that aggression is so much played down makes people the more afraid of it. There being virtually no legitimate outlets for aggressive behaviour and few effective external sanctions against it, once the internal controls do break down it can get quickly out of hand, and so there is good reason to be afraid. Herein may lie some of the explanation of the extreme violence of an aroused Chinese mob. Contrariwise, the relative ease with which a riot can be brought under control may possibly be partly due to the ease with which the internalized controls take over automatically once the hysteria has been checked.

Obviously there must be many individual personality differences. Some people are quick to take offence, and some tempers do flare up easily. The point is, however, that in Kau Sai everyone rallies to prevent a quarrel if possible, and even the offender himself deplores the lapse once he is restored to equanimity (or sobriety).

But it is obvious, too, that this cannot be the whole story. One cannot fall back upon 'personality differences' and temporary failures in self-control to explain such recurring phenomena as, say, banditry, clan warfare, or oppression by unscrupulous officials. Even the incidence of village bullies and other local delinquencies of the kinds I have already mentioned has been far too regular in traditional China to be entirely accounted for in terms of individual psychological peculiarities. Either the argument so far has no general validity and people in other parts and strata of Chinese society do not exhibit the same degree of control as in Kau Sai or something more than a psychological explanation is required. I am inclined to think that both these objections have some truth in them.

Kau Sai people are boat people,[7] and the boat people of

Kwangtung and Fukien have long been a despised group, at the bottom of most local systems of stratification and hitherto largely without wealth, education, or connections with the ruling elites. Moreover, being water-dwellers they are potentially completely mobile; it is always possible for them to up anchor and run away. For these reasons they probably are an extreme case. Few other groups in China are likely to show such a high degree of non-aggressiveness. On the other hand, even a Kau Sai fisherman would not disapprove of, say, the use of firearms (or, lacking them, sticks of dynamite) against pirates – provided only that it was successful and did not provoke still more trouble.

Are we to say, then, that aggressive behaviour is considered deplorable only because it is likely to provoke retaliation? Rather I would suggest that this way of posing the problem is mistaken. Instead of concentrating upon some supposedly unitary concept called 'aggressive behaviour', as this paper has done so far, it would be more useful to switch our attention from the actor to the situation, and to argue that, whereas in certain situations any kind of aggressiveness is thought wrong, in others some kinds of aggressiveness may be considered correct though possibly inexpedient. Kau Sai people themselves do not say 'we deplore violence' or 'we try to inhibit aggression'; rather, they say 'we fishermen are desperately afraid of trouble' and 'we people of Kau Sai are just like brothers and sisters and so we do not quarrel'. The first of these sentences refers to their situation *vis-à-vis* non-Kau Sai people, clashes with whom might provoke 'trouble' (perhaps a lawsuit, perhaps future retaliation, perhaps further squeeze – there is a large range of possible trouble); the second refers to their situation at home – strife there would not provoke trouble in the same ways, it would just be bad in itself, making community life insupportable. For the boat people, and indeed for the majority of Chinese most of the time, open manifestations of aggressiveness against outsiders must nearly always have been unwise, but there were quite a number of other groups in traditional China to whom this disability did not apply. Those who, for whatever reason, could oppress outsiders with impunity often (usually) did so. In so far as childhood training and experience did succeed in inculcating self-control of aggressive behaviour, it seems that this could be relied upon only within narrowly limited situations.

The last topic I should like to raise for discussion is the fascinating and astonishing Chinese ability to live successfully in conditions of overcrowding which would drive most other peoples to crime and/or despair. A foreigner is usually struck first by the, to him, intolerable overcrowding of such towns as Singapore, Hong Kong, and Shanghai. He tends to put it down to something called 'the early stages of urbanization', talks about 'population explosions', and wonders at the apparently successful adaptation the populace has made. But, generally speaking, crowded conditions and an almost complete lack of privacy are as typical of the villages and, of course, of the boats as of the towns; Chinese peasants who 'become urbanized' are usually moving only from one kind of crowding to another.[8]

No doubt this does go far to explain the seeming ease of transition from rural to urban living (and often back again), but we are still left to wonder what are the factors that make such crowding tolerable anywhere. And here it does seem that there may be a much more direct connection with childhood's temper tantrums and their treatment than any we have so far been able to uncover, for it is at least plausible to suggest that early habituation to frustration and interference may do much to make possible the kind of living on top of each other that is so common. This and the playing down of aggressive behaviour, which we have already discussed, probably also contribute to the remarkably low crime-rates typical of even the most densely crowded Chinese communities.

But there is a further kite here that I should like to fly. I earlier referred to my observation that village children seemed to be peculiarly self-composed and in emotional matters self-reliant. I connected this on the one hand with their experiences over temper tantrums and on the other hand with their apparently unstressful adolescence. But I mentioned also that young men going to town faced at least an initial period of uncertainty such as did not exist in the village, and suggested that their childhood experiences, by giving them emotional self-reliance, fitted them well to cope with this. Whether or not I am right in connecting emotional self-reliance with the kind of treatment given (or, rather, not given) to temper tantrums, there seems to be no doubt that it is a marked feature of Chinese personality structure. And it seems at least very likely that it contributes significantly to the success with which Chinese adapt themselves to new circumstances – whether these involve moving into a bed-space in a tenement crowded to the brim with strangers, or migrating overseas, or accepting extremes of social change at home.

NOTES

1. I wish to record my warmest thanks to H.M. Treasury Committee for the Study of Foreign Languages and Cultures (the Scarborough Committee) and to the London-Cornell Project for East and Southeast Asian Studies for making this fieldwork possible.

2. The traditional rule that marriage may be contracted only between persons of different surnames is strictly adhered to. Many villages in S.E. China are 'single surname' (i.e. localized lineage) villages, containing only bearers of one patrilineally inherited surname and their wives.

3. Not simply sons; they deeply desire girls, too, especially among their older children, for a daughter can give really useful help with the everlasting domestic work at least eight years sooner than a daughter-in-law.

4. The water people form the lowest category in the Hong Kong stratification system.

5. I.e. the division of property among sons which takes place, usually, some time after the death of their father.

6. The two major indigenous languages in Hong Kong are Hakka and Cantonese. Cantonese dominates in both numbers of speakers and prestige. The fishermen speak a dialect of Cantonese but are in other respects usually considered lower in the local prestige ranking than Hakka speakers.

7. Often called 'Tanka', a term used only in S.E. China; see Ward, 1965.

8. And traditional towns were no less crowded than modern ones; see, for example, Doolittle's description of Fuchow in the mid-nineteenth century (Doolittle, 1865).

REFERENCES

DOOLITTLE, (REV.) JUSTUS. 1865. *Social Life of the Chinese: with some account of their Religious, Governmental, Educational and Business Customs and Opinions. With Special but not Exclusive Reference to Fuhchau.* New York.

SMITH, ARTHUR H. 1890. *Village Life in China.* New York.

—— 1894. *Chinese Characteristics.* New York.

WARD, BARBARA E. 1954. A Hong Kong Fishing Village. In *Journal of Oriental Studies* **1** (1). Hong Kong.

WARD, BARBARA E. 1965. Varieties of the Conscious Model. In M. Banton (ed.), *The Relevance of Models for Social Anthropology.* A.S.A. Monographs 1. London: Tavistock Publications.

— 1966. Sociological Self-Awareness: Some Uses of the Conscious Model. *Man* (n.s.) **1** (2): 201–215.

Paul Spencer

The Function of Ritual in the Socialization of the Samburu Moran

THE CONTEXT OF SOCIALIZATION AMONG SAMBURU MORAN

Socialization has a narrower and a broader sense. In the narrower sense it tends to be confined to the social learning of children, to the processes whereby they acquire the values of adult society so as to participate fully within it (e.g. Parsons; Newcomb). In the broader sense, it may be extended to adults whenever they join a new social group and are expected to acquire a new set of values before participating fully within it (*Dictionary of Social Sciences*) and even, logically, to social deviates who have to be taught to conform. In each case there is a certain adjustment on the part of the individual and a set of expectations on the part of the wider group or society; and in each case there will be a certain conflict between the old values that have to be discarded and the new values that have to be acquired. However, the actual processes of adjustment are not identical, and the extensive body of theory linking the socialization of children to their physical and psychological development is not strictly applicable to the socialization (or rather *resocialization*) of adults. In this paper I am primarily concerned with the socialization of Samburu men who are no longer quite in the first flush of youth, and in a later section I shall consider the relevance of Pavlovian psychology to the socialization of adults and also to the analysis of ritual.

The Samburu are a Masai-speaking nomadic tribe of northern Kenya, with a pastoral economy and an age-set system whereby young men pass through an age-grade of warriorhood and are popularly known by the Masai term, *moran*. Traditionally, the moran were the younger unmarried men, who up to the age of thirty or thirty-five years were principally engaged in protecting the tribe and its cattle from hostile raiders of other tribes, although they would also initiate raids on their own account against these people. Inevitably, the tribe tended to isolate itself from its more hostile neighbours and to remain as compact as economically feasible. Inevitably also, some of the best grazing areas were in the vicinity of the no-man's land where pressure for grazing was least, and it was here that the moran would often set up camps in order to give their cattle the best food obtainable.

Traditionally, therefore, the tribe is seen as having consisted of a nucleus of Samburu elders who lived in settlements with their wives and families and were surrounded by a defensive ring of encamped moran guarding the settlements and a large portion of the most treasured cattle. Traditionally (and I must emphasize the use of the term 'traditionally' and not necessarily 'historically'), this was considered the correct place for the moran – away from the settlements and occupying a strategic position economically and militarily in the bush. Meanwhile, at the nucleus, the tribal elders held a monopoly of internal power: it was they who would decide when and where migrations should take place, who would monopolize all marriages, resolve all forms of dispute including those among the moran that they could not settle among themselves, and even direct the more strategic and organized raids of the moran. Popular attention, glamour, and interest focused attention on the embellished warriors of the society who were economically and ideologically associated with the bush, but real power lay at the centre: with the elders.

The traditional form of Samburu society could have provided an interesting example for the study of adult socialization. In the course of their social development, all the men would have to pass through three distinct age-grades: boyhood, moranhood, and elderhood. For each of these there would be different social expectations, values, and attitudes. There would therefore have to be two distinct periods of transition: from boyhood to moranhood, and from moranhood to elderhood, and each transition would involve the promotion of an entire age-set and a 'changeover' of the system. The transition from moranhood to elderhood in particular would be a radical one: from being in a position of bachelors and warriors associated with the bush and military glory (or ignominy), they would become married men and decision-makers, associated with the settlement and peace (especially within the tribe). The process of socialization should have entailed forces and pressures which enabled and encouraged the moran to make this transition.

The significance of this traditional view of the society today is that, warfare or no warfare, it defines the position of the moran with respect to the rest of the society, and inasmuch as virtually everyone still subscribes to it, it is a tradition in the fullest sense. No doubt in the past, as at present, the transition from moranhood to elderhood was essentially gradual. Thus the moran are encouraged by the elders to settle their internal disputes by discussion ('the way of the elders') rather than by violence ('the way of the moran'), and are thereby introduced to the gentle art of the debate. The elders teach them in advance what standards will be expected of them before they can be accepted into elderhood. Again, there is no precise point at which they reach elderhood: getting married, associating more closely with the elders, discarding the adornments of moranhood for the more sombre cloth of elderhood, and taking a more active part in the elders' discussions occur over a period of years, and as the moran show positive signs of settling down, so implicitly they accept elderhood and come to be accepted by the elders. This transition, then, is not altogether abrupt or unexpected, but it is at least far-reaching, especially for men at the age of thirty or more.

The contemporary situation is modified by the absence of warfare. Except for spasmodic raids and the ever-present possibility that there could be a reversion to inter-tribal warfare, the moran have no military reason for remaining as warriors or for associating with the bush away from the settlement. Any 'reason' is only to be found within the values of the contemporary society and the vested interests of the elders in power, wives, control over stock, etc. In other words, it is *still* in the elders' best interests to keep the moran as outsiders to the remainder of the society, to keep them away from the settlements, away from their wives (especially their wives), and to prolong the period during which they do not acquire the social wisdom expected of a fully mature elder. If a moran does not settle down and marry until he is, say, thirty years old, then he is hardly likely to be able to free himself from initially building up his herds until he is, say, thirty-five (or even forty, at least if he has to herd his own cattle until he has a son old enough to do this), and he is unlikely to be in a position to join actively in the elders' debates until he is forty or to acquire much local influence until he is forty-five or fifty. By this time, he will probably be in a position to take on a second or even a third wife and will belong to a comparatively small elite of survivors to that age.

By this time, he has a strongly vested interest in the system. If moran were suddenly to be allowed to marry ten years earlier, then not only would they acquire more knowledge of the society and hence power at a younger age, but also there would be fewer marriageable girls for the second and third – or even the fourth and fifth – wives of elders. Polygamy on the scale in which it is practised by the Samburu implies a delayed age of marriage for the men (but not the women). Needless to say, power in the society, and the ability to marry several times and to control marriage, are closely related. In fact it is through their power to control marriages that power chiefly resides in the hands of the elders.[1]

The elders, therefore, have every reason for wanting to maintain a *status quo*. Even those starting at the bottom at the age of thirty or thirty-five would not want to see younger men of twenty or twenty-five promoted to a position of equality. The system is one of gerontocracy and in such a system, once a man's career has been delayed at its outset so as to enhance the power in the hands of the older men, he has an investment in the system which increases year by year as he climbs towards the top of the pyramid as a very much older man.

Only those at or near the bottom of the pyramid, in other words the initiates and younger moran, have little to lose, and therefore it is at this point that the elders have to focus their attention in order to maintain the system. They have to ensure that those junior members of the society accept it in its pseudo-traditional form, and accept especially their marginal role within it. If, one way or another, these younger men can accept this situation, can accept the attractiveness of being moran, can come to regard elderhood as entailing an essentially colourless set of responsibilities, and if they can continue to accept these views for the ensuing decade after their initiation, then they too will have a stake in the system, and it will most probably be maintained. There is no idea in the minds of the Samburu today that the institution of moranhood should be scrapped. The moran, with their ostentatious norms of behaviour, their plaited red-ochred hair and fashionable adornments, are quite the most colourful feature of the society. General attention is focused in their direction. Young boys and women of all ages dote on the notion of moranhood. Elders remember with horrified affection their own period spent as moran (quite apart from having a very good gerontocratic reason for wanting to retain the institution). And the moran themselves are fully aware of this general attention and play up to it; only as they finally approach elderhood do some of them admit that they are prepared to see themselves displaced by a new age-set of newly initiated moran and to settle down to elderhood.

But, today, the general attitude towards the moran is ambivalent. They are a sector of the society without a precise role. They are no longer warriors in the most literal sense defending the society, yet no alternative role has been assigned to them. The traditional imbalance of power in terms of wives, in terms of a decision-making elite, and in terms of independent stock ownership, depends on them being somehow apart from the elders. For up to fourteen years of their lives they are in a state of social suspension between boyhood and elderhood, during which in a sense their social development is arrested. With no warfare to divert their energies and endow them with a strategic role, they have no defined purpose. Ideologically, they are still associated with the bush, but for a large portion of the year they live either in or in the vicinity of the settlements.

It is in this vacuous situation that the moran are prone to behaviour displaying various forms of anomie. Their notions of honour and prestige are brittle and can lead only too easily to small incidents which may quickly build up into affrays between different clans. It is at this point that the elders may have to intervene and assert their authority to keep the matter within reasonable bounds. At the other extreme, there may appear to be a certain purposelessness in the behaviour of the moran. Without warning, a moran may leave his home and not be seen for months; the general ebullience typically associated with the moran may be interspersed with moments of depression; euphoria leads to dysphoria. Other Samburu accept this as the 'way of the moran'; now that they are no longer warriors exactly, they have become angry young men. The moran are recognized to be under a certain stress: there is high expectation of them from all parts of the society, yet to no purpose except that they should continue to be moran and no more.

It is in this context that the Samburu themselves point out a form of nervous behaviour among the moran in which they frequently begin to shiver when under stress. In extreme moments this may develop into insensible shaking in which certain moran have to be held by as many as five men to avoid hurting themselves and other people. When this occurs, it frequently acts almost as a trigger for shaking by other moran who up to this point have only been shivering. Once a shaking fit is over, the moran generally returns to a normal state without seeming to have suffered as a result of his breakdown. In the next section, this shaking is seen to occur in two ritual contexts.

SOCIALIZATION AND CEREMONY AMONG THE MORAN

It has been noted that there are two fundamental periods of transition during the lives of Samburu men which entail new sets of expectation for their new roles. At first sight, the later transition (from moranhood to elderhood) seemed to be the more radical in terms of a conflict of values, but further consideration has suggested that in certain respects it may be the earlier transition (from boyhood to moranhood) that poses a more far-reaching problem: the older moran already have a stake in the total system, and therefore an incentive to settle down sooner or later to a peaceful elderhood, whereas boys and younger moran have not yet acquired this stake, and the continuity of the whole system depends on their acquiring it.

This section is primarily concerned with the process of socialization of the moran in order to account not only for their attachment to the values of warriorhood and their loyalty to their clans, but also for the way in which they are taught to respond to the remoter control of the elders, ultimately enabling them to dissociate themselves partially from these ideals so as to settle down to elderhood.

In one sense, the transition from boyhood to moranhood is not altogether sudden or unexpected. So much popular attention and admiration in the society, amounting in some quarters almost to an adoration, focus on the moran that it is the ambition of virtually all boys from a very early age to become moran and pseudo-warriors. When they are old enough to herd cattle, they are exposed to the full dangers of the bush and learn its lore, thereby learning to identify themselves with it and with a position of danger in the protection of their families' herds. They join the cattle camps with their elder moran brothers and cousins, and listen to their gossip in the evenings and pick up their slang. When they rejoin the settlements, they often hover on the edges of the dances of the moran and learn the motions and the accompanying songs. As they grow older and the time for their own initiation to moranhood draws near, so they keep one another's company, form their *own* gossip groups, and develop their *own* form of slang and songs: in these ways they take on various attributes of an age-set of moran.

By the time that boys are initiated – at ages varying from perhaps thirteen to twenty years or more – many of them are quite old enough to assume a warrior role and have identified themselves with such a role for a number of years. They have had both opportunity and incentive to acquire the notions and values of warriorhood, and have responded to the general expectation that they will in their turn become moran and the general focus of interest and attention. Even before initiation they have at least a small stake in the system.

But at this stage they do not identify themselves with any developed sense of responsibility towards the society of today or of subservience to the elders. In regarding themselves primarily as potential warriors, together with all that this may mean in terms of brittle notions of honour and prestige, they may be dangerously near the brink of anarchy. The years of waiting culminating with their initiation into moranhood could potentially lead to sudden and widespread disorder. It is at this point that the elders wish to assert their control and to bring the initiates to heel; they do not wish to destroy their incentive to become moran, but they do need to quell any desire in them to become complete rebels. The vital quality that the initiates are seen still to lack is 'a sense of respect' (*nkanyit*). It is this above all that the elders treasure and wish to inculcate into the younger moran. It is not simply that as warriors they may sometimes become involved in inter-clan affrays, but also that they may show their disrespect for the elders by stealing their cattle and seducing their wives. It is worth adding that there is an element of prestige quite apart from personal satisfaction in all these exploits, and frequent boasting among the moran. Potentially, the elders have a delinquent problem on their hands.

During the period of initiation when boys are promoted to moranhood the main focus of interest and concern is the circumcision operation itself. This four-minute ordeal is the supreme test as to whether a boy has the necessary courage to suit him to warriorhood. Any flinch or even the bat of an eyelid as primitive razor sears into flesh is interpreted by the Samburu as a desire to run away and will entail, first and foremost, the boy's own honour, which can never be redeemed during his lifetime; second, that of his family, which will be tainted for many years to come; and third, that of his settlement and clan, who will be derided by other settlements and clans. The prospect of a flinch engenders anxiety not merely among the initiates but also among their kinsmen and ultimately the whole clan. A timid boy would be made to wait rather than be circumcised at the earliest opportunity.

The following example illustrates one such circumcision and shows the extent to which it brought hidden anxieties to a head. Events leading up to the initiation of the *Kishili* age-set had taken their normal course and all the necessary ceremonial preparations had been completed in order to hold the first circumcisions in July 1960. Excitement ran high in the circumcision settlement where I was staying: a new age-set of moran would shortly be brought into being. On the evening of 6 July, the elders agreed that two of the initiates should be circumcised on the evening of the next day and the remainder on the morning of the 8th.

'Throughout the next day a major topic of conversation was whether or not any of the initiates would flinch. More and more elders and moran (of the previous age-set) gathered with pliant sticks up to ten feet in length; these, they said, were to discourage any initiate who had thoughts of running away to hide himself in the bush before the operation. The initiates themselves stood around in small groups, apparently nervous at the prospect of the operation and aware of the general lack of confidence which the moran and elders had in them. The previous evening their singing had been pointed out to me as distinctly unsteady, and now they were silent. They afterwards told me that it was the fear of flinching rather than of pain which had worried them most; the ordeal of the ceremony was not so much one of physical endurance during the operation itself as of maintaining confidence beforehand in the face of unknown pain.

One elder saw them standing around in dejection and shouted at them. "Sing your circumcision song," he demanded. "Show us that you are not afraid . . . Or don't you want to be circumcised?" One or two of the boys started to sing, and then another elder, the father of one of them, ran towards them and ordered them to stop singing. This, I was told, was because he was quite certain that his own son would flinch and he considered it less ignominious for him to be silent than for him to sing and boast and then afterwards to flinch.

This general anxiety came to a head just before the two circumcisions of that evening were to take place. The two initiates had to drive their fathers' cattle into the settlement, and one of them started to sing:

> "My light brown bull – roar! For I will not bring dishonour (*nyileti*)."

This boast caused some consternation and the boy's eldest brother, an elder, at first raised his whip to strike him and then checked himself. His gesture, coming as it did at a moment when nerves were frayed, sparked off a general release of tension. One moran ran up to strike the initiate himself and was seized by an elder and thrown to the ground. Other men, both elders and moran, seized any person who showed signs of wanting to strike the initiate or to start an affray, and in some cases were themselves seized on this assumption. At least five moran broke down and had to be held firmly while they shook insensibly. The first two circumcisions were then carried out in a confusion of babbling and shouting, mostly aimed at the initiates undergoing the operation and the circumciser performing it, although the latter seemed to be the one man present who had a clear notion of what should be done. Once these two circumcisions had been performed, there was less anxiety, and the ceremony was completed the following morning still in an atmosphere of confusion and shouting, but without any signs of flinching from the initiates or fighting from the adult males.

Especially interesting in this incident was the reaction to the initiate's boasting to the bull of his family herd: his elder brother nearly struck him and his father, a very old man, seemed to be on the point of having a stroke. The boast itself was made to the bull of the family herd, and it was the same herd of cattle to which previous members of the lineage had boasted when they had been circumcised. If he had flinched then the herd itself would have been driven ignominiously through the thorn fence and so long as the event was remembered no future member of this lineage would dare to make a boast of this sort. This is the one context in Samburu life where there is a recognized way of openly shaming a person and his family, and a specific word for dishonour (*nyileti*). In retrospect, the elders did not criticize the initiate for showing too much confidence in himself before the operation: this boast was expected of him if he had any spirit, and as he kept his word and did not flinch he brought credit to his family for his boldness. But they did criticize the father and the elder brother who had shown too little confidence in him, thus publicly betraying that they regarded it as quite possible that a member of their family and lineage might flinch during circumcision. Other persons in private admitted that they too had felt the same way about the circumcision of their own kinsmen, but would not want to betray this in public. The news that reached the circumcision settlements of other clans in the area was not that someone had actually flinched in this particular settlement, but that the elders had expected someone to flinch. The incident was a minor humiliation which dampened the general elation once the ceremony was over' (Spencer, 1965).

After the circumcision ceremony, the initiates spend a period of a month under strict ritual prohibitions governing their behaviour and diet, and encouraging them to keep close company with the other initiates. These prohibitions end with a further ceremony at which the initiates formally become moran; they start to grow their hair, and to plait it and embellish it with red ochre. This is the first of a series of ceremonies known as *ilmugit*, and the initiate vows to his mother not to eat any meat seen by a married woman. This is more or less symbolic of the various other norms associated with the moran: meat not seen by married women is essentially meat that has been nowhere near a settlement; it is meat of the bush where the moran belong and where they share one another's company. Likewise, a moran should not drink milk except in the company of other moran; he should not be permitted to die inside a settlement; he should not take any form of alcohol or other non-traditional form of food; he should avoid all young married women; and he should always acknowledge his obligations towards other moran of his age-set. To ignore these norms would be sometimes a matter of shame (e.g. to eat meat seen by married women – as if he were a child), sometimes a matter of unpropitiousness (e.g. to die inside a settlement), or a matter of disrespect for his age-set (e.g. to drink milk by himself), or a matter of disrespect for the elders (e.g. to seduce their wives). All these can be broadly summarized in the general formula that the moran belong to the bush where they should keep their own company.

At each defined stage of their transition to elderhood the moran of each clan perform an *ilmugit* ceremony, each of which has certain basic features which bear some similarities to their initial circumcision ceremony. Thus both circumcision and *ilmugit* ceremonies are performed separately by each clan; both entail the promotion of essentially the same group of moran and both ceremonies are controlled by essentially the same group of elders; both ceremonies draw attention to the order of birth of full brothers and the huts are laid out in order of genealogical seniority for the various families within the clan. Far from being spurious similarities, they provide the justification for various ritual details which are repeated from the circumcision to the *ilmugit* ceremonies, and the elders themselves point this out.

Altogether there are six of these *ilmugit* ceremonies associated with stages of transition of the moran from the time of their initiation to that of their reaching the brink of elderhood some sixteen years later, by which time a new age-set of younger moran will have been initiated for some years. In addition, there may be other *ilmugit* ceremonies performed at times when, in the opinion of the elders, the morale or the sense of responsibility of the moran is at low ebb. Pre-eminently, the *ilmugit* ceremonies are regarded by the elders as an occasion when they can collect the moran together, harangue them, and engender in them a sense of respect, thereby maintaining some form of control over them.

The elders instil into the moran not only a sense of respect, but also a sense of awe regarding their power to bless or to curse them. A harangue will last for several hours as one elder after another hurls a tirade against the moran over their shortcomings and points to examples which 'prove' the effectiveness of the elders' power to curse. Actual cursing is comparatively rare, but it is a very apt topic for a harangue. These harangues end with a conditional blessing by the elders.

As an example of such a blessing, consider the following incident that occurred during one of the more important *ilmugit* ceremonies.

> 'For about ten days before the performance of the *ilmugit* ceremony, the elders and moran periodically held separate discussions; and the moran were given four or five harangues, each lasting several hours. The main theme of these harangues was that the moran did not have a sufficiently developed sense of respect and that this retarded them in their progress to elderhood. This was, they said, most apparent from the open way in which they stayed close to certain settlements where there were attractive young wives and from the large number of accusations of adultery recently levelled against them. They argued that it was dangerous for the moran to provoke the anger of the elders by their bad behaviour since this might tempt them to use their curse. They urged the moran to discuss the matter among themselves so that they

could reaffirm their sense of respect. In their own discussions the moran did in fact acknowledge the essential truth of the accusations levelled against them and did not express any open or hidden hostility for the elders.

At about 9.00 p.m. on the evening before killing the first ox in the ceremony, the moran were called over to the elders' enclosure for a blessing. There were about 25 elders and 40 moran. This was preceded first by separate discussions by the elders and by the moran, and then by a harangue. At each new stage of the evening's activities a spiral kudu horn was blown by a moran at the instigation of the elders. Finally, it was time for the blessing. To the sound of the horn an intense fire was built up between the elders and the moran: the former protected their bodies from the heat by drawing up their blankets, but the moran only had short loin-cloths and were exposed to it.

Two elders led the blessing invoking the protection of God on the moran. "May *Nkai* look after you . . . May *Nkai* give you life . . . May *Nkai* look after you . . . May *Nkai* give you peace . . . May *Nkai* give you good fortune . . ." At each pause the other elders waved their up-raised staffs and chanted, "*Nkai* . . . *Nkai* . . . *Nkai* . . ." rhythmically, and continued to do so even when the invocations were drowned by the general tumult. A moran was also blowing the horn in time with the rhythmical chanting.

As they began their invocations, the two leading elders splattered the bodies of the moran with a mixture of milk and water. The touch of the cool liquid on their bodies exposed to the heat of the fire caused many of them to squeal and jump. And immediately three started to shake and perhaps a dozen started to shiver. Relentlessly the blessing continued, and the gasps of the shaking moran and the chant of elders and the sound of the horn practically drowned the words of the invocation. Some shaking moran partially recovered, and others started to shake and had to be held. Eventually the moran blowing the horn fell shaking and had to be held by about five other moran. Another moran picked up the horn and started to blow, but he began to shake immediately, and the horn was taken over by a third moran who had some difficulty in keeping the time and just blew it continuously. After about six minutes, there were five shaking moran who were being forcibly held by both moran and elders, and a dozen other moran who were either shivering or shaking. There was no moran who was not either shivering or shaking or holding a shaking moran. At this point the blessing stopped' (Spencer, 1965).

Blessings similar to this one with equally devastating effects on the moran have been witnessed on other occasions besides *ilmugit* ceremonies. Perhaps one of the most impressive occasions was the final stage of reconciliation between the moran and elders of one clan after an attack by a large group of moran on some elders had led to their being cursed by the elders. However, this case was exceptional in that it is very seldom that the moran express their hostility for the elders so positively or that the elders are faced with so acute a need to demonstrate their ascendancy over the moran.

These two examples should suffice as illustrations of the general ceremonial context of the socialization of the moran to allow consideration of various theories on the function of ritual and the development of social attitudes.

THEORIES OF RITUAL BEHAVIOUR AND THE DEVELOPMENT OF SOCIAL ATTITUDES

The age-set system of the Samburu controls the rate of development of younger men and serves to retain power in the hands of the older men. However, in doing so, it produces essentially a discontinuous process: instead of a uniform progress towards elderhood and the top of the pyramid, there are a series of discrete promotions from one stage to the next, and at each of these promotions there has to be an adjustment, not only of those promoted, but also of all other men who are inevitably affected by this promotion, and by the implicit change in the distribution of powers and privileges. With these changes, the same broad structure remains, but it induces within itself a series of more or less controlled mutations rather than a smooth continuous process. It is in this context that the function of ritual behaviour is examined.

Initiation and other ceremonies that mark transitions in the social development of individuals may be regarded as 'rites of passage' in the sense in which Van Gennep coined the term.[2] The three stages that he has noted – rites of separation, transition rites, and rites of incorporation – are present at least to some extent in each of the ceremonies. Thus, prior to their circumcision the initiates are obliged to keep one another's company more or less constantly and are thereby *separated* from the younger boys who will not be circumcised yet and from the older moran of the preceding age-set whose values they have learnt over the years to emulate. After the circumcision they are in a *transitional* state with defined ritual constraints and in a position when they are more than boys but less than moran in the fullest sense. And at the end of the month they perform their first *ilmugit* ceremony and formally become moran: they are now *incorporated* into the age-grade of moranhood.

The subsequent major *ilmugit* ceremonies may also be divided along the same lines, though less obviously, and each marks a phase in the promotion of the moran towards elderhood. Van Gennep's approach to the analysis of ceremony leaves much unaccounted for, but at least it fits as a first approximation.

One point that should be clarified immediately is exactly what is meant by 'ritual'. To what extent are ritual behaviour and practice a direct response to social pressures and expectations and to what extent are they a response to beliefs in mystical forces? What is the relationship between ritual and mystical beliefs? Certainly, my own impression from discussions with boys, initiates, and younger moran is that they really had a very limited perception of any religious or magical reasons for performing in the ceremonies. They did as they were told in response to the directions of the elders. They were, it is true, vividly aware that honour was at stake during the operation itself, but this was one of the essentially secular values associated with the ceremony: it was not expected to lead to mystical misfortune if an initiate flinched.

Thus, so far as the initiate was concerned, he was the focus of an essentially secular separation from boyhood, transition and incorporation into moranhood, and he observed 'ritual' prohibitions only because he was told to do so. For the elders supervising the ceremony, however, it was a different matter. There was an acknowledged mystical danger involved in the changeover of age-sets, and if certain details of the ceremony from the initial separation to the final incorporation were ignored or mishandled, then it was thought that this could well lead to some unexpected misfortune entailing possibly the lives of the initiate, his family, and their cattle. An additional aspect of the socialization of youths, therefore, is the process whereby they subsequently assimilate these mystical beliefs so that they have, if not always a precise knowledge of what is and what is not dangerous, at least an acceptance that such forces are at work and that the older men alone know most of the ritual prescriptions.

For further analysis of the processes involved in ceremonial activity, it is useful to consider the work of a Pavlovian psychologist, William Sargant (1957).[3]

> 'Sargant is primarily concerned with the physiological mechanisms which make it possible for the beliefs and attitudes of individuals to be modified or radically altered, and this leads him to consider the physiological basis of techniques of political and religious conversion. He first of all draws attention to Pavlov's experiments on dogs, especially his later ones. Pavlov's earlier experiments had shown that certain behaviour patterns (conditioned responses) could be built up in dogs under controlled laboratory conditions. In his later experiments he examined ways in which these behaviour patterns could be removed and supplanted by new ones. He found that by submitting the dogs to abnormal mental stress, or by debilitating them in some way (such as by inducing excessive fatigue, fever, intestinal disorders or by castrating them) a breakdown could occur which would interfere with their normal conditioned responses. Sargant refers to this breakdown as "transmarginal". Pavlov also found that while these dogs were in a transmarginal state, new patterns of behaviour might be induced in them which would remain after recovery. Thus during some floods in Leningrad when a number of his laboratory dogs were nearly drowned, some of them no longer responded to stimuli to which they had previously been conditioned, but were highly sensitive to the sound or sight of trickling water. These new

patterns tended to be more permanent in dogs of an inherently stable temperament than in other, and *not* vice versa.

Pavlov evidently felt justified in applying his conclusions on animal behaviour to processes of human thought [Sargant, 1957, pp. 6, 12, 18–19, 37], and Sargant has no hesitation in doing so [ibid., pp. 7–8 and Ch. 2], equating positive and negative conditioned responses with positive and negative emotional attitudes. Thus, the emotional attitudes of men towards one another or towards ideologies may alter when they are subjected to abnormal mental stress, and these changes may remain when the cause of anxiety is removed: the two situations are, Sargant says, analogous. He also notes that this change is liable to be more permanent if the subject has a stable personality, and if he tries at first to oppose the change. Mental stress may be produced by fasting, ordeal, threats, prolonged social isolation, debilitation or torture; and under these conditions brainwashing in both religion and politics and eliciting confessions are quite practicable. It is only necessary to force the subject to accept the fact that there is no other way of achieving peace than to accept what is being indoctrinated' (Spencer, 1965).

Sargant's work has a fairly obvious relevance to the circumcision ceremony itself.

'The period preceding circumcision was shown to be one of considerable strain for the initiates: the prospect of pain involved in the operation and the possibility that they might flinch seemed to be a greater ordeal than the operation itself; and the way in which elders and moran were losing confidence in them as the time drew near must have increased their apprehensiveness. During the 24 hours before the first circumcision they were generally subdued, a number of them shivered, at least one of them developed a facial twitch and another a fixed frown.

The thought present in everyone's mind at this moment was whether any initiate would flinch, and this entailed honour. Inasmuch as the anxiety created by the ceremony could induce any new attitude in the initiates it might well be the association of this notion of honour with their new relationship to family, clan and age-set. Honour would not be an entirely foreign notion to them, but the gravity and intensity of the ceremony could introduce a new significance. Such incidents as this might, I suggest, explain to some extent why honour is of such importance during moranhood. Almost as if by accident, it becomes the crucial issue during circumcision, but the very fact that it is a crucial issue could, it is suggested, have a pronounced effect on the values accepted by the initiates after their circumcision' (Spencer, 1965).

Honour for them could have become what the sound of trickling water was for Pavlov's dogs.

My material does not seem to justify any pseudo-psychoanalytical analysis of circumcision as a symbolic form of castration to prepare the initiates for the years of impotent bachelorhood that lie ahead. But it is still worth noting that circumcision is a form of debilitation which, following Sargant, could be one other factor that drives them to a state of mind where they are exceptionally suggestible to new ideas. The operation itself was instigated by the elders, and another aspect of the ceremony that might have impressed the initiates besides the notion of family honour was that, in every detail and at every stage, it was under the control of the elders. This could have instilled or reinforced the attitude that they belonged to a society which was controlled by the elders. As we have seen, it preceded a time when the initiates were to be subordinated to the will of the elders.

As the first example (cited pp. 134–136 above) shows only too clearly, it was not only the initiates that were visibly anxious during the ceremony. Older men of their clan showed signs of anxiety and in the event it was *their* nerve that broke, leading to a minor affray, and not the initiates' nerve.

'The period of changeover is one full of intense interest for the Samburu. It has far-reaching implications for most people in the society and concerns not only their membership of various age-grades, but also, in certain cases, of clans.

The circumcision ceremonies are the climax of this changeover which altogether takes a number of years. In the first example, the concern which elders and moran showed during the circumcision of their close kinsmen, especially at the prospect of their own sons and brothers flinching, suggests that the situation was sufficient to revive their own ingrained notions of honour associated as it was with circumcision, the lineage, and the herd. It seems possible that this anxiety may have helped to induce them to accept the change in relationships which this changeover involved. Once everyone could be made to accept it, it would be fully accomplished and the problems it raised would be solved.

This general approach to ceremony may be compared with the views of Malinowski and Radcliffe-Brown as to the relationship between ceremony and anxiety. Malinowski, referring to "magical" rites with some specific end, maintains that these are performed in situations in which there is considerable uncertainty from chance factors, and that they serve to allay anxiety and give confidence [1948, pp. 59 ff.]. Radcliffe-Brown points out that the opposite may also be true: that the rites and associated beliefs may induce anxiety in situations were it might otherwise be absent [1952, pp. 148–149]. Radcliffe-Brown then fits this into his general theory of the social function of ceremony, which is that ceremony (rites) serves to "regulate, maintain and transmit from one generation to another sentiments on which the constitution of society depends" [ibid., p. 157]. For instance, taboos observed by the parents during pregnancy and childbirth among the Andamanese may, he says, engender anxiety in the father; but anxiety over childbirth is a sentiment he should have and hence the taboos help to maintain appropriate social sentiments.

In his analysis of ceremony, Radcliffe-Brown is concerned with the maintenance and transmission of sentiments rather than with a marked change in sentiments, and he regards anxiety as a sentiment appropriate to specific occasions rather than as a means of modifying social sentiments to a new set of relationships. Here, I am suggesting that at a time when social relationships are undergoing change, the uncertainties of the occasion which Malinowski saw as a cause for anxiety, and the beliefs and ritual prescriptions which Radcliffe-Brown saw as an additional cause for anxiety, may serve to induce a mental state in the participants which implements these changes; changes which Van Gennep realized to be disruptive to social existence.[4] They increase the suggestibility of the participants so that they come to accept the changes' (Spencer, 1965).

In an extreme instance when a ceremony marks a fundamental change in social status, as when a boy is circumcised, the ceremony may be more than a temporary embarrassment: it may amount to a relentless ordeal. The anxieties of the elders appear principally to have extended sentiments that they already had (towards the senior moran) in new directions (towards the initiates whom they would shortly have to accept as moran) and to have reinforced these sentiments; the initiates' ordeal, on the other hand, may have served to instil into them altogether new sentiments. For the elders, it was a switch of social relations within a well-known social structure and a reinforcement of existing attitudes; for the initiates, it was, I suggest, a unique introduction to the social structure and their role within it.

> 'This general approach to Samburu ceremony has certain affinities with Turner's treatment of his Ndembu material [Turner, 1957, Ch. 4]. Turner has suggested that where conflict leads to a mounting crisis and ultimately to a realignment of social ties, the process commonly follows a set pattern which he has called "social drama". The ceremonies we have examined here are of a different order, since they concern the conflicts that *arise from* prescribed changes in relationships and shifts in status, rather than conflicts that *lead to* such changes. But, both Ndembu social drama and Samburu ceremony are only intelligible with reference to the structural forms of the two societies, they are critical points at which relationships (and hence attitudes) are changing, and anxiety over these changes becomes evident. Samburu ceremony, then, is not a social drama in Turner's sense of the term; but it could be regarded as a controlled social drama in which the element of individual spontaneity and freedom is heavily suppressed' (Spencer, 1965).
>
> 'A characteristic feature of moranhood which follows initiation is that it constantly points back to it: for the age-set

system, circumcision can be regarded as an "initial situation": words commonly used with reference to this system, *Imurani* (a moran, warrior) and *murata* (an age-mate, the correct reciprocal term of address to any age-mate who is not known by a more familiar term) are basically similar to *Imura* (a penis) and *emuratare* (circumcision). In *ilmugit* ceremonies, too, there is an identical layout of the settlements to that of circumcision with an emphasis on the order of birth of full brothers and performance by each clan separately. And, of course, the *ilmugit* ceremonies are in the hands of the elders.

In order to consider the social function of *ilmugit* ceremonies, it is convenient to follow Chapple and Coon's elaboration of Van Gennep's "rites of passage". Chapple and Coon [1947, Chs. 20 and 21] point out that certain ceremonies are performed periodically and do not mark any change in social relationships. They refer to these ceremonies as "rites of intensification". The authors state that, in rites of passage, individuals are conditioned to adapt themselves to a new pattern of interaction that follows from a change in social relationships, whereas, in rites of intensification, the existing pattern of interaction is periodically reinforced [ibid., pp. 484, 527]. Sargant also draws attention to the need for new doctrines to be consolidated through periodic reinculcation and communal meetings (and hence the relative permanence of Wesley's sect and the impermanence of Billy Graham's). In certain respects Chapple and Coon's rites of passage correspond to Radcliffe-Brown's "transmission of sentiments" and their rites of intensification correspond to his "maintenance of sentiments".

It is with reference to rites of intensification that the *ilmugit* ceremonies can most clearly be understood. The hypothesis here is that at circumcision certain values were instilled into the initiates, and that these are reinstilled at the periodic *ilmugit* ceremonies. The elders regard *ilmugit* ceremonies essentially as times when they can gather the moran together and harangue them. They are a means by which the moran can gain a sense of respect. This, they often say, is the prime purpose of *ilmugit* ceremonies. It was only when I asked them specifically what would happen if the ceremonies were not held that they said it would be unpropitious.

It cannot be denied that certain *ilmugit* ceremonies are also rites of passage, but their principal function does appear to be the reinforcement of the notion of a sense of respect rather than a fundamental adjustment of social relationships. Of the two types of *ilmugit* ceremony previously distinguished the first type, performed at each point of promotion of the age-set, was a rite of passage as well as of intensification; whereas the second type, performed when misbehaviour was expected from the moran and when their corporate unity and morale were low, were rites of intensification pure and simple.

It is worth noting that Chapple and Coon treat rites of passage and intensification as being intelligible in terms of Pavlovian psychology, and throughout their work they emphasize the relevance of Pavlov's "conditioned responses". They outline his findings in an early chapter, but make no mention of his later experiments which form the basis of Sargant's book, and in neglecting this they seem to have missed a very important aspect of these ceremonies: the relationship between anxiety or transmarginal states and the reorientation of social attitudes.

In trying to account for the nature of symbolism in ceremony, Chapple and Coon point out that through the mechanism of conditioned responses men come to associate certain objects with certain patterns of interaction (social relationships); they then follow Radcliffe-Brown in suggesting that through this association such objects acquire a symbolic significance in ceremony and the ceremony reinforces the relationships involved. These objects are largely derived from the technology of the society in question [Chapple & Coon, 1947, p. 508]. Thus immediately before an evening circumcision, the cattle of the homestead have to be driven into the yard, and it may be argued that the cattle, an essential part of Samburu economy, are closely associated with the family, and that the status of the initiate with respect to his family is undergoing a change; thus after his circumcision a boy with no father or elder brother can alienate stock from the herd without reference to his guardian. Similarly, the sharing of meat by moran at an *ilmugit* ceremony might be related to the importance of food in the society, confirming their solidarity and fellowship through commensality rather as Robertson Smith argued [1907, p. 265].

Sargant, on the other hand, suggests another approach to the study of symbolism which supplements this one. He points out that just as Pavlov's dogs caught by the floods became highly sensitive to the sight or sound of trickling water, so in primitive societies men may have become sensitive to objects or actions originally associated with their initiation [Sargant, 1957, p. 97]. It follows that such symbols would acquire a far greater emotional significance. This may account for all those characteristics of moranhood which, it was noted, are associated in the first place with initiation ceremonies. The cattle driven through the gateway before circumcision are more than just the means of subsistence for the family over which there is a change in rights and duties: they become associated with family honour. Similarly, it is not just shared meat at an *ilmugit* ceremony which brings the moran into closer fellowship: there are also those countless occasions when they must go hungry together, even when food (seen by married women) is available, and share many other anxious and dispiriting moments. These also serve to bring them together' (Spencer, 1965).

The second example quoted in the previous section concerned a blessing by the elders that followed a harangue of the moran. The word for 'to harangue' in Samburu (*a-ikok*) is incidentally the same as 'to hit a person in a sore place'. Sargant points out that brainwashing for religious and political ends can be effectively done by finding a 'sore spot' in the victim's experience and working away at it (1957, pp. 145, 158). In these harangues, the 'sore spot' is the waywardness of the moran. They are in a powerless position, and they simply cannot win in any circumstances. If a small group of them, or even just one individual, shows any irresponsibility through, say, stealing stock, flirting with wives, or showing less than full respect for the elders, then they are *all* held to be thieves, adulterers, and psychopaths. In their advancement towards elderhood, they are allowed to crawl only at the pace of the slowest and most unresponsive members; as there are several minor initiations into the age-set during the first seven or so years that follow its first major initiation, the older moran are constantly joined by new young recruits and have to retrace their steps with them. Added to this, there is the frustration of constantly losing girls of their own clans with whom they have formed attachments as the elders marry them off to elders of other clans; and there is the ordeal of having to wait up to fifteen or even twenty years after their own physical maturity before they can marry and are accorded even the minimum social maturity. Any reaction to these circumstances, whether expressed positively by violating some of the prohibitions placed on them or negatively by withdrawing interest and showing less than full respect, is playing into the hands of the elders.

At these harangues, the elders emphasize that they want to teach the moran a sense of respect so that they may attain full elderhood. But from attendance at such harangues it seemed evident that at heart the elders really wanted to maintain the moran in their state of social suspension and prolonged adolescence in order to keep them out of the running for elderhood. It was not simply that they tried to teach the moran respect, but that they constantly accused the moran of being incapable of learning respect. Instead of inviting them to keep company more often with the elders, they would tell them to go back into the bush where they belonged and (figuratively) to stay there until they acquired this respect. In private, no one seriously suggested that the moran could learn the true meaning of respect from other moran alone: rather, this could be seen as a way of ensuring the continued responsibility of the moran.

'Sargant pays particular attention to John Wesley's techniques of gaining converts among his hearers. And certain aspects of Wesley's meetings resemble to some extent a harangue of the moran. Wesley would first agitate his audience with threats of eternal hellfire (just as the elders warned the moran of the unpropitious consequences of their behaviour) and then he would suggest to them that salvation could be gained through conversion (just as the elders would persuade the moran of their general security from ill-fortune once they acquired a sense of respect). Wesley's preaching would have a powerful effect on his hearers: "Some sunk down, and there remained no strength in them; others exceedingly trembled and quaked; some were torn with a kind of convulsive motion in every part of their bodies, and that so violently that often four or five persons could not hold one of them."[5]

Sargant points out that religious conversion, political conversion, or for that matter conversion to any absolute philosophy, have similar basic physiological explanations although the contents of belief may belong to quite different spheres. It is quite natural, then, that the inculcation of certain values in the moran, such as honour, respect, avoidance of married women, and acceptance of their own childishness compared with the maturity of the elders, should have a similar basis. And as was stated earlier, the gaining of respect is one of the prime purposes of *ilmugit* ceremonies, harangues and blessings; and the moran acknowledge this purpose' (Spencer, 1965).

This leads once again to the topic of shaking among the moran. Viewed as a form of transmarginal breakdown, shaking can be related to the general state of anxiety among the moran. It was also seen to occur when boys were being circumcised and honour was at stake; it is common during their dances when rival clans are present and tensions build up between them in the vying for supremacy, and at times when they ceremonially hand over their girls to the elders to be married elsewhere. The period of moranhood is one of duress, and shaking tends to occur in situations when this duress is rather greater than usual. Following Sargant's general approach, at times of distress, higher nervous systems are strained beyond the limits of normal conditioned responses, suggestibility is increased and, when it leads to a transmarginal breakdown (i.e. shaking), it may accompany either a release of nervous energy (abreaction), or a change or an intensification of sentiments, or both.

Thus, in the first example, the minor affray and the shaking among the senior moran seemed to be the climax of a general state of anxiety. The moran who had shaken told me afterwards that during the whole period of the changeover they had hated that day more than any other, but, once it was over, they accepted the fact that a new age-set, which was to replace them as moran and as the focus of so much attention, had indeed been brought into existence.

Similarly, in the second example, the sentiments of the moran were being reinforced by the elders and they were given a minor form of brainwashing.

'In this incident, the blessing started abruptly and there was a sudden and relentless build-up to the climax which was maintained throughout. At one moment, the moran were standing half-naked before the blazing fire and waiting, and then it started: their heated bodies were suddenly stung by the cool mixture of milk and water, the leading elders were shouting the invocations of the blessing more or less at them, the other elders were chanting "*Nkai* . . . *Nkai* . . . *Nkai* . . .", and the horn was blowing almost deafeningly in time with the chant. The association of so many of these features with circumcision and the power which the elders hold over them may well have been sufficient to increase the apprehensiveness of the moran and induce shaking. It has much in common with the circumcision operation where each initiate has first to wash himself quickly with a similar mixture of milk and water, and then he is suddenly surrounded by a crowd of shouting elders excitedly telling both the initiate and the circumciser what they should do.

The constant use of the horn, only used at ceremonies, important discussions, or when some enemy raiders are discovered in the vicinity, added to the impressiveness of the occasion, and it, too, has powerful associations for the moran; they say that the sound of it, especially in the presence of the elders, makes them feel angry and want to shake. In other words, such features as the mixture of milk and water, the horn, the concentrated attention of the elders, may retain their potent associations from previous occasions. It also seems feasible that any extent to which the elders managed to impress the moran with the weight of their power over them on this occasion when there was a blessing would also engender a greater dread of their curse. Paradoxically, both the curse *and* the blessing over the moran are oppressive, and not as complementary as they may seem at first sight.

Another important factor which may have helped to

induce the shaking was the rhythmic chanting of the blessing, for "certain rates of rhythm can build up recordable abnormalities of brain function and explosive states of tension sufficient even to produce convulsive fits in predisposed subjects" [Sargant, 1957, p. 88]' (Spencer, 1965).

It was earlier noted that initiates had little conception of the mystical forces involved in Samburu ceremonial activity and that respect and even fear for these forces were something that they acquired as they matured. It is during their harangues that the elders interpret the misfortunes that befall the moran from time to time as a consequence of their lack of respect. In so far as they instil new attitudes into the moran, and teach them a new wisdom, it is, among other things, a respect for supernatural forces of which the elders' power to bless and to curse is just one aspect. By the time that the moran themselves become elders, they have to a very large extent assimilated the philosophy of mystical misfortune associated with ritual mishandling and disregard for social obligations towards those they should respect. They in their turn hand this on to a new generation of moran and the sentiments are maintained: sentiments which, among other things, emphasize the powers of the elders to assert at least some degree of control over these mystical forces.

In so far as the elders can be said to have been brainwashing the moran in various ways – and they certainly made individual moran admit to being immature, unworthy, and thoroughly irresponsible in front of the others – it is worth noting that brainwashing is more permanent and effective with persons (and dogs) whose temperament is essentially stable. Thus it is the more stable moran who are likely to respond more readily to this treatment by the elders, and later on as elders it is precisely these same men who are most likely to wield influence among their fellows: it is the stable men who conform best, who show most respect, and who have sway in the debates and discussions of the elders. There are many Samburu elders today who were brave, influential, and irrascible as moran and hence in some ways typical of moran, and yet they were unable to adapt themselves successfully to elderhood and tried in the debates and at other times to dominate rather as though they were still moran. Such men tend to have all the signs of instability in their temperaments and seem never to have quite achieved the transition from moranhood to elderhood.

There is one final point worth making regarding the peculiar status of the moran.

> 'Van Gennep notes [1960, p. 11] that in any rite of passage there tend to be many stages which can broadly be classified as a process of separation-transition-incorporation. Initiation rites can, he notes, last as long as six years in exceptional cases [ibid., p. 81]. But unaccountably, when discussing early material available for the Masai tribe [ibid., pp. 84–87], he fails to note that the whole period of moranhood, with its many ritual prohibitions and ceremonies, can be regarded as an extended period of transition between circumcision when a youth is separated from his mother's home and his eventual incorporation into his own home many years later, after his marriage.
>
> Among the Samburu – and I assume that the situation is essentially similar among the Masai – circumcision is a rite of separation; moranhood, with its prohibitions, association with the bush and *ilmugit* ceremonies, is a prolonged rite of transition; and the final blessing by the elders when a man is allowed to relax the food restrictions of moranhood is a rite of incorporation into elderhood.
>
> "Rites of transition" is the term used by Chapple and Coon and by the recent translators of Van Gennep's work for the second stage of a rite of passage. But Van Gennep himself refers to *rites de marge*. The term *marge* is particularly apt when referring to the separateness of those implicated from the remainder of the society: they have a marginal position. The ritual and social separateness of the moran from the remainder of the society has been stressed previously. Throughout their moranhood they are marginal. And the duress under which they are continually placed may perhaps be regarded as a counterpart of the anxiety noticed among participants in other rites of passage' (Spencer, 1965).

CONCLUSIONS

The relevance of various theories of ritual behaviour has been examined with respect to the socialization of Samburu youths, or moran, in their climb towards elderhood. Van Gennep has pointed out that the transition of an individual from one social group to another is generally enveloped in ceremony, and that this is more pronounced in societies where the differences between social groups are accentuated.

> 'The Samburu, with their age-grade system through which age-sets are promoted in a series of jerks, are no exception to this. Changes in status are inevitably disruptive to the society and engender anxiety amongst those most closely affected.
>
> Sargant, following Pavlov, has pointed out that anxiety accompanies an increased suggestibility and this may induce a change of attitude or reinforce existing attitudes of those concerned. And hence one infers that the anxiety brought about by changes in status helps those concerned to adjust themselves to the new relationships involved. But the Samburu have a number of additional devices which serve to increase this anxiety largely by overaweing those most directly concerned; and these, it has been suggested, implement the change in attitude necessary for a change in status to be accomplished.
>
> The devices through which the participants are overawed include physical debilitation (circumcision), haranguing, blessing, and insisting on the meticulous performance of ceremonies which perplex by their profusion of detail and dismay through the mystical beliefs surrounding them. The participants find public scrutiny turned in their direction and this makes them intensely aware of certain important social values such as honour and a sense of respect, for the possibility of shame and ridicule hangs over them' (Spencer, 1965).

Paradoxically, it is the anxieties aroused by possibilities of dishonour and mystical misfortune that seem to be more relevant to the structural processes involved than the values in themselves.

> 'But such ceremonies need not only be regarded as means of transmitting and maintaining social sentiments (Radcliffe-Brown) or of facilitating change in status in a society where status differences are very pronounced (Van Gennep); they may also be regarded as a means by which elders, by accident or by design, assert and maintain their control over the remainder of the society. Respect for the elders and for the will of the elders is perhaps one of the most significant sentiments induced in the participants, who are made fully aware that society sanctions the occasion and all that it implies. Ceremony, in the hands of the elders, is another means by which they retain their powers' (Spencer, 1965).

Any comprehensive theory of the socialization of adolescents should, it is suggested here, recognize the flexibility of the concept of adolescence. Thus it is hardly enough to relate theories of adolescence to sexual and physical pubescence when such societies as the Samburu have a power structure in which adolescence in the purely social sense overruns adolescence in a more physiological sense by some ten to fifteen years. Rather, adolescence and socialization should be examined in the context in which power (in a very broad sense) and responsibility are withheld by an older elite, and in which there is a succession of transitions from one set of values to another as new interests, new roles, and new possibilities develop. In the final resort, there is never an ending to the socialization process for the social learning of the individual.

NOTES

1. Precisely how they do this is beyond the context of the present paper, but has been discussed more fully in Chapter 7 of *The Samburu* (Spencer, 1965). Quotations appearing later in this paper are taken from pages 104–106 and 246–275 of this book. In order to clarify the relevance of these passages to the present paper, certain minor modifications have been made to the wording.

2. Van Gennep, *Les Rites de passage* (1909). The terms used here are those of the English translation by Vizedom and Caffee, 1960.

3. In his book, *Battle for the Mind* (1957), Sargant does consider the significance of initiation rites in West Africa and New Guinea (p. 94), and the present paper is to some extent a confirmation of his analysis by extending his arguments to the Samburu.

4. Van Gennep, p. 3. It is not altogether clear whether Van Gennep regarded such changes as a possible source of 'discomfort or injury' because of the action

of supernatural forces or because of purely social ones. I have taken him to mean the latter.

5. Sargant, 1957, p. 82. Quoted from Wesley's *The Journal of John Wesley*.

ACKNOWLEDGEMENT

For permission to quote passages from *The Samburu* by Dr Paul Spencer, thanks are due to the publishers concerned: Routledge & Kegan Paul Ltd, London, and the University of California Press, Berkeley, California.

REFERENCES

CHAPPLE, E. D. & COON, C. S. 1947. *Principles of Anthropology.* London: Cape; New York: Holt.

GENNEP, ARNOLD VAN. 1960. *The Rites of Passage.* (First published 1909.) Translated by Vizedom & Caffee. London: Routledge & Kegan Paul; Chicago: University of Chicago Press.

MALINOWSKI, B. 1948. *Magic, Science and Religion, and Other Essays.* Glencoe, Ill.: The Free Press.

RADCLIFFE-BROWN, A. R. 1952. *Structure and Function in Primitive Society.* London: Cohen & West; Glencoe, Ill.: The Free Press.

SARGANT, WILLIAM. 1957. *Battle for the Mind: A Physiology of Conversion and Brainwashing.* London: Heinemann.

SMITH, W. ROBERTSON. 1907. *Lectures on the Religion of the Semites.* Burnett Lectures, delivered 1888–89. Edinburgh: Black.

SPENCER, P. 1965. *The Samburu: A Study of Gerontocracy in a Nomadic Tribe.* London: Routledge & Kegan Paul; Berkeley, Calif.: University of California Press.

TURNER, V. W. 1957. *Schism and Continuity in an African Society.* Manchester: Manchester University Press.

Philip and Iona Mayer

Socialization by Peers

The Youth Organization of the Red Xhosa[1]

OUTLINE OF THE YOUTH ORGANIZATION

This paper is concerned with socialization of the young by their peers and near-seniors. The field material is from rural 'Red' (tribally conservative) Xhosa-speaking people in the Ciskei and Transkei of South Africa. We shall be specially considering patterns for youthful sexual and fighting behaviour, practice in political and judicial techniques, and also the attainment of 'national' Xhosa identification transcending kin and community.

Red Xhosa have a strong militaristic tradition. Warfare in the traditional sense is a thing of the past, but fighting behaviour is still deliberately taught and practised at all ages up to early manhood. Sexual gratification is valued positively at all ages. Adolescence is seen as a time when both sex and fighting should be practised vigorously. As in any society, however, practising by adolescents carries new risks in that this age is newly potent in both respects – is fertile and also able to inflict death. A broad problem, therefore, is how to encourage the proper vigorous practice and gratification in sex and fighting without the price being paid in terms of social disorder, slaughter of fellow Xhosa, and/or impregnation of potential wives. Put the other way, the problem is that of achieving control without too much inhibition.

Both in sexual matters and in fighting, the adolescents are afforded some 'negative' guidance – i.e. practice in restraint or inhibition – in the contexts of family, kin group, and neighbourhood. But those are scarcely proper contexts for 'positive' guidance or active practice. The gap is met by youth peer groups. There the youth, without any adult supervision, carry on sexual and fighting activities, and there they receive from their peers and near-seniors both encouragement and restraint. These groups also provide a forum where male youth acquire politico-judicial skills and develop a concern with 'law' – both highly valued in Red Xhosa culture. In these groups, too, social contacts with peers are progressively widened, in a way that makes for eventual self-identification as a Xhosa, over and above kinship and community identifications.

These are not 'informal' peer groups, as often encountered in sociological literature, nor do they operate with merely diffuse sanctions. The system has firm enough formal outlines to be referred to as the youth 'organization'. On the other hand, it is not a classical 'age-set system' either: there are no age-set names or other symbols of corporate feeling, no promotion ceremonies, etc. It has interested us to reflect that this youth organization, with such important functions as we shall attribute to it, might pass quite unnoticed in a classical structural analysis of a Red Xhosa community. It does not obviously enter into any of the other classical 'systems' (of kinship, politics, law, ritual, etc.) although in our view it serves important functions in regard to nearly all of them by inculcating appropriate values and patterns of behaviour. The Red youth organization seems to have escaped description in previous ethnographic literature, although Wilson, Kaplan, and Maki (1952, pp. 158–164) have dealt with 'School' (Christian) Xhosa youth institutions, which furnish an interesting comparison by virtue of their difference.

The outward visible signs of Red youth organization are parties, dances, and meetings for sport, held by groups of young people in their own or each other's neighbourhoods at weekends. Most of these gatherings last all through Saturday night and well into Sunday, dispersing only in the afternoon. They are elaborate affairs and follow strict conventions. Dancing and singing are prominent features, with both sexes taking part together, in the full splendour of their beads and other decorations. Cudgel games are arranged for each sex separately. There is also a great deal of sweethearting. *Intutu* denotes a gathering of young boys and girls (roughly from nine to thirteen); *mtshotsho* of bigger, adolescent ones; and *intlombe* of initiated young men – from perhaps nineteen or twenty onwards – with their girls. Each term applies not only to the party but to the group concerned:

e.g. the boys of appropriate age in a given neighbourhood, who habitually *tshotsha* (hold *mtshotsho* parties) together, are collectively known as 'the *mtshotsho* of' such and such place. It is taken for granted that every Red boy, youth, and girl participates in the local recreations of the youth organization at its successive stages. To hold aloof would be considered 'not normal'.

The dividing line between *mtshotsho* and *intlombe* is manhood initiation – a great event in the Xhosa life-cycle – performed at the late age of about eighteen to twenty-three. Initiations take place every year. Small neighbourhood groups of candidates are circumcised, then secluded in the bush for up to four months. There is emphasis on courage (not flinching at circumcision) but also on control of aggressive impulses (not fighting during the seclusion period). Youths in seclusion go naked and covered from head to foot in whitish clay. They are suspended from normal domestic and community affairs, including those of the youth organization, but they go about visiting each other's lodges. The coming-out ceremony is held jointly for a community or location, and is a massive affair watched by crowds of people. The novices, muffled in white blankets, are harangued by elders about the dignity and responsibilities of manhood. Initiation makes ego an *umfana*, young man (at first only an 'unripe' one, *ikrwala*). He is free to marry, and obliged to behave in an adult way (cf. p. 165 below); and he is also admitted to the *intlombe*. Normally a new initiate first goes away to town for a few months to earn money for his new adult clothes (*ukutshintsha*, 'to change' clothes).

There is no corresponding female initiation. Girls move up individually from *mtshotsho* to *intlombe* (without ceremony) to 'accompany' their boy friends.

The upper age-limit of the youth organization is indeterminate. Girls drop out of *intlombe* activities at marriage; men need not. Many men gradually cease participating after they are twenty-eight or so, but some go on much longer, perhaps until their late thirties. So this is 'youth' organization in a somewhat generous sense. The common situation of all these so-called youth is most easily defined negatively. They are no longer or not altogether dependent children but neither are they yet admitted to full participation in the main adult systems, whether domestic, political, judicial, or ritual. From the mature adult point of view they form a somewhat marginal category.

A corollary of their marginality is that they are allowed considerable autonomy. This can be seen as a condition of non-interference in the adult world, and vice versa. The recreations of the youth organization are kept entirely extra-domestic, and in some senses extra-community. No adults ever take part in them. The meetings are held in 'empty' huts or out on the veld. From the adult point of view this separation means that the violence and sexuality of youth are being kept at a convenient distance; from the point of view of the youth the distance means freedom for a modicum of self-expression and self-organization, even though real power in the family and community (domestic, political, legal, or ritual) is still being withheld.

This separation makes all the more remarkable the conservative tendency of the Red Xhosa youth organization. Unsupervised as they are, the youth train themselves and each other (by play and by instruction) to interpret their present and future roles in very much the same ways as their parents have done. People of all ages said approvingly that the young 'learn many things' through the youth organization. 'These are the schools of Red children' was a common formula.

At every stage of life Xhosa culture requires ego to show submission to those even slightly senior, concurrently with dominance over those even slightly junior. As ego ascends through the youth organization he is sometimes required to combine active teaching or guiding roles in one group with passive learning or following roles in the next highest group. This is why we speak of socialization by near-seniors as well as peers. The pattern of transitional overlap (so to call it) also operates for the exit from the senior stages of the youth organization into mature adult affairs. A man gradually drops out of the *intlombe* when he starts seeing himself as an *umdoda* (mature family man) instead of an *umfana* (young man) – perhaps with marriage, perhaps only several years after it – but before he stops participating in the *intlombe* he is already participating (in a junior or 'following' capacity) in adult institutions such as the local moot (*inkundla*) and the mature men's beer drink. The fact of this gradualism throws into relief the congruence of values, which is one reason for the harmonious relation of the youth organization to the adult world.

The Red Xhosa youth organization strikes us as notably successful, in a number of senses. It maintains itself as a flourishing institution in face of competition from (e.g.) Christian youth organizations and the lures of the town. The participants appear to find tremendous pleasure and satisfaction in it, so much that it materially helps to bind them to their traditional culture: young migrants say that they 'must' come home from town at frequent intervals because they would not like to miss too many youth meetings. Above all, the organization is successful in the purposes mentioned earlier: it does both encourage sexual and fighting behaviour and channel them into desired directions. Rural Red Xhosa do not have a 'youth problem' on their hands. Their daughters are sexually active but have fewer premarital pregnancies than either the 'School' (Christianized) or the urban Xhosa girls. Their sons learn to fight but are far less often involved in senseless violence. Both sons and daughters on the whole show more lasting attachment to home and more general respect for the parental generation and its values. All sections of Xhosa are unanimously agreed that 'Red children are the best controlled' (Mayer, 1961). And all this is attained without any direct adult participation in the youth organization. Paradoxically, although the parallel organizations that exist in the same countryside for the Christianized youth (under church or school auspices) usually have the benefit of adult leadership (at least nominally), they often fail to remain within the bounds prescribed by the adults. Many of them have foundered for this very reason.

It is not part of the present purpose to pick a way among the many different theoretical models of socialization that have found a place in the literature – some of them taking in virtually the whole of cultural transmission, or role-learning, and others concerning themselves more narrowly with the channelling of dangerous 'drives'; some being focused on overt social action, others on personality configurations, or psychological dispositions, and so forth. Further, in singling out fighting and sexual behaviour, we are not taking a stand on the question whether either or both of these represent universal endogenous 'drives', in youth or at any stage of life. We postulate only that some individuals appear to have greater and others lesser inclination to fight and/or to be active sexually; that a culture will prescribe behaviour somewhere along each spectrum as its ideal norm for a given stage of life; and that to have been socialized means to act in awareness of the cultural norms, though not everybody will become equally highly motivated to conform, and not all endeavours to conform will have the same success. We have no material on psychological internalization, but base our judgement of the 'successfulness' of Red Xhosa youth organization on observed social facts like those just mentioned (rareness of premarital pregnancies, etc.) and on the near-universal approval expressed by Red Xhosa of all ages and both sexes.

The following sections give an outline of the socializing practices of the youth organization – practices for which Xhosa themselves claim or imply an educative effect – under the four headings which have been indicated: fighting, law, sex, and self-identification or reference group. For reasons of space, only the first can be given much documentation.

FIGHTING CODES: CUDGEL PLAY IN THE YOUTH ORGANIZATION

A Red Xhosa adolescent boy, up to the age of manhood initiation (i.e. from about thirteen to about twenty), is seldom seen out of doors without a pair of cudgels. These are fairly heavy sticks, one longer and one shorter. Even at a distance a figure moving over the veld will be recognizable as a boy by the characteristic silhouette with the two sticks over the shoulder. The youth organization is largely concerned with cudgel games, 'playing sticks'. *Intutu* boys are too young to play expertly, but besides their own spirited though amateurish practice they get coaching from their seniors in the *mtshotsho*. In the *mtshotsho* itself cudgel games are a regular and prominent feature of the weekly meetings. The *intlombe* do not hold cudgel games, but *intlombe* members are called on to supervise and referee *mtshotsho* games. Girls are not allowed to attend or watch any of the boys' games but can and do 'play sticks' among themselves.

Besides the organized games of the *mtshotsho*, boys are apt to use their cudgels in two other contexts – for private fights between individuals and for public 'battles' (*idhabi*) between *mtshotsho* groups. Xhosa hold that boys are naturally pugnacious, like dogs, and 'always like to settle things by the stick'; to that extent boyish fights and battles have to be tolerated. But with the attainment of manhood the fighting urge is supposed to be sublimated and the use of the cudgel becomes improper. Xhosa see this as one of the primary meanings of manhood initiation, and it is sometimes given as a reason for hurrying initiation on in the case of a boy who has been too prone to brawling and violence. True, initiated young men were traditionally the official fighting force of the Xhosa; the new initiate was – and still is – presented with an assegai, in token of his warrior status. But he is also presented with a plain stick, to be blackened in the initiation fire – a token of his newly attained legal personality as a Xhosa man, who, as far as possible, should assert himself *vis-à-vis* other Xhosa only by words and not by blows. Nowadays the assegai is put away for good when initiation is over, but the black rod will always be carried whenever the man goes on any major business with legal implications.

Thus the training in the use and control of fighting behaviour belongs above all to the *intutu* and *mtshotsho* stages of the youth organization. It is a training that simultaneously elicits fighting behaviour in the boys, directs it against approved antagonists, and regulates it by fair-play rules and conventions. This training begins indeed at a much earlier age – as soon as the little boy can walk. But at those early stages it is in the hands of adults. In the important years of adolescence it is left to peers and near-seniors.

In what is called *thelelekisa*, women will catch hold of the hands of two little boys, two or three years old, and make them hit each other in the face, until the children get excited and angry and start lunging out on their own account, scratching and biting for good measure. The women look on with loud laughter. Slightly older little boys are given reeds or other soft 'weapons' and encouraged to have a bout together; or an adult (man or woman) will pretend to fight the child with a prodding finger, and encourage him to show how hard he can hit back. Boys of five or six are taught the use of the second (shorter, left-hand) stick for defence, and may often be seen battling away at each other with pairs of leafy branches, while other children and adults stand round watching and loudly commenting. At this stage the adults no longer show open amusement but smile indulgently as they urge the children on. Sometimes a grown boy or man takes up a stick and invites a child to fight back, teaching him meanwhile the use of terms like *mela* (wait) and *masiyeke* (lay off), and – most important – discouraging crying or any show of pain or fear.

Thus by the time a boy starts to join in *intutu* activities, at about eight or nine, he has some grounding both in techniques and in values. He knows that, unless one is specifically giving instruction, one takes up the cudgels only against an *intanga* – an 'equal' or age-mate – never against a junior or a person of the other sex. He knows that it is good to bear pain without flinching; and that whereas a fight may be private a game has an audience, both to cheer the contestants on and to safeguard fair play. The *intutu* stage now brings the first opportunity to fight regularly without an adult audience. Being also herdboys the *intutu* fight a good deal among themselves in the long hours spent out on the veld with the cattle. Occasionally they 'play sticks' at their own *intutu* meetings on Saturday afternoons or Sunday mornings. However, it is from their near-seniors, the *mtshotsho* boys, that they get their formal training. They are entitled to watch the *mtshotsho* games on Sundays and, when the games are finished, to take turns in being coached.

In watching these coaching sessions one is struck by the combination of serious purpose and good nature on the part of the youthful coaches, and by the pains they take to train the younger boys in valour on the one hand and fair play on the other. The boy who is coaching will make each small *intutu* boy choose a suitable age-mate to play against, and will keep a close eye on the game, which is limited to a few minutes for each pair. The following incidents were observed at one coaching session: One small boy was taught not to hit on the head; a second who tried hitting up and down in one quick movement – a dangerous trick – was promptly shouted at by the coach: 'No, boy, you can't do that.' A third who appeared timid was gently encouraged: 'Don't tremble, boy, you are not going to stab a goat. First *qula* (get ready). You are not going to die.' Every sign of courage or prowess was warmly praised.

The actual *mtshotsho* games are of two kinds: duels between boys of the same local group, which help to establish ranking and prestige, and those where boys of two or more local groups participate by invitation. These may be called 'games' and 'matches' respectively. Both are distinct from the *idhabi* or serious battles (see p. 171 below), though tempers sometimes run high.

Every local *mtshotsho* group has its regular place for games and matches – somewhere on the veld where there is a natural 'stage' for contestants fronted by an 'arena' for the boys who watch. On Sundays about noon boys will be seen pouring out of the *mtshotsho* dance hut towards this place. Horns blow, guitars thrum, formations are made and broken, with occasional quick rushes, and 'inspiring' songs called *amagija* are sung.

> '*Amagija* are to make you go ahead boldly – like setting a dog on somebody. The hair grows stiff, the whole body feels excited, with cold shivers down your back, and the heart becomes big and strong like a lion.'

The rules of cudgel play are taken seriously whether at games or at matches. Every boy uses his own sticks, not only because he is used to them but as a protection against possible interference by 'medicines'. Many things are forbidden as foul play, e.g. to *qusha* (hit an opponent on the ground); to inflict any needless hurt or humiliation; to ignore the call *mela* (wait) from an opponent who has dropped his stick, slipped, been hurt, etc., or the cry *masiyeke* which means the opponent is giving up; or to force him to go on too long after he suggests *khulula* (stop playing). (To *khulula* is to loosen the *iqulo* – cloth protecting the knuckles; to *qula* is to wrap it on, and is the sign of challenging or being ready.)

Enforcement falls to the audience which is entirely of peers and near-seniors. Mature men may and do watch, but from a distant spot: their voices are not supposed to be heard. Women and girls are excluded altogether.

Anyone in the audience can shout encouragement, but the near-seniors are especially responsible for stopping bouts, i.e. when these have gone on long enough or if they become bad tempered. It is done by interposing one's own cudgel between the two contestants. There is a formal division of the *mtshotsho* into three grades which is relevant in this connection. The first grade are *dala*, seniors, soon to be candidates for manhood initiation; the second are *dyongo* (from Afrikaans *jong*, 'boy'); the third are the latest recruits from the *intutu*. (The *intutu* itself comprises the fourth and fifth grades.) Boys should play within their own grade, and some of the senior grade should watch and referee. First-grade boys are usually trusted to 'control each other' but may be watched by young men.

Fighting prowess directly affects ranking and prestige. A good cudgel player may be promoted to a higher grade individually, by successfully challenging and beating boys of that grade, instead of awaiting automatic block promotion (when the seniors leave the *mtshotsho* for their manhood initiation). Promotion from boy to manhood is of course decided outside the youth organization, by way of initiation, but being a good cudgel player is some reason to expect one's initiation early. As to prestige, older Xhosa say that cudgel games used to be a recognized training for proper war and that therefore 'every boy was keen to prove his own fighting worth', since after initiation he was going to have to face the enemy. For the same reason (they say) prowess in cudgel games used to be a matter of public concern.

> 'The chief himself would know who were the champion fighters among the *mtshotsho* boys in his area, though today, if you asked a chief, he would say, "I know nothing about it; do you take me for a boy?" '

The great change, then, is that *mtshotsho* cudgel fighting has become 'just a sport', 'just for pleasure'. But even today masculine physical courage is greatly esteemed by Red Xhosa of all ages and both sexes, and a *mtshotsho* boy who fights well and fearlessly 'will be admired', 'will be respected', 'his word will carry more weight'. 'It is like having a lot of money among Europeans, it is a thing that gives him good standing.' 'He will be popular with girls.' Even women and girls who said that they 'hated the games' because 'boys only hurt themselves' agreed in this judgement.

Conversely, the stereotype of the coward is that 'nobody will think well of him'. Two men proudly invited attention to a boy (related to them by marriage) in action at a cudgel game, 'to show you what a good fighter is like'. When the boy unexpectedly retired without daring to strike a blow they were loud in their disgust: 'He had better go and work in town. He has shown fear and it will be a long time before he is brave again.'

These points can be illustrated by a brief account of an actual match:

On 18 February 1963 the Khalana *mtshotsho* were hosts to those of Nqontsi, Shushu, and Mabhongo. Mabuti, a senior boy of the Khalana group, was the first to invite challenges, and got one from a Nqontsi boy called Ngqumba. Before long Ngqumba was bleeding freely from cuts on the head, but he did not give up, perhaps because of a challenging song the Khalana boys were singing to their guitar. ('He thought it was just playing a game', ran the refrain.) In due course he fell. Mabuti went on hitting him as he lay on the ground. Immediately several Nqontsi and Shushu boys (Shushu being 'allies' of Nqontsi at this time) charged across and threatened to hit Mabuti. Mabuti slowly drew back. Another senior Khalana boy, Galata, shouted to Mabuti: 'What are you doing, fellow? Why don't you wait for the other boy when he is down?'

Ngqumba recovered and was prepared to go on, when Qhinga, who was next to Mabuti in seniority, stepped forward and hit with his stick between the two opponents. Mabuti turned to Ngqumba: 'We are being stopped, fellow.' Mabuti loosened his *iqulo*. But Ngqumba still would not give up. So Qhinga picked up the *iqulo* dropped by Mabuti.

Ngqumba's face was now covered in blood. Qhinga, a good fighter, soon added to the cuts on Ngqumba's head. Then he called on his own side to 'stop this boy; he is bleeding'. A senior boy of Mabhongo (allies of Khalana) came forward and hit with his stick between the pair, as Qhinga loosened his *iqulo*. Other boys from both sides surrounded Ngqumba, trying to make him do the same. He finally agreed, but sullenly.

A fight between a Mabhongo and a Shushu boy followed.

It was very even, and continued a long time, until Salati Bomse came forward and 'stopped' them.

Bomse put on his *iqulo* and Molo of Nqontsi took up the challenge. During this fight Molo appeared to catch hold of Bomse's defence stick. Bomse shouted, 'Don't hold me, my equal.' Molo declared he had not meant to hold. Some discussion followed. Bomse was prepared to go on, but Molo accepted defeat, saying, 'When I am beaten, my friend, I have to sit down.' To which Bomse replied: 'I am not fighting you, my friend.'

The fifth bout was between a Mabhongo and a Shushu boy. The Mabhongo boy performed extremely well. The watching Mabhongo boys were jubilant. Some of them ran up to their hero as he came down after the game, and milled round him playing the guitar, dancing and singing the fashionable song: 'Why is he silly? He thought it was just playing a game.'

The next pair were Mondile and Molo (of Nqontsi). After a while Mondile's head was cut and started bleeding badly. The Khalana boys asked him to retire but he refused. Some Mabhongo boys had to surround him and take his *iqulo* off by force.

Next, Bomse fought a boy from Shushu. The game went evenly for a long time, the Shushu boy putting up a skilful defence against the redoubtable Bomse. At the end Bomse offered his hand: 'Shake hands my equal, you are becoming tough.'

Mabuti of Khalana came forward again and another Nqontsi boy accepted his challenge. He proved a superior fighter, and Mabuti began to bleed from a cut on the head. The Nqontsi boy had a clear advantage but did not care to go on. 'Are we not being stopped?' The senior Khalana boys took the hint: 'The game is stopped.'

After this, Offisi from Shushu came forward but nobody would take him on. The Khalana and Mabhongo senior boys shouted 'Loosen (*khulula*), Offisi'. Offisi is a left-handed fighter: left-handers are much feared, except by those who have specially trained against them.

All the best fighters among the first-grade boys had now had their turns and it was the turn of the weaker brethren. A bout between a Mabhongo and a Nqontsi boy was slow and cautious. The spectators were not impressed. Bomse called out, 'This won't do, let me stop it, fellows.' Another Khalana boy supported him: 'Stop these people, they are not doing anything.'

After these it was the turn of the *dyongo* (boys of the second grade), for whose game the first grade act as referees. If the seniors like they can order which *dyongo* is to oppose which other. One senior ordered the *dyongos* to 'fetch this boy's sticks so he can play'. The Khalana–Mabhongo alliance did not put up a good show against the Nqontsi–Shushu boys. One Mabhongo *dyongo* said disgustedly: 'Man, lend me a defence stick, our boys are all being beaten, I don't know why.'

Finally, the third-grade boys played. The game became fast and furious but less organized. The older boys had their work cut out to control the young ones, and even to make sure that only two were on the 'stage' at a time.

A battle (*idhabi*) differs from a match in being far less governed by 'rules'. Battles are fairly rare occasions, but boys recall them singly in detail with a mixture of awe and glee. It is not unknown for a boy to be killed, maimed, or permanently crippled in the course of a battle. Such incidents are mentioned with regret but not as any argument against the battles as such and still less against the sport of cudgel fighting.

No two battles are exactly alike. Some reflect adult tensions between the locations involved as well as tensions between the *mtshotsho*. But more often the boys fight on a point of honour all their own. Shixini boys recalled a major battle four years earlier, when with their allies from Kulomali they had fought the united *mtshotsho* of Groxo, Bojini, and Ngcizela. 'There were so many boys it made you nervous to look at them.' The official challenge had been given by Shixini boys after some Groxo boys had attacked a few of them at a *mtshotsho* which both were attending in Bojini. But the real reason (clearly understood) was animosity over girls:

'Their (Groxo) girls liked our (Shixini) boys, but our girls did not like their boys. We were more attractive; they had a lot of *izishumana* (males without sex appeal). Our boys were better at stick fighting too. So we altogether overshadowed them, and they hated us for it, though they were our allies then.'

The challenge was taken over to Groxo in style, with much blowing of horns, and a time and place were agreed on for the battle – near the trading store 'because it was away from our homes and there was flat ground for fighting'.

'We armed ourselves with every sort of weapon – even pickaxes. Some of the Groxo boys fell and were hurt but there was only one serious injury. It was the very Groxo boy who had led the attack on our Shixini boys at the Bojini *mtshotsho*. He fell, but one of our boys went on hitting him with an axe. We tried to make him stop but he wouldn't. He kept chopping at the boy. He put the sharp edge of his axe against the boy's spine, as he lay on the ground, and rammed it in with his foot. All the time the Groxo boy was begging for mercy. This was a very cruel thing to do. The Groxo boy has never walked again to this day.'

This incident of course could not be concealed from the adults. The boys were eventually brought before the (white) magistrate, who sentenced each to a £5 fine or six months in jail. The one who had done the cruel deed was also ordered to pay his victim an allowance over the next fifteen years. Relations between Groxo and Shixini boys have been strained ever since. They do not *tshotsha* together, and hardly venture into each other's areas.

Incidents like the one just described are for once beyond the control of near-seniors, though sometimes *abafana* attend a battle especially to restrain the boys. In this particular case matters had to be adjusted by mature men representing the official political system. But even official reconciliation on the political level is unlikely to restore good relations at the youth level, at least till the generation of boys concerned has passed out of the *mtshotsho*.

'LAW' IN THE YOUTH ORGANIZATION

Red Xhosa set great store by the idea of law, and not only the law represented in the official adult legal and judicial systems.

Every corporate body is felt to have its own laws which it can and should enforce on its members. Even a group of three or four youths sharing a lodging in the town where they are labour migrants will speak of 'the laws of our house'. In the country the 'laws' of the *mtshotsho* and *intlombe* respectively are a familiar concept, and with this goes the idea that the group as a whole is responsible for wrong done by one member, since they ought to have restrained him in the name of their laws.

The idea of law becomes central at the *intlombe* stage of the youth organization. Fighting will no longer do, as a means of asserting one's will or settling disputes. '*Abafana* are adults and it is shameful if they fight.' Hence leadership and prestige come to depend more on 'political' and 'judicial' capacity (including eloquence) and less on physical courage or strength. In the words of a man of about thirty: 'The *intlombe* is a training school of the Red people for whom all life is led by law.' When Red Xhosa talk about education or maturing, there is no theme they harp upon more constantly than that 'boys settle things by the stick' but 'men should settle things by law' (or 'by words', implying judicial or quasi-judicial disputing). This is supposed to be a prime lesson of initiation. Initiation harangues (see p. 161 above) convey the message in a dramatic context, but to assimilate it thoroughly (as Xhosa think) requires long and careful practice, and this is provided by the *intlombe*.

> 'Men should attend the *intlombe* for many years, even up to fifteen or twenty. Those who attend for only five years may be liable to hit their "fathers" [i.e. the older generation] at beer drinks.'

The lesson to be learnt is that 'law is there to punish wrong done' and 'it is not right for a man to take law into his hands'. 'A man is not to solve problems with a stick.' Insults to which *mtshotsho* boys might react with blows will become the subject of a formal case-hearing in the *intlombe* instead. To give a single illustration: a young man was tried by the assembled *intlombe* for calling another member 'dog', and was fined heavily – four four-gallon barrels of strained beer, worth about £8 altogether. He was not able to pay this all at once but was ostracized till he did, not being allowed into any *intlombe* meetings. 'He had to eat all alone, like an animal.' This follows the general pattern for the ultimate sanction of Red Xhosa laws – one who fails to respect them will be rejected by the group (whatever it may be) in which they are vested. 'He will find himself neglected'; 'nobody will cooperate with him'. Since 'nobody is the only human being' and 'one lives by cooperation', there is every incentive to pay the fine demanded by one's group as the price of readmission (Mayer, 1961, pp. 131 ff.).

Becoming a man means learning to respect the law but also learning to enforce it. The *intlombe* trains in both. As a headman put it:

> 'These young men are expected to be future councillors and headmen. They are to deal with the *inkundla*, the headman, the chiefs, Bantu Commissioners, and magistrates. These will not respect one for one's strength in fighting but for eloquence and skill in solving problems.'

The *intlombe* is to the *inkundla* rather what the Oxford Union was supposed to be to parliament – a junior forum whose members, in a kind of earnest play, practise the political skills they will need in the 'real' forum later on.

The *intlombe* sets aside a special time for its legal matters, usually on Sunday morning. Older *abafana* may prefer to attend only at that time, missing out the Saturday dance. Three or four officers act as legal spokesmen. They are senior members with the necessary abilities. 'Magistrate' and 'Sergeant' are some of the titles used; a humbler executive type of officer is known as the 'Policeman'. But every man will have a chance sooner or later to show his powers of directing the *intlombe*, e.g. on an occasion when the regular officers are away and he is the most senior member present. In adult Xhosa affairs the seniority and achievement principles are combined in much the same way.

Intlombe discipline hammers away endlessly at the theme of obedience to seniors. Senior members can order around the *ikrwala* ('unripe fruit', novices – a phase which may be prolonged for several years) and even order them out of the hut if they like. A special dance, *iketile*, is the prerogative of the most senior. *Intlombe* members can 'take away' girls from the *mtshotsho* group, by virtue of their seniority. And so on. This respect for seniority is essentially the same as respect for law as against mere force. As a twenty-year-old *mtshotsho* 'boy' put it:

'If a man is beating a boy even for a wrong reason the boy does not hit back – just runs away. This is respect. An elder of sixty is no stronger by virtue of his age than a boy of twenty. If we did not learn to respect punishment by seniors there would be fights daily.'

THE YOUTH ORGANIZATION AND THE ENCOURAGEMENT AND DIRECTION OF SEXUAL 'PLAY'

Important as is all-male cudgel play in the youth organization, cross-sex relations and sweethearting have an even greater place. This sexual activity too is classed as 'play', with rules of its own. As with cudgel play, it serves two functions – encouragement, and direction into harmless channels. And, as with cudgel play, entire responsibility is left to the participants, their peers and near-seniors, the adults holding quite aloof.

Early sex play is regarded indulgently by adults, including the play of children out herding who 'learn' by seeing animals mate and 'may try to copy them'. 'All this is only childishness.' With puberty the children must learn to refrain from any mention or hint of sexual things in their parents' presence. This does not indicate guilt or shame about sexuality as such; it is merely the *hlonipha* (respect behaviour) due to parents. Girls in the *intutu* grades – pre-adolescent or barely adolescent – are already learning about the permissibility of *metsha*, external sexual intercourse. Invariably this instruction is said to be given by the older girls and never on any account by the mother, for *hlonipha* reasons.

Metsha is the erotic technique proper to the whole period from puberty to marriage. Keeping to *metsha*, as against full intercourse, is a cardinal rule of youthful sex play. It is bad to break the rules but it is also bad not to play at all. Both sexes disapprove of a girl 'who is not caressed by males'. 'She becomes stiff and her blood does not flow properly.' 'Girls who don't want it are likely to become witches. They are being caressed by *impundulu* (familiars).' Similarly, a male who has no sweethearts – an *isishumana* – is unlikely to enjoy prestige in the youth organization, though his fellows may try to encourage him as they would a timid cudgel fighter. Girls say they prefer as sweetheart 'a boy who has many girl friends'. 'I don't mind how many he has besides me; I like it, for I am proud of him.'

Premarital sweethearting ought always to be extra-domestic and actual lovemaking to be conducted in privacy. But they must not be clandestine. It is as important for the peers to know what is going on as for the parents not to know. The way to fetch a girl for lovemaking is to come to her *ikoyi* hut, where she sleeps with other girls, take her out 'into the bush', and bring her back afterwards. Similarly, at *mtshotsho* and *intlombe* parties: the youth makes a sign to the girl and everyone sees them leave the hut together.

Throughout the youth organization 'private love' (a stock phrase) is vigorously discouraged. There are various ways of ensuring publicity. In some *intlombe* groups it is an accepted practice that 'those who have fallen in love' are announced at the weekly meetings, with elaborate formality. At Tshabo a girl will publicly give her lover a decorated stick to hold. She steps forward from the line of clapping girls and offers the stick to one after another of the male dancers, but always withdraws it, till at last the lover is allowed to grasp it. He holds it proudly for the rest of the dance. In other places the corresponding sign is for the girl to take off the towel she wears round her waist and wipe the sweat from her lover's face.

One of the young people's stated objections to 'private' love is that a girl might have more than one lover at a time. This would be a bad training for marriage (in which the woman must confine herself to one sexual partner though the man need not). The other objection is that the couple might be tempted to full intercourse instead of *metsha*, with danger of pregnancy ensuing.

Prevention of pregnancy is a matter in which the youth organization adds its own heavy sanctions to those to be expected from adults. An impregnated girl can never become a wife; she must content herself with becoming an *inkazana*, a woman available for love affairs with mature (especially married) men. *Inkazana* status carries certain disabilities in the adult world but it means instant complete exclusion from the pleasures of the youth organization. The 'fallen' girl 'no longer belongs to us from the moment she is pregnant. She has become a grown-up person. We must *hlonipha* her.' She cannot come to any dances, meetings, etc., though she is not ostracized in daily relations. Obviously *hlonipha*, sexual reticence, cannot be combined with participation in such gatherings. Besides, if the girl came she might set a bad example to other girls. 'It is not right that she should join us in the happiness of our dances', or even continue sweethearting with any of the male members. Girls say that they would never knowingly accept as sweetheart anyone who has relations with an *inkazana*. Thus the girl who becomes pregnant must expect a dull, lonely life.

Apart from the fear of sanctions girls seem readily to internalize the teaching they get from their near-seniors at puberty, that *metsha* is right for them but full intercourse is wrong.[2] 'I would dislike a boy who wants me to do what I was taught not to do.' Some boys, especially if they have had experience of town, are said to plead for full intercourse, but girls always say that 'one should never agree to such a thing'. Even boys concur:

> 'The girl ought to stop me. She should not let me impregnate her because this is an offence against me. One who lets you do anything is dangerous. She wants to take away all your cattle' [force you to pay seduction fine or bridewealth].

One of the values the youth groups teach to boys is 'protecting our girls' (or 'sisters') – not only against impregnation but against any unwanted advances. 'A girl has a right to refuse.' If a boy tries to pull a girl out of the dance hut by force, or to keep her outside the door by force, the group will shout at him to let her alone. Girls say that boys are only 'beggars' and must learn to ask politely.

Mtshotsho and *intlombe* groups also tend to guard the girls of their own group against too much attention from males of other neighbourhoods – partly out of genuine protectiveness, if partly only to safeguard their own prior rights. A girl who insists on accepting an 'outside' lover is sometimes heavily penalized, e.g. made to stand in a highly uncomfortable position all night long at every dance. This is likely to be explained as an effort to protect her – an outsider could be a dangerous type and do her harm. Similarly, the youths sometimes threaten drastic steps (e.g. thrashing) to prevent girls going away for seasonal work on white-owned farms. 'They might get private lovers there: suppose they become pregnant?' These are just the kinds of argument to be expected from parents. They seemed more remarkable coming from age-mates.

Premarital pregnancy is certainly rare among Red Xhosa, by contrast with the School Xhosa where it constitutes a major problem. School people are very much aware of the sad difference. One factor is that School people have abandoned the *metsha* technique – originally because of Christian moral disapproval,[3] but also because it is now considered out of date. (The moral disapproval seems odd to Red people; as an elderly woman remarked, 'How can there be immorality (*ukungcola*) in it, seeing that they do not "spoil" each other?') But a more important factor is surely the 'privateness' typical of School love affairs, as against the publicity and control in the Red youth groups.

WIDENING SCALE AND SELF-IDENTIFICATION

The youth organization provides for a progressive widening of social horizons, which is significant for self-identification. 'Upward' and 'outward' extension go together.

The *intutu* is just a neighbourhood group. A reason cited for organizing it separately from the *mtshotsho* is that 'young boys can't travel far'. Social rather than physical incapacity is meant. The young ones do cover long distances herding, but their home duties keep them in at night (e.g. returning the cattle to the kraal every evening and taking them out every morning), whereas *mtshotsho* expeditions generally involve one if not two nights away from home.

The *intutu* party is held on a Saturday afternoon or Sunday morning, not too far from home. Home duties are not forgotten. Boys dash in and out as word comes that somebody's cattle are straying. Girls, too, emphasize that they must not stay away from home too long because 'we are always being sent on errands'. Both sexes would say they feared a thrashing if they stayed out at night.

The *mtshotsho* stage signalizes an intense awareness of local-community allegiance, transcending that of the home. Reciprocal visiting by *mtshotsho* groups brings new contacts with outside age-mates; at the same time, it is very much a community business, the group always going as a whole and identifying itself as 'the *mtshotsho* of such a place'. Lone visitors are not accepted: 'you would be beaten'.

On a first visit the group (boys with their girls) arrive at the party unannounced, as gatecrashers. They are asked to identify themselves by location and headman, and then, if all is well, the boys surrender their sticks to the hosts as a token of peaceful intentions, and join the ring of dancers, and the girls stand in the file that is clapping and singing. To be refused admission is a pointed rebuff, but if rebuffed they must leave quietly, with the choice of either avoiding that place in the future, or else going back another time to pick a fight.

Relations become friendly when the visitors have been allowed to return two or three times and have subsequently invited their hosts back. Only then can it be said, 'They have danced together and established harmony.' After this, visits are exchanged regularly, and sequences arise, each group knowing where it is going to *tshotsha* next week.

Mtshotsho relations are shifting and quasi-political. At the time of fieldwork, Shixini boys would *tshotsha* with those from Emangweni, Mtshayelwini, Qaukeni, Kulofombatha, and Mandluntsha; their relations with three or four other groups had been broken off after the 'battle' described above. Khalana boys had a circuit embracing three other groups, but a few years earlier they had had to '*tshotsha* alone' owing to their many quarrels. Group-conscious and trigger-happy as *mtshotsho* boys are, there is no knowing when trouble may break out. For this reason among others, boys say that the most relaxed (though least 'interesting') meetings are those they call *icawa* or *imbutho*, at which no outsiders are present.

Intlombe visiting is different. An *intlombe* may likewise visit and be visited by other *intlombe* groups en bloc, but the circuits are wider than those of *mtshotsho* groups, sometimes covering amazing distances. More significant, the young men can also visit other *intlombe* groups individually. It is a fundamental rule that a young man 'can dance at any *intlombe*' regardless of whether he or his group has had any relations there before. In principle 'an *umfana* can ask for *intlombe* anywhere from right across the Bashee to right across the Great Fish River'. This is like saying anywhere from Land's End to John o'Groats; it takes in hundreds of miles of the Ciskei and Transkei. The visitor is entitled to all the privileges of the dance, e.g. he can ask the master of ceremonies to have his favourite song sung, or take any of the girls out to 'propose love'.

This wide-range peaceful visiting, contrasting with the tense group visits of the earlier stage, is always said to begin in principle at manhood initiation. While in seclusion the novices are supposed to roam around visiting other lodges. 'This is the first time they can really make friends far away, as fighting is not allowed' to novices.

Given this permissive spirit, which substitutes the concept of 'visitor' for that of 'gatecrasher', formal invitations have less significance than in the *mtshotsho* circuit. A visiting *intlombe* group may invite its hosts back but it does not greatly signify whether the invitation is accepted or not. 'If not, they can continue going over there till friendship is established.' A refusal is not an insult, 'no reason why they should not make friends'.

Abafana, then, at the same time as they lay their sticks aside in favour of 'law', are supposed to lay aside the intense, suspicious, local-group preoccupations of the *mtshotsho* boys, much as the *mtshotsho* boys lay aside the earlier *intutu* preoccupation with the home. Of course this is a simplification. Family and local community loyalties will always be important. But the youth organization adds new possibilities for self-identification with something wider, namely with the Red Xhosa 'nation'. Youth visiting does not only provide an outlet for the youthful urge to roam (noted in many studies of adolescent psychology). It does not only supplement the total networks of relations between families, and the networks of political relations, by adding a new network independent of either. It also gives ego first-hand experience of the community of expectations that exists among his age-mates – all enjoying themselves in much the same ways, all governing themselves by much the same 'laws'. By the *intlombe* stage he has achieved effective self-identification as a member of a category that extends 'from across the Bashee to across the Great Fish River'.

THE CONGRUENCE WITH ADULT VALUES

The Red Xhosa youth activities outlined here are noticeably like those reported from some very different social contexts. Superficially they duplicate features of Western urban teenage parties – heavy petting, pop music, gang-mindedness and gang conflict, gatecrashing, organized sport, and preoccupation with personal adornment. A good deal that has been written sociologically about youth culture in the United States (in particular) might well be applied to the Red Xhosa. Talcott Parsons, for example, characterized American youth peer groups by their 'compulsive conformity, sharp loyalty to the group . . . along with this goes a strong romantic streak'. In a fuller account of American youth culture as something 'unique and highly distinctive for American society', Parsons observed:

> 'One of its dominant roles is "having a good time", in relation to which there is a particularly strong emphasis on social activities in company with the opposite sex. A second predominant characteristic on the male side lies in the prominence of athletics . . . [there is] emphasis on the value of certain qualities of attractiveness, especially in relation to the opposite sex' (Parsons, 1949, p. 221).

Or again, one could cite Erikson's list of youth characteristics, which implicitly relates to Western material (Erikson, 1963, pp. 1 ff.). It includes: fidelity, or the search for something and somebody to be true to; new physical energy contributing to aggressive drives; a psychosocial moratorium between the advent of genital maturity and the onset of responsible adulthood; psychosexual powers used for enhancing a sense of style and identity; grandiosity and playfulness, amplified by genital potency and locomotor maturation; a craving for locomotion, as in travel or in dancing, sports, etc. All these seem very apt to the *mtshotsho* and *intlombe* patterns.

It could be an ethological datum that human youth just 'are like that' – prone to play and display, to roaming and tussling, to exploring territorially and adventuring sexually. Alternatively, it could be a common response to a not uncommon social situation – the situation where a gerontocracy excludes youth more or less from 'real' public and domestic responsibilities, and also perhaps from adult sociable gatherings and recreation. These are broader questions. Our present question is more specific, namely how it comes about that Xhosa youth can freely enjoy themselves 'like that' without either falling foul of the adults or endangering the adult systems. The question is the more necessary in that the Xhosa youth organization – as was stressed – operates autonomously, without adult guidance or supervision, and away from adult activities. While this separation averts immediate occasions of conflict it could also hypothetically facilitate evasions of social control, e.g. youthful delinquency, or the development among youth of radical or rebellious values and expectations.

It is in this regard that Xhosa youth culture seems most distinctive or at least most different from its counterparts in the West, where the image of youth as 'forward looking' and/or 'out of hand' has become practically stereotyped. Parsons includes in his list of American youth peer-group characteristics 'a compulsive independence in relation to certain adult expectations, a touchy sensitivity to control, which in certain cases is expressed in overt defiance'; or, as he has it elsewhere, 'a certain recalcitrance to the pressure of adult expectations and discipline' (Parsons, 1963, p. 111; 1949, p. 221). Xhosa youth peer groups by contrast are allowed their freedom from adult *discipline* precisely because they do not show independence in relation to adult *expectations*. Of course, boys or young men or girls do sometimes behave 'badly' even within the framework of the youth organization, but the point is that by and large the same kinds of behaviour will rank as bad with their peers and near-seniors and the parental generation alike.

A youth culture may be called 'radical' if it substitutes its own expectations for those of the older generation to the extent that the outlook for the future appears open-ended. In the common phrase the youth would be 'shaping the world of tomorrow' – or mis-shaping it, as is alleged, for instance, by those who fear that modern Western youth are 'undermining' the institution of marriage or the values of industry or thrift, etc. Radical youth culture means accelerated social change. Prima facie one might have expected the Red Xhosa youth to import radical values and accelerated social change into their own environment: for their society is partially involved with the fast-changing 'Western' systems of the white-dominated towns, and in every generation it is the youth who have most direct contact with these, by way of labour migrancy.

Alternatively, a 'rebellious' youth culture would be one that challenged expectations of the parent culture but still remained well contained, and, indeed, served cathartic functions for the parent culture: e.g. a youthful bohemianism, defiantly exalting play above earning, or free love above marriage, to be renounced by each participant in due course as he 'settles down and comes to his senses'. This youth culture would be just a ritual of rebellion. The model would be less of a rapidly changing society than of one in which youthful roles had some ambiguity, the peer group proffering one set of expectations while seniors proffered a different, incompatible set. The seniors would always win in the end.

The fact that Red Xhosa youth groups function autonomously, and yet (as elders freely concede) are *neither* uncontrolled *nor* rebellious *nor* radical, can obviously not be explained in terms of the youth organization alone, being a matter of the relation between that and the wider society or culture. We offer a few tentative comments on this relation, without trying to answer questions in the 'why' form.

First, agreement of expectations between youth peer groups and seniors seems relatively easy in the Red Xhosa context in so far as the culture prolongs romantic and 'fun' values right into old age, though the mature sense of responsibility is supposed to be added on at the same time. Red men, for instance, are entitled to enjoy both sociable drinking and romantic sweethearting to any age they like, the latter being provided for by the *inkazana* women (p. 176 above). Thanks to the militaristic ideology, too, they can follow (though not participate in) boys' sports without loss of dignity. Thus in the general setting the youth activities and values appear only mildly – not wildly – romantic; those of the gerontocracy only slightly stodgy.

A more basic cultural value which aligns Red youth with their seniors is strong nationalistic pride, particularly in the form of opposition to the Christianized or white-style elements in School and urban Xhosa cultures. This is one of the factors that insulate Red youth against 'new' ideas and prevent them from importing cultural radicalism whether from town or elsewhere (cf. Mayer, 1961).

THE 'SECTARIAN' DANGER AND SOME FACTORS LIMITING IT

If a youth group, or any social group, does set great store by 'different' or radical values, it must also seek to play down the moral force of its members' relations with outsiders. A dual repudiation, of the other people's values and of morally effective ties with the other people, is necessary to keep the distinctive message pure. Another feature of sect-like bodies – whether youth organizations, religious or political groups, or ethnic minority associations – is that, while insulating members against moral and social control from outside, they also provide a strong internal control of their own. This is effected by a demand for intense participation and loyalty, and for mutual watchfulness, facilitated by a 'cell' type of structure. One example of a youth organization turned sect-like in these regards is the German *Wandervogel*; another is urban gang life on the fringes of criminality or beyond. The former could be ranked as dangerous on account of its ideological radicalism, the latter as being resistant to law and order.

Red Xhosa youth organization fits the sectarian pattern in so far as it demands intense participation and loyalty and mutual watchfulness, with a cell type of structure. The resulting effective control over members is exemplified in the successful direction of sexual and fighting behaviour and the bringing to book of those who offend against the 'laws' of the group. But the other element of sectarianism is absent – there is no attempt to play down the moral significance of a young person's ties with adults. The separation which we have emphasized does not have this implication because, however intensively the youth participate in their autonomous activities, each is still heavily dependent on his parents and paternal kin in other fields. The Red Xhosa is a peasant and still sees land inheritance as his best economic hope. Town earnings are important and necessary but there is no security for old age in town, and the Red person who goes off to work there typically expects to 'come home to die' – or preferably a good deal sooner. The continued strength of Red patriarchalism is indicated by the flourishing ancestor cult, which is still the main religious system (cf. Mayer, 1961).

Along with this patriarchalism, a second factor which prevents cutting off is, of course, that the youth organization operates in the context of rural communities where 'everyone knows everyone'. The youth can enjoy autonomy but never anonymity. Ego's associates in the youth peer group are the children of his father's associates in the face-to-face community. Even across the bounds of community, a battle between Shixini and Groxo boys can never be anonymous in the same sense as one between London gangs on Margate beach, since the groups are identified specifically by community. For all these reasons, latent control remains with the adults and comes into play on the rather rare occasions when youth-group activities involve some major transgress against adult interests or dictates: a girl impregnated, a boy killed or maimed in a battle, or property seriously damaged.

Third, cutting off is precluded by the mechanism of transitional overlap, which operates for the eventual exit from the youth organization into the adult world. As we saw, it is a characteristic feature of the youth organization up to the end of the *mtshotsho* that those who have reached senior or leading positions in one group or grade are already attending the next one in a marginal or receptive capacity – as spectators, hangers-on, apprentices, or pupils – the effect being that ego receives complementary experience in active and passive techniques during one and the same period. So also with the exit into the adult world. Ego will gradually drop out of *intlombe* activities when he comes to regard himself as a mature man (*umdoda*) rather than a young man (*umfana*). For the mature man, as for the elder, the proper scene of recreation and sociability is the domestic beer drink, and of judicial-political activity the locational moot or *inkundla*. Young men who are still participating in the *intlombe* can begin to attend these too, as respectful juniors or learners. At the *inkundla* they listen, or speak when specially called upon; at the men's beer drink they accept the beer portions allotted to them; meanwhile the *intlombe* gives them practice in the corresponding 'positive' or 'initiating' techniques – leading or controlling a discussion or dispensing hospitality.

But there is no transitional overlap from *mtshotsho* to *intlombe*, separated as they are by the great divide of initiation (see p. 161 above). True, young men may be called on to referee boys' games or control their battles (pp. 167 and 172), but boys cannot attend *intlombe* even as spectators, and young men cannot fight as boys do. Initiation is a 'total' status change, so to speak. Hence it may be said to score a point for the gerontocracy on the principle of divide and rule. Initiation makes initiates the focus of community attention; it offers them agreeable instant rewards in the shape of *intlombe* membership, as well as meaningful future rewards in the shape of advancing status; but the price for all this is not only to be physically disarmed, but to be sharply divided off from one's former cronies in the *mtshotsho*. There is thus an effective barrier between the two potentially dangerous groups – the boys (youths) and the young men; and, concurrently, an effective bond between the young men and the mature men, in the form of the transitional overlap just described.

A comparison suggests itself with the Pondo, a Xhosa-speaking group in the Transkei, who are rural and patriarchal like the Red Xhosa but who do not have manhood initiation. Besides traditional-style Red youth groups (*igubura*), which somewhat resemble the *intlombe*, there are in Pondoland the so-called 'rascal' youth groups, *indlavini*, which are truly sectarian and much more dangerous. *Indlavini* are organized in all-male gangs which meet secretly in lonely places. They defy adult standards of dress and manners, and they not only clash with rival gangs but sometimes terrorize home people, elders and girls, as well. An interpretation suggested here is that Xhosa initiation offers youth a flattering reception by adult society at just the age (eighteen on) when *indlavini* are pitting their wits against it.

The example of the *indlavini* also recalls Parsons's observation that all-male youth groups are naturally more dangerous than those that emphasize cross-sex ties. It seems relevant that the infertile *metsha* technique enables Red Xhosa youth to invest heavily in cross-sex ties without thereby endangering adult interests of marriage or family.

To sum up: Red Xhosa youth organization seems to owe much of its success as an autonomous yet non-trouble-making institution to particular characteristics of the parent culture: rural, proud, conservative, patriarchal, not puritanical, and not pacific. Not being puritanical or pacific, Red society can easily tolerate in principle the sexual, playful, and aggressive activities of marginal youth; while being rural, patriarchal, and so forth it does not need to fear major disobedience or 'getting out of hand'. Red seniors are rightly proud of their 'well-controlled youth' in contrast to the School and urban youth with their various symptoms of anomie, and they are right in giving some of the credit to the youth organization – 'the schools of Red children' – but it seems clear that the organization as it stands could not just be transplanted.

It is certainly not remarkable for a youth culture to emphasize sex, play, display, roaming, athleticism, and physical conflict. What we have tried to underline as more remarkable is the way Red Xhosa youth culture interprets these activities, harnessing them to conservative social values, not subversive ones.

Appendix

Gang Formation among Xhosa and Samburu

A COMMENT BY MAX GLUCKMAN[4]

There appears to be some ground for saying that in Western countries organized gangs (delinquent and non-delinquent) tend to develop where youths over a fair spread of ages continue to associate together. The youths or young men, who are likely to be in their twenties, are the organizers, and the auxiliaries are a number of peer groups, each of three or four younger youths. This was so in the classic *Street Corner Society* gangs (non-delinquent); and although Whyte does not deal with this point clearly, it seems that the older young men passed out and the younger became leader(s), with new recruits in peer groups coming in from below.

Where the older youths are quickly absorbed into the adult society, through early marriage, the development of this form of organized gang, sometimes delinquent, is prevented. Absorption into the adult society through marriage is possible during periods of full employment and affluence; as the older youths move out in this way, there are left small peer groups of coevals, with a strong egalitarian ethos, and therefore not moving into organized crime. These peer groups may indulge in sporadic violence, rather than organized crime.

If there is something in this thesis, we have in the Mayers' paper a very stimulating analysis of a situation in a tribal society where tribal organization controls the development of more extensive age-spread groups. Boys slightly older than others are their teachers; but they are at the same time pupils to a yet older group, with older boys guiding younger towards approved modes of action. Their own vested interest in the system, to take over Spencer's phrasing, is that they are looking forward to their own promotion. The rewards in the system of advancement to young manhood are partly in the right to freer *ukumetsha* (intercourse *inter crura*) with girls, but also in liberation from herding and in freedom to go to the towns where they can earn money. They are dependent on their seniors for the land they will inherit, but money and cattle are the other essentials for full social development, and town is an opportunity to earn these. Thus, as with affluent young men in Britain in the 1960s, adult life is possible for them and draws them into itself; note the difference from *Street Corner Society* in the depression.

For the Red Xhosa, then, circumcision-initiation would appear to be trebly rewarded: first, it opens the way to manhood; second, it opens the way to economic independence and married adulthood; and, third, it gives a young man individuality – he can move alone.

Comparing Spencer's Samburu, one would expect the Xhosa initiation to be much less of an ordeal, with less emphasis on not flinching. For the Samburu, I think, contrast strongly with the Xhosa in some significant respects, despite their similarities. There is a wide age-spread of youths and young men in the Samburu warrior grade at any one time; the sharply institutionalized age-grades (boyhood, warriorhood, elderhood) are fairly wide apart; and the social adolescence in the warrior grade is as long as fifteen to sixteen years. Samburu warriors are herding the cattle of their elders; it does not seem that they go out to earn money with which they could buy their own cattle, and since they can no longer raid they are dependent on their elders for cattle And for these they are compelled to wait till they leave warriorhood. Hence, as not among the Xhosa, they are suspected of wanting to steal cattle, and perhaps they actually do. Spencer rightly emphasizes that Samburu elders have a potential delinquent problem on their hands; and with this, he argues convincingly, they deal in a drastic circumcision ceremony, in which anxieties are over-created in advance. It fixes the glory and acceptance of the under-privilegement of warriorhood, and it is renewed periodically in the *ilmugit* ceremonies.

NOTES

1. This paper forms part of a project supported by the National Council for Social Research (South Africa), to which acknowledgement is due.

2. The teaching may be more easily given and received in that the instructors themselves have to practise what they preach, which would not be the case if it were given by mothers.

3. McLaren's *Xhosa–English Dictionary* (1950) gives *metsha* as 'to hold unclean intercourse', and *mtshotsho* as 'immoral night dancing of boys'.

4. Extracts from the commentary given by Max Gluckman in introducing discussion of the two preceding papers.

REFERENCES

ERIKSON, E. H. 1950. *Childhood and Society*. New York: Norton; London: Imago, 1951.

—— (ed.). 1963. *Youth: Change and Challenge*. New York: Basic Books.

MAYER, P. 1961. *Townsmen or Tribesmen*. Cape Town: Oxford University Press.

PARSONS, T. 1949. *Essays in Sociological Theory, Pure and Applied*. Glencoe, Ill.: The Free Press.

—— 1963. Youth in the Context of American Society. In E. H. Erikson (ed.), *Youth: Change and Challenge*. New York: Basic Books.

WHYTE, W. F. 1955. *Street Corner Society*. Chicago: University of Chicago Press.

WILSON, M., KAPLAN, S. & MAKI, T. 1952. *Social Structure*. Vol. III of *Keiskammahoek Rural Survey*. Pietermaritzburg: Shuter & Shooter.

J. S. La Fontaine

Two Types of Youth Group in Kinshasa (Léopoldville)[1]

The material[2] on which this paper is based derives from an urban survey on which I was engaged from October 1962 to May 1963. During this time, one of the obvious features of the life of this city, which was undergoing sudden and uncontrolled change, was the proliferation of youth groups, many of them deliquent gangs. By 'youth' I mean the age-category ten to twenty, although it is hard to draw a clear-cut distinction dividing senior members of this group from junior members of the category referred to as adult. However I shall not be concerned with young children or with mature adults. My aim is to present some material for comparison with studies in English and American towns and also to estimate the degree to which the fluid social situation, which characterized the period of my fieldwork, affected the nature of the groups themselves.

By 1962, Kinshasa (at that time still known as Léopoldville) had recovered somewhat from the most violent post-Independence struggles of 1960–61. Although throughout the period of my study there was an officially proclaimed State of Emergency, which involved police road-blocks from time to time and a curfew imposed with irregular strictness, the city was relatively calm. The main political problem was the struggle between the central government and the provincial government of Kongo Central, which adjoins the urban area. Apart from its aim of federal autonomy, the provincial government, controlled by ABAKO,[3] the nationalist party of the Kongo-speaking peoples, laid claims to territory in the peri-urban area. In the course of the fight to obtain control of this area, the provincial government used as a political weapon the city's dependence on the province for most of its supplies of fresh foods. A blockade of the city was organized in early 1963; it lasted three weeks, causing disruption of food supplies and so intensifying the already widespread economic distress in the city.

THE POPULATION OF THE CITY: STRUCTURE AND CHANGES

A major factor in the city's economic crisis after Independence was the sudden influx of rural migrants, resulting both from the lapsing of pre-Independence controls on population movements and from rural unrest. The city's Congolese population, which had numbered about 400,000 in 1959, rose to a figure which was variously estimated at between 800,000 and $1\frac{1}{2}$ million. My own estimates put it at about a million. While this population rise caused intolerable pressure on housing and other facilities of the city, the influx also resulted in the creation of an extensive squatter zone whose spread, by the end of the period I refer to, almost equalled in extent the original metropolitan area. The squatter zone was the territory disputed between the central and provincial governments and for this and other reasons it was effectively outside the control of the administrative and law-enforcing authorities of either.

Before Independence the bulk of the city's working population depended on wage labour, despite a flourishing commercial class, so that the dislocation of industry in the post-Independence upheavals severely affected Kinshasa's inhabitants. The problem of unemployment, already severe in 1960, had by 1962 reached a pitch at which the unemployed heavily outnumbered the employed. Some of the unemployed found a living in marginal commercial activities and others subsisted by begging and borrowing from kinsmen and tribesmen who were more fortunately placed. Many were forced to resort to criminal activities; prominent among them were gangs of youths.

The changes the city had undergone since 1960 were thus considerable but in general they acted to distort or intensify factors already crucial in the city's structure, rather than to alter it radically. Independence had provided the Congolese with a range of political offices, exercising far greater power than ever before, but no organized political parties. The new posts were rapidly filled so that, for the new graduates of Lovanium, opportunities were almost as restricted as in pre-Independence times. The influx of population and the economic collapse of the Congo had resulted in massive unemployment but the bulk of Kinshasa's workers had always been unskilled and had faced the threat of unemployment, with its accompanying poverty. Since the Second World War unemployment had been steadily increasing; the events of 1960–62 aggravated this problem rather than introduced it as a new factor. Hence, although Kinshasa's inhabitants found their problems intensified, at the level of the ordinary citizen, life appeared to have changed remarkably little.[4]

Kinshasa draws on a wide geographical region for its population. The city's lingua franca is the mother-tongue of none of its inhabitants, who represent widely differing cultural backgrounds. The largest grouping is that of the matrilineal Kongo-speakers from the Lower Congo, who still, in 1962, formed about half the total population. Their main rivals constitute an ethnic category rather than a tribal community and do so by virtue of the contrast with the Kongo that they represent, both by area of origin and by the dominant mode of transmitting property and authority. These are the people known as Bangala, migrants from the Upper Congo, who are typically patrilineal. Migrants from other areas come from widely differing types of social system and add to the city's heterogeneity. Kinshasa could be said to constitute a meeting-ground for the two types of descent system, but 'traditional' tribal values do not appear to be of great significance in determining the status of the young; there is also a considerable minority of children of unions which are tribally mixed.

In 1959 over half the city's population was under eighteen; in the estimates I was able to make during 1962 it appeared that the proportion had not changed significantly. Kinshasa has for many years been regarded as the educational centre for the western Congo and many children of school age were, and are, sent to live with kin in town, in order to attend school. Their numbers swell the already large population of juveniles. However, by far the greater part of this section of the population is not in school or attends for a few years only. Educational facilities were inadequate even for the pre-Independence population; by 1962, in spite of the establishment of some independent schools and the expansion of higher education, schooling was available only for a minority.

J. S. La Fontaine

THE URBAN FAMILY IN KINSHASA

In the literature on youth groups, and particularly delinquent gangs in Western cities, it is common to find the breakdown in parental authority attributed as a causal factor. It is thus necessary to examine the nature of the urban Congolese family in order to ascertain its effectiveness as a means of exerting control on its younger members.

As in other African towns, the conditions of life in Kinshasa have tended to make the nuclear family both more isolated as a social unit and of more fundamental importance in the life of the individual. Although a network of kinship ties does link it to other similar units, their dispersion within the city and between city and country inevitably diminishes the intensity of relations and the degree of interdependence between kin. Accommodation is such that, in most instances, household and nuclear family are coterminous. Except for the owners of plots, who can build up an extended family unit, housing is designed for the nuclear family. Although Congolese still manage to fulfil their duties to kin and provide them with the hospitality that traditional obligations demand, they do so by overcrowding their houses and such arrangements are, of necessity, only temporary. A further factor which adds to the isolation of the nuclear family is that each must be economically independent, depending for the major portion of its income on the earnings of its members, primarily those of its head, whether male or female. Although gifts and loans help to distribute a share of the good fortune enjoyed by one man among his close kin, households of related men and women may show a considerable range of economic standing. No family can afford to rely on aid from kin or neighbours, however welcome help may be.

Within the household the position of the parental generation is weakened by a number of factors deriving from the urban situation. However, it is important to distinguish various components, which may not all be present in any one situation. Children may be separated from their parents or from one parent, either temporarily or permanently, a not uncommon situation in towns. In a survey of 317 households in two communes of Kinshasa, we found 149 nuclear families (of which three were dependants in a kinsman's household), twenty-seven units consisting of a mother and her child or children and three units of father and children. Thus in thirty cases the children concerned were not subject to the discipline of two parents. In addition, there were a further sixty-one instances in which children were living with kin other than parents: in thirty-five cases the kin tie was that between members of one genealogical generation, in twenty-four the tie was with a sibling or a parent, and in two cases the children were dependants of a member of the grandparental generation. This situation reflects the migration of children to town to seek education but it adds to the proportion of children for whom the authority of seniors is exercised by different persons at different times. More data would be required to determine the effect this might have on the relations of such children with their peers and their seniors.

The urban situation emphasizes the economic responsibilities of the head of the household, who is in most cases the husband and father. This may strengthen his jural position, particularly in the case of matrilineal peoples where the effective authority of the maternal uncle, living either at a considerable distance or even in the provinces, may be undermined. However, 'traditional' principles of descent appear to be secondary to economic considerations in determining the degree of control a man, whether nominally subject to the jural limitations of the avunculate or not, may exercise over his children.

Poverty weakens the authority of the head of the household, by eroding both his economic power over his dependants and the basis for the respect he is generally thought entitled to expect. This happens in various ways: by removing a powerful sanction or by forcing a breach of paternal obligations which therefore implies that the reciprocal obligation of obedience and respect need not be offered. The rich wield a powerful sanction over their children in that they can withhold pocket money or school fees as a punishment; this sanction is denied to the poor, particularly in the most deprived families where the head of household is unemployed and dependent on casual earnings and the contributions of his wife and children. Kazadi (1960) reports that many unemployed complained that they were despised by their children and their orders flouted, because they were no longer able to provide for them in a manner acceptable in the neighbourhood.

It is generally accepted in Kinshasa, even among the matrilineal Kongo, that a father has the duty to provide, not only the daily needs of children, but their training for adult life. The most usual way in which this is done is by sending them to school or by arranging an apprenticeship to a skilled craftsman. In more and more cases a man is unable to do this, and few women who are responsible for their children can earn enough to fulfil this obligation. Many teenagers are thus not provided by their parents with a means to establish themselves in the adult world.

The inability of Congolese parents to provide for their children may be extended by the very nature of urban life in the Congo. While there is a small proportion of the young who are the children of men and women born in Kinshasa and thus fully urbanized, many have parents who are recent immigrants from the country. They are unfamiliar with urban society and may retain behaviour which marks them off as provincial.[5] They can neither educate their children in urban values nor keep their respect. A symbol of the discontinuity that urbanization introduces into the values transmitted within the family is the fact that the city-born often speak its lingua franca before the vernacular of their parents.

SOCIALIZATION AND YOUTH GROUPS

In fully industrialized societies, the socialization of young members of the society entails training in occupational skills whose scope makes it necessary for specialized institutions to take over this aspect of the acculturative role of the domestic group. Schools are thus the means by which the young are equipped for adult life. In the modern Congo, this is only partially true, for schools are seen not as a necessary training but as a means to the social advancement of the younger generation. Nevertheless it is thought proper for parents to do their utmost to provide such advantages for their children. However, only a small proportion of Kinshasa's youth can go to school. Apart from the difficulty of finding the fees, there are only a limited number of school places. In 1960–61 there were 50,867 boys and 36,567 girls in school out of a total juvenile population of school age of about 140,000. Nearly two-thirds of the children were being occupied, instructed, and trained.[6]

Two years later, the number of school places cannot be said to have increased substantially whereas the juvenile population had increased to about 354,000. A round figure of 100,000 boys and girls in school during 1962–63 is probably a liberal estimate. Thus at the time of the study roughly only 29 per cent of school-age children were actually going to school.

What, then, does the majority of the juvenile population do with the time that the fortunate few spend in school? The circumstances of life in Kinshasa free the young from the supervision of parents or other senior kin to a considerable degree. Many women work, either to support their children or to supplement the earnings of their husband. Younger members of the household have few traditional domestic tasks to occupy them. This is particularly true of boys, for girls help with the younger children and with cooking and housework. However, there is often not enough to do to make these chores either onerous or time-consuming. As a result, while younger children are supervised and restricted in their movements, children over the age of ten have both freedom and opportunity to engage in activities outside the household. Some earn a little money in casual employment, although it is illegal to employ persons under eighteen for heavy work and children under fourteen even for light duties. Nevertheless such children are to be found in the markets, carrying baskets, touting for custom for stall-holders, running errands, and begging. Many resort to theft and confidence tricks of all sorts in order to obtain food and money. This is no new phenomenon in Kinshasa, as can be seen from articles written as early as 1955 (e.g. Charles, 1955), but it has been intensified by post-Independence events.

As an attempt to cope with what is seen as a social problem, many organizations have instituted youth associations which aim to provide occupation and some instruction for the city's youth. The different churches, including the Kimbanguist church, run youth groups as recreational bodies and offer some instruction as well. The emphasis, however, is on moral rather than practical instruction and, although office-holding in them may offer attractions to a few, they are not a functional alternative to the schools. Most of the political parties and some of the larger tribal associations have youth sections which played an important part in the canvassing that took place before the

1960 elections and during the political struggles that followed. With the disorganization of their parent bodies, the youth wings have also ceased to be effectual. During 1962–63 there was some attempt at reviving them, in part for welfare reasons, but also in order to take advantage of the dissatisfaction of youth with politicians with a view to strengthening the opposition parties, particularly ABAKO. There also exists a large number of other organized youth groups, most of them belonging to a federation of such groups, the Conseil de la Jeunesse. Leadership within the federation offers considerable attractions for the ambitious but all these groups are maintained, and to a certain degree controlled, by parent bodies and are thus evidence of adult concern with youth rather than autonomous youth groups. My impression is that they reach only a small proportion of young people.

This paper is concerned with a different type of youth group which is established as a voluntary association, not as part of the social programme of an adult organization. Such groups can thus be characterized as informal or spontaneous in contradistinction to the organized youth groups already described. They can also be distinguished from informal peer groups or cliques of friends by virtue of their self-conscious formalism. Members of such associations consider themselves to be a distinct group, with a name and hierarchy of office-holders, even though its duration as such may be relatively brief. I wish to consider two varieties of this type of group: street gangs; and political discussion groups, which flourish among students of secondary schools, technical institutions, and Lovanium University. The latter I propose to call scholars' associations to distinguish them from the students' organizations which are a feature of the structure of the educational institutions themselves. Both gangs and scholars' associations show common structural features but their activities and aims differ. Yet both take part in a 'youth culture' with distinctive characteristics, which I shall describe before discussing the groups themselves.

YOUTH CULTURE IN THE CITY

Young urbanites in Kinshasa participate in a teenage 'pop' culture which distinguishes them from their seniors in a manner familiar to us from our own society. This culture is permeated by the symbols and mythical figures of the cinema and advertising. A striking feature of it in Kinshasa is the 'Cowboys and Indians' motif, of which perhaps the dominant figure is 'Buffalo Bill'. He and his Indian opponents, who are also taken as symbolic for teenagers, represent the use of force in pursuing individual ambitions. Both cowboys (Buffalo Bill) and Indians fight openly for their aims; for this reason they are also, to a certain extent, asocial beings, representing competitiveness unrestrained by social mores. The names of gangs show a recurrent theme – the collectivity of powerful persons known from mass communications. Some names I collected were: Russians, Cowboys, Indians, Americans, and 'Onusiens' (ONU being the French version of UNO). The titles of gang leaders and other officers reflect the theme chosen, although lack of information results in some odd associations: the Onusiens were led by Khrushchev with Kennedy as second-in-command! The name Bill with various additions is a common sobriquet. Teenagers may also refer to themselves as 'Indians'.

Kindoubil[7] is the name for the teenage slang which is youth's diacritical sign in Kinshasa. It is thought of as a secret language, designed to be unintelligible to non-initiates such as newly arrived migrants and, particularly, adults. Raymaekers (unpublished MS) states that key terms are changed periodically when they have been current long enough for their meaning to have been discovered by outsiders. Whereas a large part of the vocabulary of *kindoubil* concerns activities which one might expect to be covert for fear of adult disapproval (for example, there is an extensive vocabulary relating to drugs and their use), there is also a considerable general vocabulary. Although Raymaekers (1963) discusses the language with reference to juvenile delinquency, my material would indicate that it is not purely a delinquent argot, but a slang whose use is widespread in Kinshasa. Speaking it has several interrelated meanings: it marks the speaker off as resident in Kinshasa, a sophisticated urbanite rather than a country bumpkin; it serves as a perpetual reminder of the separation between youth and the world of adults; and, by providing the means to talk freely about activities which are frowned on by adult society, it defies the mores of that society. The first two aspects are closely related, for, as I have said, in general youth is more committed to the urban way of life than is the majority of its seniors. Fashions in dress serve also as diacritical signs to mark off the young urbanite both from the parental generation and from those of his contemporaries who are only newly arrived from the provinces.

Young people also appear to differ from the older generation in their view of heterosexual relations and roles, although it would perhaps be more accurate to say that the young accept more fully a view of relations between the sexes that is only partially accepted in the adult world. It is common to find this view described as 'Western' and 'modern'. In brief, it is the acceptance of the idea that relations between the sexes based on mutual attraction and qualities of character are to be distinguished from the institutionalized bonds of marriage. The essence of the relationship is a voluntary association of two people that is based on sentiment and a flow of gifts between them, and is unsanctioned by anything other than the desire to maintain the relationship. This type of relationship is distinguished from the relationship between spouses, for young Congolese, in that it implies companionship as well as sexual relations whereas the conjugal relationship includes joint leisure activities only rarely. Lovers enjoy themselves together visiting bars and markets; the educated write long letters exchanging news and their views of life and professing their sentiments in flowery language. The pair may set up house together or eventually get married. Usually, however, love affairs are broken off and most young men and girls have several affairs before they are married.

This conception of romantic love has been called European, and in Kinshasa certainly songs and films in the European idiom serve to disseminate and encourage it. Advertising also acts as a medium for the education of the Congolese public in European personal values. However, the Congolese interpretation of the ideas behind such advertising is perhaps more literal. This is that success in the sphere of sexual life is a demonstration of personal superiority. Sexual success results from physical attractions (smartness of dress, clearness of skin, vitality, etc.) and also from personal qualities of persuasion and charm. This success earns the successful the admiration and envy of others, who thereby acknowledge his superiority. These values are firmly held by young Congolese, some of whom take the claims of advertisements almost too literally. Certain objects (for example scent and scent bottles) have acquired magical properties and feature as essential ingredients in love-spells. Those young people who can afford it spend a considerable sum on cosmetics, which are believed to have a quasi-magical effect on a person's sexual attractiveness.

These are new ideas of what constitutes success. The competitiveness of economic and political life is mirrored here in personal relations. The successful young man is the man with many mistresses who are also desired by others. This type of personal fame depends on the only qualities over which the juvenile has control, his personal physical and mental attributes. This fact is central to the values of youth groups, as will be seen later. It also has some importance in adult life.[8] Since sexual success is so important to Kinshasa's youth it is not surprising that there is a rich and varied pharmacopoeia of magic associated with it. Raymaekers discusses in detail (1963, pp. 305–306) the magic designed to enchant a girl who is desired or to give the owner of the charm sexual irresistibility. Here only certain features of the magic of sexual conquest will be noted. There are two themes: the acquisition of power over the desired object and the enhancement of personal prestige and influence. It is clear, then, that underlying the sexual life of young people there is competition for personal success and the associated prestige.

One final characteristic of teenage culture must be noted: this is the prevalence of drug-taking. The usual drug is Indian hemp, which is easily obtained and relatively cheap. Raymaekers notes (1963, p. 300) that in one commune one in every fifty-six houses was involved in the drug trade. Adults also use drugs, but adult society disapproves of this activity whereas the young do not. Motives for drug-taking cluster round two ideas: that it dulls discomfort (especially that of hunger) and increases sexual desire and performance; that is, it improves the individual's ability to gain status within the cultural mores of youth. In addition, use of drugs appears almost ritual in gang meetings, which often consist of the communal smoking or eating of hemp in various forms. Hemp thus serves as a general symbol of the solidarity of youth in opposition to authority in general and its use serves as a solidarity-enhancing ritual for the subgroups within the general category it denotes.

Teenage culture is thus competitive, urban, and self-consciously distinct from that of society in general. In describing it, it has been impossible to avoid the implication that all young people are equally committed. This must now be corrected. There are variations in the degree to which particular individuals participate in the world of *kindoubil* and subscribe to its values. In particular, the significance of taking drugs differs among members of the gangs and among the scholars, where it is an individual pastime, to be indulged in with a few friends, but not a group ritual. In addition, there is more prestige for the scholars in demonstrating their education by using French or scattering their conversations in the lingua franca with French terms, than in using *kindoubil*, although they do not totally disdain the latter, merely use it less frequently. So that generally teenage culture as represented in individuals shows a variety of facets which may be emphasized or ignored by different individuals and groups according to their own view of themselves and their place in the city's social life.

I now turn to the examination of the two types of youth association: street gangs and scholars' associations.

STREET GANGS

As their name implies, street gangs recruit their members by locality. They are associations based on a street or part of a street and usually have well-defined territories within which they operate. Raymaekers indicates (1963, p. 121) that in 1961 street gangs included all classes of young people but that later the cleavage between educated and uneducated youth resulted in the withdrawal of the educated from the street gangs, so that an element of class definition has altered the composition of neighbourhood groups. My information confirms this development for areas which show populations of a wide range of socio-economic class. Many communes are more homogeneous and in these communes street gangs try to include all available recruits. Tribal affiliation does not appear to constitute a basis for gang formations although it is said to do so in some areas. Membership is usually informal although some gangs insist on a rite of qualification, usually proof of the ability to smoke hemp or engage in the gang's pursuits with success.

Most street gangs consist of boys although girls may be associated with them as the mistresses of older members. In some areas groups of girls are associated as a body with a local gang and a few gangs are alleged to have members of both sexes. The main emphasis is, however, on the group of boys between puberty and the early twenties. Age is a stratifying criterion and younger boys are used as messengers and helpers in exchange for the prestige they acquire by association with the gang. However, although age provides a general ranking, leadership within a gang is fiercely competitive. Rivalry for control of a gang may lead to individuals leaving the group, or the gang itself may split or dissolve. Thus the size of a gang at any moment in time is a function of its structure and the nature of the leadership within it, as well as of the prestige accruing to the group for its activities. Large gangs normally comprise a wide age-range, show a well-established leadership with an established hierarchy of subordinates, and have a record of successful defence of their territory against the incursions of outsiders.

Gangs usually meet at convenient public places within the neighbourhood, but in the older parts of the city they may also establish a permanent headquarters in a small bar or shop. In some of these the members paint on the wall the name of the gang, with the titles of its officers underneath, surrounding the list with coloured decorations and drawings. The proprietor agrees to the association, either because of the profit he draws from having a regular clientele or because he is forced to do so by threats to intimidate other customers or break up the bar. Whether there is a criminal association between bar-owner and certain gangs it is not possible to determine without further study. Some gangs may use an abandoned shack or the room of the leader; the newspapers in Kinshasa occasionally printed stories of the kidnapping of young girls by gangs, which implies that established gangs usually have some building to house their meetings.

The activities of street gangs vary from the mischievous to the criminal. The public regard them with suspicion and even fear, and so are ready to condemn all street gangs as delinquent.

However it seems clear that delinquency is the result of activities pursued not entirely for their own sake but as a means to certain common ends. Where these ends can be achieved without coming into conflict with society at large (and some of them, such as theft and drug-taking, cannot be) deliquency is not an inevitable aspect of a street gang's existence. These common aims are: first, to establish and maintain a 'territory', some geographical area in which the gang can dictate to juveniles. The concept of the territory includes the sole right to recruit members within it, sexual access to young girls living within it, and the right to use the area to satisfy requirements for money, food, and drugs. A large part of a gang's time is spent in fighting other gangs for exclusive control of a territory or in endeavouring to encroach on the territories of other gangs, particularly by kidnapping or seducing the girls 'belonging' to other gangs. A second aim is to provide the gang with food, money, and drugs for its communal feasts. Members of gangs who are in part-time employment can contribute legitimate earnings to the common fund; others may give pocket money, or gifts received or begged from kin. However, given the general economic distress of Kinshasa's citizens in 1962–63, it was likely that most gangs would have to resort to theft or organized deception in order to satisfy their wants. In the case of the most deprived sections of the population the gang's activities might be vital to the support of its members. Nevertheless, it is known that street gangs exist, as they formerly did in Kinshasa, where near-starvation is not a recurrent threat, so that economic deprivation cannot be said to account for the existence of these groups, although it probably accounts for the increase both in the amount of delinquent activity and in the degree to which organized and violent crime has become a particular gang's main activity.

In the period of my study, certain parts of the city, in particular the squatter areas, were especially subject to the activities of criminal gangs, who would set out to impose a virtual curfew in the territory under their control. The curfew was backed by violence directed against anyone found outside his house compound after a certain hour. Adults returning home late would be assaulted and young people who were not gang members were attacked. Gangs were particularly active in the middle and at the end of the month (for employees are paid on these days) but robbery was not their only aim, for victims were usually attacked before being robbed. So widespread were these nocturnal predations that in areas that were badly lit or ineffectively policed (of which there were many) a curfew was indeed maintained. Although the inhabitants of Kinshasa who suffered these attacks did not distinguish between youth groups and adult criminals when speaking of robbery with violence, it was clear that in many cases the 'bandits', as they were called, were relatively young. It is significant that all such footpads were referred to as *la jeunesse bandite* – bandit youth. These criminal activities show, to a heightened degree, the mixture of aims that is characteristic of street gangs: the attainment of power, and of a reputation that ensures their dominance over both adults and peers, and the acquisition of material goods. In some areas gangs were known to have directed their curfew specifically against adults, an interesting demonstration of the extreme form the teenage/adult opposition could take.

It is not easy to discover what proportion of the juvenile population is involved in the street gangs. It is clear that not all the eligible youth of a locality belong to its gang or gangs, because an important concern of each gang is the recruitment of new members. Schoolchildren are expected, by both adults and their less fortunate peers, to stay out of the gangs; they may often be persecuted by the gangs for this reason. One schoolboy described it as virtually impossible to avoid the street gangs, and said that this was particularly true for girls, who were in effect forced to take a gang member as a lover in order to ensure protection from the gang as a whole. Another youth from a different quarter stated that he and other secondary schoolboys in the neighbourhood had been forced to form a group for their own protection and did not go out alone. Others apparently pay to be left unmolested. Raymaekers has shown (1963, pp. 120–122) that, as the economic situation worsened, the opposition between youth in schools and the unoccupied grew in intensity between 1961 and 1963. The opportunities that education apparently offered the fortunate scholars became greater, whereas those for the illiterate dwindled rapidly, and the division between the two groups became a matter for hostility. Before 1961 gangs apparently often contained a mixture of both types; by 1963 they were largely confined to those not in school. Another change is that gangs are no longer restricted to heterogeneous or 'poor' neighbourhoods: many informants remarked that, whereas formerly street gangs were characteristic of the Old City, now they were to be found even in prosperous suburbs, such as Bandalungwa, a white-collar housing estate. This spread can be related to the decreasing opportunities for employment even for the children of the wealthy.

SCHOLARS' ASSOCIATIONS

To turn now to the voluntary groups I have referred to as scholars' associations, who recruit their members from the section of the juvenile population which contributes least to the formation of street gangs: those in schools and training colleges, who are, *de facto*, the children of the more prosperous. The scholars' association is typically a small group recruited within the organizational framework of a school, formal youth movement, or church. The associations are more restricted in age and tend to interest boys in later adolescence, although some include younger boys as well. Girls do not usually participate. Unlike the street gangs these groups are 'respectable'; they must, however, register themselves with the authorities, giving the names of their office-holders as well as a brief description of the organization, which may not be more than a fuller version of its name. Many of them do this; I was unable to obtain a full list from the authorities, but, of some fifty-one registered groups, including the youth sections of political parties and churches, fourteen were scholars' associations.[9]

These associations are recruited within an organization and have no territorial base. They prepare elaborate, usually written, constitutions, with wide-ranging programmes for political, social, and economic reform. The groups uphold democratic procedures for the election of officers in theory, but the founders normally assume the major titles, which are those of a political party – president, secretary, etc. Offices may be offered to individuals whom the group wishes to recruit and a characteristic feature of the groups, which duplicates that of existing political parties, is the proliferation of titles. Some groups may contain very few members without formal office, or even none. Membership is formal and an obligation to pay a regular subscription is usually written into the constitution, but actually contributions are somewhat irregular. The aims of the group are generally vague and idealistic, at least on paper, and have a clear bias towards political activity or, less commonly, social welfare. The elaboration of a constitution generally exhausts the initial energies of the founders, and it is my impression that membership lapses as struggles for control of the group eventually disintegrate it. Raymaekers (1963, p. 121) states that these groups have a duration he describes as 'fairly long', but my data suggest that scholars' associations suffer the same strains as street gangs: leadership struggles tend to disrupt the group, although these conflicts take place at the level of diplomacy and verbal debate, violence being disapproved. In this the scholars' associations differ strikingly from the street gangs; their typical activity is talk and their approved skills are those which most closely resemble the qualities of the adult politicians they emulate.

THE STRUCTURE OF VOLUNTARY ASSOCIATIONS AMONG THE YOUNG

Street gangs and scholars' associations represent two poles near which most of the juvenile population can be grouped. These extremes are the schoolboy and the unemployed (*chômeur*). In his analysis of the youth of Kinshasa, Raymaekers (1963, p. 21) presents his findings on youth groups in tabular form, which emphasizes the differences between them. My impression is that recent changes have had the effect of polarizing the two types; the differences were formerly less striking.

I wish to examine the structural similarities rather than the differences between the groups, similarities which indicate that they are sub-types of a similar phenomenon. The delinquent activities of street gangs are a function of their lack of occupation (in both senses of the word) and their inability to obtain entry to adult society via regular employment. The emphasis on Western associational organization found in pompous florescence among the educated young relates also to the world of adults from which they are, at the moment, still excluded. In a sense, both types of group are a reaction to exclusion and as such can be compared to tribal associations. Like tribal associations, the youth groups react to exclusion by emphasizing their own exclusive culture and language. Both gangs and scholars' associations underline the cultural distinctness and autonomy of the young. The argot which is common to both explicitly prevents communication between adults and teenagers, by excluding adults. Reformism and delinquency can both be seen as symbols of opposition to established adult society.

However violently teenagers and adults oppose one another, the distinction, which is the greater for not being emphasized, lies not between teenagers and adults but between the world of teenagers and that of children proper. In Kinshasa, the structure of the domestic group within which a child is normally confined until puberty or its approach allows for little competition. Within the household, whether it is based on a legal marriage, common-law union, or group of kin, the child is subject to a clear hierarchy of authorities, with definite obligations towards him. Their positions, like the child's, are a function of age, sex, and kinship status. While greater or lesser contributions to the household economy may alter the effective power of particular individuals, in general their status is fixed. Ranking within a domestic group is ascribed rather than achieved.

Within youth groups, members are ranked by achievement, not by virtue of ascribed characteristics. Age may be a stratifying criterion but leadership is achieved by exercising initiative and successfully eliminating rivals of whatever stratum. Scholars' associations provide openly for competition by instituting elective posts, and in both types of group a leader must aim to maintain his leadership by preventing rivals displacing him or splitting the group. The youth groups thus differ sharply from domestic groups and resemble adult society in their emphasis on achievement.

Despite the obligations of kinship and the use of tribal loyalties in a number of situations, Kinshasa is a competitive society. Rank and power depend on achievement. The exclusion of youth from access to the means essential to engage in competition, economic resources, means that, with youth groups, this competitiveness is phrased in terms of resources over which they do have control. These are personal qualities: physical or mental. Sexual rivalry, physical violence, and intellectual debate have this in common: they are the means by which individuals may demonstrate their superiority and so win both prestige and power. They are the shadows of the political and economic competition of adult society. In the case of some scholars' associations this may even be recognized by the participants. One leader of such an association told me that even if his association met with failure he would not regret the time he had spent on it because it would have given him experience in how to control people (*controller les gens*).

Similarity between the aims of adult society and youth groups should not, however, obscure an important characteristic of the latter. Their goals do not normally form part of the system of goals for which adults compete; success in the juvenile world does not equal success in adult society. In this respect the street gangs and the scholars' associations differ. Members of certain street gangs were said by the public who complained of them in 1962 and 1963 to have become very rich from their nefarious activities. They could thus be said to have achieved the adult goal of prosperity but by socially disapproved means. Scholars' associations, on the other hand, might achieve a legitimate place in the adult hierarchy through recognition by the authorities and membership of the Conseil de la Jeunesse, which had a certain official position. An important youth group might hope to acquire a politician as patron and, though few that were not founded by politicians as pressure groups had done so during the period of my study, the goal was not completely unrealistic. Nevertheless, a youth group that appeared to support politicians who opposed the government might be proscribed. The degree of disjunction with adult goals is thus not complete but few youth groups enable their leaders to achieve parity with adults. The great majority of members contend fiercely for insubstantial goals which become an end in themselves rather than a means to force an entry into the world of adult status.

YOUTH GROUPS AND SOCIAL CHANGE

In that youth groups clearly have the effect of teaching their members the social skills of adult society, they can be said to be socially adaptive. In addition, they facilitate the adolescent's transition from the domestic group to the world of adult society. Youth groups achieve this by generating solidary relations which derive from voluntary association rather than ascription by kinship. In some (usually small-scale) societies there is little contrast between the values upon which the domestic group is founded and those of the wider society: rank and power derive largely from ascriptive criteria in both. Kinshasa is clearly not a society of this type. Yet there exist institutionalized means by which the transition from dependent childhood to full adult status is mediated. The most important of these was the school, explicitly a training-ground for the 'modern', i.e. Westernized, Congolese. Another training-ground was apprenticeship. Yet for many young citizens of Kinshasa the peer group, in whatever form, is equally important. For the young migrant from the villages it is vital, for it bridges the discontinuity between village and town, teaching a new cultural pattern.

The socializing function of teenage groups is provided for the fortunate youth in Kinshasa by education. Academic competition parallels the rivalry of members of a gang, although in this case the goals are useful steps to attainment in the adult world. The school provides a world where voluntary association among equals is the basis of social relations, although the role of teachers makes an important difference to the structure of relations in school. Nevertheless, as I have already remarked, schoolboys participate less in street gangs. They also appear to participate less in other associations. I have the impression that students join scholars' associations less frequently than the out-of-school boys belong to gangs. Thus membership of an institution which mediates between childhood and the adult world appears to perform some at least of the functions of teenage groups. Other institutions in non-industrialized societies may have a similar function. The nature of the activities of members of the age-set immediately post-initiation in some East African societies would seem to represent an institutionalization of this intercalary stage which emphasizes the distance between its members and 'normal' society. The marginal position of *moran* in Arusha and Sambura society[10] is reflected in the almost antisocial qualities of character they are expected to display. These qualities serve to distinguish the intermediate stage of youth from that of childhood and that of responsible adulthood.

There is some evidence that youth groups in Kinshasa too can be considered part of the 'normal' social organization of the city. Their existence antedates the crisis of 1960 and in some respects they can be regarded as an aspect of one phase of the life-cycle. In times of normal employment, members of youth groups ceased to participate in these activities as they became increasingly involved in the competitive adult world of socio-economic ranking. Even in the period of my study it was noticeable that youths in full employment were members of youth groups less often than their unoccupied contemporaries. Marriage effectively cuts them off from the world of youth altogether.

These remarks need some qualification. Kinshasa is to a large extent part of a modern world that is committed to change, that is in which change is both expected and regarded positively, as opposed to a society in which people see the social order as unchanging. In 'progressive' as distinct from 'traditionalist'[11] societies, it is not expected that the younger generation should resemble its seniors exactly, even though it eventually takes over the same social roles. Thus the differences in outlook which what I have called 'youth culture' uses to assert its autonomy may indeed act to change the society with the passage of time by altering the playing of adult roles. Peer groups among the young may then be seen as the means by which what Mitchell (1966, p. 44) calls processive change is accomplished.

In Kinshasa, however, we have a situation in which violent and rapid change has occurred. Moreover, there is the effect of situational change (Mitchell, 1966, p. 44) on large numbers of individuals to consider. To take the latter first. Youth groups can be said to facilitate situational change by encapsulating the young immigrant in a group which imposes its cultural patterns on him. It is significant that neither scholars' associations nor street gangs concern themselves with tribal membership; they emphasize urban mores and for the purpose use a uniquely urban language. Tribal associations largely concern themselves with adult tribesmen, although some have youth wings (usually as part of their political role), so that the voluntary, informal youth groups, in particular the street gangs, are of vital importance to the young newcomer from the provinces.

I have indicated where possible the effect that recent changes in the Congo have had on urban youth groups; undoubtedly these changes have not themselves caused youth groups to appear for the first time. Politically there is a paradox as far as the young are concerned: while the transfer of power to the Congolese has meant that the powerful offices are filled by compatriots, the latter are all young men (the Congo had no experienced political leaders), so that new opportunities, except in the rather hazardous sphere of national politics, are still limited. Economically there have been two major repercussions. Deprivation has driven more street gangs to outright delinquency. Unemployment has made the transition from the marginal position of youth to adult responsibility ever more difficult. Far more youths are excluded from a 'normal' adult existence. This has meant that the upper age-limit of street-gang members has slowly risen and these older youths appear likely to form the nucleus of a class of permanent criminals. In addition, the products of secondary schools find their opportunities curtailed and leave school only to enter the world of the unemployed. The street gangs are thus in the process of re-acquiring the educated members that Raymaekers (1963) showed them to have lost between 1961 and 1963. These youths oppose adult society in a much more revolutionary way; their disenchantment with politicians makes them inflammable material for the revolutionary. The Mulelist uprising of 1965 made good use of it.

NOTES

1. I am grateful to Mrs E. Hope, Dr Philip Mayer, and Professor Michael Banton for their comments on drafts of this paper.

2. In addition to my own material I shall use more detailed information on street gangs and the activities of young people collected by Paul Raymaekers over a number of years (Raymaekers, 1960–61, 1963).

3. The Alliance des BaKongo, founded originally as a cultural association of the Kongo-speaking peoples in Léopoldville and the party of Joseph Kasavubu, the first President of the independent Congo Republic.

4. Dr V. Pons, in a private communication, has confirmed that he found a similar situation in Stanleyville in 1965.

5. Cf. Eisenstadt (1956, pp. 171–178).

6. Roels-Ceulemans (1960).

7. The term uses the Bantu prefix ki-, which indicates a language but which is also explained as referring to *Ki*nshasa; *indoubil* is a corruption of *indien* or *hindou* and Bill, meaning Buffalo Bill. Young inhabitants of Kinshasa may also refer to themselves as *les indoubils*.

8. Success with the opposite sex is also considered an attribute of the powerful personality in adult life and a man of repute will earn prestige from accounts of his numerous and glamorous mistresses, notwithstanding the still-powerful influence of the Catholic Church and the need for respectability. Such a reputation makes a man 'known', i.e. establishes his name as a person whose personality is commanding, and is an aspect of the public relations campaign that a would-be politician must pursue. In the adult world, however, it is only one of many ways of gaining prestige; among youth it has far greater importance.

9. I also know of one which was not registered.

10. See Gulliver (1963, pp. 220–221) and Spencer (1965).

11. I use these terms as a convenient means of referring to the two broad categories I establish above and not in any evaluative sense.

REFERENCES

CHARLES, V. 1955. La Protection de l'Enfance Délinquante à Léopoldville. *Zaïre* **10** (3).

EISENSTADT, S. N. 1956. *From Generation to Generation.* London: Routledge & Kegan Paul.

GULLIVER, P. H. 1963. *Social Control in an African Society: A Study of the Arusha: Agricultural Masai of Northern Tanganyika.* London: Routledge & Kegan Paul.

KAZADI, F. 1960. *La Vie du Chômeur à Léopoldville.* Mémoire de Licence en Sciences Sociales. Université Lovanium, Léopoldville.

MITCHELL, J. C. 1966. Theoretical Orientations in African Urban Studies. In M. Banton (ed.), *The Social Anthropology of Complex Societies.* A.S.A. Monographs 4. London: Tavistock Publications.

RAYMAEKERS, P. 1960–61. *Matériaux pour une Etude Sociologique de la Jeunesse Africaine du Milieu Extra-Coutumier de Léopoldville.* Institut de Recherches Economiques et Sociaux. Notes et Documents no. 1. Université Lovanium, Léopoldville.

—— 1963. Prédélinquance et Délinquance Juvénile à Léopoldville. *Inter-African Labour Institute Bulletin* (*Quarterly Review of Labour Problems in Africa*) **10** (3): 298–328. London.

ROELS-CEULEMANS, M. J. 1960. *Problèmes de la Jeunesse à Léopoldville: Analyse Quantitative de la Population.* Institut de Recherches Economiques et Sociaux. Notes et Documents no. 18/SC 3. Université Lovanium, Léopoldville.

SPENCER, P. 1965. *The Samburu: A Study of Gerontocracy in a Nomadic Tribe.* London: Routledge & Kegan Paul; Berkeley, Calif.: University of California Press.

William Wilder

Socialization and Social Structure in a Malay Village

INTRODUCTORY REMARKS

Professor Fortes has recently reiterated the principle of structural opposition which, he says, 'has its roots in the structure of the nuclear field of social reproduction' (Fortes, 1958) – 'the constellation of parents and children in which the complementarity of the sexes and the polarity of successive generations are the critical factors' (Fortes, 1967, p. 10). This paradigm bears a close similarity to Parsons's view of the nuclear family: 'The two fundamental axes of differentiation of the nuclear family as a small group' are categorization by sex, and the difference of power (superior/inferior) exhibited in the relations of proximate generations (Parsons & Bales, 1956, p. 121).

Both these paradigms derive from observations of the family or domestic group in relation to social structure, and both presume mechanisms of differentiation or opposition which, in the views of the authors, are virtually indispensable in the socialization of *pre-adolescent* children. Beyond that phase of socialization, differences of view arise. I think it is questionable whether socialization can be regarded as 'complete' by the time of initiation ceremonies and/or sexual maturity, as Fortes appears to hold, even for the more 'primitive' cultures. He says. 'The basic educational tasks required to produce an adult person capable of playing a full part in maintaining and transmitting the social capital seem to be complete at about the same time as the attainment of physical and sexual maturity . . .' (1958, p. 10), and he speaks in this context of a 'finished product'. He admits, however, that the period of 'jural infancy' may extend into the stage of physical adulthood.

What seems to be 'complete' at around puberty is rather *the family's* role in socialization. Referring to American society,

Parsons states that after puberty 'the problem of a clear delineation of the social structure in which socialization takes place is much more difficult than at the earlier level' (Parsons & Bales, 1956, p. 125). In this phase the community at large plays the most important part in the processes of socialization. In Parson's socialization scheme ('norm'), the analogy between small group task performance and socialization in the nuclear family (as a small group) becomes more difficult to apply.

On these views, the paradigm is applicable throughout socialization but the role of the family/domestic group is reduced or eliminated for children after they attain sexual

FIGURE 1 *A paradigm*

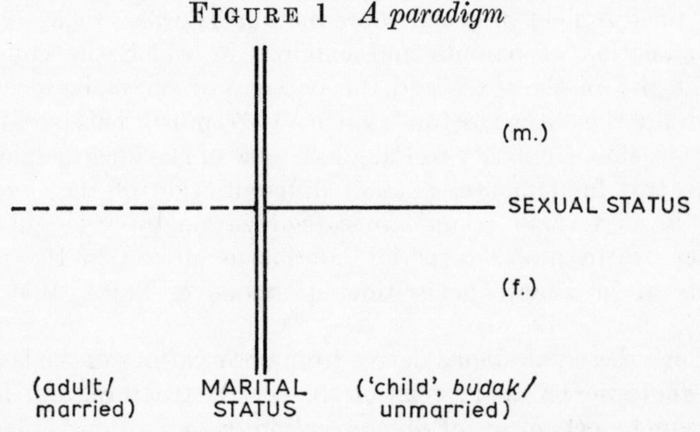

maturity. I shall take the position in this paper that socialization must be regarded as the process of social differentiation taking place throughout the entire jurally pre-adult period of the individual's life. In concrete terms, the period of socialization will be understood to correspond with the *unmarried* phase. Thus the problem becomes one of discovering what continuities there are in socialization in terms of the critical oppositions and differentiations that constitute the paradigm as applied in a variety of situations, and not simply in the domestic group.

The present paper is concerned with Malay socialization and social structure in the phase of the life-cycle from male circumcision to marriage, that is, from the point of view of the category of more or less sexually mature persons whom village Malays refer to in certain contexts as *budak*.[1] I propose to examine socialization in this phase by treating *the village* as a socializing unit, using the paradigm already developed by reference to the 'nuclear field' (*Figure 1*).

Figure 1 is a simple two-dimensional matrix for arranging data according to significant contrasts at the village level. The single horizontal rule (partly broken) indicates sexual status (opposition of sex); the double vertical rules indicate marital status (the categories married and unmarried).

While it serves to emphasize the critical factors, a paradigm does not, of course, *explain* the facts. More immediate and specific interpretations are suggested by certain empirical observations (from which, indeed, this paper grew):

1. the fact of male circumcision and the more or less straightforward question of its significance;
2. the marked segregation of the sexes from circumcision or earlier;
3. the conspicuousness of virtually all circumcised/unmarried boys in spending a large part of their time apparently doing and saying little or nothing and instead acting as spectators.

The last two observations raise a particular problem that makes the data somewhat difficult to deal with, viz. the virtual absence of the more formal, 'positive' systems of action which, perhaps for convenience, one would have hoped to see – clubs, 'gangs', schools (none after the age of twelve for most children), and games; and the restrictions on heterosexual relationships and work.

To facilitate handling of the data, it seems reasonable to postulate, as indeed do Fortes and Parsons, fields, or 'content', which are of more or less prime importance in systems of socialization generally, in addition to the 'structures' of *Figure 1*. Fortes states that the basic educational tasks of domestic groups are centred on a paramount concern of society at large, that is, the regular and adequate replenishment of persons capable of productive and reproductive activities in society (1958, p. 10). In Parsons's general theory of socialization the two dominant aims of adolescent socialization are family of procreation, and occupation (Parsons & Bales, 1956, p. 123f.). From this (admittedly limited) consensus and the observations already given for the Malays I studied, there seem to emerge two objects, or categories, of socialization in the phase after circumcision/puberty: sexual behaviour and work. I would maintain that the socialization of sexual behaviour and the socialization of work are specific 'problems' in any social system, and that socialization formulated in such terms is capable of observation through the paradigm set out in *Figure 1*. Socialization is therefore transitive, it must be socialization *of* something.

Such a formulation immediately throws into relief a striking and problematic feature of Malay socialization: this is the apparently equally (or nearly equally) *restricted* behaviour in the areas of *both* sex and work, especially in the case of boys during the phase with which we shall be concerned.

In what follows, then, I shall attempt to give a general description of socialization from school-leaving (and circumcision) to marriage and explain this in relation to social structure. Part of my analysis will be devoted to explaining the possible significance of the 'double negative' mentioned. I hope to show that it is possible to resolve this and some other difficulties in understanding Malay socialization without resorting, as some writers have done, to psychoanalytic speculations or historical-causal factors.[2]

My examination is by no means exhaustive. The materials to be cited were collected almost incidentally in a study carried out in 1964–66 of a Malay village in central Malaya.[3] Moreover, I treat the data from one point of view, that of 'dynamic social theory' (see Firth, 1964), in attempting to embrace discontinuity and movement within a given system. Such an approach would appear a natural one in studying socialization, but it is plainly not the only one possible. I take the opportunity during the course of my analysis to sound notes of caution in discussing other attempts that have been made to treat comparable problems in Malaysian studies. If in the end I can provide tentative answers to, or even tentative questions about, some of the outstanding perplexities, this may enable further investigations, by myself or others, to proceed on firmer ground.

The background to the field of study may be summarized briefly. Malays are for the most part peasants and are settled in many parts of Southeast Asia. They are Shafi'i Muslims and have a sophisticated culture and an ancient literary tradition.

For the States of Malaya (West Malaysia), excluding Singapore, the total Malay population was estimated at nearly 4 million in 1964. Roughly three-quarters may be classified as 'rural', or villagers. These villagers – young people especially – have in recent years been increasingly affected by bureaucratic administration, state primary education, and the modern media: the cinema and the transistor radio. My conclusions are valid mainly for this sector. The rules enforceable in the villages are probably not observed as widely in towns, even though Malays in towns preserve in many ways a strong rural background.[4]

BOUNDARIES IN THE LIFE-CYCLE

I have already suggested that socialization can conveniently be considered as having an upper limit in marriage rather than in sexual maturity; and that I am concerned with the important phase of the life-cycle among Malays that immediately precedes marriage. In this phase, as stated, Malay children are most frequently known as *budak* ('youngster');[5] towards the end of it they may be referred to as *bujang* ('bachelor') and *anak dara* ('virgin', 'spinster'). In chronological terms, children can be said to begin the phase at about the age of twelve and to end it several years later in marriage – for girls at around sixteen to eighteen, for boys around eighteen to twenty.

Verbal and age classifications, however, are only approximations, and are in some contexts too narrow or too wide. More distinctive are ceremonials, school, and dress, and the differences between the sexes for each. For boys the boundaries are comparatively well signposted. Entry into the immediately premarital phase is marked by circumcision (*sunat*), in addition to school-leaving, which is at present (1965) at twelve when the boy finishes primary school. For circumcision there is no ideal age, except approximately. Circumcision can take place from seven or eight to fourteen. Thus it may or may not coincide with school-leaving. A boy may leave school early and be circumcised later, or the order may be reversed. In my experience, the two appeared to coincide closely at about eleven to thirteen years. Actual puberty is always slightly later than circumcision.

For girls, the transition and the period itself are far less clearly defined. Most apparent is the shift from primary school, which is coeducational, to a distinctively female domain, viz. housekeeping. There is no attempt to bar girls from school, but they do tend to leave one or two years before boys. Thus social changes for females seem to take place, even more than for boys, by degrees, without strongly marked cultural boundaries. For all girls there are sooner or later the usual physical changes (e.g. menstruation). I would judge that it is with the physical and physiological changes of sexual maturity that all those girls who do not go beyond primary school enter definitively into the tasks of housekeeping by helping in the parental household.

There is in the few cases of daughters of wealthier parents an especially marked tendency to stay inside or near the parents' house almost all the time. With suitable reservations, this may be called 'seclusion', the result of which is that certain girls have a markedly whiter skin at the time of marriage, a very desirable thing.[6]

On the other hand, the *farther* the progress in school beyond primary level for (some) girls, the greater the similarity of their life to that of boys. In 1965, state education beyond primary level was available only at places approximately ten or more miles from the village I studied, and entailed boarding at the schools during term-time. During that year, there were five girls at secondary school, as compared with seven boys. In this situation the marked social dissimilarity of boys and girls does not appear as strongly as among those boys and girls who are more or less 'confined' to the village.

There is a female circumcision (clitoridectomy), also called *sunat* like the boy's circumcision, and a village woman specialist who in the context is called *mudin* ('circumciser'), but this operation is apparently carried out on very young girls before the age of about three (cf. Djamour, 1959, pp. 107–108; see note 29).

The period is for both sexes marked by certain styles of dress. At about school-leaving age, when they cast off school uniforms, boys and girls – but more especially boys – begin to show greater concern for their dress. Boys acquire underwear, fine shirts, and long, very tight-fitting trousers for wearing in their leisure hours. The trouser style is sometimes called *yanki*, i.e. American, and is derived from cowboy films of American,

American-style Japanese, or other origins. No sunglasses or brash colours are worn, and the effect is on the whole neat and restrained.

Girls undergo less marked changes of dress. They probably begin earlier than boys to care for their clothing – covering the upper part of their bodies consistently, and wearing the undershorts that serve as underpants for women at all times rather than sporadically, as seems to be the case with pre-pubescent girls. All girls acquire brassières later, as their breasts develop.

As in schooling, there are in dress some instructive exceptions in the typical girl's transition. There is generally little overt prejudice against Western-style dresses for older girls – and simple little dresses are almost universal for girl toddlers. Several older girls in the village owned dresses, but there were two girls in particular who wore them long after their age-mates had adopted the women's characteristically patterned *sarong* and *baju* (blouse). One of these girls is the youngest daughter of a retired schoolteacher, and the pair lived near one another in the village. They were also together in middle school near the District capital. Both girls were clearly 'progressive' in matters of dress, in that they adopted dresses for everyday wear (which is not to say exclusively). This means not simply that there are certain cultural influences at work, as in the case of boys' clothes, but also that, in school and dress, these two girls (and some others) closely paralleled aspects of the 'male' transition.

In short, there are different kinds of boundaries that serve for Malays to 'mark off' a period of their children's lives. It is important to notice that these boundaries, at the lower end, need not always be clear – or even present – in terms of social recognition. At neither end – more particularly with regard to the upper end, or marrying age – can parallels to *social* transition necessarily be fixed even approximately by judging from the *physiological* situation. Chronology aside, I would venture that an 'average' (male) sequence runs as follows: school-leaving; circumcision; new dress, and a keen consciousness about dress and style; puberty; marriage. These are various 'signs' of transition; they are associated with different aspects of status – aspects that are not equally well recognized and that nowadays involve an increasing latitude of choice among them.

The kinds of variation in chronological succession and marking of boundaries are mainly related to economic level. If a child, particularly a boy, leaves school before finishing the Sixth Standard (sixth year of school),[7] it is usually because of illness, or poverty.[8] For such a boy the boundaries of the life-cycle are much less clear. He may not be able to afford good clothes, or even be circumcised. (When a boy is poor, that is, if his household is poor, there is of course less opportunity for wearing fine clothes anyway.) The end of the phase in marriage comes sooner for poorer boys and girls; they are married at seventeen or eighteen and fifteen or sixteen respectively. The evidence I have points, in general, towards a correlation of: economic situation of the household, marrying age of the children, and the initiation of demands for work upon the children, especially the boys.

The village I studied is one where differences of wealth are not, for various reasons,[9] easy to show off. The grosser distinctions, such as large pension/small pension/no pension, large house/small house, etc., do exist and are recognized. But distinctions of wealth and refinement seem to be *best* displayed by 'managing' the lives of *budak*; the 'display' consists in increasing the degree of dependency of the unmarried children as far as possible without, however, going to ridiculously extreme degrees of parental self-denial or cash indebtedness for that specific purpose – in short, without *openly* competing. Thus the average age at marriage is rising nowadays, as are the expenses of marriage; but in accounting for the changing situation, I would link not simply marriage and the rising standard of living but rather these two together and the household, the heads of which still negotiate and to a very great extent subsidize the initiation of first marriages.

THE CIRCUMCISION CEREMONY

Circumcision is an important part of the average Malay boy's life and illustrates a very general feature of Malay culture, that is, it is male-dominated. This is true not only in religion and law strictly speaking (Islam) but also in the many features of cultural life not specifically dictated under Islam – the various ceremonial aspects of marriage, feasting, and etiquette, the general theory for all these being: men before women.[10] In line with this principle, the boy's transition to marriageability is clearly designated by circumcision; and in the circumcision ceremony there is explicit reference to the prospect of marriage and sex. By contrast, as we have seen, the girl's transition at this point is relatively unmarked and the terminus in marriage tacitly assumed.

Circumcision is performed by a specialist, called *mudin*. A *mudin* visited the village at least twice while I was living there, upon the invitation of the parents of certain boys who were judged ready for circumcision, that is, aged eleven to fourteen. The *mudin* lives at Gombak Setia near Kuala Lumpur and travels around the country as a circumcision specialist. He is also an expert in ear-piercing (of females), and sells cloth (*kain sarong*) on the side.[11]

According to the *mudin*, 'Mohammedan law' (he used the English term) lays down that circumcision may be carried out from about seven to twelve or thirteen, after which a boy may not be circumcised.[12] However, at the other extreme, the *mudin* said that he had circumcised babies of six weeks ('forty days'). He also said that circumcision should preferably *not* be done at a hospital. Even a doctor he knew had had his sons circumcised by a *mudin* (a point that will be mentioned below).

The ceremonies I attended on 14 and 15 August 1965 were held in the morning, beginning at about 8 a.m. They were attended by the boy or boys to be circumcised, also by some small girls on the second day to have their ears pierced, by parents, the *mudin*, guests who were kin (*saudara*) of the parents of the boy, and other persons of standing in the village, mainly *hajis* and, on the first day, the *khatib*. Attendance was by invitation, though invitations were not as formal as they would have been for a wedding. The size of the gathering in every case was limited to the number of people who could be fitted into one house. Where several boys were operated on, the gathering consisted of several sets of parents related to one another. *Figure 2* shows the genealogical relationships of boys circumcised in the series I attended.

The village I studied, in common with a great many Malay villages, is strung out along the bank of a major river (the Pahang), and the houses are often widely separated. As a result of this dispersal, the gatherings at each house differed in composition (not shown in *Figure 2*). Yet genealogical ties, which are recognized, clearly link most of the participants in all the ceremonies. (In effect, two spheres of kinship association came into play: one in the inviting of the *mudin*; the other in the inviting of guests for the circumcision 'feast'.)

FIGURE 2 *Genealogical relations of circumcised boys*

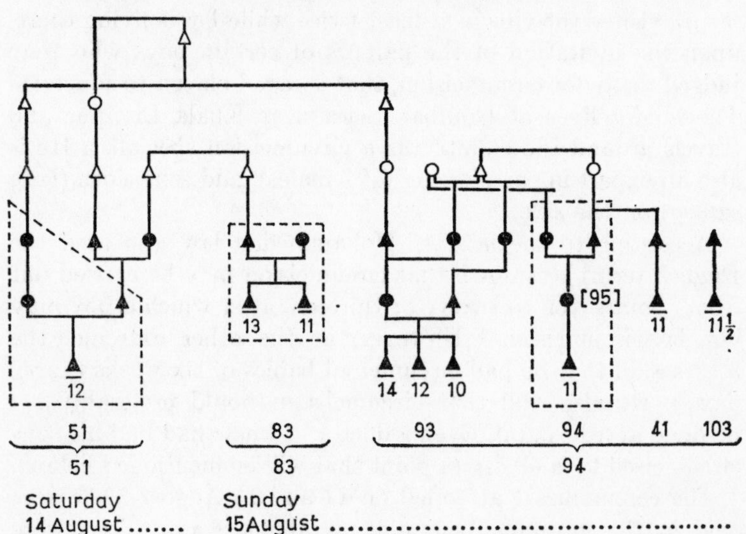

Underscored signs indicate boys undergoing circumcision, with ages. Houses in which the boys live are numbered, from lower (lying up-river) to higher (lying down-river). The houses in which ceremonies were held on successive days are indicated by broken rules. Horizontal brackets show in which houses the boys were circumcised.

The following description is based mainly on the ceremony at the first house, in which one boy was circumcised.

Upon arrival at the house the *mudin*, dressed in a rather ordinary way (shirt and trousers plus a [man's] *sarong*), immediately called for various materials he needed: a small bottle, white cotton cloth, a banana stalk for the boy to sit on (already prepared), some water and talcum powder. The boy came from the inner part of the house onto the veranda, apart from the general gathering of men. He was clad only in an unsewn *sarong* of a coloured *batik* type ordinarily worn by women. The boy was seated astride the banana stalk, facing the *mudin*. He opened the *sarong*, allowing it to hang from his shoulders. His father sat nearby, prepared to hold him. Where more than one boy had to be operated on, each was held by a father of one of them, and the father was helped by one of the guests.

The *mudin* prepared a red salve in the bottle supplied, and tore strips of white cloth to be used as a bandage. With his fingertips, he applied a powder-and-water paste to the boy's chest, forehead, and foreskin to 'cool' the boy (*kasi sejok*). At the same time he muttered (silently) a spell (*jampi*). The *mudin* then pushed back the foreskin (*hujong*, lit. 'end') to be sure it was loose (*isi* [*boleh*] *keluar*, lit. 'the glans [may] come out', or again, *chelék*, 'unshuttering', as when the eyelid opens).

In one or two cases, the foreskin could not be pushed back without causing pain. When this happened, the *mudin* forced the skin back, pointed out if the glans was 'dirty' (*kotor*), and pulled it forward again, saying, 'That will set it [the penis] right (*kasi betul*). You want to use this [penis] later. If it isn't right it will 'miss' (*lari*, lit. 'flee'), it will not be straight when you get an erection and the girl (*anak dara*, 'virgin') won't like this!' As the operation proceeded there were further references to virility, a tactic which is relevant 'traditionally' (see below) and served to hearten the boys.

If the foreskin was loose, the *mudin* remarked that the boy must have been 'playing' with his penis (*main butoh*, i.e. an allusion to masturbation). He asked at every stage – when manipulating the foreskin, preparing it for cutting, and performing the operation itself – if the foreskin hurt (*sakit*) or, less frequently, if its condition was 'tolerable' (*geli*).

As he prepared the foreskin, the *mudin* referred to the necessity of the operation to ensure virility in later life. The foreskin was pressed in a clamp (*tekan*, 'to press', hence a 'tweezer'): two sticks hinged together at one end and pointed at the other to be stuck into the banana stalk to keep the foreskin steady. The *mudin* finally instructed the boy to shut his eyes and hold his breath; his father held the boy's head facing up. The *mudin* swiftly cut away the foreskin with a straight razor. Salve and gauze were applied and the gauze was finally bound up with string. The boy was given the foreskin wrapped in cloth, and salve and gauze to apply to the wound for three days. He then limped away to the company of the women at the rear of the house.

When a boy cried or appeared afraid, the *mudin* said the boy was *takut hati* (lit. 'afraid in his liver'). If there was much blood, this was said to indicate fear. When one boy cried after the operation, a man nearby said loudly, 'You don't want your bride to know this made you cry, do you?' There was laughter from those around and from the women. Two or three boys showed signs of tears even before the operation, the youngest of two or three brothers seeming the most susceptible. When a boy showed no fear or pain, he was said to be *hati berani* (lit. 'free in the liver'). There was no reference to *semangat*, but I did hear this mentioned upon the ear-piercing for three little girls (cf. Cuisinier, 1951, especially Part II, Chs. VI–VIII).

When circumcision was completed, whether of one boy or of several, the *mudin* moved to the company of the guests, and a small 'feast' (*kenduri*) followed: tea, cakes, and glutinous rice (*nasi pulut*; prepared on special occasions), and, in two houses, a small sauce (*lauk*) with fish, all of which were paid for and served to the guests by the host.

After the refreshments, the boy's father (or one of the fathers) presented the *mudin* with a cash payment. For one boy the sum was M$20, for six M$45. At the first house, the gathering concluded with a short prayer led by the *khatib*. At the other two houses there were also short prayers. At the house where ear-piercing was carried out (No. 94), the operation was done immediately after the feast. Three girls aged two to four were operated on. Two of them were so frightened that they urinated on the laps of their holders, and the operations were interrupted while the holders (man and woman) retired or recovered from the discomfort. Payment for ear-piercing for two sisters was M$2 (handed over by their mother), and for another girl, their second-cousin, M$0·70 (by the father, through whom the girl was related).

It is worth noting that one boy volunteered on the spot for circumcision; his case (*Figure 2*, No. 41) provides the one irregularity in the 'genealogical progression' of relatives from up-river to down-river shown in *Figure 2*. It was remarked afterwards apropos of his action that some boys want very much to be circumcised, while others are afraid and will climb a tree to escape (the reference being to a *kabong*, or sugar-palm; since there are few of these around and they are not economically important, it is possible that the remark alluded to an actual event).

The form of the circumcision ceremonies described above is probably the usual one nowadays. It can be seen that the ceremonies are fairly small in scale. There is not, in this village, the great procession during which the boy, exquisitely dressed, is born aloft on a palanquin.[13] As far as I could determine, ceremonies were probably larger in the past but not of the order of the well-known east coast ceremonials. A comparable reduction was claimed for wedding ceremonial, though with less justification. People were keen to impress upon me that Malays are too poor to be able to pay for the frills demanded by tradition (*adat resam* [Alwi, 1962]) for the various ceremonies, weddings and the like. They stated, too, that people are less willing to help out than formerly.

Circumcision therefore – at least in this village – is largely a household or domestic affair. This is shown in the fact that the host took charge, serving food and dressing informally in his household dress, a *sarong* and shirt. Guests as a whole, as would be expected, tended to be more formally dressed, but all wore the *songkok* (the Malay [black] 'fez'; called *kepiah* in the dictionaries), including the *hajis*, who have the privilege of wearing the white prayer-cap, and the kin who attended were those who lived comparatively near the respective houses.

Other features of the circumcision ceremonials are of special note. First is the importance of the *context* of circumcision – the village. It was several times pointed out to me during the ceremonies that if circumcision were carried out at a hospital, i.e. outside the village, there would have to be an injection (*chochok*), which makes the penis 'weak' and results in loss of potency. The condition was illustrated by an index finger bent in a downward curve.[14]

There is behind this notion the belief in the connection between the circumcised state and virility. This has been seen several times: a good circumcision assures a good sexual performance (and particularly satisfies the female). The connection was brought out in another way when the *mudin* said jokingly to a respected village man, a *haji* of about sixty-five whom the *mudin* had evidently known for some time: 'Perhaps you need an "overhaul" [English term used]. You should be circumcised again. After all, you are an old man (*orang tua*), not like me [the *mudin* was about fifty-five], and with nothing else to do you can copulate all day!'[15]

It should be stressed at this point that it is not incumbent upon circumcised boys to 'prove' their sexuality. This comes with marriage.[16] The circumcision ceremony marks a significant change, the consequences of which will be described in the following sections; but it is not by any means an induction into manhood generally.[17]

THE DEVELOPMENT OF SEXUAL STATUS

I come now to a central topic of this paper – the notion of complementarity.

School-leaving, male circumcision, and sexual maturity confer different aspects of status – the status of 'marriageable person'. The accumulation of these features – although they are in some ways heterogeneous – is a symptom of the 'pressure to abandon . . . familial dependency and to form independent attachments outside the family' (Parsons & Bales, 1956, p. 44). When these attachments are looked for, as expressions of status, the things that impress the observer of everyday life most of all (at least this one) are the *limits* in their formation: strict spacial separation of the sexes, the extreme bashfulness of the girls, the reserved even glum watchfulness of the boys, and the general lack of emphasis on cooperative or group activities. These may be explained as elements in the development of sexual status.

At the beginning of the sequence, i.e. after the age of about twelve, it becomes a general rule that boys and girls do not associate (unless, of course, they are members of the same household). The restrictions in the village I studied seemed to be more *de facto* than *de jure*, which I attribute in part to the dispersed nature of the village (two miles long) and the small number of children of the appropriate ages (about 100 between eleven and twenty), as well as to the fact that this is not a 'violent' or apparently repressive culture. Two examples may serve to underline the nature of this restriction:

> *Teasing.* I witnessed only one instance in public of teasing between unmarried but more or less marriageable persons. It took place between a girl of about thirteen (the daughter of the retired schoolteacher mentioned earlier) and her cousin (mother's brother's son) of about twenty-three, a student at a teachers' training college (and himself about to be engaged to the daughter of another retired schoolteacher). This pair, as is probably plain, are rather more free from the strictures of village life than are most boys and girls.
>
> *Seclusion.* A daughter of a wealthy villager, sequestered in the sense already noted, excited much (good-natured) comment once when she made an excursion to a village shop, i.e. ventured out in public, unescorted.

Both these observations point to the emphasis on the separation of older boys and girls in village life.

Given this feature, it is not surprising that the lives of *budak* during the phase leading to marriage are uneventful. Unless their parents are very poor, boys especially are able to lead a life entailing only a small amount of work. Even when a boy expects to tap rubber for a living and plant rice for subsistence when he reaches adulthood, i.e. after marriage, it is only at about sixteen that he will begin tapping in a desultory way, while he learns the work. Except in special circumstances no unmarried boy takes part in rice agriculture. All boys, however, do some fishing in the rice-fields. Their work is mostly devoted to rubber-tapping, because from this they get money. Yet boys make no cash contribution to their own households (cf. Swift, 1965, p. 107; Geertz, 1961, p. 118); they supply only their own small needs and not even these entirely. For example:

> There was a widow, three of whose six children were married. The oldest unmarried child was a boy 'about twenty-one years old' who earned money from tapping rubber and, recently, from drill-training with the LDC (paramilitary corps recruited in the villages, revived as a result of the confrontation with Indonesia which was in full swing in 1964–66). He was living not with his mother but with a young schoolteacher. When asked how he contributed to their housekeeping and specifically where the rice came from, he said, 'My mother gives it to me.' Thus the woman apparently

supported herself, a daughter, and in part her unmarried son; in fact, she did this partly through her own work, and partly with contributions from her *married* children.

Girls help their mothers in the house, in cooking for instance, which they will probably not have done, at least regularly, up to now. If the household is large, with two or more girls, the shares of work are correspondingly small. Although the harvesting of rice is the woman's share of rice agriculture, only in the last resort would unmarried girls have to work in this sector.

Thus there is a simple but radical separation of male and female from about the time they begin to attain physical and social maturity, that is, when they become legally marriageable. This separation is spacial; it is also more generally social, as, for example, in the economic positions of adolescents. The position of the girls is simply defined by their incorporation into the household. This in itself undoubtedly creates a solidarity across generation lines among females not paralleled on the male side, where there is a disjunction of generation levels. The marriageable boy is 'marginal' (cf. Lewin, 1939). The situation is bound up with the unchallenged rights of adult men to negotiate the marriage of their children (which is at the same time the children's sexuality).[18] Any solidarity between generations of males (or, of course, the legal ability of females to negotiate) would upset the authority of the adult men in this sphere.

There is an important alternative open to some boys and girls in adolescence, viz. the secondary school, as we have seen. Because they spend the term-time away from the village, life for them is more eventful. In 1965, there were sixteen boys and six girls in all types of school above primary level. Of the boys, nine were in religious schools (Sekolah Arab); of the girls, one was in religious school (Taman Pendidekan Islam, Kuala Lumpur). The other boys and girls, as mentioned earlier, continued in state secondary schools. Role definition of this sort is, of course, a strong force orienting children away from the village, though it is too early to tell what the effects are more specifically.

If, as I have suggested, the strict segregation of the sexes at about the onset of sexual maturity and afterwards emphasizes the significance of their 'natural' complementarity, there are also social relations that emphasize age discrepancies. These social relations are important in understanding the everyday life of boys and girls – that is, the life of *budak* at another level. In both respects it may be remarked that asymmetries are given social values in apparently simple and direct ways.

In the recognition of age differences a premium, backed by diffuse sanctions, is placed on the 'manner' (*bahasa*) in which social relations are actually conducted. This has primarily to do with speech. For present purposes, one set of values may illustrate the point. On the whole, all Malays are quiet and undemonstrative. Because of this they are stereotyped by casual observers as 'gentle'.[19] The underlying values of comportment have been described by the Geertzes as: emphasis on 'emotional stasis' (Geertz, 1961, p. 147) and, among upper-class Javanese (*prijaji* [= *priyayi*]), 'a certain flatness of affect' (Geertz, 1960, p. 240). Village Malays of my acquaintance are rather less formal than this; quite simply it can be said that most of their relations involve a diffuse kind of respect behaviour (*hormat*, 'honour', 'respect') governed most generally by relative age.

As indicated, there are likely to be variations in behaviour among people of all ages: one finds garrulous Malays of either sex and age, and they can be instructive. I learnt, however, to regard such persons in the contexts of village life as 'different' (*lain*) in some way other than as the result of the usual and expectable differences of personality. Thus, excessive talk or demonstrativeness is always likely to be considered reprehensible, humiliating, or simply characteristic of the 'outsider' (*orang lain*; including the ethnographer); this is so almost regardless of circumstances, not the least so, of course, in anger. This general and diffuse sort of propriety has sanctions: all Malays – including young ones – are sensitive to the possibility of direct comments on their behaviour, that is, that it is 'coarse' (*kasar*) or bad mannered (*kurang ajar*).[20]

Given the 'marginal' status of boys who are, in effect, simply playing a 'waiting game', awaiting marriage, an exaggerated form of respect behaviour might well be expected. It tends to take the form of marked reticence, usually described as *malu*. *Malu* is almost always noticeable to a degree (even among boys with several years of English language education). The following is one example:

> I sat in a small shop (which is an excellent place to talk) while the shopkeeper questioned a boy of about seventeen who had wandered in. The boy was not a stranger although he did not usually travel to this end of the village. He was related to the shopkeeper ('grandfather/grandchild') and was being questioned on a matter of mutual interest: a house being built by the road (up-river) for a relative who was the boy's 'grandfather' and the shopkeeper's second cousin. The boy had had to pass by the house on his way to the shop, since he was on foot. To every question, the boy mumbled 'don't know' and stared out across the nearby rice-field.

In other instances, boys who have information to volunteer will not give it, and one often hears the irritated or puzzled reactions of adults when this reticence results in inconvenience to them.[21]

Girls (also younger married women) are even more reserved or 'bashful' (*malu*) than are their counterparts among the boys, and this applies to relations *vis-à-vis* almost all males outside their own household (who are bound to be older for the most part anyway).[22] The older a woman is the freer she is, according to inclination; very old women – widows for the most part – often enjoy considerable freedom of association and may be very talkative.[23] (Some of this behaviour, however, must verge on senility and is probably recognized and tolerated as such.) Children of about eight to ten years are frequently a noticeable exception, albeit a 'fringe', among persons of whom excessive 'reserve' (or bashfulness) is generally expected. Such children are regarded as old enough to know how to act, yet they may be loud, occasionally insolent (*jahat*). I would suggest that these children are at the stage of beginning to adjust their behaviour in extra-domestic situations and that their more than occasional 'deviance' at this stage is a result of this early transition.

It seems clear that in a society as insistent as this one on the *asymmetry* of social relations, the various features of separation and 'respect' (*hormat*) have a function of avoiding incongruities or improprieties which are bound to arise when the social adherence to 'natural' differences fails to carry the day in particular situations.[24] Within the system, the category of persons *least* well adjusted to it are the approximately sexually mature but unmarried: those aged roughly fourteen to twenty. They are socially a 'danger', and consequently seem to receive the greatest extreme of prohibitions (cf. Douglas, 1966).

How do boys and girls act within these limitations on social expression and social relations? What is the extent of participation and self-organization? I shall deal mainly with boys.

One simple kind of association that falls within the limits of the system, and is mostly peculiar to those boys who have left school, is 'age magnetism', the gathering together of youths of similar size and age. Based as it is on similarity, or 'identity', this principle really provides a contrast with the tendencies to reserve and asymmetry so characteristic of the broader field of relations. Aside from groups formed for certain games, this kind of grouping is virtually the only means of self-organization in the village I studied. It does not seem to lead to the 'gangs' (*geng*) which occur in more cosmopolitan parts of the country (cf. Swift, 1965, p. 144). Age magnetism occurs, in addition, among younger children of around ten, whose principal activity, in such groups, is fruit pilfering.[25]

Among those boys who are no longer in school the phenomenon of age magnetism is more marked as the groups are smaller, as indeed one would expect. A mere pair of boys (or girls), if not siblings, tends to be almost exactly matched in size, shape, and dress. As the group becomes larger, more disparity appears. However, I did not see boys of, say, fourteen habitually grouping themselves with boys of sixteen or eighteen, nor even boys of eighteen with boys of twenty or so.

The largest, or at least the most active, groups were made up not of teenagers but of persons from about twenty to thirty, younger married, and unmarried, men who gathered to play cards, listen to the radio, and eat (someone else's) food. It was much less usual to find crowds or 'clubs' of younger boys doing this. The reason may be that persons of over twenty or so are less easy to discourage. Shopkeepers manage to suppress such activities among younger boys; and the etiquette of visiting and hospitality in dwelling-houses is strict enough to discourage the activities in that sector. It would not be permissible even to use empty houses for carousing. Thus, men who live alone tend to attract such groups. When this happened to a young schoolteacher of about twenty-two, he deliberately avoided moving back into his small house upon return from holiday for fear of its becoming again what he described in English as the village 'youth club'. Instead, he moved in with a family. Such groups are, on the whole, therefore disapproved of.

Another focus of group activity is the game of *sépak raga* (or *bola sépak*; a kind of netball). There is in fact an inter-village league for this. The game involves boys from about seventeen to eighteen and older married and unmarried men. I saw few if any boys under sixteen or so at it. There is in addition a credit 'ring' (*kutu*) of ten members aged eighteen to thirty, i.e. roughly the range of the *sépak raga* players.[26]

In this range of activities and the formation of groups around them, as in work, boys of around twelve to fifteen are apparently left out. They are the ones who are especially involved in a 'waiting game'. They are seldom seen around the village, they generally 'potter' about the house or frequent some out-of-the-way spot, e.g. a corner of a graveyard. If seen loitering around a shop in late afternoon, they are noticeably 'out of it': standing or sitting silently, perhaps admiring their seniors.

It is precisely in this age-range – twelve to fifteen or so – that the forces of socialization are most explicit, where all the aspects of *transition* are most apparent (school-leaving, circumcision, puberty). At this point their parents' interests in them as potentially marriageable are crystallized and become a matter of concern, though not at this stage very active.

Generally speaking, age magnetism, which affects all ages of boys from around twelve to twenty or over, is an elementary sort of age-grading, but it is sporadic and largely functionless, except perhaps for purposes of a vague solidarity of age-mates; it indicates how weak or rudimentary the tendencies to social expression are. An example may illustrate the anomalies that arise when the age principle, rudimentary though it may seem, is ignored, or, more generally, the narrow limits it represents:

> A boy said to be about twenty was (like his father) a willing and frequent helper, rather more than most people in com-

munal activities, and was generally ubiquitious around the village. But he was equally a 'difficult' boy (*jahat*). He did not join his age-mates to any great extent, and tended to run around with boys in the eight to twelve range – stealing fruit. He was especially active in the *durian* season. (*Durian* is the most highly prized and rare fruit in the village. There being only a few producing trees, a watch had to be mounted day and night if the fruit were not to be spirited away as soon as they fell.) At one time he 'bothered' a girl of about sixteen as she was walking on a deserted path (not ordinarily regarded as a 'dangerous' or improper thing to do). He entered people's houses when they were out and damaged goods by fooling with them. None of this behaviour was culpable by police standards, but it was a nuisance by village standards and not at all usual.

The boy's enterprise and energy, therefore, 'cut both ways'. It seems to me that his dual nature – generous and diligent, but at the same time troublesome – is the necessary result of the especially narrow limits imposed on persons of his category (*budak*).

These limits are also, to some extent, reinforced by the style of dress which has been described. The distinctive style is strongly associated with leisure. To maintain this association, as I have suggested, is a way of showing the ability of a household to keep a boy or boys to a greater or lesser degree dependent on it and confers an implicit prestige. The boys themselves frequently display a concern for both dress and general appearance that seems to maintain the limits on work and, ultimately, independence. Once, when a man called for help to lift some fence-posts, he happened to be at the edge of a nearly dry rice-field. The danger of splashing and muddiness was not in fact very great, but a smartly dressed boy of about twenty who was watching nevertheless declined to help, saying, 'It'll finish my trousers' (*habis seluar*). Such concern is in part understandable but it also reflects a certain inflexibility, and flat refusals are surprisingly common.[27] It was all the more of an achievement another time when a man, who happened to be the village headman (*tok empat*), working near the road, succeeded in getting help in the task of splitting wood for fence-posts. He managed this by setting the situation up as a trial of skill. He attracted several youths who tried their hand; he even reinforced his appeal by saying he had a pain in his back! But, for the most part, boys remain aloof in such situations.[28]

The degree to which personal appearance can be emphasized is shown in the following example:

> I was surprised to see a young man (a friend and 'nephew' of the one just mentioned) wearing a handkerchief tied over his mouth. I thought at first that he did this to avoid the dust, since it is common in Malaya to see people, especially Malays, with a handkerchief clamped over the mouth and nose to avoid dust or a fetid smell. (It does not occur to Europeans, in Malaya or most other places, to avoid temporary nuisances such as these.) But this was not the reason for his action. I found out later that the boy had cut his upper lip accidentally and fairly seriously – seriously enough to have to go to the out-patient clinic at the hospital (thirty miles away) to have it dressed. And rather than display the dressing and, when this was removed, the temporary scar to strangers and to persons in the village, he covered his entire mouth. Even after he ceased to wear the handkerchief, he would automatically cover his mouth with his hand when near enough to speak to people (it is, incidentally, an accepted gesture among Malays to speak to a superior while screening the mouth from the gaze of the person spoken to).

Most boys, especially those who earn their own money, manage to get to town at intervals of perhaps once a month. The town is twenty-four miles away by bus, car, or motor-scooter. Village boys do not form or join groups in town, but it is not uncommon to see a pair of boys or young men walking hand-in-hand (actually, with fingers interlocked). These are boys (or young men) from different villages who often meet in town. I did not see this type of pairing in the village.

In the village, a boy (or younger married man) may have a friendship relation (*rodong*) with some other boy. This is usually explained as an especially close relationship. It was my impression, however, that it is a somewhat formal arrangement, usually having a useful purpose, for example, to go hunting together.

It is a general rule that boys who have been circumcised and are 'big enough' can attend Friday prayer (*sembahyang jumaat*) at the mosque. Anybody at all, women and children included, can go to the mosque (*masjid*) or a prayer-house (*surau*) in the evening for the prayers held at that time of day (*maghrib* and *isha*); boys may – and women often do – pray, everyone can talk, and once a week there is a *kenduri* ('feast'). In the evenings, the mosque is divided by a curtain, and the women pray in the half reserved to them for that purpose, parallel to the men.[29] At the evening prayers, too, young boys who have not yet been circumcised often sneak up behind the men who are praying and imitate the *rakaat* (prostrations) though they may not be able to recite the prayer itself.

On their own admission, nearly all boys and men of the broadest category we have discussed, i.e. up to thirty, do not pray daily (unless they attend a religious school) although entitled and even obliged as Muslims to do so 'five times a day'. As stated, Friday prayer is usually fairly well attended by men and to a lesser extent by youths. Other congregational activities in the evenings of the week, however, those held in the mosque and the two *surau*, mentioned above, are attended regularly only by older men. Attendance follows age very closely and is much less frequent the lower the age. It is of some interest in the present argument, concerning *budak*, that there were three regular communicants who did *not* follow this pattern. There were two boys and a somewhat older man who were, quite unusually, regular attendants at mosque not only for Friday prayer but also every evening for the prayers and teaching:

> A boy of about fourteen had recently been orphaned and had had an illness as a result of which, it was said, his mind was affected. He was a very docile, friendly boy, but people said that he stole things (in a village where stealing from houses was unheard of) or suddenly lost his memory, and that he hardly ate enough to stay alive.
>
> Another boy, about nineteen, was adopted and at the end of 1964 he lost his adoptive father (his 'uncle') who was himself an outsider married into the village. He was rather shy and 'slow'.

> The man, about thirty-five, had been married once, but now lived alone. He apparently lost his temper very easily (people would occasionally provoke him to see what would happen) and it was often remarked that he had 'something missing' (*kurang otak*), though he never assaulted anybody (for example, *amok*, 'running wild', as abnormal for Malays as for any other people).

In these cases the occasions of worship provide status or expression for socially deprived persons – those, it should be noted, whose marriage prospects are poor by reason of natural or social deficiencies. It is significant that they seek expression in a place where women are either excluded or strictly segregated.

Generally, however, boys tend to adopt an irreligious attitude and deny that they pray 'except when [they] go to the mosque' (rarely). Younger adult men say that 'religion is for old men'. This attitude signifies in another way the disjunction of young men and old men as categories, whether it be fathers and sons, or fathers-in-law and sons-in-law, the opposition between them centring on marriage and marital status.

The position of girls in the phase initiated by school-leaving and continued with puberty is very different from that of boys and may be briefly remarked on. As *budak*, or *anak dara*, girls occupy a clearly defined position. It may be this, more than any other process, that influences the development of sexual status. In contrast to boys, who tend to grow away from the household, girls are firmly attached to it. More generally they are in important respects 'stationary'. For instance, females travel beyond the village less frequently than boys and men, if they travel at all.

> A man who had been with the forest service during his working life, and still travelled very widely, said that he 'liked to travel', and travelled when he liked. But with regard to his wife and especially his two unmarried daughters, about fourteen and seventeen, he said that women and girls should not travel about, and he never allowed them to accompany him even when he went to town.

Not all parents are as strict, but the attitude is a fairly common one. Indeed, it is possible to see this attitude as one particular expression of a rule of social life: women do not 'move'. It holds also in marriage ceremonial, which is conducted at the girl's parents' house[30] and after which, for at least a short time, the couple expect to remain with the girl's parents. Upon divorce it is felt that the woman should have the children, a house, and some goods or money to tide her over (cf. Swift, 1963, pp. 274–275). By inheritance women should, if possible, receive a house and moveable wealth. In practice these are not always the results, but the *notion* that women should remain, as it were, in one 'place' always seems to receive first consideration, and a decision initially in favour of it often holds.

THE ROLE OF ADULTS

We have seen that one of the pre-eminent means of control of adolescents is the separation or segregation of the sexes. Perhaps because such a rule tends to be absolutistic, it seems to have associated with it adult suspicion about illicit or vicarious sex among the unmarried. One of the commonest notions held by adults (though not very openly) is the suspicion of clandestine encounters between boys and girls, or between boys and adult women (divorcees), for purposes of sexual play or sexual intercourse.

> I happened to remark to an old man that on a visit to Kuala Pahang I had seen a woman of about thirty-five running a business making *kerpok* (fish-paste slivers or wafers). She was economically independent and living on her own. He immediately commented that in our part of the country a woman, unless very old, could not stay alone in a house at night because she was certain to be visited by young men (*budak*). They would 'knock on her door', and she would 'make love with them' (*nanti chinta*).[31]

There is, too, a strong suspicion expressed by adults, which also comes out in teasing among older boys, of voyeurism among the boys of the village.[32] Malay houses are raised on posts or pillars about five feet above the ground, and so watching or listening at night would be especially easy. Such a possibility attains hyperbolic expression when people recall, albeit in other contexts, that, in the wars and violence that were said to prevail among Malays before the British came, attackers could kill people inside a house by running daggers through the slats of the floor. Awareness of this 'transparency' of the Malay house probably makes the suspicion of illicit or vicarious sex an especially abundant source of anxiety.

How far are these suspicions confirmed? The indications are that incidents that can be construed in any way as heterosexual 'adventures' are rare. The most serious breach of the 'rules' prohibiting close association (or proximity) of the sexes that occurred in 1964–66 involved two unmarried men, about twenty-two and twenty-one, and two unmarried girls, who had been 'meeting together in a house'. The bare fact was scandalous enough, or so people thought. I first heard of the affair while visiting a house late at night after attending prayers at the mosque, but was given only a skeleton account and that on condition that I told no one! I then overheard some quiet gossip later; no scandal erupted. In more detail what had happened was as follows:

> A young schoolteacher (mentioned earlier) lived with a village boy, on the principle that no one, least of all a young male or a sexually accessible female, should sleep alone in a house. The girls concerned were cousins (mother's brother's daughters) of the boy and lived nearby. The visits – despite the fact that one may have taken place in the evening after dark – appeared to be quite innocent, but their discovery brought forth a severe scolding for the village boy from his older brother (acting as 'guardian' in place of their dead father). On the other hand, nothing that would have conveyed a sense of outrage was said to the teacher by older people, nor was there scurrilous talk about him. Presumably some of the reactions were reported back by the boy.

It is understandable that the teacher was not openly reproached, not simply because he was a complete outsider and a teacher, but also because wherever possible Malays avoid open expression of strong personal differences. It was not possible to avoid conflict between 'guardian' and 'charge' (brothers). Serious though this indiscretion was felt to be at the moment of discovery, all signs of it disappeared within a few days. The incident was soon buried; moreover, no stigma would attach to those involved, unless they repeated their actions. Still, it is evident how unsettling such behaviour seems to be.[33]

These suspicions are engendered ultimately, I think, by the long-continued dependence of (unmarried) boys on the adult-managed domestic group and the comparative lack of real autonomy of (extra-domestic) youth groups. In most households, as we have seen, a boy will do little work of any kind, at least regularly; any money he does earn does not cover even his own needs and therefore forms no contribution to the household. He will, on the contrary, be given money to buy the clothes he wants and, of course, he will have the leisure to sport his clothes. If the household is poor, there is necessarily some deviance from this ideal. A boy may be tapping rubber fairly intensively at the age of fifteen or sixteen and may have begun helping a parent, mother or father, much earlier, carrying latex, water, etc. In such cases, there is little to be gained by marrying the boy off because the household could well lose his labour, but on the other hand it is even more plain that marriage is necessary and there is little profit in waiting.

On the whole, boys up to sixteen or so are regarded by adults as 'too young' (*kechik lagi*, 'still small') to engage in regular work, even seasonal work, although boys of all ages do some fishing. No boys help with 'women's work' (transplanting rice) though boys of eighteen or twenty may in a desultory way help to prepare the fields, which in most of Pahang have to be weeded and cleared entirely by hand – work that can be, and frequently is, done by women. Husbands join wives who would otherwise have to harvest rice singlehandedly, but (unmarried) boys *watching* the women, even their own mothers, harvesting rice will say, if asked why they are not working, 'I'm no good at it' (*tak pandai*). Adults in turn say that working in the rice-fields is dirty anyway, and that leeches are a constant menace, so young people should not have to work in the fields. Indeed, all the while I was in the village, it seemed to me that every effort was made to *prevent* youths from having to contribute labour or cash until they were ready to be engaged and the demands of marriage payment arose, or until other kinds of economic necessity could not be forestalled.

The rising standard of living, however, and the greater number of uses to which cash can be put, make the parents objects of more and more requests for money. Parents attempt to regulate requests, if possible, without flatly refusing. Boys who are sent away to school are not allowed too much pocket money at one time because, it is said, they immediately spend it. Several times I met or heard of a father who was making a trip to visit his son at school to give him his allowance. This is a trip of sixty or more miles, and is necessary because there is no other way to regulate the boy's spending.

A common complaint of fathers in the village generally is that their sons of about eighteen or twenty, who may be earning money themselves, ask for money for no other reason, they believe, than to squander it (*buang*, 'throw it away') in town. Yet it appears that money is rarely refused. Still, no youth in the village owned a transistor radio, which is a sign of economic achievement (or at least credit-worthiness). A single unmarried man of about twenty-two, who taught adult education classes and tapped rubber (in the mornings), had his own radio, a small transistor set.

The full range of productive activities open up for a boy only when he is married (possibly for the first of several times) and takes on the responsibility of maintaining a household and a position in the community. The overriding importance of marital status [34] here is further underlined by the arrangements at formal meals (*kenduri*) at which youths are not allowed to eat with adult (i.e. married) men. Boys eat with the women at the rear of the house. This was particularly well illustrated at an engagement feast I attended:

> It was held a few days after the negotiations between the parents and relatives of the couple being engaged had been concluded; yet the bridegroom-to-be ate with the women; like the women, he occasionally crossed to the front of the house during the celebration simply to look in on the assembled (male) guests.[35]

This certainly indicates that male roles involve the recognition of a sharp social distinction, in the transition to adulthood, and in the expression of sexual status generally. Although one risks becoming metaphysical in making assertions about the 'energy' of a system, the 'float' or suspension in the life of *budak* by contrast with adults marks an enormous difference in the levels of social dynamic, perhaps equivalent to that between potential and kinetic energy, which does seem to give adults a considerable security and perhaps satisfaction in their own positions. The rigorous interpretation of the total process will be more carefully considered below. It is plain that the facts are liable to different approaches; I should like to discuss some of these before rounding out my own attack.

OTHER MALAYSIAN STUDIES

I have touched on the socialization of economic behaviour, religious belief, adult character generally, and social control. These problems are also dealt with to some extent in two recent monographs on Malay and Indonesian societies – those by Swift (1965) and Hildred Geertz (1961) – but from different points of view from the one I have adopted.[36] I shall consider in this section how far the authors' attention specifically to socialization in these studies – whether it is socialization in terms of a 'life-cycle' or otherwise – adds to, or confirms, their respective analyses and the relevance of their conclusions to my own argument.

In his study of Malay rural economy and social structure in Negri Sembilan, Swift suggests a link between inconsistent punishment or encouragement of children and poor appreciation of economic reward potentialities by adults. As a social anthropologist drawing upon Weberian ideas, he carefully avoids a causal statement:

> 'A . . . *consistency* exists, I feel, between [the] two fields [economic behaviour and religious belief] and that of the socialization of the individual within the family . . . I suggest that the observable features of Malay child care are connected with the equally observable tendency to see only a loose connection between reward and effort in economic affairs . . ., or in life generally . . .' (Swift, 1965, p. 30; my emphasis).

According to Swift, this 'consistency' explains in part the Malay short-run orientation in economic behaviour, which puts Malays at such a disadvantage in competition with Chinese (1965, pp. 29–30).

Swift does not offer enough evidence to support his contention. There are mentioned (rather invidious) comparisons with 'the Chinese', the deleterious effects of Malay religion (Islam), and some aspects of socialization (discipline, reward, punishment) in the Malay home.[37] He appears to feel that a description of the life-cycle – not explicitly set out by him – would not provide evidence for or is unnecessary to the proposition that 'Malay child care' is closely related to (adult) economic behaviour and religious belief. Nor does he consider the possibility that, as has been argued for the Javanese case, Islam does not necessarily hinder at least a degree of economic 'success' (Geertz, 1956, 1963; also 1965, pp. 40–41; cf. Wilder, 1968). The picture is on the whole dim, as well as gloomy.

Hildred Geertz's study contains a much more extended application of socialization theory (1961, Part II). It makes extensive use of formulations derived largely, it seems, from *The People of Alor*, by Cora DuBois (1944), and, like that study, is concerned with personality development. Much of the analysis is made from the point of view of the child in the family, since 'the family, in any society, is the bridge between the individual [sc. child] and his culture' (1961, p. 146). This empirical assumption about 'the individual' in *The Javanese Family* facilitates conclusions about the Javanese 'conception of the self' and 'the personality makeup of the Javanese' (1961, pp. 123, 81). It encourages the use of psychoanalytic terms to describe social relations (that between spouses as 'almost paranoid' [1961, p. 133]), and the stress on affective relationships and conditions: 'psychological preparations', 'psychic equilibrium', 'general psychological effects on the child', and 'the emotional tone or ethos of familial relations' (1961, pp. 146, 150, 151, 152; cf. p. 112).

The theoretical paradigm for *The Javanese Family* appears to lie in the work of Kardiner and his school of psychoanalytic anthropology. The main concept for Kardiner is Basic Personality Structure; this rests upon a background of modified Freudian theory (Kardiner, 1945), what Gerth and Mills would characterize as one type of genetic theory of socialization (1954, p. 140), and Young has more recently described as the 'psychogenic' view (1965, pp. 2, 33 ff., 158 ff.). As Kardiner says, the concept of Basic Personality Structure 'offers us a basis for examining the structuralizations in society and for relating institutions to each other, not directly but through the medium of the individuals who compose it' (1945, p. 30). In his analysis of Alorese culture, Kardiner states that extensive consideration of institutions, beyond that of 'parental care', 'is obviated by our access to the individual and our opportunity of examining his mental processes [through projective tests]' (1945, p. 256).

> 'The more the ethnographer tells us about the traits of these people, the greater the number of institutions that we can place as derivations of this basic personality structure' (1945, p. 29; see also p. 30, and *passim*).

Among Kardiner's results, on this theory, are that the male sector of the Alorese economic system is 'meaningless' (1945, p. 254), and that maternal care is 'poor' (e.g. 1945, p. 239) resulting in adult characters in which 'aggression patterns are poor in organization' (1945, p. 251). (In fact, DuBois describes conventionalized combat and dancing among Alorese that only once threatened to turn into a violent fight [1944, p. 119; also pp. 120–121]. Again, she knew of only three cases of rape [1944, p. 113]. These facts seem to indicate that aggression is well organized in approved channels.) Kardiner then concludes his analysis of the Alorese by stating that 'it is certain that they are not aware of their wretchedness' (1945, p. 253).

Much of Mrs Geertz's study of the Javanese family shows – and, in my estimation, suffers from – the influence of this socialization theory. Her theory, like its precursor, conceives of the individual as a medium through which culture operates, who is, therefore, a conceptual unit of study. It is assumed that individual personalities are formed in the family at the start of the life-cycle. The family provides the 'basic models for social relationships with the rest of the world' (Geertz, 1961, p. 146). For example, the ranking system of Javanese kinship (and outside of this field) is found in the nuclear family 'in miniature' (1961, p. 148).[38] Meanings in the adult world are acquired in and persist from the family surroundings by congruency (Geertz, 1961, p. 151), or, as others have put it, by 'consistency' (Swift) or a 'tendency to spread' (Kardiner in DuBois, 1944, p. 10). In other words, it is presumed that there is an analogy[39] between consistent, or inconsistent, child-training practices and general adult behaviour. (Further criticism of this view may be found in Young, 1965, pp. 158–64.)

When, for example, we consider a typical statement from *The Javanese Family*, it is evident how prominent are the notions of the substantial individual and of the functional similarity of earlier and later patterns of behaviour. It is stated that 'the child is fed whenever he asks for food – initiating an informal, irregular pattern of eating that is to continue throughout his life' (Geertz, 1961, p. 98). On comparative grounds, this is difficult to accept as a plausible interpretation; and there is a simpler answer.

I found among Malay villagers that children indeed ate snacks more frequently than did adults, but adults themselves were very orderly in their eating habits, most of all with regard to time. (I should state that during the period I was living in the village all eating was based on the household. There were no coffee shops, though there were several small provision shops run by Malays.) It therefore appears that there is no necessary connection between earlier and later food habits; it is just that in one instance they are apparently similar. I am inclined to think that, far from all Javanese having 'an informal, irregular pattern of eating' (whatever aspects this description is supposed to include), the eating habits of Javanese in Mrs Geertz's sample are conditioned very much by their occupations in the town, and by town life in general in an 'almost completely modern' economy (Geertz, 1961, p. 2).

The statement is, I feel, an example of the distortion that seems to arise from certain theoretical preoccupations. The summoning of detailed evidence can show how statements about 'consistency' or a 'pattern' may rest on assumptions in which, as Young aptly puts it, 'the obvious facts of everyday life are tacitly denied' (1965, p. 25).[40]

What is it that robs these interpretations of their potential relevance? Or, to put it more concretely, why is it at least doubtful that there is 'inconsistency' in the punishment and reward of Malay children which, in another form, recurs and even amplifies in adult life (Swift), or that there is an 'informal, irregular pattern' in the eating habits of Javanese which have an overall structural consistency (Geertz)? What is the reason, in other words, for supposing that discontinuities or irregularities in everyday life (which doubtless exist) are *significant*? I would suggest three reasons.

First, the very use of such terms as 'consistency' is ambiguous: it is not clear what aspects of behaviour are being referred to, whether we are being presented with actions or reactions (cf. Bateson, 1936, p. 176), attitudes or actual decisions. (Firth has recently noted a similar ambiguity in the use of the term 'conflict': it is not always plain whether *conflict* refers to the empirical level (between persons) or to the structural level (between categories) (Firth, 1964, p. 23).) To take two examples:

1. For Malays I know, it is useful – indeed necessary – in speaking of economic behaviour, to make a clear distinction (which Swift does not) between the *theoretical appreciation* of the relationship between reward and effort, and the *ability* to achieve superior rewards (cf. Wilder, 1968).

2. Again, a man once told me that he did not allow his son (now grown up and living in Singapore) to feed himself until the boy was six years old because otherwise the child 'made such a mess'. But this is not in fact the usual practice. I often saw children who could not walk attempting and being encouraged to feed themselves. The man's remark seems rather to reflect a prevalent *attitude* towards socialization, viz. that children are given time to learn.[41]

Thus it can easily be argued – as has been done (Djamour, 1959, especially p. 105, and *passim*) – that child-training (socialization) is perfectly consistent in terms of other parameters (certain *attitudes*) and that 'inconsistent' or 'irregular' patterns of adult behaviour (whether or not they are noticeably conditioned by child-training) are the exception rather than the rule. Similarly, I would argue that *adolescent* patterns of restraint, austerity, and the like are highly significant and 'consistent' features and cannot be ignored.

Second, there seem to be arbitrary limits on the selection and interpretation of data. The justification for psychological interpretations of *child* development appears to lie in the assumption that the motivations and world view of the adults whose character is at issue are almost entirely formed by the time of puberty or even before, and that therefore the field for the internalization of institutional imperatives in each and every member of society is in childhood. (Fortes and Parsons seem to lean towards this view.) The validity of such assumptions for (some) observers concerned with psychosocial development may lie at least partly in the requirements of psychological observation: this is best done in a clinical situation; but in many cases, for instance in the study of illiterates, primitives, or young children, this is not feasible or not desirable, so an acceptable substitute or even analogous situation may be found in the nuclear family, in which, in any society, psychodynamics are more sharply defined and much more readily observed than in the community at large.[42] Such an approach is developed to good effect by Parsons and Bales (1956).

The danger comes when it is assumed in grosser terms that childhood is *best* explained in psychoanalytic or psychological terms, and adulthood in sociological terms (with adolescence relegated to a few perfunctory paragraphs). Here, indeed, may lie an explanation of the lively interest in childhood exhibited in so many studies. Childhood, which is relatively ill-defined sociologically, seems often to be regarded as an 'open book' psychologically (see Gerth & Mills, 1954, p. 153). Adulthood appears in an opposite light.[43] And the phase between the two (adolescence) is simply 'lost'.[44] It then becomes difficult to reconcile the various levels.

This is not to say that it is wrong to delimit a field more or less strictly for purposes of analysis (cf. Gluckman, 1964). I have done this tentatively in the preceding parts of this paper. But it should at least be recognized that the study of a restricted field may in fact be an *arbitrary* limitation of data leading to inconclusive or even incorrect interpretations – interpretations that derive significance from the manner of selection and not from an exhaustive analysis.[45]

Finally, there is a difficulty in the way child behaviour is articulated in these studies: citations are strongly biased towards whatever is 'weak', or 'poor', or 'negative', in other words, whatever is frustrating in the sociological analysis of adult behaviour (e.g. problems of 'emotional stasis', 'short-term outlook', or the tendency to evade obedience to commands). In attempting to explain such matters, Mrs Geertz finds qualities of personality which she sees as 'costs or *undesirable* indirect consequences of modelling their behaviour in the direction of their ideals' (1961, p. 147; my emphasis). (DuBois speaks of 'liability in human relationships' [1944, p. 79].) Thus, while it is no longer fashionable in anthropology to say that 'change is destructive' or 'inbreeding is bad', we still read that child-training is 'poor' or 'inconsistent', which accounts for apparent weaknesses in adult character and behaviour. It is hard to escape the conclusion that much of the concern with 'socialization' in this vein is misplaced.

CONCLUSION

In discussing socialization in a Malay village I have dealt principally with a concrete feature – the developing complementarity of the sexes in relation to social structure, especially in relation to aspects of marriage. The paradigm of *Figure 1* is a representation which emphasizes the different factors; it is intended to provide a 'space' for the facts of socialization. I have assumed, additionally, that since any social system is bound to socialize values appropriate to the two sexes, male and female, two important aspects of these values must be considered: that of heterosexual relationships, and that of productive work. In neither respect, of course, will the values be brought to full development before marriage, but they will be brought a long way.[46] I have also assumed that marriage, besides being a heterosexual and work relationship, in effect 'divides the generations', that is, marital status is another way of expressing the polarity of successive generations;[47] *it is a factor that is especially critical as the borderlines of 'married' and 'unmarried' are periodically redefined by individual marriages.*[48]

The implications of the problem may be set out as follows. For Malay boys and girls, the various incidents after school-leaving – circumcision, modes of dress, work, etc. – appear to develop in the direction of sexual asymmetry, i.e. sexual roles are clearly separated and unequal. This development is, of course, to be expected in an Islamic society; in such societies, there is a well-recognized asymmetry in the legal statuses of male and female, and there are almost always other expressions of marked inequality. Indeed, taken in isolation, the processes of *un*married social life among Malays appear at first glance to form a fairly typical system of 'honour and shame' – with males active and superior, females passive and inferior, and with considerable importance attached to wealth and prestige for purposes of contracting marriages (Peristiany, 1965).

When, however, we come to marital status as distinct from sexual status among Malays, the balance is different, in that complementarity is not maintained as strictly. It is this process that I wish to enlarge upon in conclusion: the complementarity of the sexes as it is 'diluted' by the tendency towards relative equality in marriage.

Various aspects of the marital relationship have been summarized by Downs as follows:

> 'The social distinction and separation of the sexes is well marked, but the division of labor is not strict . . .
> The theory and outward appearance of male superiority are maintained in all matters, but women have considerable freedom in their everyday activities, and generally play a by no means submissive role in the family. They may own more property than their husbands and they frequently manage the household finances' (Downs, 1964, pp. 258, 260).

Or, from another point of view,

> '. . . the relations between husband and wife . . . are much more egalitarian than at first sight they appear, *and than the people themselves say they are*' (Swift, 1963, p. 279; my emphasis).

In short, the tendency to sexual equality that develops in marriage appears to contradict the clear separateness and contrast of male and female roles prior to marriage. The contradiction is noticeable to some extent in the position of women: unmarried girls, as I have shown earlier, are tied to the household and subject to strict canons of 'modesty'. *In theory*, this also holds in married life, but we have seen that the apparently subordinate and 'stationary' position of women is misleading and may conceal a considerable independence. This is seen in the distinctly preferential treatment of women in inheritance and, often, in divorce, and in the scope that they have with regard to subsistence or even enterprise, for women can provide completely for themselves if necessary, and can even compete with men by running their own business (or they may utilize capital in land or fishing boats which they own to gain an income). On the other hand, it is clearly recognized by Malays that the prominence and preferential treatment of women in some ways conflict with important maxims of the law (*shari'a* or *sharak*) as they know it, for instance, that in law a woman is equal to 'half a man'. In symbolic aspects of ceremonial and in etiquette the male is predominant.

In general, the conflict is that between theory and practice, as already mentioned. It may be seen in another way in the discrepancy between the (male) roles of father and husband: the role of father implies authority in at least one important sphere – marriage contracts; these are conducted closely in accordance with the Islamic rules and consequently presuppose clear and distinct sexual status, with authority and the active roles variously delegated to males. The role of husband, on the other hand, for most peasants involves, in practice, a cooperative, egalitarian relationship, and the marriage bond is, statistically, an unstable one.[49] The role of father, therefore, is easier to reconcile with the theory enunciated by Islam, and from it prestige, for one thing, may be derived. The role of husband represents a compromise in terms of this theory; but the theory is nevertheless plainly cultivated by all concerned in the incidents of life immediately preceding marriage.

So we may say that marriage undermines sex complementarity. Does this 'ambivalence' in the marital sphere (cf. Lévi-Strauss, 1958, pp. 172–178)[50] affect the 'polar' relation of successive generations? Swift reports that there is 'very little specific to be said about parent–child relations [in adolescence], or sibling relations with regard to the question of relations between opposite sexes' (1963, p. 282). He does say that relations of father and son are 'often poor' (1965, p. 108) while those of females (mother and daughter) are solidary. These observations agree with mine (above, p. 230). But this is too restricted a view of the matter.[51] By shifting the focus from household to community we can see that there is more to it.

The position of marriageable persons is a major concern of parents, especially fathers, who formally negotiate their children's marriages. For success in this arena parents must have certain expectations fulfilled concerning the behaviour of their children. The maximum separation of the sexes and their deliberately restricted economic participation during the critical period are important controls that help to guarantee such virtues as dependence and chastity; these in turn support parents' positions as negotiators.

Restrictions imply order (cf. Douglas, 1966, p. 94), in the present case a largely Islamic order and a prestigious one. Thus the elaborate restrictions on *practice* in Malay adolescence certainly appear to have, as an immediate (sociological) aim, the support of a prestigious theory. But if restrictions are extreme or impractical (so that they sometimes even frustrate or baffle investigators), there is likely also to be discomfort, or contradiction, or hypocrisy (Douglas, 1966, p. 163). Parents may experience 'reactive guilt over subjecting their children to much stress' (Cohen, 1966, p. 358). How are such effects avoided, or exorcised (assuming that systematic alternatives along these lines probably exist in most societies)? In other words, given various possibilities of structural conflict, what accounts for the systematic success or continuance of the controls in adolescence?

(As we have seen, there are in fact relatively few signs of friction or anxiety over sex [as pollution ideas, or fears of impotence or homosexuality, cf. Douglas, 1966, Ch. IX]. There are no role-reversals or ridicule which would reflect concern about 'masculinity' or 'femininity'.)

One reason is fairly obvious: it is that the whole overt purpose of the restrictions is self-extinguishing; at the time of marriage the success of the parents is measured and the 'waiting game' is ended for the particular boy (and girl). It may also be noted that in some ways typical 'adolescent' activities (e.g. games) are, significantly, taken up *after* adolescence, by those aged twenty to thirty, i.e. normally young *married* men.

Another less obvious but, in my view, no less important reason for the 'success' of restrictions in adolescence may be seen in religion and its influence on daily life: this is the tendency of Muslims to prohibit or, in the case of circumcision, to enjoin in practice many things that the Koran or such *hadith* as are known do not lay down specifically. This is, I would argue, part of the 'spirit' of Islam and it underlies or is interpreted in the Malay case in such a way as to reinforce attitudes towards sex in particular. In other words, the 'spirit' of prohibition and abstemiousness in the Malay adaptation of Islam underlies the field of social control and affects unmarried persons as much as adults (the married), despite outward appearances and declarations (as when young men exert a kind of habitual levity towards their neglect of regular worship).

There remains one factor which I have already alluded to and which interpenetrates the other two – the general one of prestige. I used the term 'prestige' in connection with those restrictions exerted upon marriageable persons and their place in the community. Now 'prestige' is the same word as 'prestidigitation', meaning sleight-of-hand, illusion; Dr Douglas observes that strong restrictions in the drive for social distinction may involve 'vicarious satisfaction' on the part of parents (cf. Cohen, cited above), or deceit (Douglas, 1966, p. 163). Prestige behaviour resembles a game.

In this light, the kinds of restriction imposed upon marriageable persons seem peculiarly apt: I am thinking here of the part played by restrictions in the control of schismogenesis (see Bateson, 1936, Ch. XIII).[52] The concept is valuable because it is dynamic and of general applicability. One feature of schismogenesis is complementarity of the sexes. Complementarity is upheld, in Malay socialization, in a way that involves controlling the very practice of status, i.e. by 'rarefying' (or slighting?) the cumulative interaction between individuals, through which schismogenesis (social differentiation) takes place. Such are the rules of play.

The significance of the socialization of marriageable persons among Malays is twofold: first, it *is* prestigious because restrictions are apparently successful; second, the *kind* of socialization process – a sort of rarefication of interaction – allows the general benefits of prestige even though the prestige is promoted in a manner that the wider social structure (the 'reality') appears inimical towards; the forms of socialization allow a degree of complementarity which can be tolerated and which does not precipitate too great a discontinuity between married and unmarried (between generations), with the resultant ambiguities and conflicts of role. These two processes constitute a general explanation of the problem of 'negativity', or social inaction, posed at the beginning of this paper.

Finally, I wish to draw a parallel which may help to clarify the position of Malay adolescents: it is not a parallel with other 'adolescents' as such, but with students. In some ways the situations are quite different, in representativeness of the total age-determined population, and in the scale of discontents and the solidarity of students, which are not displayed in the Malay case. Yet the perennial features (and, perhaps, sources of strain) of traditional (male) *student* life, which follow, show an intriguing similarity to those of Malay *budak*:

1. isolated from society, emotionally self-sufficient;
2. unmarried;
3. (temporarily) privileged status *vis-à-vis* society, but at the same time economically dependent;[53]
4. traditional sexual segregation and perhaps even celibacy (presumed) – the limiting case to be found in the learning career of monkhood; and
5. distinctive mode of dress (e.g. gowns, still worn in ordinary academic activities at Durham and the Oxbridge universities, for example).

I am not sure that the Malay case suggests any solutions to student difficulties but the points of similarity seem to be salient ones. Particularly striking is the suggestion concerning monkhood and learning (no. 4). In his study of the life of Martin Luther, Erikson called Luther's student phase a *moratorium*.[54] This ties in with my similar formulation in speaking earlier in this paper of a 'waiting game', which, as I have tried to show, is ultimately connected with marital status.

This is not to say, however, that the Malay case requires a special interpretation; taken this way, the parallel, it seems to me, merely illuminates certain implications of a general social value I have called 'prestige', hinging on the status of married person in one society and of degree-holder in others. On the contrary, the usefulness of the parallel is greater in that it broadens the scope of explanation. Perhaps this is obvious. Perhaps not: I could have dealt with *budak* in the relatively conventional framework of 'marginality', 'peer groups', and the 'universal' problems of adolescence. It is all very well to do this, just as it may lend an air of authority to say that 'the family is universal' and proceed to find facts to support the statement, but such a way of asking questions narrows the scope of interpretation. Similarly with the study of social personality, e.g. in psychologically slanted approaches to socialization as such: frequently, 'the psychological formulation is only a translation on the level of the individual psyche of what is really a sociological structure [une structure proprement sociologique]' (Lévi-Strauss, 1950, p. xvi; see also Leach, 1958; Cohen, 1966, pp. 357–358).

The results of some studies seem to tell us only what we already know,[55] however well the studies appear to be worked out on first glance. This is a beginning, of course, but it is possible to go further, after all. Anthropologists study non-Western cultures, such as those represented in this volume, to explore the range of human possibilities, not merely to find out, by extending the geographical coverage, what was already known. They are concerned to discover what the data *mean*. The tasks may perhaps best be tackled if for a start we ask what it is the society wants to socialize, as well as how it does it (cf. Cohen, 1966, p. 358); this should at once take us beyond substantial individuals. If it does not, then we are surely on the wrong track.[56]

NOTES

1. The orthography of Malay words in this paper follows that of Wilkinson, Coope & Mohamed Ali (1963). The final *-k* represents the glottal stop, the indeterminate e is written *e* and the long e written *é*.

2. In an exercise which stems in part from the present paper, I have considered the place of 'personality' and 'history' in explaining Malay economic behaviour (Wilder, 1968).

3. My fieldwork, lasting eighteen months, was carried out in Pahang state in the Malay Peninsula (West Malaysia). It was made possible by a grant from the London-Cornell Project for East and Southeast Asian Studies, which I gratefully acknowledge. The Project is supported jointly by the Carnegie Corporation of New York and by the Nuffield Foundation. I am indebted to both the London and Cornell Committees of the Project. I wish also to thank Professors R. W. Firth and Maurice Freedman and Dr H. S. Morris for their help. They, of course, bear no responsibility for the views expressed here.

4. The Malay settlements in Kuala Lumpur, Singapore, or Malacca, although by no means recent developments, have a distinctive rural character, if not origin. Thus an anthropologist recently working among 'urban' Malays found it worth while to trace the comparative origins of some of his subjects in far-flung rural areas as part of his study.

5. I shall not be making very great use of the term *budak* (for reasons to be

explained), but it is as well to note its significance. In the overall context of pre-adult social categories, three terms are relevant: *budak*, *anak*, and *adek*.

The term *budak* refers to any child who can walk and talk. This is its most frequent use. However, it can be applied, in reference, to *anybody younger than the person using the term*, in the sense of 'young fella' or 'youngster', e.g. to an old man by another man yet older than he – which would be rather informal but still respectful usage.

Anak means 'child', but in general it implies a different kind of relation from that expressed by *budak*; *anak* is applicable not only to people, but also to animals or things. A brassière, for instance, is called locally *anak baju* (*baju* = 'shirt'). *Anak* thus implies relation of descent or certain kinds of similarity, that is, it means 'offspring, or miniature, *of* . . .' (see Wilkinson, Coope & Mohamed Ali, 1963, p. 7, 'anak'). It cannot signify relative physiological or social development as can *budak* (hence 'youth', 'adolescence', etc. as possible translations of *budak*). But *budak* in its turn cannot express any idea of relationship other than that of a certain degree of physiological or age difference.

Thus, *budak* means 'he, or they, younger than I (and not otherwise related or relateable to me)'.

Neither term is used in address. In addressing persons they think of as *budak*, elders use a personal name. Similarly with *anak*. I found nothing comparable with Javanese practice where, according to Geertz,

> 'a term of address that is affectionate and preferred . . . [to] the standard *nak* [Mal. *anak*], meaning child, is *lé* for little boys, thought by Javanese to derive from the word *kontolé*, meaning penis, and *nduk* for little girls, thought to derive from a word meaning vagina' (Geertz, 1961, p. 102).

Adek is relevant mainly as a term of address signifying the limits of the social proper: it is a term for babies, i.e. those who cannot walk or talk. (In other ways *adek* may *refer* to younger collaterals, including siblings, among others.)

Therefore, in occasionally translating *budak* as 'adolescent' (or the objective phase as 'adolescence'), I shall be tentatively 'carving out' a section of socialization and the life-cycle, whereas there is, in social reality, only a single verbal categorization – as *budak* – of almost the whole developmental period, from the age of walking and talking to the age of marriage. As I am about to explain in the text, there are transitions or boundaries, but they are only a series of incidents, i.e. degrees towards the attainment, in marriage, of maturity. The term 'adolescence' can serve only as an approximation for the congeries of significant incidents of socialization; it is a fairly good one, nevertheless, because of the extent of the impact of modern schools on village life.

I would not attach this degree of importance to the difference of linguistic categorization between Malay and English were it not for the tendency for terms like 'child', 'child-training', 'adolescence', and even 'socialization' (which have to be used) to develop special connotations and usages. (I am indebted to Peter Wilson for sensitizing me on this point.) As Conklin observes, English terms may become 'descriptive rubrics . . . derived only from a priori notions of expected occurrences on a prearranged grid' (1964, p. 28).

The problem is ultimately one of judicious translation. I would take the position that we must *deliberately* provide inaccurate translations for the simple reason that this is all we can do in order to carry out any analysis at all. (Two of the pitfalls of this necessary procedure have been usefully distinguished by Conklin as translation-labelling analysis and translation-domain analysis; see Conklin, 1964, p. 29.) Thus, while I shall use Malay terms, I shall also try to avoid as far as possible the exclusive use of Malay terms or – though perhaps to a lesser extent – dependence on adscititious qualifications or glosses.

6. 'Marriageable girls are very restricted in their movements and contacts, *ideally* being confined to the house and closely watched even there' (Swift, 1963, p. 269; my emphasis). The following instance gives an idea of how this ideal is conceived:

> Winstedt (1963) gives the meaning of *peram* as to ripen fruit indoors and 'fig., [to] keep (marriageable girl) cooped up at home . . .'. I had often heard *peram* used in the first sense but not in the second. When I asked a friend – a bachelor of about twenty-six (whose sister, about twenty, was 'cooped up' rather like this) – if *peram* could be used of girls, he said no, '*simpan s-ja*', i.e. to keep or hoard, as in a box.

7. Only school registration was compulsory at the time I was in Malaya; actual attendance was, in fact, not compulsory. (The policy was under review in 1965.) However, my census indicates that the proportion of children who do attend school for, say, two years or more is very high indeed. The village, relatively isolated though it is even now, has had a primary school since 1914.

8. I refer here not to 'Malay poverty', which is used to characterize Malays as a cultural (racial) group in other contexts, but to 'poor' Malays within the Malay population. A poor Malay is defined by Malays as being without land or property of any kind, or being poor as a result of inability to exploit his property, i.e. to make it productive. The term used is *miskin*, 'permanently poor', as opposed to *sesak* (occasionally *bangsat*) 'hard up', or 'collectively poor' as compared with other races in Malaya. It should also be noted that economic differentiation is comparatively slight within village society, less marked than that in the plural society of Malaya as a whole. An astute examination of social stratification in a 'Malay' (immigrant Javanese) village has been carried out by Husin Ali (1964).

9. The primary reason is a rudimentary technology as compared with most other parts of the country. This is evident in house styles and agricultural technique. House styles, for example, are modestly distinctive of the region but only slightly differentiated in the range of styles (see Hilton, 1956, which contains a description of houses of Temerloh District, Pahang). Pahang rice cultivation is generally done in fields which are not drained and where the principal tool is consequently the human hand rather than the plough or hoe. Also, the village has no electricity or piped water. On the other hand, transistor radios (and a few valve-type sets) operating on batteries are present in no less than 40 per cent of the households.

Conditions such as these do not permit a differential display of (material) status symbols. The community described by Husin Ali (Johor) is a good example of the more usual type of stratification, and is culturally much more sophisticated than the village I studied. I was especially struck by the differences between Pahang and Kelantan when Manning Nash kindly showed me his field notes on technology and house styles in Kelantan taken in 1964–65. I also recall that during a meeting of London-Cornell workers and other field-workers held in Kuala Lumpur in February 1965 Peter Wilson mentioned a figure of more than sixty when speaking of distinctive house-style features in a village in Selangor. Such degrees of complexity and specialization are, I believe, generally absent from most Pahang villages.

10. The generalization holds even for the areas in and around Negri Sembilan

where Malay kinship is strongly matrilineal in emphasis. (In most of the Peninsula Malay kinship is cognatic, or bilateral.)

11. Probably no Malay village has ever been so isolated or self-contained that outside experts were unknown. Many Malay magicians are great travellers. Alligator hunters and honey collectors as well as circumcision experts are sometimes in demand. I was told, however, that in two neighbouring sub-districts (*mukim*), up- and down-river, respectively, villagers still held the traditional ceremonies with processions and, it seems, local experts.

12. '. . . though the "schools" differ as to whether [circumcision] is indispensable . . . Muslims, with a few doubtful exceptions, in practice regard it as an essential of the faith' (Levy, 1957, p. 251).

13. Compare, for instance, the elaborate public circumcision ceremonial of Kelantan Malays (Cuisinier, 1951, pp. 101–102; Plates V, VI).

14. There is here a problem in the 'modernization' of circumcision which may take different forms in different societies. Alwi bin Sheikh Alhady states, concerning Malays:

> 'Allah be praised, today this ceremonial circumcision is no longer looked upon or practised as an adat [custom] even by the kampong [village] Malays. They have now made the best use of the services of the medical clinics and hospitals, and found them to be very much more economical, healthier, and safer, and thus this old practice is fast disappearing from even the rural areas in the Malay Peninsula' (Alwi, 1962, p. 11).

All this may be true in some areas, but there is probably not such a widespread decline as Alwi claims. Certainly *some* Malays, as I found, look upon medical circumcision with disfavour. (It should be added, however, that Malays, like very remote Brazilian Indians, regard injections as an excellent cure for *illness*; cf. D. Maybury-Lewis, 1967, p. 51, n. 1.)

Compare with this an Australian aboriginal situation reported by Gould (1968). Like (some) Malays, the Gibson Desert aborigines (Western Australia) practise more or less full traditional circumcisions. When it was discovered in 1966 that a lad being prepared for traditional circumcision was already circumcised and that it had been done at a hospital while the boy was working as a stockman near Kalgoorlie, the elders were in no way upset. Instead, they were 'amused by the way everyone had been fooled'. Younger men, however, said the boy 'lacked courage'.

The author specifically remarks that this incident does not necessarily signal a breakdown in tradition: the boy continued his learning of the sacred traditions 'as though he had been circumcised in the accepted way', and there has generally been a rise in the frequency of initiation ceremonies as a result of the ready availability of food and transportation for aborigines living close to white settlements (Gould, 1968, pp. 62–64).

Some aborigines are – so far – indifferent to modern techniques of circumcision. It seems possible, however, that if hospital circumcisions were carried further in the Australian case they could in time lead to a decline in 'tradition' by causing boys to refuse subincision, which is performed in a later rite and is more painful than circumcision. It is subincision, as Gould seems to suggest on the basis of Meggitt's similar Walbiri material, that is supposed to give heightened sexual gratification to the female, something that Malays attribute to a traditionally circumcised penis (see next paragraph in text).

In short, hospital circumcision, as is certainly indicated by Malay attitudes towards it, could destroy the rationalizations for circumcision (virility and erotic satisfaction) and thus undermine 'tradition'. This is precisely what, by implication, Alwi claims has *already* happened among Malays, but the cases I have described seem to indicate the contrary: that 'tradition' has continued, and may continue, to stand up rather well under such changes. It is rather the relation between the sexes that is the primary factor, as I show further on.

15. 'Immediately after this operation [cutting off the foreskin], the *mudin* takes [a] live cock and pushes its head towards the boy's penis once or twice, and notes the response of the cock; should the feathers round the cock's neck puff out when it comes close to the penis, it is traditionally believed to be an omen showing that the boy will be highly sexed, liable to marry more than once, or to be polygamous' (Alwi, 1962, p. 10; cf. Wilkinson, 1920, pp. 17–18).

16. Javanese townsmen seem to be the direct opposite of rural Malays. In a Javanese town, adolescent boys 'are expected to be sexually experienced by the time they are married' (Geertz, 1961, p. 119). Moreover, although sexual maturity marks a change in a Javanese boy's life, and Javanese boys are circumcised, 'sex is rarely discussed openly or joked about or directly symbolized in any ritual' (ibid.). Here there is a sharp contrast with rural Malays, who stress sexual symbolism but frown on premarital sexual experience.

17. Cf. Djamour, 1959, p. 106. Young remarks that 'initiation does not confer the status of responsible adult. When one reads the ethnographic reports closely, it is clear that even initiated youths are still under close supervision' (1965, p. 13). See also Van Gennep, 1960, pp. 65–71.

18. There are, however, few 'shotgun' marriages (*kahwin paksa*, 'forced marriage'; having, of course, nothing to do with premarital pregnancy), even though, strictly speaking, a guardian need not consult either the boy or the girl. Long engagements (*tunang*) are common and, as is implied by this, the concurrence of at least the boy is always sought implicitly or explicitly. But it is acknowledged that a son or daughter has no formal *authority* in arranging marriage.

19. An ethnographer has pointed out that this feature is developed early among Javanese: 'Javanese children are markedly well behaved, obedient, and quiet' (Geertz, 1961, p. 115). I may say, however, that while this is certainly true of children in the presence of a stranger-ethnographer, in *some* domestic situations Malay children are importunate and mischievous!

20. Lit. 'poorly taught'. This is comparable to the accusations of regression to 'childish' behaviour, *durung djawa*, a form of control described by Geertz for Javanese (1961, p. 105). The phonetic similarity is notable. People may also be compared with (domesticated) animals. A form of control that is *not* used is to impute to a person characteristics of the opposite sex, 'He is acting like a woman', etc.

21. An observation on Balinese children is probably relevant here: of two boys of about eight who worked in his house, Colin McPhee remarked:

> 'What went on in the inner life of these two, what they were thinking or absorbing, was an utter mystery to me. In true Balinese fashion they were completely uncommunicative, at least as far as I was concerned, about their real activities. . . . What they did when not around was not withheld from secrecy, for we were old friends. It merely did not occur to either one to mention anything about himself or anything which might be happening in our *banjar* [village]' (McPhee, 1955, p. 75).

Of course, boys of all ages can be used as messengers, that is, they can be specifically entrusted with messages by adults, but this is quite clearly a different matter.

22. '. . . this is a society which does not make a demonstration of its affections [!] at all except with very small children . . . [A] couple may be shy of plainly showing affection, *even privately*' (Swift, 1963, p. 281; my emphasis).

23. Women as young as forty-five perhaps (not past childbearing) are capable of quite sarcastic or lewd remarks in mixed company, though this is by no means a usual thing. Here, wit and sophistication presuppose status (that of older married women). These same women (about forty-five and older) may also go about the house, or near it, at times dressed only in a *sarong* and nude from the waist up, though this also is not a very usual thing. Neither sort of behaviour is necessarily a flouting of the delicate rules of etiquette. It is simply that the canons of 'modesty' are more relaxed for this class of women, symptomatic of the ongoing development of sexual and marital status.

24. Harmony, which is disrupted in such situations, is formally described as 'being in accord' (*sa-suai*; cf. *selesai*, 'settled', 'satisfactory'). Disharmony is *seliseh* or *berseliseh*. This is formal, however; the people are not *preoccupied* with 'harmony' (cf. Geertz, 1961, p. 143; also Peristiany, 1965, p. 3).

25. The formation of such groups among young children is described by Margaret Mead. A group of children watching their father at work on a canoe breaks up

> 'depending on the accident of who passes next along that bit of beach. . . . Within a matter of minutes five or six little boys, all of about the same size, may be playing together, and the group may then break away from the canoe-making central figure and wander off on its own' (Mead, 1964, p. 58; Manus, expedition of 1953).

It may be remarked that Dr Mead considers this behaviour to be part of a broad learning (or socialization) process, an instance of 'mixed empathy-imitativeness' or 'general identification behaviour' (ibid.). A more convincing hypothesis on peers as an agency of socialization is, I think, offered by Parsons & Bales (1956, pp. 122–123).

On the socializing function of fruit-stealing, Aschmann writes:

> 'Memory of taking a neighbour's fruit seems to make a noteworthy contribution to one's sense of belonging and attachment to a home neighbourhood, an important asset in the generally rootless land of Southern California' (Aschmann, 1963, p. 76).

26. I suspect the *kutu* is a recent introduction in the village I studied. It is referred to by Swift (1965, pp. 75–76). While Ardener (1964, p. 203) mentions rotating credit associations among Malays, she is apparently unable to establish what the indigenous term is.

27. A common response to the requests of parents addressed to a child, of adults to older boys, and even of husbands to young wives is, *Malas*, 'I don't want to', lit. 'lazy' (given by Wilkinson, Coope & Mohamed Ali, 1963, as Kelantan dialect for 'reluctant'; though Winstedt, 1963, says it is archaic in this sense).

28. Undoubtedly this aloofness is partly the result of the accepted means of cooperation in labour, which is more or less exactly reciprocative or, alternatively, paid for in cash; it therefore has to be calculated in advance; consequently, it is almost always adults who are involved.

29. I believe Swift underrates the place of women in practical religion in saying that

> 'there is . . . no place for women in village Islam. Women have religious

duties, but these provide no opportunities for them to hold public positions, or to participate in public worship' (1963, p. 282).

It all depends on how you define 'village Islam' and 'public worship'. In the village I studied women play an important part in the *haj* and in the *organization* of religious or mosque-centred feasts (labour in cooking, sewing, etc.) as well as in evening prayers in the mosque. It is only at Friday prayer that they are totally excluded from the mosque, and, in effect, from 'village Islam'.

An observation by Wilkinson shows that females are given a definite place in village Islam by being assigned a status clearly complementary to that of males. Writing on the religious education of Malay boys and girls, he describes the ceremonies marking completion of the boy's education, which are combined with circumcision (Wilkinson, 1920, p. 17; cf. Djamour, 1959, p. 106 f.). He adds that girls also have ceremonies on completion of their Koran training, but that these are 'much simpler and less public' (ibid.). He seems to argue, therefore, that boys and girls follow a parallel development. (There is no mention of clitoridectomy.) But he remarks in a note that in Patani (a predominantly Malay state in southern Thailand) the girl's ceremony, which includes ear-boring, 'is performed in infancy' (Wilkinson, 1920, p. 19). The last-mentioned fact would particularly lend support to the argument that women's role in practical religious organization is definite and is socialized as such.

30. There are two parts to a marriage: the Islamic (legal) rite (*nikah*), usually performed in the evening, and the Malay traditional festivities (*kahwin*), held the next day. For first marriages, the whole is conveniently termed *kahwin* and in virtually every case takes place in its entirety at the girl's parents' house. If either party – certainly the woman – has been married before, only the *nikah* is performed.

31. 'This belief . . . – that it is the woman who seduces, who is passionate – is a common Javanese attitude' (Geertz, 1961, p. 130).

32. In his discussion of this paper (tape-recorded), Professor Banton remarked that Malay youths appear to learn not by doing but by watching (and waiting). I doubt that he had this kind of situation in mind!

33. It has occurred to me that in both the cases I have cited where there has been unusual familiarity between boy(s) and girl(s) (public teasing and surreptitious visiting) the persons are first cousins. I can think of no special reason for the coincidence except social proximity.

34. It should be noted that marital status among Malays is primarily signified by having gone through the ceremonies of *nikah-kahwin*, and does not necessarily require actually having a spouse at any given moment.

35. The sharpness of the distinction between 'married' and 'unmarried' (e.g. betrothed) is reminiscent of the Manus case as described by Fortune:

> 'In Manus boys and girls are usually betrothed several years before marriage . . . Betrothal is as sacrosanct as marriage. The unmarried adolescent girl is required to remain virgin. The boy . . . nowadays is without exception required to remain chaste' (n.d., p. 124).

The consistency of these imperatives is carried to an extreme:

> 'The men of Peri, without exception, do not know that women menstruate between puberty and marriage. The young women, without realizing that all their men are so ignorant, faithfully conceal the facts from them' (Fortune, n.d., p. 149; see also p. 82).

36. Wilkinson (1920) and Djamour (1959) deal briefly with adolescence and socialization respectively.

37. Parkinson (1967) has drawn upon Swift's material and made similar points to Swift's. I have discussed Parkinson's argument (Wilder, 1968).

38. It is also stated that 'the process of socialization is a continuous one throughout the life of the individual; and it is a man's closest relatives [members of his two families] who, by their day-to-day comment, both verbal and non-verbal [*sic*], keep him from deviating too far from the cultural norms' (Geertz, 1961, p. 5). It seems reasonable to infer from this and statements already cited that Mrs Geertz believes: (a) that the family is Javanese society writ small, and (b) that childhood experiences are continuously relived. Both naïve propositions Parsons and Bales would reject strongly:

> 'Looked at as a part of the society, the family is, even in primitive societies, a *specialized*, i.e., differentiated, part of the larger system; it is quite erroneous to regard it as a "microcosm" of the whole. We will maintain that at one stage the evolving personality is a kind of "mirror-image" microcosm of the nuclear family, but it is crucial that it *cannot* be such an image of the whole society, since this is inevitably a more complex system than any family, and the family is specialized in relation to it' (1956, p. 33; their emphasis).

Parsons has also made this point in earlier publications.

They point out, further, that the socialization process is 'inherently time-bound', i.e. irreversible (1956, p. 37), a view that does not seem to be taken account of in Mrs Geertz's theory.

39. Indeed, in his zeal to avoid a causal statement, Swift prefers to see a functional *identity* of childhood discipline (domestic) and adult attitudes (extra-domestic) (see Gerth & Mills, 1954, p. 156; also Young, 1965, p. 162). The view seems to me hardly tenable.

40. As indicated by various citations in this paper, not all facts are distorted or obscured in Mrs Geertz's presentation. Yet methodological weaknesses, and omissions, are still such as to detract considerably from the value of the analysis. Some of these follow.

Although the title of the book is *The Javanese Family: A Study of Kinship and Socialization*, the study was actually carried out in a single town and the original report was entitled *Family and Life-cycle in Modjokuto* (see Koentjaraningrat, 1962, p. 872). In its published form the coverage is extended to 35 *million* Javanese. The book abounds with 'typical characteristics' and 'typical patterns', which have clearly been arrived at on the basis of seven or eight main informants and about fifteen families in a single locality, which is in fact a town (Geertz, 1961, pp. 169–170). In consequence there are a vast number of facts, such as, importantly, the 'matrifocal family', which are at least partly the result of local conditions. There is a tendency to rationalizations, 'just so' phrases introduced with the words 'because' or 'in order to'. Aside from their questionable bases, such rationalizations do not in many cases ring true (see below, note 41). Many facts said to be 'distinctively Javanese' are not distinctive. There is in some places an obfuscating use of jargon. It is also curious that Mrs Geertz does not include in her analysis the results of projective tests (thematic apperception tests) administered during fieldwork (see Geertz, 1961, p. 168). One result is mentioned in the book (at p. 139, n. 1). (Many of these points are also made in the tactful review of *The Javanese Family* by Koentjaraningrat, 1962.)

41. This seems to me closer to the mark than Mrs Geertz's observation on the same fact among some Javanese:

> 'Many mothers continue to feed their children themselves until after they are five or six *in order to keep the diet balanced* by seeing to it that the child does not eat all of the minute quantity of protein (usually simply soy-bean cake) first and then not want to finish out the rice which is the main body of the meal' (Geertz, 1961, p. 98; my emphasis).

42. 'Family life is like a hall endowed with the finest acoustical properties. Growing children hear not only their parents' words (and in most cases gradually ignore them), they hear the intentions, the attitudes behind the words. Above all they learn what their parents *really* admire, *really* despise' (Wilder, 1967, pp. 261–262; emphasis in original).

43. Psychoanalysis has developed from the study of adults to include prominently the study of young children (cf. Sebag, 1964, p. 220).

44. Of the six studies of child-rearing in *Six Cultures* (Whiting, 1963), one deals with adolescence (Gusii). Four of the field teams 'did not feel that they had enough knowledge' to include a description of adolescence (Whiting, 1966, p. xxiv; see also Cohen, 1966, p. 359).

45. '. . . there has been a tendency to analyze arbitrarily delimited segments rather than complete sets. While such a restriction may simplify componential treatment, *its arbitrary quality may also lead to the distortion of significant ethnographic relations*' (Conklin, 1964, p. 45; my emphasis).

46. '[Non-family] life to newcomers presents itself as a brightly lighted stage where they will be called upon to play roles exhibiting courage, fair dealing, magnanimity, wisdom, and helpfulness. Hoping and trembling a little, they feel that they are almost ready for these great demands upon them' (Wilder, 1967, p. 262).

47. The married pair in the nuclear family is a 'power-coalition' (Parsons & Bales, 1956, p. 80).

48. Parsons observes that as a child grows up 'the inequality vis-à-vis his parents is lessened' (Parsons & Bales, 1956, p. 46), but he does not refer to marriage and seems to see no special problems in relation to the lessening of the relative difference of power.

49. In a sample I took of 317 marriages, 155 (48·9 per cent) resulted in divorce (this includes desertion, treated in Muslim marriage contracts as leading to an automatic divorce called *pasah*). The average for the whole of Malaya and Singapore among Muslims (Malays) seems to be around 50 per cent. No convincing explanation has been offered for diachronic and regional variations in this rate (see Djamour, 1959, Ch. VI; Swift, 1965, pp. 119–134). Recent legislation in Singapore, however, has markedly reduced the divorce rate (Djamour, 1966) and a similar result may perhaps be expected soon in the Peninsula.

While there is no stigma attached to divorce among Malays, divorce has social effects which cannot be discounted. People expect, and deplore, frequent divorce *as a general phenomenon*, and presumably the attitude affects the esteem of individuals in divorce.

50. Lévi-Strauss implies, in speaking (rather dangerously) of 'la pensée indonésienne', that symmetrical and asymmetrical forms of social process (the dualism of male and female and an asymmetric marriage rule), while contradictory, coexist fairly generally in Indonesia. Though made from slightly different premises, this assertion corresponds with my argument.

51. Swift would prefer to bring in Freudian theory at this point (1965, p. 108, n. 1).

52. Schismogenesis is '*a process of differentiation in the norms of individual behaviour resulting from cumulative interaction between individuals*' (Bateson, 1936, p. 175; italics in original). One of the forms of schismogenesis is socialization; I have defined socialization in terms similar to Bateson's for schismogenesis (above, p. 216).

53. One of the sources of ambivalence in student life today has been remarked upon as follows:

> 'For example, young manual workers gain such a large measure of financial independence at a time when students and technical apprentices lead an economically restricted life, that the working youths propose fashions and models of behaviour which are copied by their cultural superiors. At the same time knowledge retains its importance as an element of social ranking. The resulting ambiguities of value orientation and of clearcut social identification are important elements in the assessment of our cultural trends' (Peristiany, 1965, p. 18, n. 5).

54. Erikson, 1958, p. 98: 'he was more nobody than at any other time.'

55. Whiting & Child recognized this state of affairs in 1953 in the following terms: many well-known culture and personality studies 'seem rather to be oriented toward obtaining and organizing sound and persuasive evidence which will convince the layman of the falsity of an extreme statement already known to the anthropologist as an overstatement' (1953, p. 7).

56. The present paper is a revised and amplified version of the one presented to the A.S.A. Conference in 1967. I wish to thank those who have helped at various stages: Dr R. Jain who, in my absence, presented an earlier version to the Birmingham conference; my father, W. D. Wilder, M.D., for drawing my attention to Dr Gould's most interesting article; especially Dr Philip Mayer who, in addition to his many other tasks, arranged to have the paper presented and has at different times offered salutary criticism on it; and Dr Peter J. Wilson who read and commented liberally on what later became an interim version of the paper; finally my wife, who accompanied me in the field, for pitting her interpretations against mine. Any inadequacies or obscurities in the final result are my fault entirely.

REFERENCES

ALWI BIN SHEIKH ALHADY. 1962. *Malay Customs and Traditions*. Singapore: Eastern Universities Press Ltd.

ARDENER, SHIRLEY. 1964. The Comparative Study of Rotating Credit Associations. *Journal of the Royal Anthropological Institute* 94 (2): 201–229.

ASCHMANN, HOMER. 1963. Proprietary Rights to Fruit on Trees Growing on Residential Property. *Man* **63**: 75–76 (Article No. 84).

BATESON, GREGORY. 1936. *Naven: A Survey of the Problems Suggested by a Composite Picture of the Culture of a New Guinea*

Tribe drawn from Three Points of View. Cambridge: Cambridge University Press. Second edition, Stanford, Calif.: Stanford University Press, 1958.

COHEN, YEHUDI A. 1966. On Alternative Views of the Individual in Culture-and-Personality Studies. *American Anthropologist* **68** (2, Part I): 355–361.

CONKLIN, HAROLD C. 1964. Ethnogenealogical Method. In W. H. Goodenough (ed.), *Explorations in Cultural Anthropology. Essays in Honor of George Peter Murdock*. New York: McGraw-Hill.

CUISINIER, JEANNE. 1951. *Sumangat: L'Âme et son Culte en Indochine et en Indonésie*. Paris: Gallimard.

DJAMOUR, JUDITH. 1959. *Malay Kinship and Marriage in Singapore*. London School of Economics Monographs on Social Anthropology 21. London: Athlone Press (University of London).

—— 1966. *The Muslim Matrimonial Court in Singapore*. London School of Economics Monographs on Social Anthropology 31. London: Athlone Press (University of London).

DOUGLAS, MARY. 1966. *Purity and Danger: An Analysis of Concepts of Pollution and Taboo*. London: Routledge & Kegan Paul; New York: Praeger.

DOWNS, RICHARD E. 1964. Malay. In F. M. LeBar, G. C. Hickey, J. K. Musgrave *et al.*, *Ethnic Groups of Mainland Southeast Asia*. New Haven, Conn.: H.R.A.F. Press.

DUBOIS, CORA A. 1944. *The People of Alor: A Social-Psychological Study of an East Indian Island*. Minneapolis: University of Minnesota Press.

ERIKSON, ERIK H. 1958. *Young Man Luther*. New York: Norton.

FIRTH, RAYMOND W. 1964. Comment on 'Dynamic Theory' in Social Anthropology. In *Essays on Social Organization and Values*. London School of Economics Monographs on Social Anthropology 28. London: Athlone Press (University of London).

FIRTH, ROSEMARY. 1966. *Housekeeping among Malay Peasants*. London School of Economics Monographs on Social Anthropology 7. Second edition. London: Athlone Press (University of London).

FORTES, MEYER. 1958. Introduction to J. Goody (ed.), *The Developmental Cycle in Domestic Groups*. Cambridge Papers in Social Anthropology 1. Cambridge: Cambridge University Press.

—— 1967. Totem and Taboo. (Presidential Address 1966.) *Proceedings of the Royal Anthropological Institute of Great Britain and Ireland for 1966*: 5–22.

FORTUNE, REO F. n.d. *Manus Religion: An Ethnological Study of the Manus Natives of the Admiralty Islands.* Lincoln: University of Nebraska Press. (Original edition published Philadelphia, 1935.)

GEERTZ, CLIFFORD. 1956. Religious Belief and Economic Behaviour in a Central Javanese Town: Some Preliminary Considerations. *Economic Development and Cultural Change* **4** (2): 134–158.

— 1960. *The Religion of Java.* New York: The Free Press.

— 1963. *Peddlers and Princes: Social Change and Economic Modernization in Two Indonesian Towns.* Chicago: University of Chicago Press.

— 1965. *The Social History of an Indonesian Town.* Cambridge, Mass.: M.I.T. Press.

GEERTZ, HILDRED. 1961. *The Javanese Family: A Study of Kinship and Socialization.* New York: Free Press of Glencoe Inc.

GENNEP, ARNOLD VAN. 1960. *The Rites of Passage.* (First published 1909.) Translated by Vizedom & Caffee. London: Routledge & Kegan Paul; Chicago: University of Chicago Press.

GERTH, HANS & MILLS, C. W. 1954. *Character and Social Structure: The Psychology of Social Institutions.* London: Routledge & Kegan Paul.

GLUCKMAN, MAX (ed.). 1964. *Closed Systems and Open Minds: The Limits of Naivety in Social Anthropology.* Edinburgh and London: Oliver & Boyd; Chicago: Aldine.

GOULD, RICHARD A. 1968. Masculinity and Mutilation in a Primitive Society. *Medical Opinion and Review* January: 58–75.

HILTON, R. N. 1956. The Basic Malay House. *Journal of the Malay Branch, Royal Asiatic Society* **29**: 134–155.

HUSIN ALI, S. 1964. *Social Stratification in Kampong Bagan: A Study of Class, Status, Conflict and Mobility in a Rural Malay Community.* Monographs of the Malaysian Branch, Royal Asiatic Society 1. Singapore: Malaysian Branch, Royal Asiatic Society.

KARDINER, ABRAM. 1945. *The Psychological Frontiers of Society* (in collaboration with R. Linton, C. DuBois & J. West). New York: Columbia University Press; London: Oxford University Press.

KOENTJARANINGRAT. 1962. Review of *The Javanese Family: A Study of Kinship and Socialization,* by Hildred Geertz. *American Anthropologist* **64**: 872–874.

LEACH, EDMUND R. 1958. Magical Hair (Curl Bequest Prize Essay 1957). *Journal of the Royal Anthropological Institute* **88** (2): 147–164. Reprinted in J. Middleton (ed.), *Myth and Cosmos:*

Readings in Mythology and Symbolism. Garden City, N.Y.: Natural History Press (Doubleday), 1967. Pp. 77–108.

LÉVI-STRAUSS, CLAUDE. 1950. Introduction à l'Oeuvre de Marcel Mauss. In Marcel Mauss, *Sociologie et Anthropologie.* Paris: Presses Universitaires de France.

—— 1958. Les Organisations dualistes existent-elles? In *Anthropologie Structurale.* Paris: Plon.

LEVY, RUBEN. 1957. *The Social Structure of Islam: Being the Second Edition of the Sociology of Islam.* Cambridge: Cambridge University Press.

LEWIN, KURT. 1939. Field Theory and Experiment in Social Psychology: Concepts and Methods. *American Journal of Sociology* **44**: 868–897. Reprinted in D. Cartwright (ed.), *Field Theory in Social Science: Selected Theoretical Papers,* Ch. VI. New York: Harper & Row, 1951.

MAYBURY-LEWIS, DAVID. 1967. *Akwe-Shavante Society.* Oxford: Clarendon Press.

MEAD, MARGARET. 1964. *Continuities in Cultural Evolution.* New Haven, Conn: Yale University Press.

MCPHEE, COLIN, 1955. Children and Music in Bali. (First published 1938.) In M. Mead & M. Wolfenstein (eds.), *Childhood in Contemporary Cultures.* Chicago: University of Chicago Press.

PARKINSON, BRIEN K. 1967. Non-economic Factors in the Economic Retardation of the Rural Malays. *Modern Asian Studies* **1** (1): 31–46.

PARSONS, TALCOTT & BALES, R. 1956. *Family, Socialization and Interaction Process.* London: Routledge & Kegan Paul.

PERISTIANY, JOHN G. 1965. Introduction to J. G. Peristiany (ed.), *Honour and Shame: The Values of Mediterranean Society.* London: Weidenfeld & Nicolson; Chicago: University of Chicago Press.

SEBAG, LUCIEN. 1964. *Marxisme et Structuralisme.* Paris: Payot.

SWIFT, MICHAEL G. 1963. Men and Women in Malay Society. In B. E. Ward (ed.), *Women in the New Asia: The Changing Social Roles of Men and Women in South and South-East Asia.* Paris: UNESCO.

—— 1965. *Malay Peasant Society in Jelebu.* London School of Economics Monographs on Social Anthropology 29. London: Athlone Press (University of London).

WHITING, BEATRICE B. (ed.). 1963. *Six Cultures: Studies of Child Rearing.* New York and London: Wiley

—— 1966. Introduction to R. A. LeVine and B. B. LeVine, *Nyansongo: A Gusii Community in Kenya.* Six Cultures Series 2. New York and London: Wiley.

WHITING, JOHN W. M. & CHILD, IRVIN L. 1953. *Child Training and Personality: A Cross-cultural Study.* New Haven, Conn.: Yale University Press.

WILDER, THORNTON. 1967. *The Eighth Day.* New York: Popular Library and Harper & Row.

WILDER, WILLIAM D. 1968. Islam, Other Factors and Malay Backwardness: Comments on an Argument. *Modern Asian Studies* 2 (2): 155–164.

WILKINSON, R. J. 1920. The Incidents of Malay Life. Second edition, revised. *Papers on Malay Subjects: Life and Customs, Part I.* Singapore: Kelley & Walsh.

WILKINSON, R. J., COOPE, A. E. & MOHAMED ALI BIN MOHAMED. 1963. *An Abridged Malay–English English–Malay Dictionary.* Pocket edition. London: Macmillan.

WINSTEDT, R. O. 1963. *An Unabridged Malay–English Dictionary.* Fifth edition, enlarged. Kuala Lumpur: Marican.

YOUNG, FRANK W. 1965. *Initiation Ceremonies: A Cross-cultural Study of Status Dramatization.* Indianapolis, New York, Kansas City: Bobbs-Merrill.

Anthony Forge

Learning to See in New Guinea

This paper concentrates on one small aspect of the socialization process among the Abelam of the Sepik District, New Guinea. It suggests that through their early experiences, particularly in the context of the tambaran cult,[1] boys and young men acquire a set of fixed expectations about what they will see in two dimensions, that is on the flat; and hence that polychrome two-dimensional paintings become a closed system, unrelated to natural objects, or to carvings and other three-dimensional art objects, or, indeed, to anything outside the paintings. These expectations act to prevent them 'seeing', that is making sense of, anything in two dimensions that is not part of the closed system; they also enable Abelam flat painting to act directly on the fully initiated adult as a system of communication and not as a representation of any other communication system such as myth. I shall not here be concerned with the problem of what is communicated, nor, indeed, with the fundamental problem of whether anthropologists have the techniques to discover what is communicated by such systems, but only with showing that such a system exists and operates.

THE ABELAM[2]

The Abelam are a group of more than 30,000 living on the southern foothills of the Prince Alexander Mountains in the Sepik District, New Guinea. They speak mutually intelligible dialects of a language of the Ndu family and as such are one of the largest language groups in lowland New Guinea. Their population density is high by New Guinea standards, averaging 120 p.s.m. for the Northern and Eastern Abelam and 200 p.s.m. for the South-western Abelam. Villages are the basic political and war-making units and have populations of between 300 and 800.

Yams form the basis of the diet, supplemented by taro,

coconuts, breadfruit, and sago; pig-raising provides virtually the only source of animal protein and a useful means of acquiring the highly valued shell rings which constitute Abelam wealth. Ceremonial exchange relationships are of great importance and, together with the exchange relationships set up by marriage, which continue for three generations, provide the main means of distributing produce within and between villages. The exchange system is also the organizing principle for all ceremonial.

Ceremonies are performed by one-half of a dual organization, who initiate the sons of their exchange partners in the other half and receive pigs from their partners in payment. The next ceremony is performed by the other half and the arrangements are reversed. Throughout most of the area, eight ceremonies of increasing importance and elaboration form a cycle. A man may be initiated only at a ceremony performed by his exchange partners; it therefore takes two full cycles to complete his initiation (see *Figure 1*).

FIGURE 1 *The structure of Abelam tambaran ceremonial*

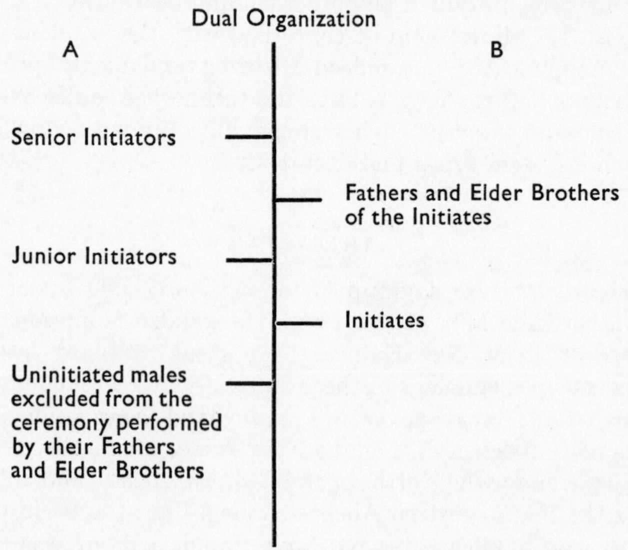

A will perform ceremonies 1, 3, 5, and 7 of the eight-part cycle; B will perform 2, 4, 6, and 8, thereafter starting a new cycle by performing ceremony 1.

The Northern and Eastern Abelam have shown remarkable tenacity in retaining their traditional cults, and in resisting the temptations of the cargo cults that have swept in waves through the Sepik ever since the end of the Japanese occupation and have affected all their neighbours. Cult activity seems to have gone through a low point in the early 'fifties, but by 1958, when I first went there, it was reviving, and in 1963, when I last left, was in full spate. Mission activity throughout the area has been intense since the Second World War; various varieties of Christian faith are represented and all were, at least initially, opposed not only to the cult but also to the art that formed the focus of the various ceremonies of the cult. The persistence of cult activity among the Northern and Eastern Abelam is so remarkable in the context of general New Guinea experience that some idea of its scale may be helpful. During two and a half years of fieldwork I attended more than twenty ceremonies, each involving considerable artistic work, and missed at least twice as many. In the six-month ceremonial season of 1958–59, fifteen new ceremonial houses were built within five miles of my base village, and in 1963 there were over 100 ceremonial houses in the Northern and Eastern Abelam villages whose total population is about 15,000. The same area is also comparatively prosperous in cash terms, selling coffee and carvings and washing gold dust from certain streams, and it is, furthermore, the area in which the first Local Government Council in the inland part of the Sepik District was set up. It is an interesting contradiction of the stereotype of development in New Guinea that this small part of the vast Sepik District, which has so strongly maintained its traditional cults, should also be one of the most 'developed' and the only part to have resisted cargo cults. This paper is no place for an attempt at explanation, but two factors that are probably relevant are, first, the peculiarly satisfying nature of the long-yam cult, a cult of fertility and nourishment of a decidedly phallic nature, and the high road to male prestige; and, second, the function of frequent performance of ceremonial in crystallizing and reordering relationships between individuals and groups, thus enabling large-scale enterprises, including those producing cash, to be undertaken among a people normally characterized by a profound and aggressive individualism.

The material considered in this paper comes mainly from the two Eastern Abelam villages of Bengragum and Wingei, and the Northern Abelam village of Yanuko, but most of the discussion would apply to the whole Abelam area.[3]

For convenience, Abelam ritual can be divided into two cults, the long-yam cult and the tambaran cult; the Abelam make the distinction themselves and the rituals for each are performed at different times. The long-yam cult involves the cultivation of certain varieties of *Dioscorea alata* in special gardens which are forbidden to women, and may only be entered by men observing a whole series of taboos, of which the most important are those on sex and eating meat. Long yams require a great deal of ritual and magic at every stage of their cultivation from planting until harvest about six months later; they are then elaborately decorated, including being provided with a wood or basketry mask, displayed, and subsequently presented to the exchange partner of the grower. Prestige depends on the length and number of such yams grown by the individual (single tubers up to 12 ft in length have been recorded, but any village will usually have a few of 9 ft or so in any one season).

The tambaran cult ceremonies are held after the yam displays and all the subsequent exchanges have been completed, by which time the yams are safely in their store houses. Any tambaran ceremony requires large quantities of food, and the main harvesting of the non-sacred yams (mainly *Dioscorea esculenta*) and taro has to take place before the preparations for the ceremony can begin. The tambaran season must end when the work of clearing the long-yam gardens is due to start; it is, therefore, limited to about four months. No ceremonies of any kind can be held while the long yams are growing. At the symbolic level the two cults are united, both being concerned with aspects of the *nggwalndu*, the spirits associated with the nominally patrilineal clans which are the basic units of the ceremonial structure and of village and hamlet organization. Both are cults of fertility and male prestige and aggression (Forge, 1966).

The tambaran cult involves a series of displays of things all loosely classifiable as art. At each ceremony the initiates are told that they are being shown the *nggwalndu*; then at the next ceremony they are told that they were tricked last time but this time they really will see it; and so on until the final ceremony when they are in fact shown the huge carved figures that are considered to be the real *nggwalndu*. Since an individual is ineligible for an initiation staged by members of his own half of the dual organization, it takes from twenty to thirty years, two full cycles, for any man to see all eight displays.

Both the yam displays and the tambaran ceremonies take place on the *amei* (ceremonial ground) that forms the centre of the hamlet; the village itself has no centre, being a collection of hamlets. The ceremonial house, inside which the majority of the displays of the tambaran cult are staged, is at one side of the *amei*; its high triangular façade (sometimes 60 ft high) is raked forward and dominates the *amei*, the hamlet, and the village; it can be seen for miles around. The façade has a base of decorative matting in which the entrance is set, then a carved board usually of heads, but the bulk of the façade is taken up by bands of polychrome painting on sago-spathe. The largest and most important of these paintings are those at the bottom – a huge row of *nggwalndu* heads whose large round eyes look down on the *amei* (*Plate I*).

CHILDHOOD

Abelam children are treated with great indulgence, although they may be scolded when older. They are very rarely beaten in secular contexts, with the exception that girls, both just before and after puberty, may be beaten by their brothers or father for secret contact with boys other than their betrothed or those approved by him. Boys are encouraged to accompany their fathers in gardening activities and will be given a corner of the father's mundane yam garden as their own and urged to tend it, but it is usually the mother who does the bulk of the work. Boys roam around in gangs, turning up to help at any communal activity where soup is likely to be distributed, often only just in time to do a little work before the distribution; but even in these circumstances children are never grudged food and are always being urged to eat more. Girls by and large accompany their mothers everywhere and start to carry burdens and perform other female tasks as soon as they can walk. A girl will usually be betrothed at about ten, and from then on will divide her time between her mother and her mother-in-law; it is the latter who should teach her to cook and perform other domestic tasks.

Children of both sexes call their mother's brother 'mother', and their father's mother's brother 'father's mother'; these relatives are not only especially indulgent and are turned to at the first sign of a cross word at home, but are specially associated with feeding. The mother's brother, in particular, has the right to provide a large proportion of the food eaten by the child – a hungry child is as much a reproach to the mother's brother as to the father. This provision of food establishes the right to perform ceremonial services for the sister's son, particularly during initiations, services which have to be paid for in the highly valued shell rings. Disputes occasionally occur about who is entitled to act as mother's brother in ceremony; on such occasions to have consistently fed a child is the strongest form of entitlement, even overriding genealogical proximity, although the blood tie can never be absolutely excluded.

Girls should be betrothed well before puberty and most of those without obvious defects are. At first menstruation girls go through an initiation ceremony involving seclusion and a series of exchanges and displays of wealth by father and father's exchange partner, followed by a beating and nettle-rubbing performed by the men. The main part of the ceremony is, however, in the hands of the women and occupies a whole day. The girl is scarified at dawn; she is held by her mother's brother, but it is the senior women who cut the patterns on her breasts, belly, and upper arms. The men are then frozen off their ceremonial ground, and the women perform their own secret ceremonial involving, among other things, transvestite women who magnificently imitate and mock the swaggering of their husbands and brothers. I have attended only the early stages of a female initiation but believe that I have seen more than any Abelam male. I understand that pantomimes of sexual intercourse and advice on the conduct of love affairs are included, and there is certainly feasting and much riotous laughter. The women abandon the *amei* only at nightfall when it is elaborately and ostentatiously cleansed from the effects of 'all those vulvas' by the returning men.

The initiated girl is then beautifully decorated and begins an

PLATE I *Ceremonial house at Kinbanggwa village, N. Abelam. The huge* nggwalndu *faces form the bottom row of the painted façade; in front is the* amei

PLATE II *A section of the chamber containing a tambaran display in a ceremonial house at Kinbanggwa village. The main display, of large and small painted heads, is to the left. The two styles of* nggwalndu *representation are seen in the centre: the carved and painted wooden figure to the left and the flat painted head and arms to the right. For detailed discussion of the differences,* *see pp. 280–1*

idyllic period during which she is not expected to work, is welcomed everywhere within the village and in neighbouring villages, and offered the finest food. It is at this time that a girl wears a small string bag of special design covering her genitalia; traditionally, this was the only time any member of either sex wore any form of clothing. Its removal about a year after scarification is a sign that the marriage has been consummated and the girl has started on the hard life of a married woman. As no art except for face-painting is involved in female ceremonial I shall not be considering women further in this paper.

TAMBARAN INITIATIONS

Since the tambaran cult with its cycle of ceremonies requires twenty to thirty years before a man is fully initiated, a child will 'attend' every ceremony performed by his father's exchange partner from birth. All that is essential is that he is physically present for at least part of the time and that his father presents a pig to the partner who acts as initiator. Babes-in-arms are to be seen at all ceremonies, held by their mother's brother, and four- and five-year-olds are expected to form part of the band of initiates and go through the whole ceremony. Children are often frightened and run away, particularly if there is a beating in prospect; the only sanction applied is the mockery of their fellows; they will be credited with the initiation even if they never set eyes on the display.

There is no form of instruction of the initiates at tambaran ceremonies; they have to undergo certain ordeals, usually beating and/or rubbing with stinging nettles, during which they are carried or held by their mother's brother, who takes a good proportion of the punishment. Men with a reputation for bravery tend to stroll down the gauntlet line of initiators and back again, scorning to dodge even though their charges suffer in consequence far more than do those of cowards, who scuttle along with as much speed as is decent. Beating is an essential part of some of the ceremonies and has to be performed for that reason alone; rubbing with nettles is, however, considered beneficial in itself to the initiate, and great efforts are made to catch every eligible child. Initiates have also to observe some taboos for a few days, and have to participate in certain rituals during the ceremony, but nothing is explained to them; they are hauled out, told to perform certain actions, and then to keep out of the way until they are required again. Although the ceremonies are ostensibly put on for their benefit they are the least important people present and their reactions vary between bewilderment and terror.

In some parts of the area there is a separate puberty seclusion for boys; in others, this is amalgamated with a tambaran ceremony but involves only those initiates of the correct age. Beatings and nettle-rubbings at the beginning of the period of seclusion are more than usually severe, and are followed by instruction in cleansing from sexual contact with women by penis-bleeding. This operation is performed by the father's exchange partner on the first occasion and thereafter by the young man himself or by some mutual arrangement. The foreskin is rolled back and the glans rubbed with nettles; after a minute or so the glans is slashed with a piece of broken bottle (previously a bamboo knife), and the blood allowed to fall into the stream on whose banks the operation must be carried out. The seclusion follows during which the initiates are stuffed with the finest food and given general instruction on the role of men in Abelam society and on the danger of sexual contact with women to long yams and sacred things in general. Instruction during seclusion does not include any interpretation of the meaning of the various tambaran ceremonies or any learning or even telling of myths, of which the Abelam know remarkably few. Seclusion lasts from three weeks to two months, depending on the part of the area, and is ended with the ceremonial re-entry into the village of the initiates, gorgeously painted and wearing huge feather head-dresses. The face-painting is in the style used for yam masks, *nggwalndu*, and initiators, except that the eyes are closed and painted over entirely and very thickly with the yellow paint that covers the cheeks, so that the returning initiates appear not merely blind, but creatures who have no provision for eyes at all.

Apart from attendance as initiates at tambaran ceremonies, boys of between about eight or nine and puberty have a vital role to play in the ceremonial life of their elders. Abelam have very strongly held beliefs about the dangers of sex to sacred activities. Although the dangers are expressed in terms of vulvas it is not women as such who are dangerous, but the sex act and the aroused vulva; thus, for the six months the long yams are growing, a man observing a sex taboo will happily take food from his wife, but should she have committed adultery the food would contaminate him and hence his long yams. Young men are considered too susceptible to the charms of their wives and paramours to be trustworthy in the strict observance of the six-months' taboo on all sexual activity. In general, a man is not considered adult until about thirty, when he should have got over all his childish enthusiasms, had a few children and many affairs, and be prepared to settle down to the really serious business of life, growing long yams. In these circumstances most young men entrust their long yams to older men, usually big men with high prestige who recruit adherents by taking charge of their yams.

In the cultivation of long yams boys before puberty are of great importance; not only are they incapable of breaking the taboo but they have never had any contact from which to be cleansed. These virgin boys are used to break the ground with digging sticks and dig the holes over which the yam is planted, although adult men usually clear away the loosened earth. Virgin boys, under the close supervision and direction of the expert, frequently perform many of the operations in the actual preparation and distribution of the magical substances used at every stage to encourage the yam. Virgin boys are also used to avoid danger of contamination in distributing the benefits of a tambaran ceremony. Villages that have helped in the preparation bring a few very large and valuable shell rings which are laid in front of the display for the three-day period of the actual ceremony. These rings, with a cassowary bone dagger stuck through the middle of them, are a symbol of peace and participation, but they have also been at the heart of the display and the focus of the sacredness of the ceremony. They are brought out and laid on banana leaves, then carefully taken home where they are washed on the *amei* in bespelled coconut milk by virgin boys, who subsequently sprinkle the mixture onto the ceremonial houses, the *nggwalndu*, and the long yams of their village, thus transferring the benefit of the ceremony.

Boys, then, are socialized very slowly, not being expected to become fully adult until they are about thirty. Few, if any, men can feed their new households by their own production for the first years of marriage. At the same time, they are exposed to a whole series of ceremonies at which they are shown paintings and carved objects under conditions of great tension and associated with various rituals of which they understand nothing but which have the recurring theme of pain. It is significant that the last and most elaborate of the ceremonies, at which initiates are shown the actual *nggwalndu*, is said to be a 'good' tambaran, and involves no beating, and rubbing only with dead nettles. This fact is concealed from the initiates and the younger ones would be unable to scream more vigorously were the nettles 'live'.

After the display and parades are over the ceremonial house and its initiation chamber are sealed and the long-yam planting season begins. The payment of pigs by the fathers of the initiates to their exchange partners is said to 'buy' the display, and after the following long-yam display the chamber is reopened and dismantled by the initiates and their fathers. It is at this time that the initiates learn how the display was constructed, and see the component parts of what was previously just a confusing mass of colour, with faces looming out of the background, when seen by the flickering light of flares made from dry coconut-palm frond. Men learn about ceremonies not during their actual initiations but while dismantling the display, and ten years or so later, when the ceremonial cycle brings the ceremony round again, the initiates are now qualified to act as junior initiators and learn how to prepare the ceremony under the direction of the 'fathers and elder brothers' of their half of the dual organization. Every Abelam man participates in four performances of each ceremony of the cycle, first as initiate and later as father of an initiate when the ceremony is performed by the other half of the dual organization, also as junior and then as senior initiator when the ceremony is performed by his own half. After these four attendances, which may involve a period of fifty to sixty years, a man can be, and often is, excluded by his juniors from any further participation.[4]

Thus boys are expected gradually to assume mundane responsibilities until, at about thirty, they should be able to produce sufficient food for their families and be able to start in yam and pig exchanges. In ritual life they are expected to show, and by and large do show, a great deal of responsibility and secrecy about the operations they perform as virgin boys. As soon as they reach puberty they are excluded from the long-yam cult and are not readmitted fully until fifteen years later when they have a settled married life and a desire for prestige, which can be satisfied only by growing and presenting long yams.

THE ART

All art among the Abelam is fundamentally cult art; decorative art exists but its motifs and usages are derived from cult art and from statuses associated with the yam and tambaran cults, and it does not involve any painting. Painting, as opposed to sculpture, engraving, and other activities that are performed by artists but are difficult to classify in our terms, is a sacred activity. Although charms, spells, and invocations may accompany other sorts of artistic work, these are solely the affair of the artist and mainly utilitarian, i.e. to prevent the timber splitting in carving or the bone breaking in engraving. Painting is an essential part of the ritual, carried out by the whole group of initiators as the final stage in preparing a ceremony. The painting phase is opened and closed by feasts and food distributions; the initiators cleanse themselves from past contact with women and observe taboos on sex and meat while the phase lasts. The taboos are almost identical with those necessary for the cultivation of long yams.

All magically and supernaturally powerful substances are classified as paint by the Abelam. Although the paint used in tambaran ceremonies is not intrinsically powerful it becomes the medium by which the benefit of the ceremony is conferred on those participating.[5] The use of paint in the long-yam cult and for sorcery is surrounded by similar taboos and ritual restrictions.

Abelam art relies very much for its effects on the brightness and magnificence of polychrome painting. Carving is ritually less highly valued; it is a specialist activity carried on in secrecy, but not as an essential part of the ritual, and the majority of men do not participate in carving in any way whatever, whereas all men take some part in painting if only in mixing the colours. Painting is applied to all carvings but in addition is done on the flat, not only on the façade of the ceremonial house, but in very large quantities on sago-spathe panels which line and form the ceiling of the initiation chamber built specially inside the ceremonial house for each initiation ceremony. In the painting of carvings the painters of course have to follow the lines and surfaces presented by the carver. With new figures the carver will usually supervise the painting himself, but for many of the more important ceremonies old figures have to be washed and repainted and there is some room for variation, particularly since some of the oldest figures are carved in a style different from that current.

In general, carvings tend to be of beings of human form, although some, especially the *nggwalndu,* have very much larger heads in proportion to their bodies than are found in the human model. The faces of the carvings are painted in a prescribed style built up of a series of elements (forehead ornaments, nose decorations, etc.) and definite areas of colour (eyes – black, cheeks – yellow, etc.) that make all painted carved faces stylistically the same as each other, and also the same as the carved faces attached to the heads of the displayed long yams, and the same as the painted faces of the initiators as they emerge from the ceremonial house and parade round the *amei* during the actual ceremony. The identification of man, yam, and *nggwalndu* provided by the stylistic unity of their several faces is one of the most important 'theological' functions of Abelam art. The unity of this trinity is given various other forms of symbolic expression, for instance in names, but it is perhaps in the exciting and highly emotional atmosphere of tambaran ceremonies and yam displays that the identification has the greatest impact. But the *nggwalndu* has more than one face: although in three dimensions on carvings *nggwalndu* faces are always the same, when painted on the flat the elements that make up the face and their arrangement are different; there are some similarities – the forehead ornament is the same and in the same place – but the eyes, nose, and mouth are represented in a completely different manner. This is not due to the problems of representing a three-dimensional object in two dimensions. The eyes, for instance, in the carving are black, triangular, or semicircular, and in about the natural proportion to the rest of the face; in flat painting they are huge – a series of polychrome rings that dominate the face. Similarly, the arms of the carvings come from the shoulders and the hands rest on the groin, whereas in flat-painted *nggwalndu* heads they are represented by three or more white lines springing from beside the nostrils, describing a graceful arabesque round under the mouth where they nearly meet (the elbows being indicated by black lunate shapes), then turning up again to finish with white diagrammatic hands beside the ears. The hands often have more than five fingers, and on the ceremonial house façade, where these faces form a band right across, each hand is shared by the adjacent *nggwalndu*, their arms uniting just under the palm (see *Plate II*).

It is perhaps as well to make clear at this stage that neither the three- nor the two-dimensional versions are representations (in the literal sense) of the *nggwalndu*: they are not attempts to show what *nggwalndu* look like, but different manifestations of the *nggwalndu*. The actual carvings called *nggwalndu* are the most sacred of Abelam objects and provide the closest contact between man and *nggwalndu*. They have on occasion been used to manipulate the *nggwalndu* to the advantage of the owning clan, as in the case of the clan that replaced its *nggwalndu* with a freshly carved one, which was given the name and place of the old one in the ceremonial house, thus halting a run of death and misfortune that had been afflicting the clan, and starting the period of fertility and prosperity that it was still enjoying when I was told of the incident and shown the rejected carving. But *nggwalndu* manifest themselves in other forms: as vicious wild boars, as a whole series of noises, and in dreams as tall, strong men in full war paint; an entirely different style of face-painting and ornamentation from that of the carvings or the flat paintings.

The point here is that neither the carving nor the painting on the flat shows what a *nggwalndu* 'looks like'; they are both arrangements of stylistic elements that mean *nggwalndu* in the appropriate context only, the carving among carvings, the painting among paintings. There is no sense in which the painting on the flat is a projection of the carving or an attempt to represent the three-dimensional object in two dimensions; the two systems are unrelated. The question 'Why, if *nggwalndu* have arms springing from their upper lips in flat painting, do they have arms coming from their shoulders in carving?' is meaningless in Abelam terms, arising as it does from the supposition that both forms are meant to be representations of something originally outside both three- and two-dimensional art, that they are meant to 'look like' something in nature. There are common aspects that bridge the two styles – for instance, the face-painting is identical, given that the faces are different shapes; again, the same decorations are to be found in the head-dress and on the arms although the arms are, as we have seen, completely different in form and placing in the two styles.

Similar considerations apply to all the spirits and natural species included in the Abelam ceremonial flat-painting style; they form a code built out of a finite number of stylistic elements; various arrangements of these elements signify *nggwalndu*, butterfly, flying fox, etc., in a way that is closer to our use of the elements PIG to signify a member of the genus *sus*, than to any drawing, however schematic, of a four-legged snouted animal. Although the examples discussed so far are fairly straightforward, all coming from ceremonial house façades, the flat-painting code has an essential ambiguity in that varying interpretations of collections of elements are possible and all are equally legitimate. The main point, however, is that in two-dimensional painting there is no desire or attempt of any sort to establish any visual correspondence with either nature or three-dimensional art.

WHAT DO THE ABELAM SEE?

Quite obviously there can be no absolute answer to this question: it is impossible literally to see through the eyes of another man, let alone perceive with his brain. Yet if we are to consider the place of art in any society, especially one such as the Abelam where the art is so highly valued and vigorously preserved, we must beware of assuming that they see what we see and vice versa. Since much of the information must be derived from what Abelam say, cognitive categorization is involved as well as perception.

Abelam have no word for colour as such, but they have a

word for paint in which they recognize four colours: white, black, red, and yellow; all these terms have a much wider reference than colours. There is also another set of colour names employed by women to refer to the vegetable dyes used for the string bags, but these are specific and are not used to indicate the colours of anything else. All other coloured substances are subsumed into the four paints – thus a pale-green powder, apparently used by the Japanese army for treating skin infections, is called yellow, and blue, either from Reckitts or in the form of cheap powder paint sold by trade stores, is called black. In some villages these non-traditional colours have been used for painting the tambarans. In such cases they are used interchangeably with the traditional colour whose name they share. In rare cases both colours have been applied to the same object so that a patch that should be all black is half-black and half-blue with an irregular boundary totally meaningless in terms of the design, and indeed to my eyes completely ruining it. Painters of such works, when remonstrated with, deny that there is any difference or that there is an inharmonious boundary. I am not suggesting that they cannot distinguish between black and blue, only that the distinction is meaningless in terms of the ritual system whose servant the art is. In fact, one façade where such mixing occurred was widely judged a failure, but although I collected some dozens of opinions on the façade, none of them mentioned the mixing of colours as a factor.[6]

All Abelam painting is done on a mud base that is either black or grey; when the base is grey a little of it is left showing, but there is no name for grey, the name for the mud base applying to both kinds; thus although the contrast of white next to grey and white next to black is quite consciously exploited by artists for aesthetic effect, the colour grey cannot be spoken about directly.

All Abelam, whether initiated or not, can see the façades of the ceremonial houses, although children do not go on the *amei* without special reason. The façades are in fact all they do see in the form of two-dimensional representation of anything, and the only other flat surfaces in an Abelam village are the earth of the *amei* and the grey thatch sides of the houses. Façades are brightly painted and one of their main stylistic features is the multiple polychrome lines that are used to outline all the principal shapes of the design. It is this feature that children seem to pick up. Whenever I have seen children drawing with their fingers in the dust the shapes are given multiple outlines. When I gave children paper and paint to work with, they produced pictures of humans and animals with round heads, oval bodies, and stick limbs as children apparently do in all cultures, but always the heads and bodies, at least, were given multiple polychrome outlines (*Figure 2*). There is no attempt to copy or reproduce the designs of the façade but the technique is taken directly from it. Many of the motifs chosen by children are not represented at all on the façade, for instance snakes, a favourite with children, are simply parallel sinuous lines of colour. Children when painting are quite happy with white paper; indeed, they positively preferred white paper because the colours showed up better, whereas their elders, the real artists who did many excellent paintings on grey and black paper for me, were unable to tackle white paper; their technique involves outlining the whole design in white on the black or grey mud, and they cannot cope with black on white. The ability of children to use white paper confirms that they paint with multiple polychrome lines because that is the way they *see* marks on flat surfaces and not because they have been taught to do so in the cult context. Children never normally have any access to paint of any sort, and since painting is a ritual activity, only to be performed by purified initiators observing strict taboos and carried out in secrecy, it is not considered a suitable activity for children; they draw in the dust only when no adult is around. They also play at initiation ceremonies, again when they think themselves unobserved, and I suspect that such mimicking of adult ceremonial forms an important part of children's secret activities.

In general, colour (or strictly paint) words are applied only to things of ritual concern. This can be seen very clearly in the Abelam classification of nature. Tree species are subject to an elaborate classification, but apart from the quality of the timber for practical purposes, the criteria used are seed and leaf shapes. Whether the tree has flowers or not, and the colour of flowers or leaves, are rarely mentioned as criteria. Broadly speaking, the Abelam had use only for the hibiscus and a yellow

FIGURE 2 *Children's drawings*

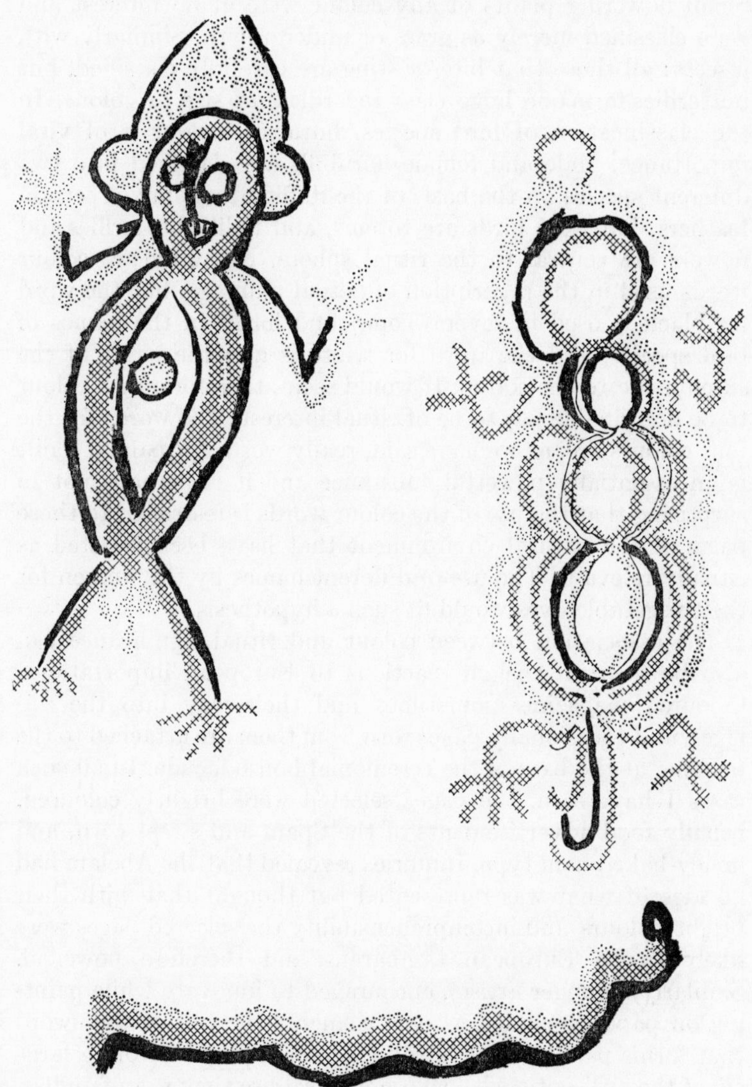

Man, Lizard, and Snake drawn in Red, Yellow, and Black on white by children aged approximately eight to twelve from Bengragum village.

flower, both of which served as decorations for men and yams. Small flowering plants of any colour were of no interest and were classified merely as grass or undergrowth. Similarly with insects: all those that bite or sting are carefully classified, but butterflies form one huge class regardless of size or colour. In the classification of bird species, however, colour is of vital importance. Male and female hornbills are classified into two different species on the basis of the different colours of certain feathers, but then birds are totems, and unlike butterflies and flowers are central to the ritual sphere. Not only are colour words used in the description of actual plumage, but the word for black is used in several compound forms in the names of bird species, and the word for white is also the name of the sulphur-crested cockatoo. It would seem, therefore, that colour to be describable has to be of ritual interest. The words for the four colours are, as we have said, really words for paints. Paint is an essentially powerful substance and it is perhaps not so surprising that the use of the colour words is restricted to those parts of the natural environment that have been selected as ritually relevant. The use of different names by the women for their vegetable dyes would fit such a hypothesis.

The association between colour and ritual significance can also be seen in Abelam reactions to European importations. Coloured magazines sometimes find their way into the villages, and occasionally pages torn from them are attached to the matting at the base of the ceremonial house façade. In all such cases I have seen, the pages selected were brightly coloured, usually food advertisements of the Spam and sweet corn, and honey-baked ham type. Inquiries revealed that the Abelam had no idea of what was represented but thought that with their bright colours and incomprehensibility the selected pages were likely to be European tambarans and therefore powerful. Similarly, younger artists, encouraged to innovate while painting on paper, included as new elements the hilt of the sword that forms part of the 'Dettol' trademark, copied from a large tin of the antiseptic with whose medical use they were familiar, and the Christian cross, believing both to be powerful tambaran-like design elements.[7]

The inability of people in cultures not used to them to see photographs is of course well known (cf. Segall, Campbell &

Herskovits, 1966), and the comparison of inabilities is a difficult task for which I have no systematic material. Nevertheless, the Abelam's lack of understanding of photographs after more than twenty years of contact remains almost absolute, and provides possible support for my hypothesis that they have very definite and limited expectations about what they will see on any two-dimensional surface made to be looked at. In other words, their vision has been socialized in a way that makes photographs especially incomprehensible, just as ours is socialized to see photographs and indeed to regard them as in some sense more truthful than what the eye sees.

Photography has been known to the Abelam since the first contacts with Europeans in 1937. Nowadays, when all young men go away for at least a two-year stint of labour on the coast, they bring back photographs of themselves in all their modern finery, usually taken by Chinese photographers. The subjects stand rigidly at attention facing the camera, either singly or in groups, against a background of either a white sheet or a wall. No Abelam have any difficulty today in 'seeing' such a photograph and in recognizing and naming the individual concerned if they know him. But when shown photographs of themselves in action, or of any pose other than face or full figure looking directly at the camera, they cease to be able to 'see' the photograph at all. Even people from other villages who came specially because they knew I had taken a photograph of a relative who had subsequently died, and were often pathetically keen to see his features, were initially unable to see him at all, turning the photograph in all directions. Even when the figure dominated (to my eyes) the photograph I sometimes had to draw a thick line round it before it could be identified, and in some cases I had the impression that they willed themselves to see it rather than actually saw it in the way we do. Photographs of ceremonial houses and objects were easier, although in black and white people could identify a house as a ceremonial house rather than say which house it was. With colour they were happier, partly because they looked into a viewer, which itself was three-dimensional, instead of staring at a flat sheet, but they could rarely identify individuals and had a tendency to regard any brightly coloured photograph with no outstanding form as a tambaran display. Since

I needed identifications from photographs of yam exchanges, brawls, ceremonies, and debates, I trained a few boys to see photographs; they learnt to do this after a few hours of concentrated looking and discussion on both sides.

CONCLUSIONS

The Abelam boy, indulged in secular contexts and violently treated in ritual ones, is proffered no explanation of the ill treatment he receives or of the ceremony of which it is a part. Abelam culture is very deficient in myth: most young men not only do not know any myths but can never remember having heard any. Ceremonies are performed because they must be, and are intrinsically good, but no one can offer much in the way of an explanation of the elements that make them up. Certain parts are self-explanatory, invocations to spirits and such like, but on the symbolism of the objects displayed, or the ritual actions performed, no one has anything to offer. The powerful substances used in yam magic are called paints, and from his experiences as a virgin boy, as well as his experiences as an initiate, a boy learns to regard paint as something associated with supernatural power, and painted objects as of great and mysterious importance; they are the foci of the ceremonies and he has to suffer before he is shown them. Just as it is only for objects or species of ritual concern that the Abelam language uses colour names, so anything painted in polychrome must be powerful and a focus of ritual attention. Colour, and its use in painting, is separated both by the way it is presented and by the attitudes displayed towards it from any connection with nature.

The experiences of Abelam boys tend to make them regard paintings as something of great importance, intrinsically powerful, but as a closed system not referring to other natural or social phenomena and a closed system the meaning of which is not explained beyond the naming of designs. It seems to me that Abelam painting could be regarded as a form of language operating on its own rules and communicating things that are not communicable by other methods. The very fact that the paintings are not described and analysed by the Abelam would, I suggest, strengthen such a hypothesis. It was, I believe, Isadora

Duncan who was reported to have replied to someone who asked her the meaning of a dance she had just performed, 'If I could tell you what it meant there would be no point in dancing it.' I am not suggesting that the Abelam youth puzzles out for himself the answers to a sort of trick questionnaire set by his elders; rather, it seems to me that neither the initiators nor the initiates are totally conscious of the significance of the designs they paint; to them they are essential parts of the ceremony and their form is dictated by tradition.

I have argued in another paper (Forge, 1966) that the art communicates some fundamental values of Abelam society, and that this communication is not fully conscious to anyone concerned. In painting on the flat one can see how a whole series of objects and animals of interest and concern to the Abelam are integrated into the ritual system by being painted in a series of elements that they share with paintings of spirits. For instance, 'legs of pork' is one interpretation of a spiral arabesque motif that occurs fairly commonly in Abelam painting. In some cases this motif will be repeated and manipulated so that many such motifs make up a face of roughly *nggwalndu* type; to this face are added the head-dress and other decorations of the *nggwalndu*, and it thus becomes a sort of personification of legs of pork. Not that the Abelam believe that there is any spirit exclusively concerned with legs of pork, but painting in this way is used to integrate legs of pork, which are extremely important in the exchange system, into the ritual sphere and to direct the attention of men to them.

There is, however, no secure iconography; the design elements and their combinations are essentially ambiguous, in the sense that translation from the language of flat painting to the language of words is not a matter of simple one-to-one correspondence. Interpretation of elements and whole compositions often varies according to the artistic and social contexts and according to the informant. Thus, although a painting of a *nggwalndu* face will always be so identified, the arabesque 'legs of pork' cited above could equally well be named as immature fern frond or a swirl in the water of a flooded river; if the element means anything in terms of words it probably means all three with all their connotations as well. But the Abelam do not ask what a painting means. The design elements all have names and they are assembled into harmonious compositions, which appear to act directly on the beholder without having to be named. Abelam art is about relationships, not about things. One of its functions is to relate and unite disparate things in terms of their place in the ritual and cosmological order. It does this, I would suggest, directly and not as an illustration to some text based in another symbolic system such as language. One of the main functions of the initiation system with its repetitive exposure of initiates to quantities of art is, I would suggest, to teach the young men to see the art, not so that he may consciously interpret it but so that he is directly affected by it.

NOTES

1. The pidgin English word 'tambaran' corresponds directly to the Abelam term *maira*. As it has become a technical term in Melanesian ethnography, I use it here without italics.

2. Dr P. M. Kaberry worked in the Northern Abelam village of Kalabu in 1938–39 shortly after the establishment of government control. Her accounts (1940–41, 1966) apply in general to the whole area.

3. My two visits to the Abelam were made in 1958–59 and 1962–63. They were made possible by generous grants from the Emslie Horniman Anthropological Scholarship Fund of the Royal Anthropological Institute and from the Bollingen Foundation, respectively. I am also grateful for assistance from the Wenner-Gren Foundation. I am indebted to Dr Edmund Leach, the sympathetic discussant of this paper when it was first delivered, whose comments have helped me to clarify my ideas, although I am afraid that they still lack the felicity and force of his original discussion.

4. This is not the place for a full account of the structure of the initiation system. It involves a series of half-generational grades split by the dual organization. In the Eastern part of the area this is cross-cut by a moiety system as well. The structure is very similar to that of the closely related Iatmul, whose system also pushes old men out at the top (Bateson, 1936, p. 165).

5. The magical nature of paint and the organization of artistic production are more fully discussed in Forge, 1962 and 1967.

6. A small group of villages in the furthest East part of Abelam territory have integrated blue into their related but different façade style as a genuine fifth colour. It is called *blu* and is used sparingly, always for parts of the design previously painted black.

7. The leader of the local branch of a fundamentalist mission had recently publically denounced the cross as a 'catholic tambaran'.

REFERENCES

BATESON, G. 1936. *Naven*. Cambridge: Cambridge University Press.

FORGE, A. 1962. Paint – A Magical Substance. *Palette*, No. 9.

— 1966. Art and Environment in the Sepik. *Proceedings of the Royal Anthropological Institute, 1965*.

— 1967. The Abelam Artist. In M. Freedman (ed.), *Social Organization: Essays Presented to Raymond Firth*. London: Cass.

KABERRY, P. M. 1940–41. The Abelam Tribe, Sepik District, New Guinea. A Preliminary Report. *Oceania* **11**: 233–258, 345–367.

— 1966. Political Organization among the Northern Abelam. *Anthropological Forum* **1** (3–4).

SEGALL, M. H., CAMPBELL, D. T. & HERSKOVITS, M. J. 1966. *The Influence of Culture on Visual Perception*. New York: Bobbs-Merrill.

J. B. Loudon

Teasing and Socialization on Tristan da Cunha

INTRODUCTORY

Towards the end of his classic paper on joking relationships Radcliffe-Brown (1952) drew a clear distinction between formalized and unformalized teasing. He emphasized that his sole concern was with standardized social relationships involving joking behaviour; but he suggested that there was a need for study of unformalized teasing or making fun of other persons, 'a common mode of behaviour in any human society' which 'tends to occur in certain kinds of social situations'. This essay is intended to be a contribution to such a study.

Since Radcliffe-Brown's paper first appeared in 1940 a good deal has been written in which analysis is directed, or incidental reference is made, to relationships between persons and between groups which are characterized by a combination of friendliness and antagonism. The emphasis in most of this work has been on joking as a prescribed form of behaviour and on the fact that the relationships of permitted or enjoined disrespect involve a combination of simulated hostility and underlying 'real' amity. Some attention has also been paid to other relatively informal modes of behaviour which share many of the features both of joking and of teasing. Firth's (1956) account of rumour is a good example; and Gluckman (1963) has drawn on other studies such as those of West (1945), Colson (1953), and Frankenberg (1957) for his examination of gossip and scandal. More recently, Paine (1967) has put forward the view that functional explanations of gossip neglect its connection with communication. And although there are a number of accounts of verbal duels such as those found among the Eskimo, relatively little work seems to have been done on the significance of teasing and making fun in social situations where the hostility appears to be at least as 'real' as the amity, where unformalized joking behaviour is permitted, expected, or tolerated because such alternative extremes of behaviour as open and avowed conflict or total and persisting avoidance, between persons or between groups, either are impracticable or seem to be regarded by everyone concerned as potentially dangerous if not disastrous.

Any attempt to assess the relative 'reality' of the hostile and friendly components of teasing behaviour therefore requires close examination of the context and content of a series of particular instances; it would also seem to demand some attempt to analyse the apparent motivations of the individual actors concerned in what must be regarded as purposive behaviour. As part of the process of informal communication between persons and groups teasing may be presumed to have not only demonstrable social functions but also effects on individual values and attitudes, by which I here mean preferences and predispositions to action. Teasing may therefore be seen as an example of human social interaction where explanation is likely to appear less than satisfactory if couched in terms which are either purely sociological or purely psychological.

In their introduction to the first four volumes of the A.S.A. Monograph series Gluckman and Eggan (1965) remark upon the apparent reluctance of some social anthropologists, especially some British ones, to make any reference to what they call 'the whole fruitful field of study in psychological anthropology', adding that it is only in the study of religion that any of the contributors to these volumes 'argue for the essential place of some psychological treatment'; and they find the British contributors less ready in general than their American colleagues 'to move outside the restricted range of the social sciences to draw on disciplines which employ quite different techniques and concepts'. No doubt this avoidance of much reference to psychological anthropology is partly a reflection of who was asked to contribute to the conference in Cambridge in 1963 from which the material in those volumes was drawn, and partly a result of what those who were invited to contribute decided to deal with. But it seems probable that there is rather more than that in the avoidance. Fox (1967) unambiguously links the rejection by structural anthropologists of 'psychology' (which he is careful to put in inverted commas) to what he calls their 'curious feeling that rules are more stable than emotions'. A number of other appeals for greater flexibility in the use made by social anthropologists of the findings and concepts of other behavioural sciences seem to indicate that some of the contributors to the first four A.S.A. Monographs may have been representative of their generation but unrepresentative of new approaches. Fox has also, in collaboration with Tiger (Fox & Tiger, 1966), made a strong case for an ethological perspective, backed up by Freeman (1966); and Freeman (1965) has further observed that anthropology must transcend what he calls the unscientific doctrine of cultural relativism if it is to bring into being a true science of man. In order to do this Freeman suggests that 'the values and discoveries of the science of psychiatry are . . . of the greatest relevance' in providing 'ways in which human behaviour – of whatever culture – can be scientifically and normatively evaluated'. Freeman does not put the word 'psychiatry' into inverted commas but it seems clear that to him it is synonymous with psychoanalytic theory; for example, he makes the suggestion, derived from the work of Money-Kyrle, that 'a neurotic person is not only *relatively* inefficient but *absolutely* inefficient . . . [and that] the neurotic is not only emotionally sick – he is cognitively wrong'. To the uninitiated, statements of this kind are not easy to understand; it is also difficult to be patient with formulations which spoil a good case by crude eclecticism and therefore tend to obscure the real need that social anthropology and psychology have of one another, whether or no one adds to the word 'psychology' such prefixes as 'clinical', 'social', 'developmental', or 'experimental'. The approach of others particularly well qualified to discuss this topic seems more encouraging, such as that of Horton (1963), who lays stress on how the 'explanatory programme' of both social anthropology and psychology 'rests on certain assumptions to which only the other has given serious thought'.

This essay on teasing among the islanders of Tristan da Cunha does not pretend to be an example of the kind of interdisciplinary explanatory study for which there is no doubt great need. I do, however, draw to some extent upon published material on the Tristan people by a sociologist (Munch, 1945, 1964) and a psychologist (Keir, 1966), and also on investigations which I undertook in collaboration with a psychiatrist (Rawnsley & Loudon 1964; Loudon, 1966).

My own fieldwork occupied a total of about seven months, spread over a period of two years, between December 1961 and December 1963.[1] For most of this period the Tristan people were living in what were, for them, somewhat trying and very unfamiliar conditions in southern Britain, to which many of the islanders found some difficulty in adjusting themselves. They were brought to Britain from their island home in the South Atlantic following the eruption of a volcano in October 1961. At first they were accommodated in temporary dwellings on a disused army camp in Surrey; they were then moved to more permanent quarters on a disused air-force station in Hampshire, where they remained until all but a handful of them returned to Tristan in October 1963. Accompanying them on their return I was able to see them very briefly on their home ground; but much of my material was obtained under considerable difficulties in almost daily competition with an assortment of fellow investigators, visiting officials from the Colonial Office and from local government and social service agencies, journalists, pressmen, and television teams, together with a variety of local well-wishers, benefactors, and sightseers. These circumstances provided me with excellent opportunities to observe the sometimes painful process of socialization undergone by almost all members of the Tristan community while they were in Britain. It is also scarcely to be wondered at that my informants required very gentle handling; for although the Tristan people, with rare exceptions, are outwardly cheerful, courteous, and stoical, much of my material was obtained from them when they were growing impatient and increasingly resentful of some aspects of their predicament as unwilling immigrants and when their hospitable attitude to strangers was being diluted by the confusion, uncertainty, and frustration of enforced exile.

TRISTAN DA CUNHA: OUTLINE HISTORY AND SOCIOLOGY

Tristan, as the island is usually called, is a fairly tough place to live, very small, very isolated, very rugged, windswept and wet. Until the first ancestors of the present population settled there in 1816 it was without permanent human inhabitants.

By 1961, when the entire population was evacuated, there were 264 inhabitants.

The island is a volcanic cone about 7,000 feet high and about seven miles in diameter, with an area of rather less than forty square miles, most of which is uninhabitable. Together with two other much smaller and uninhabited islands about eighteen miles away, it forms the tip of that part of the submarine Mid-Atlantic Ridge which lies roughly half-way between South America and South Africa. The nearest inhabited land is the island of St Helena, about 1,500 miles to the north; the nearest mainland, the Cape of Good Hope in South Africa, is about 2,000 miles to the east.

The only part of the island which is suitable for permanent settlement is a low coastal plateau about four miles long and about half a mile wide, situated on the north-western shore and exposed to the prevailing winds. The people live at one end of this plateau in about sixty small stone and thatched single-storey houses which, together with a church and a number of modern administrative buildings, are clustered together to form a village close to the principal landing-place and to the only perennial supply of drinking water on the island. Also on the plateau are a number of small stone-walled cultivated plots in which the islanders grow the potatoes which were, and to some extent still are, their principal food item. These plots are a little distance from the village and most of the plateau is used as grassland for cattle, sheep, and donkeys. Poultry are also kept in and near the village. On the southern shore of the island are two other smaller grass-covered plateaux where cattle are kept and allowed to run wild. When meat is required they are killed with rifles by parties of men who generally go round to that part of the island in boats, since going there on foot involves a stiff climb across the shoulder of the mountain which takes several hours. Boats are also used for catching fish, of which many edible varieties abound in the seas around Tristan, including the crawfish or 'rock lobster' which has proved of considerable commercial importance in recent years. Two or three times a year visits are made by boat to the two neighbouring uninhabited islands; in the past these islands were economically important to the Tristan people as their main source of supply of wild birds and their eggs, principally albatross shearwaters, and penguins. Apart from use as food, these birds were the regular source of oil for use in cooking and as fuel for lamps, supplemented as occasion offered by oil obtained by killing whales, seals, and sea-elephants. Visits to these islands remain very valuable to the people, partly as a recreation and as a way of getting away for a short time from the somewhat restrictive environment of the settlement.

The islanders are all linked to one another by ties of blood and marriage and are descended from fifteen original settlers of mixed European, North American, African, and Asian stock. Until the Second World War, that is for about 120 years, the people practised a peasant economy and used their agricultural surplus to carry on barter with passing ships. For the first fifty years or so of the community's existence these ships were mostly men-o'-war, East Indiamen and whaling ships from North America, ships long at sea whose crews welcomed the chance of replenishing their stocks of fresh water, meat, and vegetables. In those days Tristan seems to have been a prosperous place, frequent contacts with the outside world being maintained by the average of about thirty ships which called there each year. Barter with them was apparently well able to provide the people with most of their luxuries and some of their necessities, including clothing, tools, tea, tobacco, flour, sugar, and so forth. By about 1880 the population reached about a hundred. Thereafter there was a decline in the islanders' fortunes.

First the island became infested with rats following a shipwreck in 1882. Then in 1885 occurred the Boat Disaster, in which most of the island's able-bodied men disappeared in high seas on their way to a passing ship. The fact that they had put out in dangerous conditions was itself related to a great reduction in the number of ships calling at or being sighted from Tristan, following the replacement of sail by steam and the extermination of most of the whales in that part of the South Atlantic. By 1888 an average of only about five ships was sighted in a full year; those that stopped were not really interested in barter and tended to give the islanders what they could spare from their stores out of kindness of heart. The people therefore became increasingly dependent on well-wishers in the outside world, particularly members of various charitable organizations in Britain stimulated by news of the Boat Disaster of 1885. In addition, a number of the islanders emigrated at this time, the population falling by 1904 to a total of seventy. Emigration as the answer to the island's problems had for long been urged by members of the Society for the Propagation of the Gospel, a Church of England missionary society which has maintained a series of Anglican clergymen on Tristan; the first was sent out in the 1850s, another in the 1880s, a third from 1906 to 1909, and since 1921 there has been a fairly regular succession of two-year incumbents. The islanders therefore came to depend more and more for all but the barest necessities of life upon the goodwill of an outside world which most of them had never seen and with which their principal negotiator and intermediary came to be the clergyman. In earlier years the people gained some acquaintance with visiting sailors, and the older islanders had, of course, themselves been born and brought up outside the island; but in later years these factors hardly applied. From the beginning of this century until the 1939–45 war almost the only outsiders with whom the people became well acquainted at close quarters were the clergymen, some of whom seem to have found it advisable to adopt a somewhat authoritarian approach to their pastoral duties. One of them set up a storehouse and made sure that all stores and supplies sent as gifts to the islanders came to him, through the Society for the Propagation of the Gospel, for distribution. He is quoted by Munch (1945) as having said to a visitor to the island that 'the way to rule Tristan is to have your storehouse full and keep the key'.

Apart from the provision of supplies of various kinds, the continued presence on Tristan of the islanders came to depend, directly and indirectly, upon the good opinion of the outside world. A number of attempts to bring about the voluntary evacuation of the island were made by the British and the Cape governments between 1850 and 1910, and a substantial trickle of emigrants left Tristan between those years. In 1856 a large party went to the United States and were followed there by a few others in later years; but most emigrants settled in South Africa where their descendants are today members of the coloured community in the Cape. Between 1910 and 1960, however, only two islanders left Tristan permanently; and no outsiders have joined the community since 1908.

In spite of inducements and deprivations of various kinds, at no time until the volcanic eruption of 1961 did it prove possible to persuade the whole population to leave. At one time substantial cash payments and the provision of small-holdings in South Africa were held out by the British government as an inducement. The regular annual visits of inspection by a British warship from Simonstown, eagerly looked forward to by the people, were discontinued in the early years of this century. These visits ensured that the people received some stores and mail and also reassured them of the continuing benevolence of the British Crown, of which – in spite, for example, of getting no mail from England between 1906 and 1916 – they remained (and still continue) vehemently loyal adherents.

Since the Second World War, when money and a canteen and general store were introduced by a garrison of British and South African forces, together with other services such as a hospital and a wireless station, the economy has changed. Operations for the freezing and canning of crawfish for the American market were established in 1949 by a South African company with support from the Colonial Development Corporation; and a factory was built which provided regular paid employment for the men and occasional work for many of the women. At the same time, the continuing series of Anglican clergymen was reinforced by a small staff of expatriates and their families, including an administrator, a medical officer, a schoolteacher, a factory manager, and a meteorological officer/wireless operator. Gradually the islanders became less dependent on the charity of well-wishers in the outside world and more dependent on their ability to obtain the good opinion of the outsiders temporarily living among them and to manipulate the fissiparous tendencies present among the expatriates: they learnt, for example, to enlist the clergyman on their side against the fishing company when seeking the right to press for higher wages, and to gain the support of the factory manager against the clergyman when attempting to gain the right to import liquor from South Africa through the canteen store run by the fishing company. After the establishment of a fishing industry they clearly began to feel that their continued survival as a community was at last assured because of their economic indispensability as a source of labour, and because of their local knowledge and their special skill and experience in handling boats in Tristan waters and weather conditions. Nevertheless they did not cease giving expression to their ideal of independence. From time to time they proclaimed their conviction that, even without the operations of the fishing company, they were well able to survive on Tristan as they had in the past by a combination of their own efforts and the charitable assistance from well-wishers overseas to which they felt themselves entitled.

MODEL AND IMAGE

The Tristan conscious model thus remained essentially an export model. The people place the greatest emphasis upon their honesty, piety, unity, and readiness to help one another; they repeatedly describe themselves to outsiders as 'one big happy family' and they take pride in claiming that strife, crime, and status inequalities are not found among them. Their principles are most commonly enunciated in the words 'fair shares', which are often on their lips and express the conceptual yardstick by which they judge their dealings with one another and with the outside world. Glaring instances of past failure to live up to these principles are regarded as aberrations almost entirely attributable to the interference of outsiders or to the intrigues of what they refer to as 'newcomers', the latter including not only persons coming from the outside to settle on Tristan but also unwelcome islanders returning home after many years abroad. Such people, it is said, always cause trouble; and a number of illustrative examples, mostly from the distant past but including some notorious cases from recent times, are often quoted by informants, old and young, to demonstrate by contrast the idyllic nature of uncontaminated social relations among the islanders. They are also used to warrant the people's reluctance, supported for many years by government ordinances, to admit immigrants, especially males, as permanent settlers.

Once they had been evacuated to Britain in 1961 they again came to feel that their future as a community and as individuals, and especially their chances of ever returning to Tristan, depended in large measure upon their 'image'. They saw anything damaging to their reputation as being likely to forfeit the sympathy of their friends in Britain; and a few of them also became aware of the possible importance of retaining the support of a wider public through the medium of the press, radio, and television. They emphasized such features of their history as the numbers of mariners saved from shipwreck to whom their immediate ancestors had given aid and hospitality. And they continued to present themselves, to themselves and to others, as conspicuously honest, sober, hard-working, clean-living, law-abiding, God-fearing, peace-loving, loyal British subjects who surely (they felt) could not fail to attract the support of those they believed to be in a position to influence or bring pressure to bear on the authorities.[2] And as time passed and they saw little sign of willingness on the part of the Colonial Office to countenance their early return to Tristan, their anxieties increased and were accentuated by a number of factors and experiences.

First of all, it soon became clear to them that the fishing company was continuing under its government concession to operate profitably off the shores of Tristan in spite of the fact that the factory had been destroyed by the volcanic eruption; indeed, it was rumoured among the people during 1962 that the fishing company was going to introduce factory ships in order to dispense altogether with the need for an island-based freezing plant. It also appeared that, since the crews of the company's ships had by then become as experienced in Tristan conditions as any islander, the company was able to depend solely upon coloured labour from South Africa to man the fishing boats. At the same time, the islanders' future in Britain seemed to some of them to be less secure than it had at first: a number of the men lost their jobs and, although most soon got other work of a kind, many began to realize that the unskilled or semi-skilled labour for which alone they were fitted, and on which most of them were engaged, by no means guaranteed the continuous and relatively highly paid employment they had come to expect in this country.

In addition to these anxieties, their image of themselves was reinforced by the contrast between their own standards of behaviour and some of the more lurid aspects of vice, crime, and violence in Britain as reported by national news media.

The impact of much of this material upon the islanders was accentuated by the fact that most of them had difficulty in grasping some of the real differences between living on a small island with less than three hundred inhabitants and living in a small corner of a large island with a population of 50 million; and a number of first-hand encounters provided further evidence for the contrast they saw between Tristan values and those of England.

For example, it so happened that among their closest neighbours outside the perimeter fence of the camp on which they lived were a number of people many aspects of whose behaviour differed markedly from that regarded as desirable by the islanders, and although such behaviour was scarcely typical of Britain as a whole, it tended to be so regarded by many of them. Particularly conspicuous among these neighbours was a constantly changing population of about twenty temporarily acephalous service families in transit between overseas postings, consisting mostly of discontented young wives with large numbers of unruly children; nearby there was also a considerable contingent of migrant labourers, many of them from other parts of the British Isles including the Irish Republic, living in hostels and employed on local civil engineering projects. And an incident that occurred soon after the Tristan people arrived in Hampshire made a lasting impression upon them: an elderly, respected, and disabled islander, who had with difficulty obtained a job as a night-watchman, was set upon after dark on his way to work and robbed, though not injured, by a couple of English youths.

The people also began to realize, from a variety of personal contacts as well as from a small number of abusive anonymous letters, that some British people no longer, if they ever had, looked upon them as colourful refugees from a much publicized natural disaster but regarded them rather as unwelcome coloured immigrants. For example, in one of the schools in the vicinity attended by Tristan children a number of cases of infestation by head-lice were discovered among the English children at a routine health inspection; the Tristan parents soon got to hear from their offspring that these cases were attributed by some of the English parents to contamination by Tristan children, among whom in fact no cases of infestation with head-lice were ever reported. Corresponding with this was the fact that some of the local inhabitants compared the islanders to gypsies, to whom many of them may indeed be said to have borne a certain resemblance both in physical features and, at least during the first few months in Britain, in some aspects of dress also. Although much of the significance of this particular comparison was lost on the islanders, many of them were well aware of being physically conspicuous and became increasingly sensitive about being recognized as 'Tristans' by passers-by in the street.

The Tristan people thus came to contrast their own standards and behaviour with those of many of their neighbours; individuals among them also took pains, when speaking to friends who were outsiders, to differentiate themselves very carefully from those few of their fellow islanders who associated too closely or too publicly with their more disreputable English neighbours or whose behaviour from time to time fell below the level of rectitude regarded as consonant with the Tristan conscious model.

To many observers with a more than nodding acquaintance with the islanders the picture they presented of themselves seemed reasonably accurate; outwardly at least the Tristan people are everything they say they are. It is true that some outsiders who have got to know them well by serving for long periods among them in an official capacity have become disenchanted: one such spoke of them as never cooperating with one another except in the matter of begging and as having developed a mendicant mentality in which untruthfulness and ingratiating cunning are associated with unbelievable improvidence. Another, faced with complaints from some islanders about the accommodation provided for them, spoke in a moment of exasperation of their incorrigible ingratitude and of their need to learn and accept the fact that they were 'working class'. Other observers, although their comments are not necessarily incompatible with such views as these, put the emphasis on other features. The most distinguished professional student of the Tristan community, writing on the basis of his first-hand experience of the people in 1937–38, emphasizes their 'great love of peace and their reprobation of any form of violence, which is the leading principle of all their attitudes and behaviour, [and] is actually the most outstanding trait of the islanders' group character' (Munch, 1945). Thirty years later, after further fieldwork, the same writer speaks of

> 'the core values of this utopian community . . . crystallized into a system of norms which strongly discourage any man from putting himself forward in any way or manner, and which promote and constantly reinforce those character traits of dignity, kindness and an alert but subtle sensitivity to the rights and feelings of others for which the islanders have so often been noted';

and writing of what he calls the 'integrating structure of selective personal reciprocity' among the Tristan people he goes on to say that

> 'this is what makes every major operation connected with the subsistence economy a social event of the greatest importance, a recreation in the true sense of the word, where sociability, play, and fun, with much joking and ribbing, are inseparably mingled with the work' (Munch, 1967).

That there may be more than pure recreation involved in the 'joking and ribbing' is suggested elsewhere by the same writer when he describes 'public teasing' as a 'frequently applied form of public accusation in Tristan da Cunha, and the only form of direct self-assertion over against a fellow socially recognized' (Munch, 1945).

THE SIGNIFICANCE OF TEASING AND RIDICULE IN SOCIALIZATION

The circumstances in which the Tristan people found themselves on their arrival in Britain in 1961 and during their stay were, as I have suggested, such as to lead them to place great emphasis on conformity to moral rules. I have also tried to show that this emphasis was no new thing but simply an emergency extension in a strange social environment of already existing attitudes. The Tristan community, through physical and social isolation, has for many years been an outstanding example of that type of exclusive group which has not only, in the words of Gluckman (1963), had exclusiveness thrust upon it but has also jealously guarded its exclusiveness. By doing so it has sustained its social identity; that is, its members have managed to establish and maintain more or less exclusive claims to land, house-sites, and other property on the island and also certain claims on goods and services almost all of which are ultimately dependent on the benevolence of government and other agencies, including the goodwill of individual outsiders among whom members of religious and welfare organizations are particularly prominent.

Like members of other exclusive groups the Tristan people gossip and scandalize among themselves and with outsiders in much the same way and for the same reasons as Colson (1953) has demonstrated so vividly among the Makah. But on Tristan there is often a need to try to combine two potentially incompatible approaches: individuals and groups are constantly displaying or asserting their own conformity to moral rules and their superiority in this respect to some, if not most, of their fellow islanders; at the same time there are great pressures on every member of the community to avoid any overt signs of conflict with other members. Thus there are a number of topics, including incest, adultery, stealing, skin colour, and hair texture, which figure frequently in gossip about other people but which are very rarely, if ever, referred to directly in confrontations with them. This has led to teasing and ridicule playing a part of great importance in exchanges between members of this very small and exclusive community, where face-to-face contact and intimate knowledge are life-long and universal. The teasing process has accordingly been refined and extended in a variety of ways to form an instrument of considerable subtlety in informal communication, in the assertion of values and moral rules, as a means of social control, and in the identification of potential leaders. Its importance is particularly well shown in some aspects of socialization.

Socialization is used in this essay in two ways, both of which seem to be generally acceptable. I use the word in its narrow sense as referring to the acquisition by children of socially approved attitudes and patterns of behaviour. But I also use it more widely to cover the learning by individuals of all ages of ways of acting regarded as appropriate for the performance of new social roles and for dealing with new and unfamiliar social situations. Teasing may be described as the deliberate and persistent irritation of another person by actions which are intended to cause pain or discomfort or exposure to ridicule. The actions may be verbal or non-verbal or a combination of both, and are usually designed to cause mental rather than physical pain or discomfort. Verbal teasing, in particular, is generally characterized by a variable combination of apparent good humour and calculated ambiguity.

TEASING AND CHILD-REARING

The importance attached to the avoidance of open violent display of aggressive feelings among Tristan people is well seen in the ways in which children are taught to behave and in the methods employed to teach them. Paradoxically it is through threats or acts of physical punishment that children are inculcated with the importance of non-violent behaviour, as I shall show.

With very few exceptions Tristan children, including infants under a year old, are remarkable for their docility and quietness; it is rare to hear Tristan babies crying and even when children are playing together supposedly out of the earshot of adults most of their games seem to involve relatively little noise and argument. The aim of parents and of other persons, such as a child's grandmothers and elder siblings, who often take a major part in child care, is to instil into an infant's mind as early as possible the idea of 'naughtiness'. Most informants said that this early training was essential if a child was to learn to avoid certain common dangers: toddlers are taught that it is naughty to go near an open fire or near water or large animals or the cliff edge. But long before a baby becomes mobile he is also taught that it is naughty to show signs of what is interpreted as wilful behaviour or bad temper; and all island women asked about this clearly felt that it was as important to prevent such displays in a child as to prevent him incurring physical danger, and that the first type of behaviour was the more reprehensible. Even when exhibited by babies of only six months old wilful behaviour is characterized as naughty and the child is threatened accordingly. The usual procedure is for the mother or whoever has charge of the child to say 'naughty' very sternly and to accompany the word either with a tap or smack on the hand or with a threat to smack. Sometimes the tap is no more than the merest token of disapproval; sometimes a mother holds the baby's hand and pretends to smack it by smacking her own hand; more usually the smack is administered in such a way as to leave no doubt in the child's mind that the pain caused was intentional. A child who then cries is often picked up and comforted; but if he persists in crying he may again be threatened and smacked.

Observation of these matters is never easy; children quickly learn what to expect and the methods employed in handling a particular child change from month to month and vary with the context. Material of this kind was particularly difficult to obtain among the Tristan people; but the procedure I have described was observed on a number of occasions with different actors and seems to be the customary way of defining and dealing with 'naughtiness' on the part of quite young children. Not only did I never encounter disapproval of such relatively mild physical punishment of babies among adult islanders; rather, all those with whom I discussed this and other related aspects of child-rearing said that the method was the best and the most effective one to employ. Indeed, none of my informants seemed able to suggest an alternative. But an additional and apparently common refinement of the method is to tease a child and provoke a show of angry or petulant behaviour which may then be punished.

For example, in one house occupied by a three-generation joint family to which I was a frequent visitor, a female infant of generally placid disposition was sometimes teased in the following way by her maternal grandmother: when a bottle of baby food had been prepared but was still too hot to drink, it was shown to the child and then put down out of reach; if, as was often the case, the child was hungry and started to whimper the grandmother spoke sharply to her, saying in baby-talk: 'No! Nanna mack' (i.e. Granny will smack you). If the child continued to whimper or burst out crying she was then sometimes soothed or distracted in some way until the bottle had cooled; but on one or two occasions when she continued to cry her grandmother smacked her and more than once the child was given the bottle to hold in order that the heat of it might cause pain and teach her a lesson. Sometimes this whole procedure took place when I was the only spectator present; but it also occurred when other visitors and other members of the household were in the room. On a number of occasions the grandmother volunteered, either directly to me or indirectly by admonishing the child in baby-talk, that it was very important for children to learn to be patient and not expect everything to be given to them at once and for them not to get 'spoilt'.

Another example of the use of teasing in child-training concerned an intelligent and active little boy of about two years of age who was the youngest member of a household of three adults and four children. I watched the following performance, or variations of it, on a number of occasions over a period of some weeks; it always took place in the presence of other members of the household and of visitors who, other than myself, were all islanders. The father played a game with the child which consisted of his repeatedly hiding the child's favourite toy of the moment in different places round the room. For a time the game would proceed happily, the father meanwhile taking some part in the general conversation but inviting us by periodic indulgent smiling glances to watch and admire the 'cute' way in which the child was performing. When, however, as usually happened sooner or later, the child began to complain or show signs of exasperation because he was growing tired of the game or could no longer find the toy or reach it down from its hiding-place, the father spoke sternly to him and, seizing the toy, would make a pretence of throwing it onto the fire or out of the window. If this produced further reaction, which it generally did, the father threatened the child with punishment and, if he continued to whimper or started crying, the father smacked him. The child then ran for comfort to his mother or to his twelve-year-old sister, both of whom had until then been apparently acquiescent spectators of the proceedings. In this case the parents explicitly stated that they saw the game as including a valuable way of training a child who might otherwise become too self-willed. Others agreed. Leaving the house one night in company with an islander with whom I was on terms of rare and easy intimacy, I asked him what he thought of the performance. 'You can't start learning them too young,' he said.

Another child was often mentioned by informants as an

example of what happened when indulgent parents failed to institute disciplinary training early enough. This was a lively and uncharacteristically noisy boy aged four, the only child of young and, by Tristan standards, rather 'advanced' parents. Unlike most children of his age, this boy had not learnt to be invariably respectful to his elders and he did not always keep quiet or leave the room when asked to do so when adults were holding conversation. On one occasion I saw him provoked by teasing into a display of bad manners which resulted in physical chastisement by a succession of adults to each of whom he appealed unsuccessfully for sympathy and comfort.

In general the manners of Tristan children are exemplary and were described by some of the people's English neighbours as 'old-fashioned'. Predictably enough, most Tristan adults found the behaviour of most English children insufferably rude. In Tristan households the slightest sign of a breach in the rules governing children's behaviour tends to lead to rough words or rough handling. Mothers and grandmothers in particular are often quick to 'swipe' young children guilty of solecisms. Older children of both sexes are threatened with the strap and boys are not infrequently given what the islanders cheerfully term a 'good hiding' by their fathers. Even when full grown, children are not immune from physical punishment by their parents as long as they remain unmarried and members of their natal household. I was reliably informed of teenage girls and youths, and even young men and women, who had been struck or beaten by their parents from time to time in recent years, mostly for disobedience, although the only instance of which I have first-hand knowledge is that of a young man aged twenty who was beaten with a leather belt by his father for jeering at him during a game of cards. Older informants often related, with a certain pride, incidents from the past in which they had undergone similar punishments at the hands of their parents. Earlier published accounts remark on this aspect of Tristan domestic life: the wife of a clergyman who lived on the island for nearly three years in the 1920s describes one woman, then a widow aged about forty-five, as 'a very strict disciplinarian . . . I have seen her take a stick to her two big sons', then aged more than twenty and still unmarried, 'if they ventured to disobey her orders' (Rogers, 1926). And a middle-aged islander told me how, when he was about twenty-seven and newly married and established in his own house, he met his elderly father out for a walk, got into a trivial argument with him and, as he would never have dared to do before, teased the old man and 'answered back' (as my informant put it); whereupon the old man raised his stick and only just recalled in time that his son was now the head of his own household and therefore no longer subject to paternal authority.

The phrase 'a good hiding' seems to be used on Tristan almost exclusively to denote legitimate physical punishment of children by parents and, occasionally, of errant wives by justifiably enraged husbands. The words are also sometimes used in jokes between adults and children. The only occasion on which I heard them used to refer to the possibility of serious and spontaneous public action was in the following connection. In the spring of 1962 the local authority in Hampshire provided a field adjacent to the islanders' homes which was divided into small plots, one for each household, in a well-meaning attempt to make them feel at home by providing land on which they could grow vegetables as they did on Tristan. One or two islanders started digging the plots allocated to them but got no further than that; for they were soon told by other members of the community that they deserved and would get 'a good hiding' if they persisted in an activity which might suggest the slightest willingness on the part of the people to settle down in England and abandon their fixed intention of returning to Tristan at the earliest possible moment. The plots thereafter remained uncultivated throughout the period in which the islanders remained in Britain.

CHILDHOOD AGGRESSION: A PSYCHOLOGICAL ASSESSMENT

One assumes that Tristan children, no less than children elsewhere, have aggressive impulses. This assumption is simply based on the idea that aggression is a universal human response to frustration, and that frustration is an invariable concomitant of living with other people, of the process of passing from the dangerous but dependent egotism of childhood to the constrained independence of being a social person (Fortes, 1959).

What seems clear is that the open display of aggressive impulses by most Tristan people is successfully discouraged by socialization processes in childhood, partly through disapproval and intimidation and partly, at a later stage, through moral and religious precepts and the model of public behaviour presented by their elders.

That these measures are effective receives some support from an account of a psychological assessment of Tristan schoolchildren carried out while they were in England by the application of tests of intelligence and personality (Keir, 1966). This study reveals that they did not show much aggression either towards each other or towards the English children with whom they went to school. Forty Tristan children attending infant school, junior school, and secondary modern school had low ratings for the three variables described as curiosity, independence, and aggression; this is said to confirm 'the picture of the Island community as lacking in interest in the outside world, and being generally rather passive, dependent, peace-loving and non-aggressive', and it is stressed that 'aggression was one of the characteristics they most disliked, according to their own statements . . . their social relations' with English children 'for the most part were marked by withdrawal rather than aggression'. This finding may in part be related to the new and unfamiliar circumstances in which the Tristan children found themselves in exile, including the fact that for the first time they formed a minority group. There is some evidence that their behaviour before they came to England was rather less passive and withdrawn. In the school on the island, which was attended from time to time by a few outside children, the offspring of expatriate officials, Tristan children were always in the majority. According to one English boy who spent some time at school there they sometimes ganged up on expatriate children and occasionally persecuted them. He also said that there were occasional gang fights, usually confined to Tristan children, although English children occasionally took part in them too; in general, however, Tristan children never joined forces with English children against fellow islanders except in play. It is also worth noting that before 1961 there were a number of what may be called outbreaks of a fashion for aggressive stone-throwing among Tristan children; the elected Island Council's attention was drawn more than once to the fact that this practice was assuming dangerous proportions and it supported its suppression by approving the corporal punishment of offenders.

Included in the psychological assessment are the results of applying the Rorschach test, from which it appears that the younger children showed records giving little impression 'of active outgoing and imaginative childhood', while the records of the children attending the secondary modern school

> 'were poorly organized and immature – and suggest passive dependent personalities, lacking drive. However, they give evidence of self sufficiency suited to a simple environment where there is easy gratification of instinctual needs and where there are realistic outlets for unruly fantasy' (ibid., p. 167).

The report concludes:

> 'Taking the group as a whole they remained for the most part closely integrated, rather passive, peace-loving children, not outstanding in ability, content with their own company and their own ways of life' (ibid., p. 172).

This rather depressing account by a distinguished educational psychologist seems to confirm in a systematic way many of my own more impressionistic conclusions. What one might question is whether the results of the psychological assessment and its theoretical basis have any explanatory value of an aetiological kind not possessed by the relationship it is possible to trace between the exercise of authority within the Tristan domestic family, the nature of the socialization process, and the kind of emphasis placed by the people on preserving at least an outward appearance of cheerful reciprocal cooperation and on keeping a good reputation in the outside world, an emphasis upon which the people seem to feel their survival as a community may partly depend.

TEASING AND AGGRESSION AMONG ADULT ISLANDERS

Among adult members of the Tristan community there are a number of socially accepted forms of behaviour which may be looked upon as offering outlets for aggressive feelings and impulses. One such outlet already mentioned is, of course, that provided for many if not all adult islanders by the verbal attacks and physical punishments involved in child-rearing and in such domestic strife as takes place behind closed doors. Another outlet, which cannot be dealt with here, and for which material is sparse if suggestive, is provided by the methods employed in dealing with and killing animals and birds, both domestic and wild. For those who accept the clinical evidence suggesting an association between repressed hostility in childhood and the occurrence of neuroticism and anxiety in later life, a third outlet which may be regarded as important, and which some psychoanalytic theorists would no doubt look upon as the displacement of aggressive feelings towards the self, consists of two related and standardized forms of psychogenic illness both of which have high prevalence among the Tristan people.[3]

For present purposes, however, the most important outlet is that provided by teasing. Two main kinds of teasing may be described, which I shall call public and domestic; they differ from one another not only in the locale in which they occur but in other important respects.

Public teasing

The essence of public teasing is described by Munch (1945) in the following passage:

> 'a sportive and humorous teasing, seemingly harmless but often with concealed hints and sharp stings, is an art in which the islanders have developed a remarkable dexterity and whenever they see a chance they like to perform it. Preferably, then, they choose a situation where they are sure to have a public – a working gang, a boat's crew – and the point is, of course, to turn the laugh against the other party.'

As this implies, public teasing is most commonly carried on by groups of men, either at work or during leisure hours; and perhaps the most characteristic teasing sessions are those in which the active participants are men of roughly the same age, even though men of other age-groups may be present. Sometimes, in fact, the presence of non-participants of other age-groups may be an important element in the effectiveness of the teasing exchanges: thus a group of young men may attempt to ridicule one of their number by making joking references to some personal characteristic or item of behaviour which the victim may have hoped to prevent becoming a matter of general public knowledge; or a group of older men may hold up one of their fellows to shame before their juniors by dragging up past indiscretions or misdemeanours. Sometimes the public teasing of a young man is initiated or controlled by older men in such a way as to encourage or even ensure the active participation of his peers in the game of exposing to ridicule his pretensions or peccadilloes; by this means senior men appear to take care to avoid divisions on the basis of age. But on other occasions young unmarried men are tacitly encouraged to act as licensed agents of the community at large in teasing or otherwise persecuting certain individuals who are generally regarded as fair game and in ridiculing certain failings among their elders. Characteristics and tendencies particularly liable to expose people to public ridicule include what may be termed cowardice, laziness, stupidity, and credulity, but above all boastfulness and self-importance and over-readiness to push oneself forward, especially if combined with difficulty in taking a joke and in putting up with teasing.

The words most commonly used by the Tristan people to describe teasing do not greatly differ from those employed by English people; they include such phrases as to 'laugh at' or 'make a joke at' someone, to 'work' or to 'chaff' someone, to 'pull someone's leg'. The adjective 'joky' is also sometimes used, as a compliment, to describe a good fellow, the important implication being that such a person does not give himself airs or show signs of trying to claim a higher status than anyone else. An outsider characterized as a 'joky person' has clearly won approval. Of the administrators who had served on Tristan the one most generally spoken of with affection and admiration was always described as a 'fair' man and a 'joky' man; that is, he never showed favouritism and, by readily taking part in teasing and joking exchanges, never tried to show that he was superior as a human being. Informants were much more reluctant to categorize the characters of islanders in this way: 'I don't want to say nothing against a Tristan person' was a common phrase. But islanders I got to know well, although rarely labelling their fellows as they did outsiders, were never slow to gossip about their relatives and neighbours. As already mentioned, the content of gossip differs in many respects from that of public teasing. In private conversations many informants laid implicit claims to higher status than most of their fellows, in terms of such things as colour ('my father was lily white') and level of literacy ('she can just about sign her name and that's it'). In open confrontations the two features most often and most ruthlessly exposed to ridicule may be summed up as tendencies to hypocrisy and apparent attempts to claim higher status. Sexual innuendoes play a part in teasing but a rather smaller part than is reported of comparable verbal exchanges in other societies, such as the Eskimo.

Tristan women are never subjected to public teasing and ridicule in the way that men are; and I very much doubt if women ever take part in the public teasing of men. It is largely in domestic affairs that men and women associate together and form small groups for such cooperative activities as hoeing and planting potatoes. On public occasions, formal and informal, at which members of both sexes are present, men and women tend to segregate themselves from each other; as they do, for example, in church and at community gatherings. Public teasing of men generally occurs when women are not present; but the accidental presence of a woman on such an occasion is sometimes seized upon and used to sharpen a barbed remark.

This is very different from the good-natured public joking and badinage which often take place, for example, when a girl passes a group of young men or when a newly married man comes within earshot of a group of middle-aged women. Mostly these exchanges are sexually suggestive in the most modest way, especially if close relatives of opposite sex to the victim are present; but sexual references considered highly obscene by many islanders are not infrequently made on occasion by particular individuals, both male and female, who are notorious for their tendency to use 'bad language'.[4] Teasing of this kind between members of the two sexes, very different in tone and content from what I have called public teasing sessions among groups of men, also takes place at dances. Indeed, one of the most popular of the island dances has as one of its main attractions the fact that it is highly suggestive and provides a context in which a good deal of relatively polite sexual banter between men and women may legitimately occur.

The behaviour of some women is often, of course, the focus of gossip by both men and women. One example is that of a woman, long since dead, whose notorious adulterous liaisons led her to be known jocularly as 'all hands' wife'. Sometimes gossip about a woman, taking place in public, may, by the accompanying nods, winks, and scarcely suppressed laughter as she goes past, come very near to public teasing. More often the menfolk of such women, particularly their husbands, are forced by other men to act as vicarious objects of open ridicule. One elderly man, whom I shall call Ezra, was often publicly baited in a merciless way, in part at least on his wife's account. She was a vigorous, capable, egocentric, and domineering woman, popular among outsiders for her friendliness and forthright manner and, especially among clergymen, for the leading part she played in church affairs; to most islanders, however, including some of her own children and grandchildren, she was a mixture of raucous bad joke and violent embarrassment. Ezra himself was a kindly, harmless, and gentle person in the early stages of senile psychosis, rather given to wearing eccentric articles of clothing and to boasting about his past prowess in various island activities. He was frequently teased by men rather younger than himself and sometimes reduced to tears in the process. As I had heard on a number of occasions, much of this teasing was concerned with his wife's behaviour, particularly her shameless currying for favour among outsiders, and with his subservience to her. One afternoon, when out for a solitary stroll, he was waylaid by a group of men and soon humiliated by references to, among other things, his waning ability to satisfy his wife's sexual demands. I happened to join the group while this was going on and found my presence being used as an unwitting means of increasing Ezra's confusion and shame. Most of the teasing was so allusive that I was unable and, I suspect, not intended, wholly to understand what was causing Ezra's distress. It was only later, with the help of an informant who had been present and who had taken little active part in the exchanges, that I was able to make much sense of what had been said; a good deal of it consisted of laughing references to animal behaviour, such as bulls getting so old and fat that they rolled off as soon as they managed to mount a cow.

This use of myself, an outsider, as a kind of catalytic agent is a good example of the stratagems employed by islanders who are skilled in teasing. Ezra, of course, while regarded by many as fair game, did not provide very good sport. Men who became angry rather than tearful were better entertainment though generally less likely to allow themselves to get caught; such men are often solitary and on the whole avoid joining groups at work or at leisure. In these cases third parties are also likely to be used in leg-pulling. For example, a young child may be sent to make a seemingly innocent request which it is known will produce an angry reaction. I was myself used in this way on a number of occasions, as the unsuspecting carrier of teasing messages; sometimes it turned out that the hidden meaning was clearly intended to cause embarrassment to me as much as to the recipient.

Most island men have at least one nickname. Some nicknames involve harmless and even complimentary references to appearance, mannerisms, and so forth, and are constantly used by almost everyone; others tend to be restricted to friends and contemporaries or to be used only within the family circle. But some nicknames, like several of the island's place names, recall past events of a trivial nature, many of them of a mildly disreputable kind; and some involve verbal abuse and are employed to effect in public teasing. One man who is particularly unpopular and is a frequent butt of public teasing and ridicule has a nickname consisting of a word used by young children to describe human faeces. Another example is that of a rather surly elderly man of unusually ugly appearance who is generally referred to as 'Karl' and is so addressed by his contemporaries; this nickname is an abbreviated form of Karloff and is derived from the film actor of that name well known for his performances in horror films. It was apparently bestowed by an outsider and, hearing it used as a mode of address, I employed it myself without realizing its significance until, when I was involved one day in a minor altercation with him, 'Karl' angrily accused me of being deliberately offensive and told me to call him by his own proper name and to stop using what he said I knew perfectly well was the name of a 'murderer'.

Domestic teasing

Women, children, and outsiders may be used in public teasing, as agents or as objects of ridicule in the way I have described, but they are not expected or encouraged to participate in it. In some ways their role may be likened to that described by Frankenberg (1957) for what he rather confusingly calls 'strangers' in Pentrediwaith. Although not excluded, and sometimes welcomed, as a member of the audience in public teasing sessions, I was left in no doubt that, as an outsider, it would not be appropriate for me to join in. The same applied in most cases to gossip, certainly when third parties were present: the surest way to cut off the flow of conversation was to provide information about other islanders or to express opinions about them and their affairs, even when asked to do so.

In what I call domestic teasing, however, the situation was rather different. Characteristically this took place in informal groups small enough for not more than one conversation to take place easily at the same time; mostly the people involved were close relatives or friends and the conversation was usually confined to the fireside or to other comparable occasions when those who were not members of the group could neither overhear what was said nor join it unexpectedly. Members of both sexes and of different age-groups took part and outsiders such as myself were not excluded from active intervention, especially if they were on joking terms with one or more members of the group.

Domestic teasing lacks the tone of aggressive ridicule found in the public variety. The content is also noticeably different. Some topics generally thought to be too dangerous for undisguised public use are sometimes mentioned openly in private teasing; for example, on a number of occasions I heard children, in their parents' presence, teasing each other in fairly good-natured rivalry about which of them had the darkest skin or the frizziest hair and about which of them took after which parent in these and other respects. On the other hand, crude obscenities and sexual innuendo, so often a feature of public teasing, seem to be unusual in domestic joking and teasing; no doubt this is partly because these weapons, to be really effective, demand that those who wield them should have a certain social elbow room and have the freedom to thrust and parry which is not found in groups containing members of both sexes and all ages. This does not mean that frank references to sexual activity do not occur in ordinary conversation in some households; nor does it mean that spouses, for example, always refrain from sexual references in domestic teasing of one another. A young woman who, to her undisguised regret, had failed to become pregnant after two or three years of happy marriage, was with her husband when an outsider, well known and very friendly to them both, with whom they happened to be passing the time in idle conversation, unwrapped a bar of nut chocolate and offered her a piece; she politely refused, saying that she did not 'go for nuts', and then, indicating her husband, jokingly added: 'Try him; his nuts ain't no good.'

Learning to take part in domestic teasing proved invaluable in the process of personal socialization among the Tristan people; I soon found myself discovering which of my informants' weak points could be used with safety and effect, and which were dangerous; and informants were quick to spot my own tender areas and wound me in them. One man ten years older and a much better physical specimen than I, without a grey hair on his head or any sign of balding, always greeted me ironically as 'old man' when I came to his house and teased me continually about getting fat, 'going to wrack and ruin', being 'past it', being unlikely ever again to attract the girls. Conversational gambits of this kind were employed by many of my male informants; but they were hardly ever used unless one or two other members of the household were present. When I met or talked with islanders on their own, even men and women I had got to know particularly well, conversation tended to be serious rather than otherwise; a good deal of what was said consisted of gossip and of nostalgic accounts of life on Tristan before the volcano, together with anecdotes and complaints about their life and work in England. Only occasionally was there a small amount of joking and mild leg-pulling. When others were present, however, conversations with the same informants were rather different.

In public and in what West (1945) calls 'loafing groups' a few of my informants tended to joke directly with me in a rather ostentatious fashion. These essentially well-intentioned sallies were generally greeted with very little response from the other islanders present and often caused them (and me) some uneasiness of mind. But most of my informants, especially those I knew well, surprised me at first by the lengths to which they would go in public to avoid seeming to claim any special acquaintance with me. I was not alone in this. Observation showed that other outsiders on comparably friendly terms with particular islanders were usually treated by them in the same way in public. And in many cases even islanders well known to be life-long intimate friends were rather reserved in their behaviour towards each other when they were together in public. In private, however, or in small groups of friends, the same individuals talked freely and good humouredly, with a lot of joking and teasing in which I was often involved to some extent and in which I was sometimes encouraged to take part. At the same time I sometimes got the impression that they were trying to prevent the talk getting too serious, especially when some of those present appeared to feel that a topic was being explored too deeply in front of an outsider. Apart from this, much of the ordinary idle conversation which took place in Tristan households over innumerable cups of tea and which may with justice be described as the principal pastime of most Tristan adults consisted of a mixture of gossip and of prolonged and sometimes almost continuous banter, through the medium of which matters of deep concern were often explored and personal rivalries expressed. This is best shown by an extended illustation.

COMPETITIVE TEASING: AN EXAMPLE ANALYSED

What follows is the transcript of part of a typical evening conversation which took place in November 1962 in the house of a middle-aged married couple I shall call Barnabas and Della.

At that time there was considerable uncertainty about the likelihood of the people being allowed by the government to return to Tristan, even though a so-called 'advance party' of six island men had been reluctantly permitted to go back and see for themselves what the conditions were like. It was also known that some of the people, especially some of the younger ones, were lukewarm about leaving England; and there was some anxiety among the remainder that the government would be less likely to facilitate the return if a united front of determination to get home were not maintained.

Five individuals were involved in the conversation. Although he was present throughout, Barnabas took no part in it at this stage, while his wife Della was one of the principal speakers. The other three were: myself (JBL), addressed and referred to by the others as 'Doc'; Bunty, the twenty-year-old daughter of the house, an intelligent and, by Tristan standards, well-educated young woman, at that time working as an assembler in an electronics factory near Southampton; and Desmond, an islander aged about twenty-eight working in a boat-builder's yard, a son of Barnabas's father's sister's son, godson of Barnabas (who is addressed and referred to by Desmond as 'Fardy', the Tristan term for godfather) and recently engaged to be married to Bunty.

Although I do not think that her parents had attempted to make any objections to the engagement, it was a matter of common knowledge that neither of them, but particularly Della, at that time welcomed the idea of Desmond as a future son-in-law. There were a number of reasons for their attitude, some of which Della had guardedly mentioned to me in private. One of their immediate objections was that they were not wholly convinced of the seriousness of Desmond's intentions in a number of respects. Some months earlier Desmond had openly admitted in an interview given to a national newspaper that he did not want to go back to Tristan. The report described him as 'a dashingly handsome figure' who found the pull of his newly purchased motor bike stronger than that of Tristan, and quoted him as having said that he had no thoughts of marriage or engagement. Not long after this report appeared he in fact sold his motor bike, denied as untrue everything reported of him in the newspaper, declared his enthusiastic determination to return home as soon as possible, and became engaged to Bunty.

The fire was showing signs of going out and the room was getting cold. In an attempt to get a blaze going Barnabas fetched kindling wood and a few small pieces of coal and Desmond took a letter out of his coat pocket, tore it in half and offered it as a help in getting the wood to catch. Della said:

Well! You'll tear her love letters up now!

Bunty indignantly denied that it was a letter from her; and Desmond said to me, with mock pitying scorn:

I'll tell you; she want to look at this; it tempt her so much. (*To* DELLA) There you are. You want to look at everything anybody else got.

DELLA (*offering evidence that this could not be true*): I can't see without my glasses.

BUNTY (*to* DESMOND, *referring to his nosiness*): You are just the same.

DESMOND (*ignoring Bunty's remark and addressing* DELLA): I never thought you'd use glasses. You tell me you'd drink straight from the bottle.

DELLA (*who holds strong views about the drinking of alcohol, especially by women – views which she shares with most other islanders*): Straight from the bottle! What do you think – I'd drink? That'll be the day you see me drink . . . (*She then changes her tactics as part of the fun.*) If I drink – if I go back to Tristan – when I know I's going back, then I's buying a bottle.

DESMOND (*incredulous*): How much are you going to drink out of it?

DELLA (*triumphant*): I's cleaning the whole bottle!

Desmond then tries to hold her to this promise, taunting Della with her often-expressed regard for telling the exact truth and keeping promises. Della tries to wriggle out of it by saying she might buy an empty bottle. Desmond appeals to the rest of us as witnesses. Della then says that when she knows they are going back to Tristan she will buy a bottle; she brings me into it in an attempt to neutralize the argument.

DELLA: I's buying a bottle of sherry and I's having it to drink to celebrate my going back. I's only waiting till Doc comes down here next time and I know I's going back.

DESMOND: That may be a long time – [may be] next year this time.

DELLA (*getting really upset and angry*): Desmond! Don't get me itching to use my fist, it would flatten you right out. If you tell me that – you get me mad. Man! It's the worst thing I hate, anybody to tell me I ain't going to go back this time. . . . Before I stop here another year I don't know what I'm going to do.

DESMOND (*in a conciliatory tone*): They say you're enjoying your job.

DELLA: Well, yeah, I don't say I don't enjoy my job up there – it takes my mind off –

BUNTY (*sarcastically*): Yes, I reckon it does take your mind off.

This remark of her daughter's has a double edge: it refers both to the fact that Della is liable to hysterical outbursts and to the standing complaint in the household that Della is always talking about the packing-plant where she works and always suggesting that she works harder there than anyone else. Della is visibly shaken by this verbal blow but ignores it.

DELLA: Well, it take my mind more or less off Tristan; quick as I leave here again I just come back again [i.e. it makes the day pass quickly].

DESMOND: You mean to tell me that the place where you work is more interesting to you than Tristan?

DELLA: No, it isn't. It isn't!

DESMOND: But it take your mind away from Tristan. I tell you one thing. Nothing takes *my* mind away from Tristan.

After a bit more of this kind of thing, in which Della is almost reduced to tears, she again brings me into the conversation as a protection. The others are laughing at her and she turns on her husband.

DELLA (*to Barnabas*): You got no sense at all! Now Doc would understand. (*To me*) Doc! Now listen –

JBL: Don't let him make you mad.

DELLA: Doc! Nobody will put me off Tristan [i.e. turn my mind away from Tristan], not even the governor if he ever come down here would put me off Tristan [by the governor she means the government embodied in the Prime Minister].

BUNTY (*in a supercilious voice*): Who's he?

DESMOND (*joining in the pursuit*): Who's he?

DELLA (*desperately searching her memory*): Well, he is –

DESMOND: What's his name?

DELLA (*racking her brains*): Mister –

DESMOND: Mister what?

DELLA (*with triumph mingled with niggling doubt that she may have got it wrong*): Mister Macmillan.

JBL: That's one in the eye for you, Desmond.

DELLA (*to Desmond in a cocky voice*): You think I don't know?

Desmond acknowledges by a wink to me that he has lost that point but then immediately returns to the attack by suggesting that Della might be a member of a deputation which was shortly going up to London to see the Colonial Secretary in order to press the authorities to allow the islanders to return to Tristan. It would, of course, be quite unprecedented for a woman to fill such a role among the Tristan people. The usual procedure was that deputations of this kind consisted of the government-appointed Chief of the Islanders plus one senior man from each of the seven patrinominal kin groups which the people speak of, in such contexts as this, as 'families'. The usual representative of the M— 'family' was Howard M—, one of Barnabas's father's brother's sons, who at this time had already left Britain as a member of the advance party for the return to Tristan. Desmond's suggestion that Della might be a member, while well known to everyone in the room to be absurd, did, however, tap two sources of polemical energy. The first was the part played by women in decision-making, which was often very considerable if informal, and the fact that the position of women on Tristan is often a matter for joking between members of the two sexes. The second was the recognition since coming to Britain, by both men and women, of the very considerable difference in this respect between the beliefs and practices of the islanders and the beliefs and practices of English people. Barnabas worked while in England in a small engineering firm the boss of which happened to be a woman, the widow of the previous proprietor. This was often a matter of humorous comment by other Tristan men when talking to Barnabas and by Barnabas himself when talking about his daily work to his wife.

DESMOND: Would you like to go up to the Colonial Office and talk to them?

DELLA (*in a loud voice*): Well, I tell you, if I know I would go back to Tristan I'd talk to the Colonial Office, I'd went to the Colonial Office, I'd talk to anybody.

DESMOND: Well, if there is one each out of the people going up to see them I suppose Fardy [i.e. Barnabas] is going to go up for the M—s because Howard is away; maybe they ought to send you up in his place.

DELLA: Send me up in his place? . . . Yeah! But listen, that's a man's [job], the men got to go.

DESMOND: Now, look! (*by which he seemed to mean, from his tone of voice, 'Come, come, after all you have said about what ought to be done' – this referring back to previous conversations in my presence in which Della had criticized the men for doing nothing*).

DELLA (*shouting and thumping her knee to emphasize the strength of her feelings*): If they say to me, if I go to the Colonial Office I will get back to Tristan, well, I'm going tomorrow!

DESMOND (*chidingly*): Now, we don't want to see you limping out of here tomorrow morning.

DELLA: I don't care if I limp or crawl as long as I get back to Tristan.

DESMOND: You just say [i.e. you mean to say] if a woman went up and talked to the Colonial Office it might be far better than if a man went up and talked to them.

BUNTY (*in a mock dreamy voice and fluttering her eyelids*): You'd just have to look in their eyes. You know.

DELLA (*showing instant disapproval of her daughter's sexy behaviour*): Well, I don't know. I tell you, their heads is as hard as stone. Nothing can do anything with them.

BUNTY: I can't see what a woman can do.

DELLA (*angrily to her daughter, referring back to a discussion some days earlier in which Bunty had boasted about what she would do*): Well, you's the first; you said you was going to write a letter up to them.

BUNTY: Well it so happens that I'm not . . .

DELLA: Well if I had the schooling as what you [have had] –

BUNTY: It would take a couple of years to understand what it all meant.

DELLA (*really angry*): Couple of years to understand what it all meant! What you mean, there's a couple of years to understand what it all meant?

DESMOND (*in a mocking tone to fan the flames of her wrath*): Never mind, Della. We'll get back one day.

DELLA: One day! I don't want to know, I want to know today . . .

BUNTY (*to her mother, in a tone of reproof*): And you keep your hair on and you will know.

At this remark Della gave me a look as if to say 'What can you do with them?' I also fancy it meant that, had I not been present, she would not have allowed Bunty to get away with a remark the content and tone of which were so much at odds with the customary demeanour of unmarried Tristan daughters. She swallowed her pride until further provoked by the next couple of exchanges.

DESMOND: We'll get back one day.

BUNTY (*provocatively*): This year, next year, sometime, never.

DESMOND: You know what they say: those that wait patiently in the Lord all good things shall come unto them.

DELLA (*shocked by the levity of Desmond's tone of voice*): Desmond, you talk too much!

BUNTY (*changing sides*): He's got to talk to keep himself warm.

Throughout this extract from a conversation Della and Desmond were the two individuals most clearly involved in teasing one another, relatively good humouredly but with a perceptible undercurrent of mutual mistrust. But there were three other important, if less obvious, rivalries between members of this particular group which sometimes found expression in similar passages at arms at other times. A few signs of them may be discerned in the transcript used for illustration. In all three cases the rivalries involved aspects of socialization, of learning how to perform new roles and adapt to new role relationships, or how to deal with new social situations. Mostly the rivalries and the learning process were made tolerable through the use of teasing.

For example, there was a fair amount of open rivalry between Bunty and Desmond; they teased each other a good deal about their strongly conflicting views on the role of women in public affairs on Tristan and in ordinary domestic day-to-day decision-making. Partly, no doubt, this was a matter of two individuals selecting or emphasizing alternative norms of behaviour at a time of rapid social change; but their differences also arose from more personal factors. Thus Bunty, as well as being better educated and better informed than Desmond, was in my view distinctly more intelligent, less likeable, and more determined and forthright than he was. She usually took no trouble when she could be bothered to tease him to conceal the fact that she regarded Desmond as in every way her inferior; but I formed the clear impression that Desmond, a singularly thick-skinned person, was generally the only person present on these occasions who completely failed to get the message, and that the message was, in fact, intended for the others.

A second situation of rivalry existed between mother and daughter. Although based on what seemed to me to be a fundamental incompatibility of temperament, their differences were expressed in terms of relative level of education, relative sophistication, and so forth. Della often teased her daughter about her laziness, her selfishness, and her conceit; Bunty often ridiculed her mother's outmoded style in clothes, her ignorance, and her verbal solecisms, and mimicked her Tristan pronunciation. Barnabas, who by no accident was usually present during these exchanges, rarely intervened; when he did so it was to support his wife; but it was clear that he took great pride in his daughter's accomplishments, boasting to me once in private that nobody would know from her appearance or her speech that Bunty wasn't an English girl. And Della occasionally showed that she knew that Barnabas was really on their daughter's side in these arguments.

This, indeed, was the third rivalry of importance in the group: it centred on a number of issues, but the most critical one, barely acknowledged directly by either of them, was that Barnabas himself was rather more keen on remaining in England than on returning to Tristan. He only once confessed this to me in private, over a tongue-loosening pint of beer in a pub; he said that the happiest time of his life had been 'working with diesel engines' in England. He added: 'I tell you, Doc, if I was a young man, unmarried and no family, Tristan would never see me no more.'

CONCLUSION

I have assumed in this essay that joking behaviour is something very different from joking relationships. I have also tried to isolate teasing as a particular element in the general field of joking behaviour; for example, if mock attack is an important component of joking behaviour, the special emphasis in teasing is on attack masquerading as friendliness; and although it can be linked on the one hand with gossip and scandalizing and on the other with direct and undisguised aggressive ridicule, teasing is distinguishable from both in that it combines direct person-to-person communication with a special kind of ambiguity. Indeed, the essence of successful teasing lies in the skilful use of ambiguity. This, if anything, is its universal diagnostic feature.

By allowing informants to speak for themselves the intention is not simply to provide an illustration of the teasing process but to bring out and underline a number of the points made earlier. I have tried to show the relationship between the special situation in which the Tristan people have for some time found themselves, a situation exacerbated by exile, and the part played by teasing in their ordinary daily interchanges. The uncertainty of their position *vis-à-vis* the outside world, and the ambivalence of their feelings towards it, may be said to be reflected in the extent to which ambiguity figures in their communication with one another. This comes out especially strongly in relation to important and potentially conflicting moral values, such as the position of women in decision-making, the need for leaders and the emphasis on equality of status, the overriding principle of fair shares and the attempts of individuals and small groups to acquire more possessions and prestige than their fellows.

In addition to separating teasing from other forms of joking behaviour, I have distinguished between two main kinds of teasing in terms of context, content, and the role relationships of the participants. There are also important differences in the functions of what I have called public and domestic teasing, although these differences are mostly a matter of relative emphasis. For example, the way in which teasing is used as a means of social control and as a way of identifying potential leaders is more apparent in public teasing than in domestic, and

I have not attempted to deal with these functions in any systematic way in this essay. My main concern has been with the socialization function: this is most clearly seen in the domestic setting, not only in the teasing of children, which, although treated separately above, is of course a part of the domestic teasing process, but also in the ways in which the learning of new social roles by individuals is carried on at the same time, and with the same instruments of competitive banter, as contests for power and influence within the domestic family.

NOTES

1. The work was undertaken as part of an extensive programme of combined care and investigation among the Tristan people carried out by a wide variety of agencies and individuals under the general auspices of the Medical Research Council and with the help and cooperation of the English local authorities concerned and of the Colonial Office. Among the very large number of people to whom I am indebted for help, support, and encouragement I wish to make special mention of the following: Sir Aubrey Lewis, lately (until 1966) Professor of Psychiatry at the Institute of Psychiatry in the University of London and Honorary Director of the M.R.C. Social Psychiatry Research Unit; Professor Sir Hedley Atkins and Dr H. E. Lewis, Chairman and Secretary (respectively) of the Tristan da Cunha Working Party of the M.R.C.; Professor P. A. Munch, of Southern Illinois University; and Professor K. Rawnsley, of the Welsh National School of Medicine.

2. A leading islander, who had previously met H.R.H. the Duke of Edinburgh on the latter's visit to Tristan da Cunha in 1957 and to one of whose ancestors Queen Victoria had sent a signed portrait and letter of thanks for rescuing some of her shipwrecked subjects, in conversation with the Duke at the opening by H.M. the Queen in November 1962 of the new Commonwealth Institute building, felt able to ask for help in getting the people home. He afterwards reported that H.R.H. replied: 'It is no good asking me. You will have to talk to those fellows over there,' indicating members of the government in attendance.

3. The illnesses take the following forms: (i) sporadic outbreaks of epidemic hysteria; (ii) endemic bi-frontal headaches associated with anxiety. A major outbreak of hysteria, affecting over 10 per cent of the population, occurred in 1937. Present-day survivors of that epidemic are particularly prone to 'psychogenic' headache (see Rawnsley & Loudon, 1964, for details). A possible link between these minor psychiatric disorders and exposure to gossip, teasing, and ridicule is suggested by the relatively high frequency of past hysteria and present headaches found among women whose husbands have the somewhat ambiguous status of leaders in a fiercely egalitarian community.

4. As Sykes (1966) has noted for a very different setting, immodest joking and teasing seem more common between those who are not, and are unlikely to become, sexual partners, particularly on grounds of disparity in age. This observation seems to hold for Tristan only in that some elderly men were liable to make jokes to young married women which were regarded by many islanders as particularly obscene but relatively harmless.

REFERENCES

COLSON, E. 1953. *The Makah Indians.* Manchester: Manchester University Press.

FIRTH, R. 1956. Rumour in a Primitive Society. *Journal of Abnormal and Social Psychology* **53**: 122–132.

FORTES, M. 1959. *Oedipus and Job in West African Religion.* Cambridge: Cambridge University Press.

FOX, R. 1967. *Totem and Taboo* Reconsidered. In E. R. Leach (ed.), *The Structural Study of Myth and Totemism.* A.S.A. Monographs 5. London: Tavistock Publications.

FOX, R. & TIGER, L. 1966. The Zoological Perspective in Social Science. *Man* (n.s.) **1**: 75–81.

FRANKENBERG, R. 1957. *Village on the Border.* London: Cohen & West.

FREEMAN, D. 1965. Anthropology, Psychiatry and the Doctrine of Cultural Relativism. *Man* **65**: 59.

—— 1966. Social Anthropology and the Scientific Study of Human Behaviour. *Man* (n.s.) **1**: 330–342.

GLUCKMAN, M. 1963. Gossip and Scandal. *Current Anthropology* **4**: 307–315.

—— & EGGAN, F. 1965–66. Introduction to M. Banton (ed.), A.S.A. Monographs 1–4. London: Tavistock Publications.

HORTON, R. 1963. The Boundaries of Explanation in Social Anthropology. *Man* **63**: 6.

KEIR, G. 1966. The Psychological Assessment of the Children from the Island of Tristan da Cunha. In C. Banks & P. L. Broadhurst (eds.), *Studies in Psychology presented to Cyril Burt.* London: University of London Press.

LOUDON, J. B. 1966. Private Stress and Public Ritual. *Journal of Psychosomatic Research* **10**: 101–108.

MUNCH, P. A. 1945. *Sociology of Tristan da Cunha.* Oslo: The Norwegian Academy of Science in Oslo.

—— 1964. Culture and Superculture in a Displaced Community: Tristan da Cunha. *Ethnology* **3**: 369–376.

—— 1967. *Economic Development and Conflicting Values: A Social Experiment in Tristan da Cunha.* (Mimeo.)

PAINE, R. 1967. What is Gossip About? An Alternative Hypothesis. *Man* (n.s.) **2**: 278–285.

RADCLIFFE-BROWN, A. R. 1952. *Structure and Function in Primitive Society.* London: Cohen & West; Glencoe, Ill.: The Free Press.

RAWNSLEY, K. & LOUDON, J. B. 1964. Epidemiology of Mental Disorder in a Closed Community. *British Journal of Psychiatry* **110**: 830–839.

ROGERS, R. A. 1926. *The Lonely Island.* London: Allen & Unwin.

SYKES, A. J. M. 1966. Joking Relationships in an Industrial Setting. *American Anthropologist* **68**: 188–193.

WEST, J. 1945. *Plainsville, U.S.A.* New York: Columbia University Press.

NOTES ON CONTRIBUTORS

FORGE, ANTHONY. Born 1929, United Kingdom; studied at Cambridge, M.A.; London School of Economics.

Horniman Scholarship, 1957–60; Part-time Research Officer, London School of Economics, 1960–61; Assistant Lecturer in Social Anthropology, London School of Economics, 1961–64; Fellow of the Bollingen Foundation, New York, 1962–63; Lecturer in Social Anthropology, London School of Economics, 1964–.

Co-author (with Raymond Firth and Jane Hubert) of *Families and their Relatives*, 1969.

GOODY, ESTHER NEWCOMB. Born 1932, USA; educated at Antioch College, Yellow Springs, Ohio, B.A.; University of Cambridge, Ph.D.

Social Science Research Council (US) First-year Graduate Fellowship, 1954–55; Ford Foundation Foreign Area Training Fellowship, 1956–57; Assistant Director of Studies in Archaeology and Anthropology, Newnham College, Cambridge, 1961–1963; Visiting Lecturer, Institute of African Studies, University of Ghana, autumn 1964; Fellow and Lecturer in Social Anthropology, New Hall, Cambridge, 1966–.

Author of 'Terminal Separation and Divorce among the Gonja' in M. Fortes (ed.), *Marriage in Tribal Society*, 1962; co-author (with J. R. Goody) of two comparative papers on kinship institutions in Northern Ghana, *Man* (n.s.) **1** (3), 1966, and **2** (2), 1967.

JAHODA, GUSTAV. Born 1920, Vienna; studied at London School of Economics (Sociology) and Birkbeck College (Psychology); B.Sc. (Econ.), M.Sc., Ph.D.

Extra-mural Tutor, University of Oxford, 1947–49; Lecturer in Psychology, University of Manchester, 1949–52; Lecturer, University College of the Gold Coast, 1952–56; Senior Lecturer, University of Glasgow, 1956–63; Professor of Psychology, University of Strathclyde, 1964–.

Author of *White Man* (1961); *The Psychology of Superstition* (1969); chapters in several books and a variety of papers.

LA FONTAINE, J. S. Born 1931, East Africa; educated at Cambridge University, B.A., Ph.D.

Lecturer, Lovanium University, Kinshasa, Congo, 1961–63; undertook urban survey in Kinshasa, 1962–63; Lecturer in

Social Anthropology, Birkbeck College, University of London, 1965–68; Reader in Social Anthropology, London School of Economics, 1968–.

Author of 'Gisu Chiefs' in A. I. Richards (ed.), *East African Chiefs*, 1959; 'Gisu Homicide and Suicide' in P. Bohannan (ed.), *African Homicide and Suicide*, 1960; 'Witchcraft and Sorcery in Bugisu' in J. Middleton and E. H. Winter (eds.), *Witchcraft and Sorcery in East Africa*, 1963; *City Politics: A Study of Leadership in Leopoldville 1962–63* (forthcoming).

LLOYD, BARBARA B. Born New Jersey, USA; studied at the University of Chicago, A.B.; Boston University, M.A. (Psychology), Ph.D.; Northwestern University (Psychology).

Senior Research Fellow, University of Ibadan, 1962–64; Part-time Lecturer in Psychology, University of Birmingham, 1964–65, 1966–67; Lecturer in Social Psychology, University of Sussex, 1967–.

Co-author (with R. A. LeVine) of *Nyansongo: A Gusii Community in Kenya*, 1966.

LOUDON, JOSEPH BUIST. Born 1921, United Kingdom; educated at Oxford University, B.A. (Natural Science), M.A., B.M., B.Ch. (Medicine); London School of Economics, Acad.Postgrad.Dip.Anthropology.

Medical appointments, 1946–56; Assistant Lecturer in Social Anthropology, London School of Economics, 1956–57; Social Anthropologist, Social Psychiatry Research Unit, Medical Research Council, 1957–64; Lecturer in Anthropology, 1964–66, Senior Lecturer in Anthropology, 1966, University College of Swansea.

Author of 'Psychogenic Disorder and Social Conflict among the Zulu' in M. K. Opler (ed.), *Culture and Mental Health*, 1959; 'Kinship and Crisis in South Wales', *British Journal of Sociology*, vol. 12, 1961; 'Social Aspects of Ideas about Treatment' in A. V. S. de Reuck and R. Porter (eds.), *Transcultural Psychiatry: Ciba Foundation Symposium*, 1965; 'Religious Order and Mental Disorder: A Study in a South Wales Rural Community' in M. Banton (ed.), *The Social Anthropology of Complex Societies* (A.S.A. Monographs 4), 1966; etc.

MAYER, IONA. Born 1923, United Kingdom; studied history at Oxford University, M.A.; Rhodes University, Ph.D. (Anthropology).

Author of *The Nature of Kinship Relations*, Rhodes-Livingstone paper No. 37, 1965; 'From Kinship to Common Descent', *Africa*, 1965.

MAYER, PHILIP. Born 1910, Germany; studied at Heidelberg

University, Dr. jur.; Oxford University, B.Sc., D.Phil.

Kenya Government Sociologist, 1946–50; Lecturer in Social Anthropology, Birkbeck College, University of London, 1950–1952; Professor of Social Anthropology, Rhodes University, South Africa, 1953–63; Professor of Anthropology, University of the Witwatersrand, Johannesburg, 1964–66; Reader in Anthropology, 1966–67, Professor of Anthropology, 1968, University of Durham.

Author of *The Lineage Principle in Gusii Society*, 1950; *Gusii Bridewealth Law and Custom*, 1951; *Two Studies in Applied Anthropology in Kenya*, 1952; *Townsmen or Tribesmen*, 1961.

Editor of trilogy *Xhosa in Town*, 1961–63.

RICHARDS, AUDREY I. Born 1899, England; educated at Cambridge University, M.A.; London School of Economics, Ph.D.

Lecturer in Social Anthropology, London School of Economics, 1931–37; Senior Lecturer in Anthropology, University of the Witwatersrand, Johannesburg, 1938–41; London School of Economics, 1944–49; Director, East African Institute of Social Research, 1950–56; Fellow of Newnham College, Cambridge, 1957–67; Smuts Reader, University of Cambridge, 1962–67; Director of Centre of African Studies, Cambridge, 1965–67; Honorary Fellow, Newnham College, Cambridge, 1967–; President, Royal Anthropological Institute, 1960–61; President, African Studies Association in the United Kingdom, 1964–65.

Author of *Hunger and Work in a Savage Tribe*, 1932; *Land, Labour and Diet in Northern Rhodesia*, 1939; *Bemba Marriage and Modern Economic Conditions*, 1940; *Chisungu: A Girls' Initiation Ceremony among the Bemba of Northern Rhodesia*, 1956; *The Multi-cultural States of East Africa*, 1969.

Editor of *Economic Development and Tribal Change*, 1954; *East African Chiefs*, 1959.

SPENCER, PAUL. Born 1932, London; studied engineering at Cambridge University, M.A.; and social anthropology at Cambridge and Oxford Universities, B.Litt., D.Phil.

William Wyse Student in Social Anthropology, 1956–59; Fieldwork in East Africa, 1957–62; Member of the staff of the Tavistock Institute, 1962 to present; Further research in planning and local government, 1963–68, and in the health service, since 1968; Seconded to the research staff of the Royal Commission on Local Government in England, 1967–68.

Author of *The Samburu: A Study of Gerontocracy in a Nomadic Tribe*, 1965; *Nomads in Alliance: A Survey of the Rendille and the Samburu of Northern Kenya*, in press.

WARD, BARBARA E. (Mrs. H. S. Morris) Educated at Newnham College, Cambridge, M.A. (History); University of London, Dip.Ed. and M.A. (Anthropology).

Lecturer in Anthropology, Birkbeck College, University of London, 1955–65; Lecturer in Asian Anthropology, School of Oriental and African Studies, University of London, 1965– ; Visiting Professor, Cornell University, 1964; Visiting Professor, the Chinese University of Hong Kong, 1967.

Editor of *Women in the New Asia*, Unesco, 1963.

WILDER, WILLIAM DEAN, JR. Born 1939, USA; educated at Harvard College, A.B.; London School of Economics, M.A.

Lecturer in Anthropology, University of Durham, 1966.

Author of 'Confusion versus Classification in the Study of Purum Society', *American Anthropologist*, 1964; and of other articles in *Man* and *Modern Asian Studies*.

Author Index

Author Index

Subject Index